Praise for *Introduction to Android™ Application Development, Fourth Edition*

"*Introduction to Android™ Application Development, Fourth Edition,* is a phenomenal read and allows those interested in Android development to be brought up to speed and developing apps with minimal fuss. Everything from an introduction to the Android ecosystem and setting up a development environment to creating and publishing Android applications is covered in depth and with technical expertise. Those who crave even more from the book will be treated to a feast of useful links at the end of each chapter to help guide them on and expand their new-found knowledge base."
—*Philip Dutson, UX and mobile developer for ICON Health & Fitness*

"With this edition, you won't find a more solid and comprehensive introduction to Android programming. Even if you already have another Android book, *Introduction to Android™ Application Development* makes a good second reference."
—*Douglas Jones, senior software engineer, Fullpower Technologies*

"*Introduction to Android™ Application Development, Fourth Edition,* is an important update to this invaluable reference for new and seasoned Android developers. It brings the latest up-to-date information about the newest releases of Android, showing you how to keep your application fresh on yesterday's, today's, and tomorrow's Android devices."
—*Ray Rischpater, senior software engineer, Microsoft*

Introduction to Android™ Application Development

Fourth Edition

Introduction to Android™ Application Development

Android Essentials

Fourth Edition

Joseph Annuzzi, Jr.
Lauren Darcey
Shane Conder

✦✦ Addison-Wesley

Upper Saddle River, NJ • Boston • Indianapolis • San Francisco
New York • Toronto • Montreal • London • Munich • Paris • Madrid
Capetown • Sydney • Tokyo • Singapore • Mexico City

Many of the designations used by manufacturers and sellers to distinguish their products are claimed as trademarks. Where those designations appear in this book, and the publisher was aware of a trademark claim, the designations have been printed with initial capital letters or in all capitals.

The authors and publisher have taken care in the preparation of this book, but make no expressed or implied warranty of any kind and assume no responsibility for errors or omissions. No liability is assumed for incidental or consequential damages in connection with or arising out of the use of the information or programs contained herein.

For information about buying this title in bulk quantities, or for special sales opportunities (which may include electronic versions; custom cover designs; and content particular to your business, training goals, marketing focus, or branding interests), please contact our corporate sales department at corpsales@pearsoned.com or (800) 382-3419.

For government sales inquiries, please contact governmentsales@pearsoned.com.

For questions about sales outside the U.S., please contact international@pearsoned.com.

Visit us on the Web: informit.com/aw

Library of Congress Cataloging-in-Publication Data
Annuzzi, Joseph, Jr.
 Introduction to Android application development : Android essentials / Joseph Annuzzi, Jr., Lauren Darcey, Shane Conder.—Fourth edition.
    pages cm
 Revised edition of first part of: Android wireless application development / Shane Conder, Lauren Darcey. c2010.
 Includes bibliographical references and index.
 ISBN-13: 978-0-321-94026-1 (alk. paper)
 ISBN-10: 0-321-94026-1 (alk. paper)
 1. Application software—Development. 2. Android (Electronic resource) 3. Mobile computing. 4. Wireless communication systems. I. Darcey, Lauren, 1977- II. Conder, Shane, 1975- III. Darcey, Lauren, 1977- Android wireless application development. IV. Title.
 QA76.76.A65A56 2014
 005.3—dc23
                                                2013035917

ISBN-13: 978-0-321-94026-1
ISBN-10:   0-321-94026-1

Text printed in the United States on recycled paper at Edwards Brothers Malloy in Ann Arbor, Michigan.
Third Printing: September, 2014

Editor-in-Chief
Mark L. Taub

Acquisitions Editor
Laura Lewin

Development Editor
Songlin Qiu

Managing Editor
John Fuller

Project Editor
Caroline Senay

Copy Editor
Barbara Wood

Indexer
Jack Lewis

Proofreader
Christine Clark

Technical Reviews
Douglas Jones
Ray Rischpater

Publishing Coordinator
Olivia Basegio

Compositor
Shepherd, Inc.

❖

This book is dedicated to Cleopatra (Cleo).
—Joseph Annuzzi, Jr.

This book is dedicated to ESC.
—Lauren Darcey and Shane Conder

❖

Contents at a Glance

Contents

VI: Appendixes

Acknowledgments

This book is the result of collaboration among a great group, from the efforts of the team at Pearson Education (Addison-Wesley Professional); from the suggestions made by the technical reviewers; and from the support of family, friends, coworkers, and acquaintances alike. We'd like to thank the Android developer community, Google, and the Open Handset Alliance for their vision and expertise. Special thanks go to Mark Taub for believing in the vision for this edition; Laura Lewin, who was the driving force behind the book and without whom it would not have become a reality; Olivia Basegio, who was instrumental in orchestrating the efforts of everyone involved; Songlin Qiu for performing countless iterations through the manuscript to make this book ready for production; and the technical reviewers: Ray Rischpater, who made many beneficial recommendations, and Doug Jones, who suggested improvements of the fine details (as well as Mike Wallace, Mark Gjoel, Dan Galpin, Tony Hillerson, Ronan Schwarz, and Charles Stearns, who reviewed previous editions). Dan Galpin also graciously provided the clever Android graphics used for Tips, Notes, and Warnings. Amy Badger must be commended for her wonderful waterfall illustration, and we also thank Hans Bodlaender for letting us use the nifty chess font he developed as a hobby project.

About the Authors

Joseph Annuzzi, Jr., is a freelance software architect, graphic artist, writer, and technical reviewer. He usually can be found mastering the Android platform, implementing cutting-edge HTML5 capabilities, leveraging various cloud technologies, speaking in different programming languages, working with diverse frameworks, integrating with various social APIs, tinkering with peer-to-peer, cryptography, and computer vision algorithms, or creating stunningly realistic 3D renders. He is always on the lookout for disruptive Internet and mobile technologies and has multiple patent applications in process. He graduated from the University of California, Davis, with a BS in managerial economics and a minor in computer science and lives where much of the action is, Silicon Valley.

When he is not working with technology, he has been known to lounge in the sun on the beaches of the Black Sea with international movie stars; he has trekked through the Bavarian forest in winter, has immersed himself in the culture of the Italian Mediterranean, and has narrowly escaped the wrath of an organized crime ring in Eastern Europe after his taxi dropped him off in front of the bank ATM they were liquidating. He also lives an active and healthy lifestyle, designs and performs custom fitness training routines to stay in shape, and adores his loyal beagle, Cleopatra.

Lauren Darcey is responsible for the technical leadership and direction of a small software company specializing in mobile technologies, including Android, iOS, BlackBerry, Palm Pre, BREW, and J2ME, and consulting services. With more than two decades of experience in professional software production, Lauren is a recognized authority in application architecture and the development of commercial-grade mobile applications. Lauren received a BS in computer science from the University of California, Santa Cruz.

She spends her copious free time traveling the world with her geeky mobile-minded husband and is an avid nature photographer. Her work has been published in books and newspapers around the world. In South Africa, she dove with 4-meter-long great white sharks and got stuck between a herd of rampaging hippopotami and an irritated bull elephant. She's been attacked by monkeys in Japan, gotten stuck in a ravine with two hungry lions in Kenya, gotten thirsty in Egypt, narrowly avoided a *coup d état* in Thailand, geocached her way through the Swiss Alps, drank her way through the beer halls of Germany, slept in the crumbling castles of Europe, and gotten her tongue stuck to an iceberg in Iceland (while being watched by a herd of suspicious wild reindeer).

Shane Conder has extensive development experience and has focused his attention on mobile and embedded development for the past decade. He has designed and developed many commercial applications for Android, iOS, BREW, BlackBerry, J2ME, Palm, and

Windows Mobile—some of which have been installed on millions of phones worldwide. Shane has written extensively about the mobile industry and evaluated mobile development platforms on his tech blogs and is well known within the blogosphere. Shane received a BS in computer science from the University of California.

A self-admitted gadget freak, Shane always has the latest smartphone, tablet, or other mobile device. He can often be found fiddling with the latest technologies, such as cloud services and mobile platforms, and other exciting, state-of-the-art technologies that activate the creative part of his brain. He also enjoys traveling the world with his geeky wife, even if she did make him dive with 4-meter-long great white sharks and almost get eaten by a lion in Kenya. He admits that he has to take at least two phones with him when backpacking—even though there is no coverage—and that he snickered and whipped out his Android phone to take a picture when Laurie got her tongue stuck to that iceberg in Iceland, and that he is catching on that he should be writing his own bio.

Introduction

Android is a popular, free, open-source mobile platform that has taken the wireless world by storm. This book provides guidance for software development teams on designing, developing, testing, debugging, and distributing professional Android applications. If you're a veteran mobile developer, you can find tips and tricks to streamline the development process and take advantage of Android's unique features. If you're new to mobile development, this book provides everything you need to make a smooth transition from traditional software development to mobile development—specifically, its most promising platform: Android.

Who Should Read This Book

This book includes tips for successful mobile development based upon our years in the mobile industry and covers everything you need to know in order to run a successful Android project from concept to completion. We cover how the mobile software process differs from traditional software development, including tricks to save valuable time and pitfalls to avoid. Regardless of the size of your project, this book is for you.

This book was written for several audiences:

- **Software developers who want to learn to develop professional Android applications.** The bulk of this book is targeted at software developers with Java experience who do not necessarily have mobile development experience. More-seasoned developers of mobile applications can learn how to take advantage of Android and how it differs from the other technologies on the mobile development market today.

- **Quality assurance personnel tasked with testing Android applications.** Whether they are black-box or white-box testing, quality assurance engineers can find this book invaluable. We devote several chapters to mobile QA concerns, including topics such as developing solid test plans and defect-tracking systems for mobile applications, how to manage handsets, and how to test applications thoroughly using all the Android tools available.

- **Project managers planning and managing Android development teams.** Managers can use this book to help plan, hire for, and execute Android projects from start to finish. We cover project risk management and how to keep Android projects running smoothly.

- **Other audiences.** This book is useful not only to the software developer, but also to the corporation looking at potential vertical market applications, the entrepreneur thinking about a cool phone application, and the hobbyist looking for some fun with his or her new phone. Businesses seeking to evaluate Android for their specific needs (including feasibility analysis) can also find the information provided valuable. Anyone with an Android handset and a good idea for a mobile application can put the information in this book to use for fun and profit.

Key Questions Answered in This Book

This book answers the following questions:

1. What is Android? How do the SDK versions differ?
2. How is Android different from other mobile technologies, and how can developers take advantage of these differences?
3. How do developers use the Android SDK and ADT Bundle to develop and debug Android applications on the emulator and handsets?
4. How are Android applications structured?
5. How do developers design robust user interfaces for mobile—specifically, for Android?
6. What capabilities does the Android SDK have and how can developers use them?
7. How does the mobile development process differ from traditional desktop development?
8. What strategies work best for Android development?
9. What do managers, developers, and testers need to look for when planning, developing, and testing a mobile application?
10. How do mobile teams design bulletproof Android applications for publication?
11. How do mobile teams package Android applications for deployment?
12. How do mobile teams make money from Android applications?
13. And, finally, what is new in this edition of the book?

How This Book Is Structured

Introduction to Android Application Development, Fourth Edition focuses on Android essentials, including setting up the development environment, understanding the application lifecycle, user interface design, developing for different types of devices, and the mobile software process from design and development to testing and publication of commercial-grade applications.

The book is divided into six parts. Here is an overview of the various parts:

- **Part I: An Overview of the Android Platform**
Part I provides an introduction to Android, explaining how it differs from other mobile platforms. You become familiar with the Android SDK and tools, install the development tools, and write and run your first Android application—on the

emulator and on a handset. This section is of primary interest to developers and testers, especially white-box testers.

- **Part II: Android Application Basics**
  Part II introduces the design principles necessary to write Android applications. You learn how Android applications are structured and how to include resources, such as strings, graphics, and user interface components, in your projects. This section is of primary interest to developers.

- **Part III: Android User Interface Design Essentials**
  Part III dives deeper into how user interfaces are designed in Android. You learn about the core user interface element in Android: the View. You also learn about the most common user interface controls and layouts provided in the Android SDK. This section is of primary interest to developers.

- **Part IV: Android Application Design Essentials**
  Part IV covers the features used by most Android applications, including storing persistent application data using preferences and working with files, directories, and content providers. You also learn how to design applications that will run smoothly on many different Android devices. This section is of primary interest to developers.

- **Part V: Publishing and Distributing Android Applications**
  Part V covers the software development process for mobile, from start to finish, with tips and tricks for project management, software developers, user experience designers, and quality assurance personnel.

- **Part VI: Appendixes**
  Part VI includes several helpful appendixes to help you get up and running with the most important Android tools. This section consists of an overview of the Android development tools, two helpful quick-start guides for the Android development tools—the emulator and DDMS—an appendix of Android IDE tips and tricks, as well as answers to the end-of-chapter quiz questions.

An Overview of Changes in This Edition

When we began writing the first edition of this book, there were no Android devices on the market. Today there are hundreds of devices shipping all over the world—smartphones, tablets, e-book readers, smart watches, and specialty devices such as gaming consoles, Google TV, and Google Glass. Other devices such as Google Chromecast provide screen sharing between Android devices and TVs.

The Android platform has gone through extensive changes since the first edition of this book was published. The Android SDK has many new features, and the development tools have received many much-needed upgrades. Android, as a technology, is now the leader within the mobile marketplace.

In this new edition, we took the opportunity to add a wealth of information about how to plan the Android application experience for users. In addition, we have included valuable and ready-to-use techniques for automating the testing of your Android applications, to ensure that you deliver high-quality code. We have also updated many chapters and accompanying content for making use of `Fragment`-based implementation approaches. But don't worry, it's still the book readers loved the first, second, and third time around; it's just much bigger, better, and more comprehensive, following many best practices. In addition to adding new content, we've retested and upgraded all existing content (text and sample code) for use with the latest Android SDKs available while still remaining backward compatible. We created quiz questions to help readers ensure they understand each chapter's content, and we added end-of-chapter exercises for readers to perform to dig deeper into all that Android has to offer. The Android development community is diverse, and we aim to support all developers, regardless of which devices they are developing for. This includes developers who need to target nearly all platforms, so coverage in some key areas of older SDKs continues to be included because it's often the most reasonable option for compatibility.

Here are some of the highlights of the additions and enhancements we've made to this edition:

- Coverage of the latest and greatest Android tools and utilities is included.
- The topic of planning the Android application experience now has its own chapter, which includes a discussion of different navigation patterns with a new code sample and presents techniques that you can use to improve the quality of the user experience.
- The chapter on testing has brand-new content to include topics such as unit testing and provides a practical code sample showing how to leverage the automated testing techniques used by the experts for testing their Android applications.
- A new code sample and a discussion of how to add an `ActionBar` to your applications have been included.
- The chapter on dialogs has been completely updated to make use of `DialogFragments`.
- The chapter on Android preferences now includes an additional code sample with a brand-new discussion of how to add preference fragments that display accordingly within single-pane and multipane layouts.
- The publishing chapter has been completely redesigned to discuss using the new Google Play Developer Console for publishing your applications, in addition to outlining new features provided within the console.
- All chapters and appendixes now include quiz questions and exercises for readers to test their knowledge of the subject matter presented.
- All existing chapters have been updated, often with some entirely new sections.
- All sample code and accompanying applications have been updated to work with the latest SDK.

As you can see, we cover many of the hottest and most exciting features that Android has to offer. We didn't take this review lightly; we touched every existing chapter, updated content, and added new chapters as well. Finally, we included many additions, clarifications, and, yes, even a few fixes based on the feedback from our fantastic (and meticulous) readers. Thank you!

Development Environments Used in This Book

The Android code in this book was written using the following development environments:

- Windows 7
- Android ADT Bundle (the `adt-bundle-windows-x86-20130729.zip` file was used)
- Android SDK Version 4.3, API Level 18 (Jelly Bean)
- Android SDK Tools Revision 22.0.5
- Android SDK Platform Tools 18.0.1
- Android SDK Build Tools 18.0.1
- Android Support Library Revision 18 (where applicable)
- Java SE Development Kit (JDK) 6 Update 45
- Android devices: Nexus 4 (phone), Nexus 7 (small tablet), and Nexus 10 (large tablet)

The Android platform continues to grow aggressively in market share against competing mobile platforms, such as Apple iOS and BlackBerry. New and exciting types of Android devices reach consumers' hands at a furious pace. Developers have embraced Android as a target platform to reach the device users of today and tomorrow.

Android's latest major platform update, Android 4.3—frequently called by its code name, Jelly Bean, or just JB—brings many new features that help differentiate Android from the competition. This book features the latest SDK and tools available, but it does not focus on them to the detriment of popular legacy versions of the platform. The book is meant to be an overall reference to help developers support all popular devices on the market today. As of the writing of this book, approximately 37.9% of users' devices are running a version of Android Jelly Bean, 4.1 or 4.2. Of course, some devices will receive upgrades, and users will purchase new Jelly Bean devices as they become available, but for now, developers need to straddle this gap and support numerous versions of Android to reach the majority of users in the field. In addition, the next version of the Android operating system is likely to be released in the near future.

So what does this mean for this book? It means we provide legacy API support and discuss some of the newer APIs available in later versions of the Android SDK. We discuss strategies for supporting all (or at least most) users in terms of compatibility. And we provide screenshots that highlight different versions of the Android SDK, because each major revision has brought with it a change in the look and feel of the overall platform. That said, we are assuming that you are downloading the latest Android tools, so we provide screenshots and steps that support the latest tools available at the time of writing, not legacy tools. Those are the boundaries we set when trying to determine what to include and leave out of this book.

Supplementary Materials Available

The source code that accompanies this book is available for download from our book's website: *http://introductiontoandroid.blogspot.com/2013/05/book-code-samples.html*. You'll also find other Android topics discussed at our book website (*http://introductiontoandroid .blogspot.com*).

Where to Find More Information

There is a vibrant, helpful Android developer community on the Web. Here are a number of useful websites for Android developers and followers of the wireless industry:

- Android Developer website: the Android SDK and developer reference site: *http://d.android.com/index.html or http://d.android.com*
- Google Plus: Android Developers Group *https://plus.google.com/+AndroidDevelopers/posts*
- Stack Overflow: the Android website with great technical information (complete with tags) and an official support forum for developers: *http://stackoverflow.com/questions/tagged/android*
- Open Handset Alliance: Android manufacturers, operators, and developers: *http://openhandsetalliance.com*
- Google Play: buy and sell Android applications: *https://play.google.com/store*
- Mobiletuts+: mobile development tutorials, including Android: *http://mobile.tutsplus.com/category/tutorials/android*
- anddev.org: an Android developer forum: *http://anddev.org*
- Google Team Android Apps: open-source Android applications: *http://apps-for-android.googlecode.com*
- Android Tools Project Site: the tools team discusses updates and changes: *https://sites.google.com/a/android.com/tools/recent*
- FierceDeveloper: a weekly newsletter for wireless developers: *http://fiercedeveloper.com*
- Wireless Developer Network: daily news on the wireless industry: *http://wirelessdevnet.com*

- XDA-Developers Android Forum: from general development to ROMs: *http://forum.xda-developers.com/forumdisplay.php?f=564*
- Developer.com: a developer-oriented site with mobile articles: *http://developer.com*

Conventions Used in This Book

This book uses the following conventions:

- Code and programming terms are set in `monospace` text.
- Java import statements, exception handling, and error checking are often removed from printed code examples for clarity and to keep the book a reasonable length.

This book also presents information in the following sidebars:

Tip

Tips provide useful information or hints related to the current text.

Note

Notes provide additional information that might be interesting or relevant.

Warning

Warnings provide hints or tips about pitfalls that may be encountered and how to avoid them.

Contacting the Authors

We welcome your comments, questions, and feedback. We invite you to visit our blog at

- *http://introductiontoandroid.blogspot.com*

Or email us at

- introtoandroid4e@gmail.com

Circle us on Google+:

- Joseph Annuzzi, Jr.: *http://goo.gl/FBQeL*
- Lauren Darcey: *http://goo.gl/P3RGo*
- Shane Conder: *http://goo.gl/BpVJh*

An Overview of the Android Platform

1

Introducing Android

The mobile development community has completely embraced Android as a first-class operating system. Developing for Android is now a major focus for companies that would like to target and retain a mobile user base for their businesses. Mobile developers are using Android to define what a mobile application experience should be. Finally, handset manufacturers and mobile operators have invested heavily in Android to create unique experiences for their customers.

Android has emerged as a game-changing platform for the mobile development community. An innovative and open platform, Android is well positioned to address the growing needs of the mobile marketplace as it continues to expand beyond early adopters and purchasers of high-end smart devices.

This chapter explains what Android is, how and why it was developed, and where the platform fits into the established mobile marketplace. The first half of this chapter focuses on the history, and the second half narrows in on how the Android platform operates.

A Brief History of Mobile Software Development

To understand what makes Android so compelling, we must examine how mobile development has evolved and how Android differs from competing platforms.

Way Back When

Remember way back when a phone was just a phone? When we relied on fixed landlines? When we ran for the phone instead of pulling it out of our pocket? When we lost our friends at a crowded ball game and waited around for hours hoping to reunite? When we forgot the grocery list (see Figure 1.1) and had to find a pay phone or drive back home again?

Those days are long gone. Today, commonplace problems such as these are easily solved with a one-button speed dial or a simple text message such as "WRU?" or "20?" or "Milk and?"

Our mobile phones keep us safe and connected. Now we roam around freely, relying on our phones not only to keep us in touch with friends, family, and coworkers, but also to tell us where to go, what to do, and how to do it. Even the simplest events seem to involve a mobile phone these days.

Figure 1.1   Mobile phones have become a crucial shopping accessory.

Consider the following true story, which has been slightly enhanced for effect:

Once upon a time, on a warm summer evening, I was happily minding my own business cooking dinner in my new house in rural New Hampshire when a bat swooped over my head, scaring me to death.

The first thing I did—while ducking—was to pull out my cell phone and send a text message to my husband, who was across the country at the time. I typed, "There's a bat in the house!"

My husband did not immediately respond (a divorce-worthy incident, I thought at the time), so I called my dad and asked him for suggestions on how to get rid of the bat.

He just laughed.

Annoyed, I snapped a picture of the bat with my phone and sent it to my husband and my blog, simultaneously guilt-tripping him and informing the world of my treacherous domestic wildlife encounter.

Finally, I Googled "get rid of a bat," and then I followed the helpful do-it-yourself instructions provided on the Web for people in my situation. I also learned that late August is when baby bats often leave the roost for the first time and learn to fly. Newly aware that I had a baby bat on my hands, I calmly got a broom and managed to herd the bat out of the house. Problem solved—and I did it all with the help of my trusty cell phone, the old LG VX9800.

So what is the point here? Today's mobile devices aren't called smartphones for no reason. They can solve just about any problem—and we rely on them for everything these days.

Notice that half a dozen different mobile applications were used over the course of this story. Each application was developed by a different company and had a different user interface. Some were well designed; others not so much. Some of the applications were purchased, and others came on the phone free of charge.

From the user perspective, the experience was functional, but not terribly inspiring. From the perspective of a mobile developer, there seemed to be an opportunity to create a more seamless and powerful application that could handle all the tasks performed and more—to build a better bat trap, if you will.

Before Android, mobile developers faced many roadblocks when it came to writing applications. Building the better application, the unique application, the competing application, the hybrid application, and incorporating many common tasks, such as messaging and calling, in a familiar way was often unrealistic.

To understand why, let's take a brief look at the history of mobile software development.

"The Brick"

The Motorola DynaTAC 8000X was the first commercially available portable cell phone. First marketed in 1983, it was 13 X 1.75 X 3.5 inches in dimension, weighed about 2.5 pounds, and allowed you to talk for a little more than half an hour. It retailed for $3,995, plus hefty monthly service fees and per-minute charges.

We called it "The Brick," and the nickname stuck for many of those early mobile phones we alternately loved and hated. About the size of a brick, with battery power just long enough for half a conversation, those early mobile handsets were mostly seen in the hands of traveling business execs, security personnel, and the wealthy. First-generation mobile phones were just too expensive. The service charges alone would bankrupt the average person, especially when roaming.

Early mobile phones were not particularly full featured (although even the Motorola DynaTAC, shown in Figure 1.2, had many of the buttons we've come to know well, such as the SEND, END, and CLR buttons). These early phones did little more than make and receive calls, and if you were lucky, there was a simple contacts application that wasn't impossible to use.

The first-generation mobile phones were designed and developed by the handset manufacturers. Competition was fierce and trade secrets were closely guarded. Manufacturers

Figure 1.2   The first commercially available
mobile phone: the Motorola DynaTAC.

didn't want to expose the internal workings of their handsets, so they usually developed the phone software in-house. As a developer, if you weren't part of this inner circle, you had no opportunity to write applications for the phones.

It was during this period that we saw the first "time-waster" games begin to appear. Nokia was famous for putting the 1970s video game Snake on some of its earliest monochrome phones. Other manufacturers followed suit, adding games such as Pong, Tetris, and Tic-Tac-Toe.

These early devices were flawed, but they did something important—they changed the way people thought about communication. As mobile device prices dropped, batteries improved, and reception areas grew, more and more people began carrying these handy devices. Soon mobile devices were more than just a novelty.

Customers began pushing for more features and more games. But there was a problem. The handset manufacturers didn't have the motivation or the resources to build every

Figure 1.3   Various mobile phone form factors:
the candy bar, the slider, and the clamshell.

application users wanted. They needed some way to provide a portal for entertainment and information services without allowing direct access to the handset.

What better way to provide these services than the Internet?

Wireless Application Protocol (WAP)

As it turned out, allowing direct phone access to the Internet didn't scale well for mobile.

By this time, professional websites were full color and chock full of text, images, and other sorts of media. These sites relied on JavaScript, Flash, and other technologies to enhance the user experience, and they were often designed with a target resolution of 800 × 600 pixels and higher.

When the first clamshell phone, the Motorola StarTAC, was released in 1996, it merely had an LCD ten-digit segmented display. (Later models would add a dot-matrix-type display.) Meanwhile, Nokia released one of the first slider phones, the 8110—fondly referred to as "The Matrix Phone" because the phone was heavily used in films. The 8110 could display four lines of text with 13 characters per line. Figure 1.3 shows some of the common phone form factors.

With their postage-stamp-size low-resolution screens and limited storage and processing power, these phones couldn't handle the data-intensive operations required by traditional Web browsers. The bandwidth requirements for data transmission were also costly to the user.

The Wireless Application Protocol (WAP) standard emerged to address these concerns. Simply put, WAP was a stripped-down version of Hypertext Transfer Protocol (HTTP), which is the backbone protocol of the World Wide Web. Unlike traditional

Web browsers, WAP browsers were designed to run within the memory and bandwidth constraints of the phone. Third-party WAP sites served up pages written in a markup language called Wireless Markup Language (WML). These pages were then displayed on the phone's WAP browser. Users navigated as they would on the Web, but the pages were much simpler in design.

The WAP solution was great for handset manufacturers. The pressure was off—they could write one WAP browser to ship with the handset and rely on developers to come up with the content users wanted.

The WAP solution was great for mobile operators. They could provide a custom WAP portal, directing their subscribers to the content they wanted to provide, and rake in the data charges associated with browsing, which were often high.

For the first time, developers had a chance to develop content for phone users, and some did so, with limited success. Few gained any traction in the consumer market because the content was of limited value and the end user experience left much to be desired.

Most of the early WAP sites were extensions of popular branded websites, such as CNN.com and ESPN.com, which were looking for new ways to extend their readership. Suddenly phone users could access the news, stock market quotes, and sports scores on their phones.

Commercializing WAP applications was difficult, and there was no built-in billing mechanism. Some of the most popular commercial WAP applications that emerged during this time were simple wallpaper and ringtone catalogs that enabled users to personalize their phones for the first time. For example, a user browsed a WAP site and requested a specific item. He filled out a simple order form with his phone number and his handset model. It was up to the content provider to deliver an image or audio file compatible with the given phone. Payment and verification were handled through various premium-priced delivery mechanisms such as Short Message Service (SMS), Enhanced Messaging Service (EMS), Multimedia Messaging Service (MMS), and WAP Push.

WAP browsers, especially in the early days, were slow and frustrating. Typing long URLs with the numeric keypad was onerous. WAP pages were often difficult to navigate. Most WAP sites were written one time for all phones and did not account for individual phone specifications. It didn't matter if the end user's phone had a big color screen or a postage-stamp-size monochrome screen; the developer couldn't tailor the user's experience. The result was a mediocre and not very compelling experience for everyone involved.

Content providers often didn't bother with a WAP site and instead just advertised SMS short codes on TV and in magazines. In this case, the user sent a premium SMS message with a request for a specific wallpaper or ringtone, and the content provider sent it back. Mobile operators generally liked these delivery mechanisms because they received a large portion of each messaging fee.

WAP fell short of commercial expectations. In some markets, such as Japan, it flourished, whereas in others, such as the United States, it failed to take off. Handset screens were too small for surfing. Reading a sentence fragment at a time, and then waiting seconds for the next segment to download, ruined the user experience, especially because every second of downloading was often charged to the user. Critics began to call WAP "Wait and Pay."

Finally, the mobile operators who provided the WAP portal (the default home page loaded when you started your WAP browser) often restricted which WAP sites were accessible. The portal enabled the operator to restrict the number of sites users could browse and to funnel subscribers to the operator's preferred content providers and exclude competing sites. This kind of walled garden approach further discouraged third-party developers, who already faced difficulties in monetizing applications, from writing applications.

Proprietary Mobile Platforms

It came as no surprise that users wanted more—they will always want more.

Writing robust applications with WAP, such as graphics-intensive video games, was nearly impossible. The 18-to-25-year-old sweet-spot demographic—the kids with the disposable income most likely to personalize their phones with wallpapers and ringtones—looked at their portable gaming systems and asked for a device that was both a phone and a gaming device or a phone and a music player. They argued that if devices such as Nintendo's Game Boy could provide hours of entertainment with only five buttons, why not just add phone capabilities? Others looked to their digital cameras, Palms, BlackBerries, iPods, and even their laptops and asked the same question. The market seemed to be teetering on the edge of device convergence.

Memory was getting cheaper, batteries were getting better, and PDAs and other embedded devices were beginning to run compact versions of common operating systems such as Linux and Windows. The traditional desktop application developer was suddenly a player in the embedded device market, especially with smartphone technologies such as Windows Mobile, which they found familiar.

Handset manufacturers realized that if they wanted to continue to sell traditional handsets, they needed to change their protectionist policies pertaining to handset design and expose their internal frameworks to some extent.

A variety of different proprietary platforms emerged for traditional handsets. Some smartphone devices ran Palm OS (later known as WebOS) and RIM BlackBerry OS. Sun Microsystems took its popular Java platform and J2ME emerged (now known as Java Micro Edition [Java ME]). Chipset maker Qualcomm developed and licensed its Binary Runtime Environment for Wireless (BREW). Other platforms, such as Symbian OS, were developed by handset manufacturers such as Nokia, Sony Ericsson, Motorola, and Samsung. The Apple iPhone OS (OS X iPhone) joined the ranks in 2008.

Many of these platforms operate associated developer programs. These programs keep the developer communities small, vetted, and under contractual agreements on what they can and cannot do. These programs are often required, and developers even pay to participate.

Each platform has benefits and drawbacks. Of course, developers love to debate about which platform is "the best." (Hint: It's usually the platform we're currently developing for.)

The truth is that no one platform has emerged victorious. Some platforms are best suited for commercializing games and making millions—if your company has brand backing. Other platforms are more open and suitable for the hobbyist or vertical market applications. No mobile platform is best suited for all possible applications. As a result, the mobile phone market has become increasingly fragmented, with all platforms sharing parts of the pie.

For manufacturers and mobile operators, handset product lines quickly became complicated. Platform market penetration varies greatly by region and user demographic. Instead of choosing just one platform, manufacturers and operators have been forced to sell phones for all the different platforms to compete in the market. We've even seen some handsets supporting multiple platforms. (For instance, BlackBerry 10 phones provide a runtime to support Android applications.)

The mobile developer community has become as fragmented as the market. It's nearly impossible to keep track of all the changes. Developer specialty niches have formed. The platform development requirements vary greatly. Mobile software developers work with distinctly different programming environments, different tools, and different programming languages. Porting among the platforms is often costly and not straightforward. Furthermore, application testing services, signing and certification programs, carrier relationship management services, and application marketplaces have become complex spin-off businesses of their own.

It's a nightmare for the ACME Company that wants a mobile application. Should it develop an application for BlackBerry? iPhone? Windows Phone? Everyone has a different kind of phone. ACME is forced to choose one or, worse, all of the platforms. Some platforms allow for free applications, whereas others do not. Vertical market application opportunities are limited and expensive.

As a result, many wonderful applications have not reached their desired users, and many other great ideas have not been developed at all.

The Open Handset Alliance

Enter search advertising giant Google. Now a household name, Google has shown an interest in spreading its vision, its brand, its search and ad revenue–based platform, and its suite of tools to the wireless marketplace. The company's business model has been amazingly successful on the Internet and, technically speaking, wireless isn't that different.

Google Goes Wireless

The company's initial forays into mobile were beset with all the problems you would expect. The freedoms Internet users enjoyed were not shared by mobile phone subscribers. Internet users can choose from a wide variety of computer brands, operating systems, Internet service providers, and Web browser applications.

Nearly all Google services are free and ad driven. Many applications in the Google Labs suite directly compete with the applications available on mobile phones. The applications range from simple calendars and calculators to navigation with Google Maps and the latest tailored news from News Alerts—not to mention corporate acquisitions such as Blogger and YouTube.

When this approach didn't yield the intended results, Google decided on a different approach—to revamp the entire system upon which wireless application development was based, hoping to provide a more open environment for users and developers: the Internet model. The Internet model allows users to choose among freeware, shareware, and paid software. This enables free-market competition among services.

Forming the Open Handset Alliance

With its user-centric, democratic design philosophies, Google has led a movement to turn the existing closely guarded wireless market into one where phone users can move between carriers easily and have unfettered access to applications and services. With its vast resources, Google has taken a broad approach, examining the wireless infrastructure—from the FCC wireless spectrum policies to the handset manufacturers' requirements, application developer needs, and mobile operator desires.

Next, Google joined with other like-minded members in the wireless community and posed the following question: What would it take to build a better mobile phone?

The Open Handset Alliance (OHA) was formed in November 2007 to answer that very question. The OHA is a business alliance composed of many of the largest and most successful mobile companies on the planet. Its members include chip makers, handset manufacturers, software developers, and service providers. The entire mobile supply chain is well represented.

Andy Rubin has been credited as the father of the Android platform. His company, Android, Inc., was acquired by Google in 2005. Working together, OHA members, including Google, began developing an open-standard platform based on technology developed at Android, Inc., that would aim to alleviate the aforementioned problems hindering the mobile community. The result is the Android project.

Google's involvement in the Android project has been so extensive that who takes responsibility for the Android platform (the OHA or Google) is unclear. Google provides the initial code for the Android open-source project and provides online Android documentation, tools, forums, and the Software Development Kit (SDK) for developers. Most major Android news originates from Google. The company has also hosted a number of events at conferences (Google IO, Mobile World Congress, CTIA Wireless) and the Android Developer Challenge (ADC), a series of contests to encourage developers to write killer Android applications—for millions of dollars in prizes to spur development on the platform. That's not to say Google is the only organization involved, but it is the driving force behind the platform.

Manufacturers: Designing Android Devices

More than half the members of the OHA are device manufacturers, such as Samsung, Motorola, Dell, Sony Ericsson, HTC, and LG, and semiconductor companies, such as Intel, Texas Instruments, ARM, NVIDIA, and Qualcomm.

Figure 1.4   A sampling of Android devices on the market today.

The first shipping Android handset—the T-Mobile G1—was developed by handset manufacturer HTC with service provided by T-Mobile. It was released in October 2008. Many other Android handsets were slated for 2009 and early 2010. The platform gained momentum relatively quickly. By the fourth quarter of 2010, Android had come to dominate the smartphone market, gaining ground steadily against competitive platforms such as RIM BlackBerry, Apple iOS, and Windows Mobile.

Google normally announces Android platform statistics at its annual Google IO conference each year and at important events, such as financial earnings calls. As of May 2013, Android devices were being shipped to more than 130 countries, more than 1.5 million new Android devices were being activated every day, and about 900 million devices have been activated in total. The advantages of widespread manufacturer and carrier support appear to be really paying off at this point.

Manufacturers continue to create new generations of Android devices—from phones with HD displays, to watches for managing exercise programs, to dedicated e-book readers, to full-featured televisions, netbooks, and almost any other "smart" device you can imagine (see Figure 1.4).

Mobile Operators: Delivering the Android Experience

After you have the devices, you have to get them out to the users. Mobile operators from North, South, and Central America as well as Europe, Asia, India, Australia, Africa, and the Middle East have joined the OHA, ensuring a worldwide market for the Android movement. With almost half a billion subscribers alone, telephony giant China Mobile is a founding member of the alliance.

Much of Android's success is also due to the fact that many Android handsets don't come with the traditional smartphone price tag—quite a few are offered free with activation by carriers. Competitors such as the Apple iPhone have struggled to provide competitive offerings at the low end of the market. For the first time, the average Jane or Joe can afford a feature-full smart device. We've heard so many people, from wait staff to grocery store clerks, say how much their lives have changed for the better after receiving their first Android phone. This phenomenon has only added to the Android's underdog status.

Manufacturers have contributed significantly to the growth of Android. In January 2013, Samsung announced that its Galaxy S line has sold more than 100 million units worldwide (*http://www.samsungmobilepress.com/2013/01/14/Samsung-GALAXY-S-Series-Surpasses-100-Million-Unit-Sales*). Within the first month after the release of the Galaxy S4, Samsung achieved sales of more than 10 million of the devices.

Google has also created its own Android brand known as Nexus. There are currently three devices in the Nexus line, the Nexus 4, 7, and 10, each created in partnership with the handset manufacturers LG, Asus, and Samsung, respectively. The Nexus devices provide the full, authentic Android experience as Google intends. Many developers use these devices for building and testing their applications because they are the only devices in the world that receive the latest Android operating system upgrades as they are released. If you, too, would like your applications to work on the latest Android operating system version, you should consider investing in one or more of these devices.

Apps Drive Device Sales: Developing Android Applications

When users acquire Android devices, they need those killer apps, right?

Initially, Google led the pack in developing Android applications, many of which, such as the email client and Web browser, are core features of the platform. They also developed the first successful distribution platform for third-party Android applications: the Android Market, now known as the Google Play store. The Google Play store remains the primary method by which users download apps, but it is no longer the only distribution mechanism for Android apps.

As of July 2013, there have been more than 50 billion application installations from the Google Play store. This takes into account only applications published through this one marketplace—not the many other applications sold individually or on other markets. These numbers also do not take into account all the Web applications that target mobile devices running the Android platform. This opens up even more application choices for Android users and more opportunities for Android developers.

The Google Play store has recently received a significant redesign, and there has been a growing effort to increase the exposure and sales of game applications. One way Google plans to increase the distribution of games is by providing the new Google Play Game Services SDK. This SDK will allow developers to add real-time social features to games, and application programming interfaces (APIs) for implementing leaderboards and achievements to help drive new users to applications, while continuing to engage existing users.

Another reason for the Google Play redesign is to help drive sales of content. Users are always looking for new music, movies, TV shows, books, magazines, and more, and Google Play's focus on content has placed it in a position to keep up with user demand for such services.

Taking Advantage of All Android Has to Offer

Android's open platform has been embraced by much of the mobile development community—extending far beyond the members of the OHA.

As Android devices and applications have become more readily available, many other mobile operators and device manufacturers have jumped at the chance to sell Android devices to their subscribers, especially given the cost benefits compared to proprietary platforms. The open standard of the Android platform has resulted in reduced operator costs in licensing and royalties, and we are now seeing a migration to more open devices. The market has cracked wide open; new types of users are able to consider smartphones for the first time. Android is well suited to fill this demand.

The Android Marketplace: Where We Are Now

The Android marketplace continues to grow at an aggressive rate on all fronts (devices, developers, and users). Lately, the focus has been on several topics:

- **Competitive hardware and software feature upgrades:** The Android SDK developers have focused on providing APIs for features that are not available on competing platforms to move Android ahead in the market. For example, recent releases of the Android SDK have featured significant improvements such as Google Now contextual services.

- **Expansion beyond smartphones:** Tablet usage is on the rise with Android users. There are many new tablets on the market with Android Jelly Bean that come in many different sizes and form factors. Some hardware manufacturers are even using Android for gaming consoles, smart watches, and TVs, in addition to many other types of devices that require an operating system.

- **Improved user-facing features:** The Android development team has shifted its focus from feature implementation to providing user-facing usability upgrades and "chrome." They have invested heavily in creating a smoother, faster, more responsive user interface, in addition to updating their design documentation with excellent trainings with best practices for developers to follow. Those principles are centered around three goals and focused on the user experience: "Enchant me," "Simplify my life," and "Make me amazing." Following these principles should help any application increase usability.

Note

Some may wonder about various legal battles surrounding Android that appear to involve almost every industry player in the mobile market. Although most of these issues do not affect developers directly, some have—in particular, those dealing with in-app purchases. This is typical of any popular platform. We can't provide any legal advice here. What we can recommend is keeping informed on the various legal battles and hope they turn out well, not just for Android, but for all platforms they impact.

Android Platform Differences

The Android platform itself is hailed as "the first complete, open, and free mobile platform":

- **Complete:** The designers took a comprehensive approach when they developed the Android platform. They began with a secure operating system and built a robust software framework on top that allows for rich application development opportunities.

- **Open:** The Android platform is provided through open-source licensing. Developers have unprecedented access to the device features when developing applications.

- **Free:** Android applications are free to develop. There are no licensing fees for developing on the platform. No required membership fees. No required testing fees. No required signing or certification fees. Android applications can be distributed and commercialized in a variety of ways. There is no cost for distributing your applications on your own, but to do so in the Google Play store requires registration and paying a small, one-time $25 fee. (The term *free* implies there might actually be costs for development, but they are not mandated by the platform. Costs for designing, developing, testing, marketing, and maintaining are not included. If you provide all of these, you may not be laying out cash, but there is a cost associated with them. The $25 developer registration fee is designed to encourage developers to create quality applications.)

Android: A Next-Generation Platform

Although Android has many innovative features not available in existing mobile platforms, its designers also leveraged many tried-and-true approaches that have been proven to work in the wireless world. It's true that many of these features appear in existing proprietary platforms, but Android combines them in a free and open fashion while simultaneously addressing many of the flaws on these competing platforms.

The Android mascot is a little green robot, shown in Figure 1.5. This little guy (girl?) is often used to depict Android-related materials.

Android is the first in a new generation of mobile platforms, giving its developers a distinct edge over the competition. Android's designers examined the benefits and drawbacks

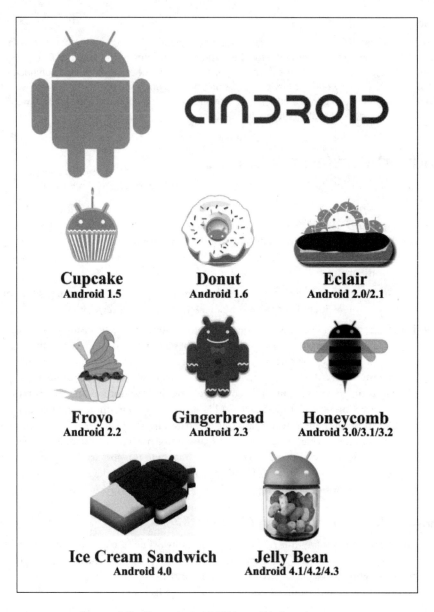

Figure 1.5   Some Android SDKs and their code names.

of existing platforms and then incorporated their most successful features. At the same time, Android's designers avoided the mistakes others made in the past.

Since the Android 1.0 SDK was released, Android platform development has continued at a fast and furious pace. For quite some time, a new Android SDK came out every couple of months! In typical tech-sector jargon, each Android SDK has had a project name. In Android's case, the SDKs are named alphabetically after sweets (see Figure 1.5).

The latest version of Android is code-named Jelly Bean, and the next version of Android is a highly anticipated release.

Free and Open Source

Android is an open-source platform. Neither developers nor device manufacturers pay royalties or license fees to develop for the platform.

The underlying operating system of Android is licensed under GNU General Public License Version 2 (GPLv2), a strong "copyleft" license where any third-party improvements must continue to fall under the open-source licensing agreement terms. The Android framework is distributed under the Apache Software License (ASL/Apache2), which allows for the distribution of both open- and closed-source derivations of the source code. Platform developers (device manufacturers, especially) can choose to enhance Android without having to provide their improvements to the open-source community. Instead, platform developers can profit from enhancements such as device-specific improvements and redistribute their work under whatever licensing they want.

Android application developers also have the ability to distribute their applications under whatever licensing scheme they prefer. They can write open-source freeware or traditional licensed applications for profit and everything in between.

Familiar and Inexpensive Development Tools

Unlike some proprietary platforms that require developer registration fees, vetting, and expensive compilers, there are no up-front costs to developing Android applications.

Freely Available Software Development Kit

The Android SDK and tools are freely available. Developers can download the Android SDK from the Android website after agreeing to the terms of the Android Software Development Kit License Agreement.

Familiar Language, Familiar Development Environments

Developers have several choices when it comes to integrated development environments (IDEs). Many developers choose the popular and freely available Eclipse IDE to design and develop Android applications. Eclipse is one of the most popular IDEs for Android development, and an Android Eclipse plugin known as the Android Developer Tools (ADT) is available for facilitating Android development. Furthermore, the Android SDK may be downloaded as a bundle that includes the Eclipse IDE preconfigured with the ADT plugin, known as the Android IDE. In addition, the Android team released an alternative to Eclipse named Android Studio, which is based on the Community Edition of IntelliJ IDEA. Android applications can be developed on the following operating systems:

- Windows XP (32-bit), Windows Vista (32-bit or 64-bit), and Windows 7 (32-bit or 64-bit)
- Mac OS X 10.5.8 or later (x86 only)
- Linux (Ubuntu Linux 8.04 or later is required)

Reasonable Learning Curve for Developers

Android applications are written in a well-respected programming language: Java.

The Android application framework includes traditional programming constructs, such as threads and processes and specially designed data structures to encapsulate objects commonly used in mobile applications. Developers can rely on familiar class libraries such as `java.net` and `java.text`. Specialty libraries for tasks such as graphics and database management are implemented using well-defined open standards such as OpenGL Embedded Systems (OpenGL ES) and SQLite.

Enabling Development of Powerful Applications

In the past, device manufacturers often established special relationships with trusted third-party software developers (OEM/ODM relationships). This elite group of software developers wrote native applications, such as messaging and Web browsers, that shipped on the device as part of its core feature set. To design these applications, the manufacturer would grant the developer privileged inside access and knowledge of the internal software framework and firmware.

On the Android platform, there is no distinction between native and third-party applications, thus helping maintain healthy competition among application developers. All Android applications use the same APIs. Android applications have unprecedented access to the underlying hardware, allowing developers to write much more powerful applications. Applications can be extended or replaced altogether.

Rich, Secure Application Integration

Recall from the bat story previously shared, where one of the authors accessed a variety of phone applications in the course of a few moments: text messaging, phone dialer, camera, email, picture messaging, and the browser. Each was a separate application running on the phone—some built in and some purchased. Each had its own unique user interface. None were truly integrated.

Not so with Android. One of the Android platform's most compelling and innovative features is well-designed application integration. Android provides all the tools necessary to build a better "bat trap," if you will, by allowing developers to write applications that seamlessly leverage core functionality such as Web browsing, mapping, contact management, and messaging. Applications can also become content providers and share their data with each other in a secure fashion.

In the past, platforms such as Symbian have suffered from setbacks due to malware. Android's vigorous application security model helps protect the user and the system from malicious software, although Android devices are not immune to malware.

No Costly Obstacles for Development

Android applications require none of the costly and time-intensive testing and certification programs that other platforms such as iOS do. A one-time low-cost ($25) developer fee is required to publish applications within the Google Play store. To create Android applications, there is no cost whatsoever other than your time. All you need is a computer, an Android device, a good idea, and an understanding of Java.

A "Free Market" for Applications

Android developers are free to choose any kind of revenue model they want. They can develop freeware, shareware, trial-ware, ad-driven applications, and paid applications. Android was designed to fundamentally change the rules about what kind of wireless applications could be developed. In the past, developers faced many restrictions that had little to do with the application functionality or features:

- Store limitations on the number of competing applications of a given type
- Store limitations on pricing, revenue models, and royalties
- Operator unwillingness to provide applications for smaller demographics

With Android, developers can write and successfully publish any kind of application they want. Developers can tailor applications to small demographics, instead of just large-scale moneymaking ones often insisted upon by mobile operators. Vertical market applications can be deployed to specific, targeted users.

Because developers have a variety of application distribution mechanisms to choose from, they can pick the methods that work for them instead of being forced to play by others' rules. Android developers can distribute their applications to users in a variety of ways:

- Google developed the Google Play store (formerly the Android Market), a generic Android application store with a revenue-sharing model. The Google Play store now has a Web store for browsing and buying apps online (see Figure 1.6). Google Play also sells movies, music, and books, so your application will be in good company.
- Amazon Appstore for Android launched in 2011 with a lineup of exciting Android applications using its own billing and revenue-sharing models. A unique feature of Amazon Appstore for Android is that it allows users to demo certain applications in the Web browser or from within the Amazon Appstore app before purchasing them. Amazon uses an environment similar to the emulator that runs right in the browser.

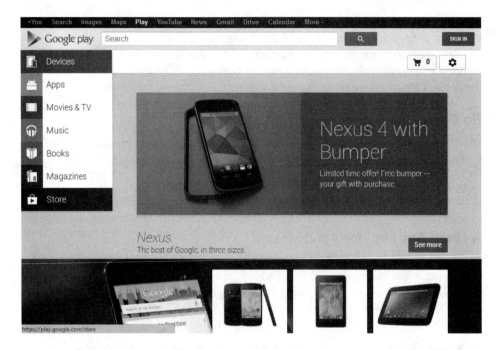

Figure 1.6   The Google Play store online, showing the `Devices` tab.

- Numerous other third-party application stores are available. Some are for niche markets; others cater to many different mobile platforms.
- Developers can come up with their own delivery and payment mechanisms, such as distributing from a website or within an enterprise.

Mobile operators and carriers are still free to develop their own application stores and enforce their own rules, but these will no longer be the only opportunities developers have to distribute their applications. Be sure to read any application store agreements carefully before distributing your applications on them.

A Growing Platform

Early Android developers have had to deal with the typical roadblocks associated with a new platform: frequently revised SDKs, lack of good documentation, market uncertainties, and mobile operators and device manufacturers that have been extremely slow in rolling out new upgrades of Android, if ever. This means that Android developers often need to target several different SDK versions to reach all users. Luckily, the continuously evolving Android development tools have made this easier than ever, and now that Android is a well-established platform, many of these issues have been ironed out. The Android forum community is lively and friendly and very supportive when it comes to helping one another over these bumps in the road.

Each new version of the Android SDK has provided a number of substantial improvements to the platform. In recent revisions, the Android platform has received some much-needed UI "polish," in terms of both visual appeal and performance. Popular types of devices such as tablets and Internet TVs are now fully supported by the platform, in addition to new devices such as Google Glass and smart watches. Screen sharing of Android devices and applications is now possible with the release of API Level 18 and a new device known as Chromecast.

Although most of these upgrades and improvements were welcome and necessary, new SDK versions often cause some upheaval within the Android developer community. A number of published applications have required retesting and resubmission to the Google Play store to conform to new SDK requirements, which are quickly rolled out to all Android devices in the field as a firmware upgrade, rendering older applications obsolete and sometimes unusable.

Although these growing pains are expected, and most developers have endured them, it's important to remember that Android was a latecomer to the mobile marketplace compared to the RIM and iOS platforms. The Apple App Store boasts many applications, but users demand these same applications on their Android devices. Fewer developers can afford to deploy exclusively to one platform or the other—they must support all the popular ones.

The Android Platform

Android is an operating system and a software platform upon which applications are developed. A core set of applications for everyday tasks, such as Web browsing and email, are included on Android devices.

As a product of the OHA's vision for a robust and open-source development environment for wireless, Android is an emerging mobile development platform. The platform was designed for the sole purpose of encouraging a free and open market that users might want to have and software developers might want to develop for.

Android's Underlying Architecture

The Android platform is designed to be more fault tolerant than many of its predecessors. The device runs a Linux operating system upon which Android applications are executed in a secure fashion. Each Android application runs in its own virtual machine (see Figure 1.7). Android applications are managed code; therefore, they are much less likely to cause the device to crash, leading to fewer instances of device corruption (also called "bricking" the device, or rendering it useless).

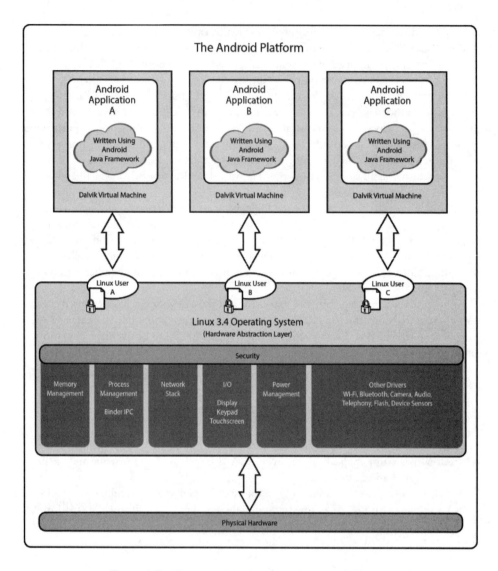

Figure 1.7 Diagram of the Android platform architecture.

The Linux Operating System

The Linux 3.4 kernel handles core system services and acts as a hardware abstraction layer (HAL) between the physical hardware of the device and the Android software stack.

Some of the core functions the kernel handles include

- Enforcement of application permissions and security
- Low-level memory management
- Process management and threading
- The network stack
- Display, keypad input, camera, Wi-Fi, Flash memory, audio, binder inter-process communication (IPC), and power management driver access

Android Application Runtime Environment

Each Android application runs in a separate process, with its own instance of the Dalvik virtual machine (VM). Based on the Java VM, the Dalvik design has been optimized for mobile devices. The Dalvik VM has a small memory footprint and optimized application loading, and multiple instances of the Dalvik VM can run concurrently on a device.

Security and Permissions

The integrity of the Android platform is maintained through a variety of security measures. These measures help ensure that the user's data is secure and that the device is not subjected to malware or misuse.

Applications as Operating System Users

When an application is installed, the operating system creates a new user profile associated with the application. Each application runs as a different user, with its own private files on the file system, a user ID, and a secure operating environment.

The application executes in its own process with its own instance of the Dalvik VM and under its own user ID on the operating system.

Explicitly Defined Application Permissions

To access shared resources on the system, Android applications register for the specific privileges they require. Some of these privileges enable the application to use device functionality to make calls, access the network, and control the camera and other hardware sensors. Applications also require permission to access shared data containing private and personal information, such as user preferences, the user's location, and contact information.

Applications might also enforce their own permissions by declaring them for other applications to use. An application can declare any number of different permission types, such as read-only or read-write permissions, for finer control over the application.

Limited Ad Hoc Permissions

Applications that act as content providers might want to provide some on-the-fly permissions to other applications for specific information they want to share openly. This is done using ad hoc granting and revoking of access to specific resources using Uniform Resource Identifiers (URIs).

URIs index specific data assets on the system, such as images and text. Here is an example of a URI that provides the phone numbers of all contacts:

```
content://contacts/phones
```

To understand how this permission process works, let's look at an example.

Let's say we have an application that keeps track of the user's public and private birthday wish lists. If this application wanted to share its data with other applications, the application could grant URI permissions for the public wish list, allowing another application to access this list without explicitly having to ask the user for it.

Application Signing for Trust Relationships

All Android application packages are signed with a certificate, so users know that the application is authentic. The private key for the certificate is held by the developer. This helps establish a trust relationship between the developer and the user. It also enables the developer to control which applications can grant access to one another on the system. No certificate authority is necessary; self-signed certificates are acceptable.

Multiple Users and Restricted Profiles

Android 4.2 (API Level 17) brought support for multiple user accounts on shareable Android devices such as tablets. With the new release of Android 4.3 (API Level 18), primary device users are now able to create restricted profiles for limiting a user profile's access to particular applications. Developers may also leverage restricted profile capabilities in their applications to provide primary users the ability to further prohibit particular device users from accessing specific in-app content.

Google Play Developer Registration

To publish applications on the popular Google Play store, developers must create a developer account. The Google Play store is managed closely and no malware is tolerated.

Exploring Android Applications

The Android SDK provides an extensive set of APIs that are both modern and robust. Android device core system services are exposed and accessible to all applications. When granted the appropriate permissions, Android applications can share data with one another and access shared resources on the system securely.

Android Programming Language Choices

Android applications are written in Java (see Figure 1.8). For now, the Java language is the developer's only choice for accessing the entire Android SDK.

Figure 1.8   Duke, the Java mascot.

Tip

There has been some speculation that other programming languages, such as C++, might be added in future versions of Android. If your application must rely on native code in another language such as C or C++, you might want to consider integrating it using the Android Native Development Kit (NDK).

You can also develop mobile Web applications that will run on Android devices. These applications can be accessed through an Android browser application, or an embedded WebView control within a native Android application (still written in Java). This book focuses on native application development. You can find out more about developing Web applications for Android devices at the Android Developer website: *http://d.android.com/guide/webapps/index.html.*

Got a Flash app you want to deploy to the Android platform? Check out Adobe's AIR support for the Android platform. Users install the Adobe AIR application from the Google Play store and then load your compatible applications using it. For more information, see the Adobe website: *http://adobe.com/devnet/air/air_for_android.html.*

Developers even have the option to build applications using certain scripting languages. There is an open-source project that is working to use scripting languages such as Python and others as options for building Android applications. For more information, see the android-scripting project site: *https://code.google.com/p/android-scripting.* As with Web apps and Adobe AIR apps, developing SL4A applications is outside the scope of this book.

No Distinctions Made between Native and Third-Party Applications

Unlike other mobile development platforms, the Android platform makes no distinction between native applications and developer-created applications. Provided they are granted the appropriate permissions, all applications have the same access to core libraries and the underlying hardware interfaces.

Android devices ship with a set of native applications such as a Web browser and contact manager. Third-party applications might integrate with these core applications, extend them to provide a rich user experience, or replace them entirely with alternative applications. The idea is that any of these applications is built using the exact same APIs available to third-party developers, thus ensuring a level playing field, or as close to one as we can get.

Note that although this has been Google's line since the beginning, there are some cases where Google has used undocumented APIs. Because Android is open, there are no private APIs. Google has never blocked access to such APIs but has warned developers that using them may result in incompatibilities in future SDK versions. See the blog post at *http://android-developers.blogspot.com//2011/10/ics-and-non-public-apis.html* for some examples of previously undocumented APIs that have become publicly documented.

Commonly Used Packages

With Android, mobile developers no longer have to reinvent the wheel. Instead, developers use familiar class libraries exposed through Android's Java packages to perform common tasks involving graphics, database access, network access, secure communications, and utilities. The Android packages include support for the following:

- A wide variety of user interface controls (Buttons, Spinners, Text input)
- A wide variety of user interface layouts (Tables, Tabs, Lists, Galleries)
- Integration capabilities (Notifications, Widgets)
- Secure networking and Web browsing features (SSL, WebKit)
- XML support (DOM, SAX, XML Pull Parser)
- Structured storage and relational databases (App Preferences, SQLite)
- Powerful 2D and 3D graphics (including SGL, OpenGL ES, and RenderScript)
- Multimedia frameworks for playing and recording standalone or network streaming (`MediaPlayer`, `JetPlayer`, `SoundPool`, `AudioManager`)
- Extensive support for many audio and visual media formats (MPEG4, H.264, MP3, AAC, AMR, JPG, and PNG)
- Access to optional hardware such as location-based services (LBS), USB, Wi-Fi, Bluetooth, and hardware sensors

Android Application Framework

The Android application framework provides everything necessary to implement an average application. The Android application lifecycle involves the following key components:

- Activities are functions that the application performs.
- Groups of views define the application's layout.
- Intents inform the system about an application's plans.

- Services allow for background processing without user interaction.
- Notifications alert the user when something interesting happens.
- Content providers facilitate data transmission among different applications.

Android Platform Services

Android applications can interact with the operating system and underlying hardware using a collection of managers. Each manager is responsible for keeping the state of some underlying system service. For example:

- The `LocationManager` facilitates interaction with the location-based services available on the device.
- The `ViewManager` and `WindowManager` manage display and user interface fundamentals related to the device.
- The `AccessibilityManager` manages accessibility events, facilitating device support for users with physical impairments.
- The `ClipboardManager` provides access to the global clipboard for the device, for cutting and pasting content.
- The `DownloadManager` manages HTTP downloads in the background as a system service.
- The `FragmentManager` manages the fragments of an activity.
- The `AudioManager` provides access to audio and ringer controls.

Google Services

Google provides APIs for integrating with many different Google services. Prior to the addition of many of these services, developers would need to wait for mobile operators and device manufacturers to upgrade Android on their devices in order to take advantage of many common features such as maps or location-based services. Now developers are able to integrate the latest and greatest updates of these services by including the required SDKs in their application projects. Some of these Google services include

- Maps
- Location-based services
- Game Services
- Authorization APIs
- Google Plus
- Play Services
- In-app Billing
- Google Cloud Messaging
- Google Analytics
- Google AdMob ads

Summary

Mobile software development has evolved over time. Android has emerged as a new mobile development platform, building on past successes and avoiding past failures of other platforms. Android was designed to empower the developer to write innovative applications. The platform is open source, with no up-front fees, and developers enjoy many benefits over other competing platforms. Now it's time to dive deeper so you can evaluate what Android can do for you.

Quiz Questions

1. What is the nickname of the first mobile phone sold for personal use?
2. What 1970s game did Nokia load onto its early mobile devices?
3. What was the name of the company that Google purchased that is credited for developing much of the technology used in the Android operating system?
4. What was the first Android device called? Which manufacturer created it? Which mobile operator sold it?

Exercises

1. Describe the benefits of Android being open source.
2. In your own words, describe Android's underlying architecture.
3. Familiarize yourself with the Android documentation, which can be found here: *http://d.android.com/index.html*.

References and More Information

Android Development:
   http://d.android.com/index.html
Open Handset Alliance:
   http://openhandsetalliance.com
Official Android Developers Blog:
   http://android-developers.blogspot.com
This book's blog:
   http://introductiontoandroid.blogspot.com

2

Setting Up Your Android Development Environment

Android developers write and test applications on their computers and then deploy those applications onto the actual device hardware for further testing.

In this chapter, you become familiar with all the tools you need to master in order to develop Android applications. You learn information about configuring your development environment both on a virtual device and on real hardware. You also explore the Android SDK and all it has to offer.

Note

The Android SDK and Android Development Tool Bundles are updated frequently. We have made every attempt to provide the latest steps for the latest tools. However, these steps and the user interfaces described in this chapter may change at any time. Please refer to the Android development website (*http://d.android.com/sdk/index.html*) and our book website (*http://introductiontoandroid.blogspot.com*) for the latest information.

Configuring Your Development Environment

To write Android applications, you must configure your programming environment for Java development. The software is available online for download at no cost. Android applications can be developed on Windows, Macintosh, or Linux systems.

To develop Android applications, you need to have the following software installed on your computer:

- The Java Development Kit (JDK), Version 6, available for download at *http://oracle .com/technetwork/java/javase/downloads/index.html* (or *http://java.sun.com/javase/ downloads/index.jsp*, if you're nostalgic).

- The latest Android SDK. In this book, we will cover using the Android SDK included in the ADT Bundle, which is available for Windows, Mac, or Linux and can be downloaded at *http://d.android.com/sdk/index.html*. The ADT Bundle includes everything you will need for working on the examples in this book and for developing Android applications. Other items included in the ADT Bundle are the SDK

Tools, Platform Tools, the latest Android platform, and the latest Android System image for the emulator.

- A compatible Java IDE is required. Luckily, the ADT Bundle provides the Android IDE, which is a special version of the Eclipse IDE. The Android IDE comes ready with the ADT plugin already installed. This book focuses on using the Android IDE. An alternative to using the Android IDE would be to use your own copy of Eclipse. You will need Eclipse 3.6.2 (Helios) or later and either Eclipse IDE for Java Developers, Eclipse Classic, or Eclipse IDE for Java EE Developers. When using your own copy of Eclipse, you should install the ADT plugin for Eclipse. This plugin is available for download through the Eclipse software update mechanism. For instructions on how to install this plugin, see *http://d.android.com/tools/sdk/eclipse-adt.html*. Although this tool is optional for development, we highly recommend installing it when using a regular Eclipse IDE. We will use many of this plugin's features frequently throughout this book, although this will be done using the Android IDE.

A complete list of Android development system requirements is available at *http://d .android.com/sdk/index.html*.

Tip

Most developers use the Android IDE for Android development. The Android development team has integrated the Android development tools directly into the Eclipse IDE. However, developers are not constrained to using the Android IDE or Eclipse; they can also use other IDEs, such as the new Android Studio based on IntelliJ IDEA. This book does not cover how to develop Android applications with Android Studio. For information on using Android Studio, read the getting-started guide at *http://d.android.com/sdk/installing/studio.html*. For information on using other development environments, begin by reading *http://d.android.com/ tools/projects/projects-cmdline.html*; it talks about using the command-line tools, which may be useful for using other environments. In addition, read *http://d.android.com/tools/ debugging/debugging-projects-cmdline.html* for information on debugging from other IDEs, and *http://d.android.com/tools/testing/testing_otheride.html* for testing from other IDEs.

The basic installation process follows these steps:

1. Download and install the appropriate JDK.
2. (Android IDE users only) Download and unzip the appropriate Android SDK ADT Bundle.
3. (Eclipse users only) Download and install the appropriate Android SDK Tools, Eclipse IDE, and the Android ADT plugin for Eclipse. Configure the Android settings in the Eclipse preferences. Make sure you specify the directory where you installed the Android SDK and save your settings.
4. Launch the IDE and use the Android SDK Manager to download and install specific Android platform versions and other components you might use, including the documentation, sample applications, USB drivers, and additional tools. The

Android SDK Manager is available as a standalone tool in the Android ADT Bundle, as well as from within the Android IDE (or Eclipse once you have installed the plugin in the previous step). In terms of which components you'll want to choose, we recommend a full installation (choose everything).

5. Configure your computer for device debugging by installing the appropriate USB drivers, if necessary.

6. Configure your Android device(s) for device debugging.

7. Start developing Android applications.

In this book, we do not give you detailed step-by-step instructions for installing each and every component listed in the preceding steps for three main reasons. First, this is an intermediate/advanced book, and we expect you have some familiarity with installing Java development tools and SDKs. Second, the Android Developer website provides fairly extensive information about installing development tools and configuring them on a variety of different operating systems. Installation instructions for setting up the ADT Bundle are available at *http://d.android.com/sdk/installing/bundle.html*, and instructions for setting up an existing IDE are available at *http://d.android.com/sdk/installing/index .html*. Third, the exact steps required to install the Android SDK tend to change subtly with each and every major release (and some minor releases), so you're always better off checking the Android Developer website for the latest information. Finally, keep in mind that the Android SDK, ADT Bundle, and tools are updated frequently and may not exactly match the development environment used in this book, as defined in the Introduction. That said, we will help you work through some of the later steps in the process described in this section, starting after you've installed and configured the JDK and the ADT Bundle in step 2. We'll poke around in the Android SDK and look at some of the core tools you'll need to use to develop applications. Then, in the next chapter, you'll test your development environment and write your first Android application.

Configuring Your Operating System for Device Debugging

To install and debug Android applications on Android devices, you need to configure your operating system to access the phone via the USB cable (see Figure 2.1). On some operating systems, such as Mac OS, this may just work. However, for Windows installations, you need to install the appropriate USB driver. You can download the Windows USB driver from the following website: *http://d.android.com/sdk/win-usb.html*. Under Linux, there are some additional steps to perform. See *http://d.android.com/tools/device .html* for more information.

Configuring Your Android Hardware for Debugging

Android devices have debugging disabled by default. Your Android device must be enabled for debugging via a USB connection to allow the tools to install and launch the applications you deploy.

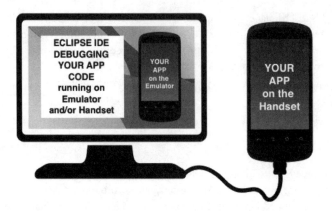

Figure 2.1   Android application debugging using
the emulator and an Android handset.

Devices that have Android 4.2+ require enabling Developer Options for testing your applications on real hardware. We will be discussing how to configure your hardware for working with Android 4.3, but if you are working with a different version of Android, check out the following link to learn how to get set up with your version: *http://d .android.com/tools/device.html#setting-up*. Different versions of Android use different setup methods, so just perform the method for the version you have.

Note

You can enable the Developer Options by selecting Home, All Apps, Settings, About Phone (or About Tablet); then scroll down to Build Number, and press Build Number seven times. After a few presses, you will notice a message displaying "You are now X steps away from being a developer." Continue to press Build Number until you are told that Developer Options have been enabled. If you do not enable the Developer Options, you will not be able to install your applications on your device.

You need to enable your device to install Android applications other than those from the Google Play store. This setting is reached by navigating to Settings, Security. Here, you should check (enable) the option called Unknown sources, as shown in Figure 2.2. If you do not enable this option, you cannot install developer-created applications, the sample applications, or applications published on alternative markets without the developer tools. Loading applications from servers or even email is a great way to test deployments.

Several other important development settings are available on the Android device by selecting Home, All Apps, Settings, Developer options (see Figure 2.3).

Figure 2.2   Enabling Unknown sources on the device.

Figure 2.3   Enabling Android developer settings on the device.

Here, you should enable the following options:

- `USB debugging`: This setting enables you to debug your applications via the USB connection.
- `Allow mock locations`: This setting enables you to send mock location information to the phone for development purposes and is very convenient for applications using LBS.

Upgrading the Android SDK

The Android SDK is upgraded from time to time. You can easily upgrade the Android SDK and tools from within the Android IDE using the Android SDK Manager, which is installed as part of the ADT plugin.

Changes to the Android SDK might include addition, update, and removal of features; package name changes; and updated tools. With each new version of the SDK, Google provides the following useful documents:

- An Overview of Changes: A brief description of the major changes to the SDK
- An API Diff Report: A complete list of specific changes to the SDK
- Release Notes: A list of known issues with the SDK

These documents are available with every new release of the Android SDK. For instance, Android 4.3 information is available at *http://d.android.com/about/versions/android-4.3.html*, and Android 4.2 information is available at *http://d.android.com/about/versions/android-4.2.html*.

You can find out more about adding and updating SDK packages at *http://d.android.com/sdk/installing/adding-packages.html*.

Problems with the Android Software Development Kit

Because the Android SDK is constantly under active development, you might come across problems with it. If you think you've found a problem, you can find a list of open issues and their status at the Android project's Issue Tracker website. You can also submit new issues for review.

The Issue Tracker website for the Android open-source project is *https://code.google.com/p/android/issues/list*. For more information about logging your own bugs or defects to be considered by the Android platform development team, check out the following website: *http://source.android.com/source/report-bugs.html*.

Tip

Frustrated with how long it takes for your bug to get fixed? It can be helpful to understand how the Android bug-resolution process works. For more information on this process, see *http://source.android.com/source/life-of-a-bug.html*.

Exploring the Android SDK

The Android SDK ADT Bundle comes with several major components: the Android Application Framework, Platform Tools, SDK Tools, extras, and sample applications.

Understanding the Android SDK License Agreement

Before you can download the Android SDK ADT Bundle, you must review and agree to the Android SDK License Agreement. This agreement is a contract between you (the developer) and Google (copyright holder of the Android SDK).

Even if someone at your company has agreed to the licensing agreement on your behalf, it is important for you, the developer, to be aware of a few important points:

- Rights granted: Google (as the copyright holder of Android) grants you a limited, worldwide, royalty-free, nonassignable, and nonexclusive license to use the SDK solely to develop applications for the Android platform. Google (and third-party contributors) are granting you license, but they still hold all copyrights and intellectual property rights to the material. Using the Android SDK does not grant you permission to use any Google brands, logos, or trade names. You may not remove any of the copyright notices therein. Third-party applications that your applications interact with (other Android apps) are subject to separate terms and fall outside this agreement.

- SDK usage: You may only develop Android applications. You may not make derivative works from the SDK or distribute the SDK on any device or distribute part of the SDK with other software.

- SDK changes and backward compatibility: Google may change the Android SDK at any time, without notice, without regard to backward compatibility. Although Android API changes were a major issue with prerelease versions of the SDK, recent releases have been reasonably stable. That said, each SDK update does tend to affect a small number of existing applications in the field, thus necessitating updates.

- Android application developer rights: You retain all rights to any Android software you develop with the SDK, including intellectual property rights. You also retain all responsibility for your own work.

- Android application privacy requirements: You agree that your application will protect the privacy and legal rights of its users. If your application uses or accesses personal and private information about the user (usernames, passwords, and so on), your application must provide an adequate privacy notice and keep that data stored securely. Note that privacy laws and regulations may vary by user location; you as a developer are solely responsible for managing this data appropriately.

- Android application malware requirements: You are responsible for all applications you develop. You agree not to write disruptive applications or malware. You are solely responsible for all data transmitted through your application.

- Additional terms for specific Google APIs: Use of the Google Maps Android API is subject to further Terms of Service. You must agree to these additional terms before using those specific APIs and always include the Google Maps copyright notice provided. Use of Google APIs (Google apps such as Gmail, Blogger, Google Calendar, YouTube, and so on) is limited to access what the user has explicitly granted permission for during installation time.

- Develop at your own risk: Any harm that comes about from developing with the Android SDK is your own fault and not Google's.

Reading the Android SDK Documentation

The Android documentation is provided in HTML format online at *http://d.android .com/index.html*. If you would like to have a local copy of the docs, you need to download them using the SDK Manager. Once you have downloaded them, a local copy of the Android documentation is provided in the `docs` subfolder of the Android installation directory (as shown in Figure 2.4).

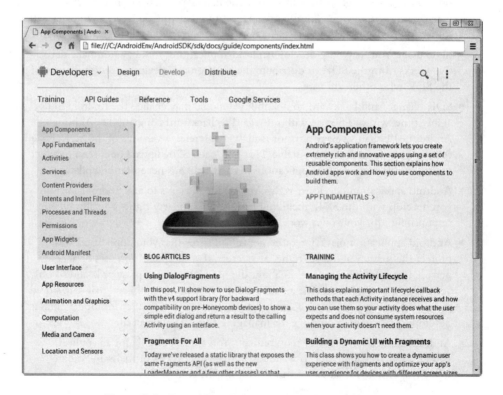

Figure 2.4 The Android SDK documentation viewed offline.

Exploring the Core Android Application Framework

The Android application framework is provided in the `android.jar` file. The Android SDK is made up of several important packages, which are listed in Table 2.1.

Several optional third-party APIs are available outside the core Android SDK. These packages must be installed separately from their respective websites. Some packages are from Google, whereas others are from device manufacturers and other providers. Some of the most popular third-party APIs are described in Table 2.2.

Table 2.1 **Important Packages in the Android SDK**

Top-Level Package Name	Description
`android.*`	Android application fundamentals
`dalvik.*`	Dalvik virtual machine support classes
`java.*`	Core classes and familiar generic utilities for networking, security, math, and so on
`javax.*`	Encryption support
`junit.*`	Unit-testing support
`org.apache.http.*`	HTTP protocol support
`org.json`	JavaScript Object Notation (JSON) support
`org.w3c.dom`	W3C Java bindings for the Document Object Model Core (XML and HTML)
`org.xml.sax.*`	Simple API for XML (SAX) support for XML
`org.xmlpull.*`	High-performance XML pull parsing

Table 2.2 **Popular Third-Party Android APIs**

Optional Android SDKs	Description
Android Support Library Packages: various	Adds several components available in recent SDKs to legacy versions of the SDKs. For example, the Various Loader APIs and Fragment APIs introduced in API Level 11 can be used, in compatibility form, as far back as API Level 4 using this add-on.
Google AdMob Ads SDK Package: `com.google.ads.*`	Allows developers to insert Google AdMob advertisements to monetize their applications. This SDK requires agreement to additional Terms of Service and registration for an account. For more information, see *https://developers.google.com/ mobile-ads-sdk/*.
Google Analytics App Tracking SDK Package: `com.google.analytics .tracking.android.*`	Allows developers to collect and analyze information about how their Android applications are used with the popular Google Analytics service. This SDK requires agreement to additional Terms of Service and registration for an account. For more information, see *https://developers.google.com/analytics/ devguides/collection/android/v2*.

(continues)

Table 2.2 **Continued**

Optional Android SDKs	Description
Android Cloud Messaging for Android (GCM) Package: `com.google.android.gcm`	Provides access to a service for developers to push data from the network to their applications installed on devices. This SDK requires agreement to additional Terms of Service and registration for an account. For more information, see *http://d.android.com/google/gcm/index.html.*
Google Play services Package: `com.google.*`	Facilitates development using Google+, Google Maps, and other Google APIs and services. For example, if you want to include the MapView control in your application, you need to install and use this feature. This add-on requires agreement to additional Terms of Service and registration for an API Key. For more information, see *http://d.android.com/google/play-services/index.html.*

Google Play APK Expansion Library
 	
Package:
`com.google.android`
`.vending.expansion.*`
	Allows developers of applications to create applications beyond the 50MB limit by hosting and serving expansion files from Google Play. This allows up to an additional 4GB per APK. This SDK requires agreement to additional Terms of Service and registration for an account. For more information, see *http://d.android.com/google/play/expansion-files.html.*

Google Play In-app Billing Library
 	
Package:
`com.android.vending`
`.billing`
	Allows developers of applications targeting the Google Play store to enable in-application purchases. This SDK requires agreement to additional Terms of Service and must be tied to your Google Play publisher account. For more information, see *http://d.android.com/google/play/billing/index.html.*

Google Play Licensing Library
 	
Package:
`com.google.android`
`.vending.licensing.*`
	Allows developers of applications targeting the Google Play store to enable in-application license verification. This SDK requires agreement to additional Terms of Service and must be tied to your Google Play publisher account. For more information, see *http://d.android.com/google/play/licensing/index.html.*

Numerous device and manufacturer-specific add-ons and SDKs	You'll find a number of third-party add-ons and manufacturer-specific SDKs available within the Android SDK and Android Virtual Device (AVD) add-ons and SDK Manager's Available Packages. Still others can be found at third-party websites. If you are targeting features available from a specific device or manufacturer, or services from a known service provider, check to see if they have add-ons available for the Android platform.

Exploring the Core Android Tools

The Android SDK provides many tools to design, develop, debug, and deploy your Android applications. For now, we want you to focus on familiarizing yourself with the core tools you need to know about to get up and running with Android applications. We discuss many Android tools in greater detail in Appendix A, "Mastering the Android Development Tools."

The Android IDE and ADT

You'll spend most of your development time in your IDE. This book assumes you are using the Android IDE that comes with the ADT Bundle, because this is the official development environment configuration.

ADT incorporates many of the most important Android SDK tools seamlessly into the Android IDE and provides various wizards for creating, debugging, and deploying Android applications. ADT adds a number of useful functions to the Android IDE. Several buttons are available on the toolbar, including buttons to perform the following actions:

- Launch the Android SDK Manager
- Launch the Android Virtual Device Manager
- Run Android `lint`
- Create a new Android XML resource file

The Android IDE organizes its workspace into perspectives (each a set of specific panes) for different tasks such as coding and debugging. You can switch between perspectives by choosing the appropriate tab in the top-right corner of the Android IDE environment. The `Java` perspective arranges the appropriate panes for coding and navigating around the project. The `Debug` perspective enables you to set breakpoints, view `LogCat` information, and debug. ADT adds several special perspectives for designing and debugging Android applications. The `Hierarchy View` perspective integrates the Hierarchy Viewer tool into the Android IDE so that you can design, inspect, and debug user interface controls within your applications. The `DDMS` perspective integrates the `Dalvik Debug Monitor Server` (DDMS) tool into the Android IDE so that you can attach to emulator and device instances and debug your applications. Figure 2.5 shows the Android IDE toolbar with the Android features (left) and the Android perspectives (right).

You can switch perspectives within the Android IDE by choosing `Window`, `Open Perspective` or by clicking the appropriate perspective tab in the top-right corner of the Android IDE toolbar.

Figure 2.5   Android features and perspectives on the Android IDE toolbar.

Android SDK and AVD Managers

The first Android toolbar icon with the little green Android and the down arrow will launch the Android SDK Manager (see Figure 2.6, top). The second Android toolbar icon, looking like a tiny phone, will launch the Android Virtual Device Manager (see Figure 2.6, bottom).

These tools perform two major functions: management of Android SDK components installed on the development machine and management of the developer's AVD configurations.

Much like desktop computers, different Android devices run different versions of the Android operating system. Developers need to be able to target different Android SDK versions with their applications. Some applications target a specific Android SDK, whereas others try to provide simultaneous support for as many versions as possible.

The Android SDK Manager facilitates Android development across multiple platform versions simultaneously. When a new Android SDK is released, you can use this tool to download and update your tools while still maintaining backward compatibility and use older versions of the Android SDK.

The Android Virtual Device Manager organizes and provides tools to create and edit AVDs. To manage applications in the Android emulator, you must configure different AVD profiles. Each AVD profile describes what type of device you want the emulator to simulate, including which Android platform to support as well what the device specifications should be. You can specify different screen sizes and orientations, and you can specify whether the emulator has an SD card and, if so, what its capacity is, among many other device configuration settings.

Android Emulator

The Android emulator is one of the most important tools provided with the Android SDK. You will use this tool frequently when designing and developing Android applications. The emulator runs on your computer and behaves much as a mobile device would. You can load Android applications into the emulator, test, and debug them.

The emulator is a generic device and is not tied to any one specific phone configuration. You describe the hardware and software configuration details that the emulator is to simulate by providing an AVD configuration. Figure 2.7 shows what the emulator might look like with a typical Android 4.3 smartphone-style AVD configuration.

Figure 2.8 shows what the emulator might look like with a typical Android 4.3 tablet-style AVD configuration. Both Figures 2.7 and 2.8 show how the popular Gallery application behaves differently on different devices.

Tip

You should be aware that the Android emulator is a substitute for a real Android device, but it's an imperfect one. The emulator is a valuable tool for testing but cannot fully replace testing on actual target devices.

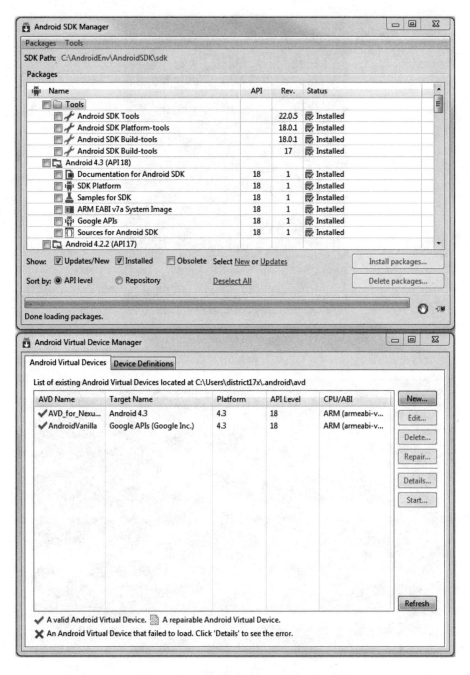

Figure 2.6   The Android SDK Manager (top)
and Android Virtual Device Manager (bottom).

Figure 2.7   The Android emulator (smartphone-style,
Jelly Bean AVD configuration).

Figure 2.8   The Android emulator (tablet-style,
Nexus 7 Jelly Bean AVD configuration).

Exploring the Android Sample Applications

The Android SDK provides many samples and demo applications to help you learn the ropes of Android development. These demo applications are not provided as part of the Android SDK by default, but you can download them for different API levels using the Android SDK Manager. Once downloaded, they will be located in the /samples subdirectory of the Android SDK.

Tip

To learn how to download the Android SDK sample applications using the Android IDE, read the section titled "Adding the Android Samples Using the SDK Manager" in Chapter 3, "Writing Your First Android Application."

More than five dozen sample applications are available to demonstrate different aspects of the Android SDK. Some focus on generic application development tasks such as managing application lifecycle or user interface design.

Some of the most straightforward demo applications to take a look at are

- **ApiDemos:** a menu-driven utility that demonstrates a wide variety of Android APIs, from user interface widgets to application lifecycle components such as services, alarms, and notifications
- **Snake:** a simple game that demonstrates bitmap drawing and key events
- **NotePad:** a simple list application that demonstrates database access and Live Folder functionality
- **LunarLander:** a simple game that demonstrates drawing and animation
- **SkeletonApp and SkeletonAppTest:** a simple application that demonstrates accepting text input
- **Spinner and SpinnerTest:** a simple application that demonstrates some application lifecycle basics, as well as how to create and manage application test cases using the unit test framework
- **TicTacToeMain and TicTacToeLib:** a simple application that demonstrates how to create and manage shared code libraries for use with your applications

There are numerous other sample applications that cover specific topics, but they demonstrate Android features that are discussed later in this book. Some other sample apps are found only online. Some of the most useful online sample applications to take a look at are listed here:

- **Support4Demos:** a sample application that demonstrates the key features in the Android API Level 4+ Support Library, including fragments and loaders
- **Support7Demos:** a sample application that demonstrates the key features in the Android API Level 7+ Support Library, including support for `ActionBar`, `GridLayout`, and `MediaRouter` (API Level 18) for Google Cast

- **Support13Demos:** a sample application that demonstrates the key features in the Android API Level 13+ Support Library, including enhanced `Fragment` support
- **SupportAppNavigation:** a sample application that demonstrates the key features of app navigation for use with the support libraries

Tip

We discuss how to set up your development environment for using the sample applications in Chapter 3, "Writing Your First Android Application." Once the environment is set up, to add a sample project within the Android IDE or Eclipse, select `File`, `New`, `Other`, and then under `Android`, choose `Android Sample Project`. The sample applications available depend on which specific build target is chosen. Proceed as you normally would, by creating a `Run` or `Debug` configuration, compiling and running the application in the emulator or on a device. You will see these steps performed in detail in the next chapter when you test your development environment and write your first application.

Summary

In this chapter, you installed, configured, and began to explore the tools you need to start developing Android applications, including the appropriate JDK, the Android SDK, and the Android IDE or ADT Bundle. You also learned that there are alternative development environments you can choose from, such as Android Studio. You learned how to configure your Android hardware for debugging. Further, you explored many of the tools provided along with the Android SDK and understand their basic purposes. Finally, you perused the sample applications provided along with the Android SDK. You should now have a reasonable development environment configured to write Android applications. In the next chapter, you'll be able to take advantage of all this setup and write an Android application.

Quiz Questions

1. What version of the Java JDK is required for Android development?
2. What security option must be selected on an Android hardware device for installing your own applications without using an Android marketplace?
3. What option must be enabled on your hardware device to debug your applications?
4. What is the name of the `.jar` file that comprises the Android application framework?
5. What is the top-level package name for unit-testing support?
6. Which optional Android SDK is provided by Google for integrating advertising in your applications?

Exercises

1. Open a local copy of the Android documentation provided with the Android SDK.

2. Launch the Android SDK Manager and install at least one other version of Android.

3. Name five other sample applications provided with the Android SDK that were not mentioned in this chapter.

References and More Information

Google's Android Developers Guide:
http://d.android.com/guide/components/index.html
Android SDK download site:
http://d.android.com/sdk/index.html
Android SDK License Agreement:
http://d.android.com/sdk/terms.html
The Java Platform, Standard Edition:
http://oracle.com/technetwork/java/javase/overview/index.html
The Eclipse Project:
http://eclipse.org

3

Writing Your First Android Application

You should now have a workable Android development environment set up on your computer. Ideally, you have an Android device as well. Now it's time for you to start writing some Android code. In this chapter, you learn how to install the Android sample applications and to add and create Android projects from within the Android IDE. You also learn how to verify that your Android development environment is set up correctly. You then write and debug your first Android application in the software emulator and on an Android device.

Note

The Android Development Tool Bundles are updated frequently. We have made every attempt to provide the latest steps for the latest tools. However, these steps and the user interfaces described in this chapter may change at any time. Please refer to the Android development website (*http://d.android.com/sdk/index.html*) and our book website (*http://introductiontoandroid.blogspot.com*) for the latest information.

Testing Your Development Environment

The best way to make sure you configured your development environment correctly is to run an existing Android application. You can do this easily by using one of the sample applications provided as part of the Android SDK in the `samples` subdirectory found where your Android SDK is installed.

Within the Android SDK sample applications, you will find a classic game called Snake (*http://en.wikipedia.org/wiki/Snake_(video_game)*). To build and run the `Snake` application, you must create a new Android project in your Android IDE workspace based on the existing Android sample project, create an appropriate Android Virtual Device (AVD) profile, and configure a launch configuration for that project. After you have everything set up correctly, you can build the application and run it on the Android emulator and on an Android device. By testing your development environment with a sample application, you can rule out project configuration and coding issues and focus on determining

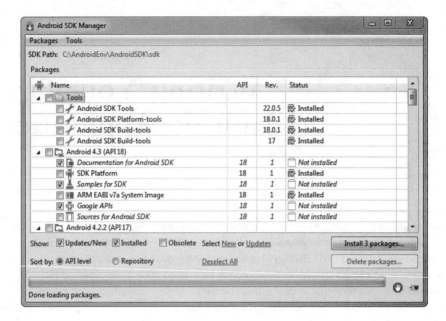

Figure 3.1   The Android SDK Manager.

whether the tools are set up properly for Android development. After this fact has been established, you can move on to writing and compiling your own applications.

Adding the Android Samples Using the SDK Manager

One quick way to learn how to develop Android applications is by reviewing an application that has already been created. There are many Android applications available for this purpose, but first we must download them. Here is how:

1. From within the Android IDE, click the `Android SDK Manager` icon (▣) to open the Android SDK Manager. You should see a dialog similar to that in Figure 3.1.

2. You now need to install the `Samples for SDK` listed under `Android 4.3 (API 18)`, so go ahead and select this item. You may also want to install a few additional items along with the samples, so select the following for installation (shown in Figure 3.1): `Documentation for Android SDK` and `Google APIs`. Then click `Install Packages`. Make sure that the proper `SDK Tools`, `Platform-tools`, `Build-tools`, `SDK Platform`, and `System Image` are installed as well; if they are not, you should select those for installation now, too.

3. A new dialog appears (see Figure 3.2) asking you to accept the license agreement for the packages that you will be installing. You may accept or reject each license

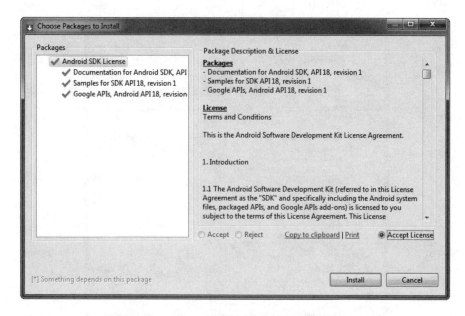

Figure 3.2   Accepting the license agreements.

individually by highlighting a particular package in the left pane and choosing
Accept or Reject, or you can accept them all at once by highlighting Android SDK
License in the left pane and choosing Accept License. Let's accept all the licenses
together by selecting Android SDK License in the left pane, choosing Accept
License, and then clicking Install. This will initiate the installation of the se-
lected packages. Wait until the installation is complete.

Tip

To learn more about how to download the Android SDK sample applications for your particular development platform, see *http://d.android.com/tools/samples/index.html*.

Now that the installation is completed, you are ready to begin loading Android sample
projects into your workspace.

Adding the Snake Project to Your Android IDE Workspace

To add the Snake project to your Android IDE workspace, follow these steps:

1. Choose File, New, Other....

2. Choose Android, Android Sample Project (see Figure 3.3). Click Next.

Figure 3.3   Creating a new Android sample project.

3. Choose your build target (see Figure 3.4). In this case, we've picked Android 4.3, API Level 18, from the Android Open Source Project. Click Next.

4. Select which sample you want to create (see Figure 3.5). Choose Snake.

5. Click Finish. You now see the Snake project files in your workspace (see Figure 3.6).

Warning

Occasionally the Android IDE shows an error like "Project 'Snake' is missing required source folder: gen" when you're adding an existing project to the workspace. If this happens, navigate to the /gen directory and delete the files within. These files are automatically regenerated and the error should disappear. Performing a Clean operation followed by a Build operation does not always solve this problem.

Figure 3.4   Choose an API level for the sample.

Figure 3.5   Picking the Snake sample project.

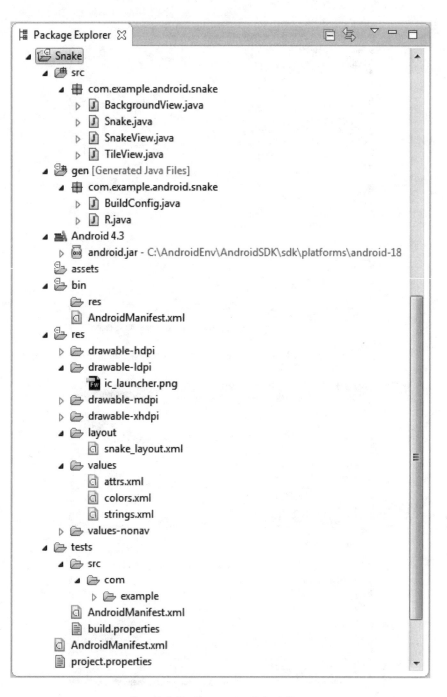

Figure 3.6   The Snake project files.

Creating an AVD for Your Snake Project

The next step is to create an AVD that describes what type of device you want to emulate when running the Snake application. This AVD profile describes what type of device you want the emulator to simulate, including which Android platform to support. You do not need to create new AVDs for each application, only for each device you want to emulate. You can specify different screen sizes and orientations, and you can specify whether the emulator has an SD card and, if it does, what capacity the card has.

For the purposes of this example, an AVD for the default installation of Android 4.3 suffices. Here are the steps to create a basic AVD:

1. Launch the Android Virtual Device Manager from within the Android IDE by clicking the little Android device icon on the toolbar (). If you cannot find the icon, you can also launch the manager through the Window menu of the Android IDE. You should now see the Android Virtual Device Manager window (see Figure 3.7).

2. Click the New button.

3. Choose a name for your AVD. Because we are going to take all the defaults, give this AVD a name of AndroidVanilla.

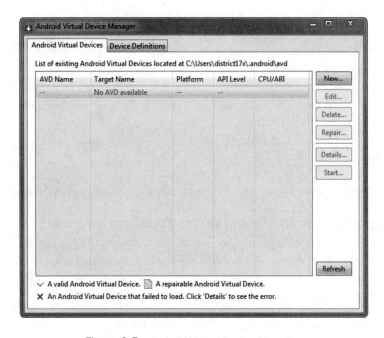

Figure 3.7   Android Virtual Device Manager.

4. Choose a device. This option controls the different resolutions of the emulator. We want to choose a typical device size, so in this case, select Nexus 4 (4.7", 768 × 1280: xhdpi). This option most directly correlates to the popular Nexus 4 Google-branded device. Feel free to choose the most appropriate device to match the Android device on which you plan to run the application.

5. Choose a build target. We want a typical Android 4.3 device, so choose Google APIs (Google Inc.) - API Level 18 from the drop-down menu. In addition to including the Android APIs, this option will also include the Google APIs and applications, such as the Maps application, as part of the platform image. Although we could choose the standard Android 4.3 - APIs Level 18 for this project, it is important to be aware of the additional options the Google APIs provide.

6. For the Memory Options setting, you may have to try different values for optimal performance depending on the memory configuration of your development machine. The default RAM value for this virtual device is 1907 and the VM Heap is 64. If your machine is older and does not have a lot of memory, you may need to lower this value significantly to something like 512. The development machine used for this book has 8GB of RAM with a fairly powerful quad-core processor, and the RAM value we decided to use is 768 with the VM Heap set to 64.

7. Choose an SD card capacity, in either kibibytes or mibibytes. (Not familiar with kibibytes? See this Wikipedia entry: *http://en.wikipedia.org/wiki/Kibibyte*.) This SD card image will take up space on your hard drive and may also take a long time to allocate, so choose something reasonable, such as 1024MiB.

8. Seriously consider enabling the Snapshot feature listed under Emulation Options. This greatly improves emulator startup performance. See Appendix B, "Quick-Start Guide: The Android Emulator," for details.

   Your project settings will look like Figure 3.8.

9. Click the OK button to create the AVD, and then wait for the operation to complete.

10. You should now see the AVD that you just created listed within your Android Virtual Device Manager (see Figure 3.9).

For more information on creating different types of AVDs, check out Appendix B.

Creating a Launch Configuration for Your Snake Project

Next, you must create a launch configuration in the Android IDE to configure under what circumstances the Snake application builds and launches. The launch configuration is where you configure the emulator options to use and the entry point for your application.

You can create Run configurations and Debug configurations separately, each with different options. These configurations are created under the Run menu in the Android IDE

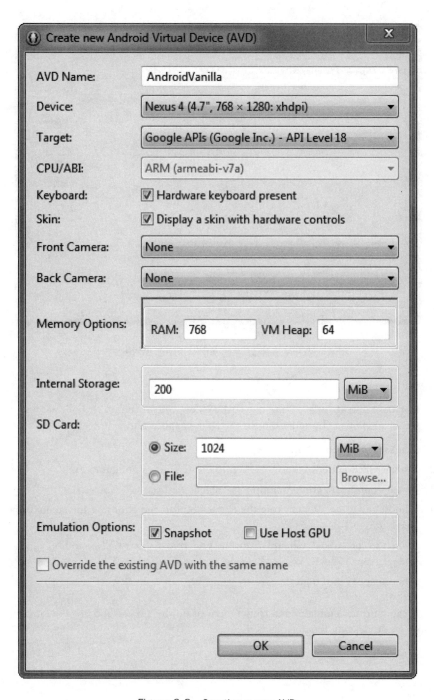

Figure 3.8   Creating a new AVD.

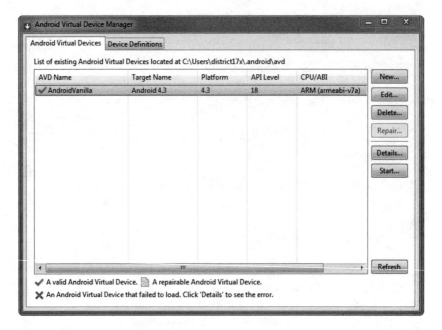

Figure 3.9   The new AVD is now listed.

(Run, Run Configurations... and Run, Debug Configurations...). Follow these steps
to create a basic Debug configuration for the Snake application:

1. Choose Run, Debug Configurations....

2. Double-click Android Application to create a new configuration.

3. Name your Debug configuration SnakeDebugConfig.

4. Choose the project by clicking the Browse button and choosing the Snake project
   (see Figure 3.10).

5. Switch to the Target tab and, from the preferred AVD list, choose the
   AndroidVanilla AVD created earlier, as shown in Figure 3.11.

6. Choose Apply and then Close.

You can set other emulator and launch options on the Target and Common tabs, but
for now we are leaving the defaults as they are.

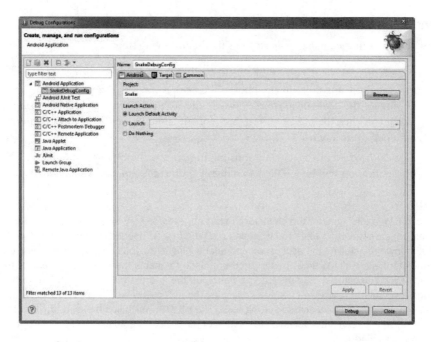

Figure 3.10   Naming the `Debug` configuration in the Android IDE.

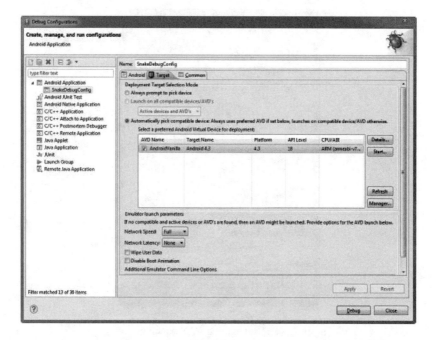

Figure 3.11   `Target` AVD for the `Debug` configuration in the Android IDE.

Running the Snake Application in the Android Emulator

Now you can run the Snake application using the following steps:

1. Choose the Debug As icon drop-down menu on the toolbar (▓).

2. Pull the drop-down menu and choose the SnakeDebugConfig you created. If you do not see the SnakeDebugConfig listed, find it in the Debug Configurations... listing and click the Debug button. Subsequent launches can be initiated from the little bug drop-down.

3. The Android emulator starts up; this might take a few moments to initialize. Then the application will be installed or reinstalled onto the emulator.

Tip

It can take a long time for the emulator to start up, even on very fast computers. You might want to leave it around while you work and reattach to it as needed. The tools in the Android IDE handle reinstalling the application and relaunching it, so you can more easily keep the emulator loaded all the time. This is another reason to enable the Snapshot feature for each AVD. You can also use the Start button on the Android Virtual Device Manager to load an emulator before you need it. Launching the AVD this way also gives you some additional options such as screen scaling (see Figure 3.12), which can be used to either fit the AVD on your screen if it's very high resolution or more closely emulate the size it might be on real hardware.

Figure 3.12   Configuring AVD launch options.

4. If necessary, swipe the screen from left to right to unlock the emulator, as shown in Figure 3.13.

5. The Snake application starts and you can play the game, as shown in Figure 3.14.

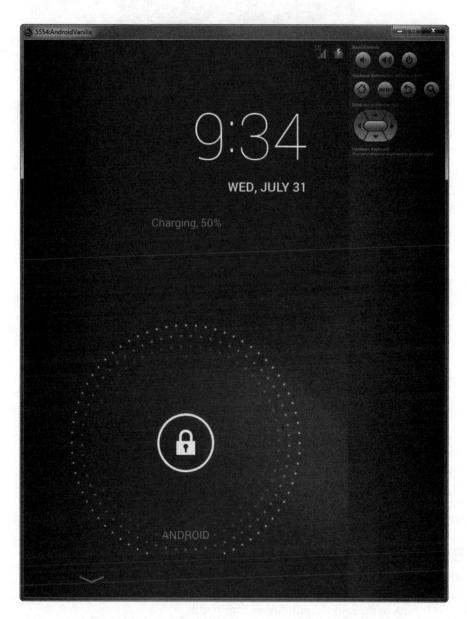

Figure 3.13   The Android emulator launching (locked).

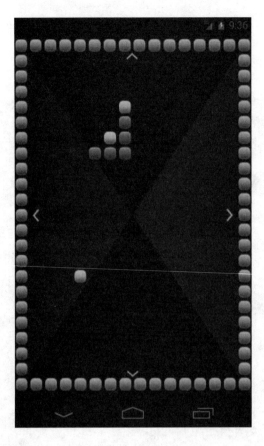

Figure 3.14   The Snake game in the Android emulator.

You can interact with the Snake application through the emulator and play the game. You can also launch the Snake application from the All Apps screen at any time by clicking its application icon. There is no need to shut down and restart the emulator every time you rebuild and reinstall your application for testing. Simply leave the emulator running on your computer in the background while you work in the Android IDE and then redeploy using the Debug configuration again.

Building Your First Android Application

Now it's time to write your first Android application from scratch. To get your feet wet, you will start with a simple "Hello World" application and build upon it to explore some of the features of the Android platform in more detail.

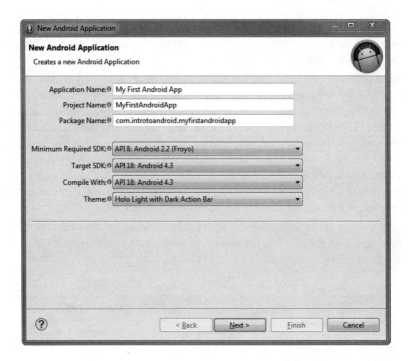

Figure 3.15   Configuring a new Android project.

Tip

The code examples provided in this chapter are taken from the `MyFirstAndroidApp` application. The source code for the `MyFirstAndroidApp` application is provided for download on the book's website.

Creating and Configuring a New Android Project

You can create a new Android application in much the same way that you added the `Snake` application to your Android IDE workspace.

The first thing you need to do is create a new project in your Android IDE workspace. The `Android Application Project` creation wizard creates all the required files for an Android application. Follow these steps within the Android IDE to create a new project:

1. Choose `File`, `New`, `Android Application Project` on the Android IDE toolbar.

2. Choose an application name as shown in Figure 3.15. The application name is the "friendly" name of the application and the name shown with the icon on the

application launcher. Name the application My First Android App. This will automatically create a project name of MyFirstAndroidApp, but you are free to change this to a name of your choosing.

3. We should also change the package name, using reverse domain name notation (*http://en.wikipedia.org/wiki/Reverse_domain_name_notation*), to com.introto android.myfirstandroidapp. The Minimum Required SDK version should be the first SDK API level you plan to target. Because our application will be compatible with just about any Android device, you can set this number low (such as to 4 to represent Android 1.6) or at the target API level to avoid any warnings in the Android IDE. Make sure you set the minimum SDK version to encompass any test devices you have available so you can successfully install the application on them. The default options are just fine for our example. Click Next.

4. Keep the rest of the New Android Application settings at their defaults, unless you want to change the directory of where the source files will be stored. Click Next (see Figure 3.16).

Figure 3.16   Configuring Android project options.

5. Leave the `Configure Launcher Icon` settings at their defaults. This option screen would allow us to define how our application launcher icon appears, but for this example, we will use the standard icon set included with the Android SDK. Choose `Next` (see Figure 3.17).

6. The `Create Activity` wizard allows us to include a default launch activity by type. We will leave the settings as is and choose `Next` (see Figure 3.18).

7. Choose an `Activity Name`. Call this `Activity` class `MyFirstAndroidApp Activity`. The `Layout Name` should automatically change to a name resembling what you just entered. Finally, click the `Finish` button (see Figure 3.19) to create the application.

8. The Android IDE should now display our first application created using the wizard with our layout file open and ready for editing (see Figure 3.20).

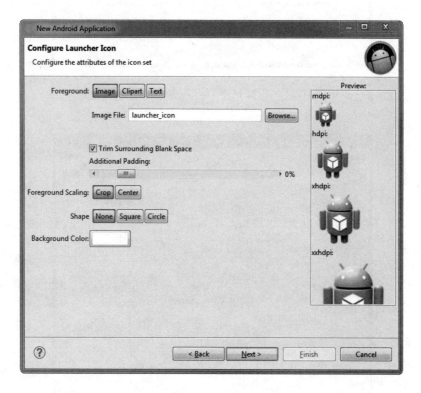

Figure 3.17   Configuring the launcher icon for our Android project.

Figure 3.18   Creating an `Activity` for our Android project.

Figure 3.19   Choosing an `Activity Name`.

Figure 3.20   Our first application created with the wizard.

Core Files and Directories of the Android Application

Every Android application has a set of core files that are created and used to define the functionality of the application. The following files are created by default with a new Android application:

- **AndroidManifest.xml**—the central configuration file for the application. It defines your application's capabilities and permissions as well as how it runs.

- **ic_launcher-web.png**—This is a high-resolution 32-bit 512 × 512 PNG application icon that is required and used for your application listing in the Google Play store. The size of this icon should not exceed 1024KB.

- **proguard-project.txt**—a generated build file used by the Android IDE and Pro-Guard. Edit this file to configure your code optimization and obfuscation settings for release builds.

- **project.properties**—a generated build file used by the Android IDE. It defines your application's build target and other build system options, as required. Do not edit this file.

- **/src**—required folder for all source code.
- **/src/com/introtoandroid/myfirstandroidapp/MyFirstAndroidAppActivity .java**—main entry point to this application, named MyFirstAndroidAppActivity. This activity has been defined as the default launch activity in the Android manifest file.
- **/gen**—required folder for all autogenerated files.
- **/gen/com/introtoandroid/myfirstandroidapp/BuildConfig.java**—a generated source file used when debugging your applications. Do not edit this file.
- **/gen/com/introtoandroid/myfirstandroidapp/R.java**—a generated resource management source file. Do not edit this file.
- **/assets**—required folder where uncompiled file resources can be included in the project. Application assets are pieces of application data (files, directories) that you do not want managed as application resources.
- **/bin**—folder for creating autogenerated files for producing your application's APK file.
- **/libs**—folder for including any .jar library projects.
- **/libs/android-support-v4.jar**—This support library can be added to your projects to bring newer Android APIs to older devices running older versions of Android.
- **/res**—required folder where all application resources are managed. Application resources include animations, drawable graphics, layout files, datalike strings and numbers, and raw files.
- **/res/drawable-***—Application icon graphics resources are included in several sizes for different device screen resolutions.
- **/res/layout**—required folder that comprises one or more layout resource files, each file managing a different UI or App Widget layout for your application.
- **/res/layout/activity_my_first_android_app.xml**—layout resource file used by MyFirstAndroidAppActivity to organize controls on the main application screen.
- **/res/menu**—folder for including XML files for defining Android application menus.
- **/res/menu/my_first_android_app.xml**—menu resource file used by MyFirst AndroidAppActivity defining a menu item for Settings.
- **/res/values***—folders for including XML files for defining Android application dimensions, strings, and styles.
- **/res/values/dimens.xml**—dimension resource file used by MyFirstAndroid AppActivity defining default screen margins.
- **/res/values/strings.xml**—string resource file used by MyFirstAndroidApp Activity defining string variables that may be reused throughout the application.

- **/res/values/styles.xml**—style resource file used by `MyFirstAndroidAppActivity` to define the application theme.

- **/res/values-sw600dp/dimens.xml**—dimension resource file for overriding the `res/values/dimens.xml` for defining dimensions for 7-inch tablets.

- **/res/values-sw720dp-land/dimens.xml**—dimension resource file for overriding the `res/values/dimens.xml` for defining dimensions for 10-inch tablets in landscape mode.

- **/res/values-v11/styles.xml**—style resource file for overriding the `res/values/styles.xml` for devices running Android with an API greater than or equal to 11.

- **/res/values-v14/styles.xml**—style resource file for overriding the `res/values/styles.xml` for devices running Android with an API greater than or equal to 14.

A number of other files are saved on disk as part of the Android IDE project in the workspace. However, the files and resource directories included in the list here are the important project files you will use on a regular basis.

Creating an AVD for Your Project

The next step is to create an AVD that describes what type of device you want to emulate when running the application. For this example, we can use the AVD we created for the `Snake` application. An AVD describes a device, not an application. Therefore, you can use the same AVD for multiple applications. You can also create similar AVDs with the same configuration but different data (such as different applications installed and different SD card contents).

Creating a Launch Configuration for Your Project

Next, you must create a `Run` and `Debug` launch configuration in the Android IDE to configure the circumstances under which the `MyFirstAndroidApp` application builds and launches. The launch configuration is where you configure the emulator options to use and the entry point for your application.

You can create `Run` configurations and `Debug` configurations separately, with different options for each. Begin by creating a `Run` configuration for the application. Follow these steps to create a basic `Run` configuration for the `MyFirstAndroidApp` application:

1. Choose `Run`, `Run Configurations...` (or right-click the project and choose `Run As`).

2. Double-click `Android Application`.

3. Name your configuration `MyFirstAndroidAppRunConfig`.

4. Choose the project by clicking the `Browse` button and choosing the `MyFirstAndroidApp` project.

5. Switch to the `Target` tab and set the `Deployment Target Selection Mode` to `Always prompt to pick device`.

6. Click `Apply` and then click `Close`.

Tip

If you leave the `Deployment Target Selection Mode` set to `Automatic` when you choose `Run` or `Debug` in the Android IDE, your application is automatically installed and run on the device if the device is plugged in. Otherwise, the application starts in the emulator with the specified AVD. By choosing `Always prompt to pick device`, you are always prompted for whether (a) you want your application to be launched in an existing emulator; (b) you want your application to be launched in a new emulator instance and are allowed to specify an AVD; or (c) you want your application to be launched on the device (if it's plugged in). If any emulator is already running, the device is then plugged in, and the mode is set to `Automatic`, you see this same prompt, too.

Now create a `Debug` configuration for the application. This process is similar to creating a `Run` configuration. Follow these steps to create a basic `Debug` configuration for the `MyFirstAndroidApp` application:

1. Choose `Run`, `Debug Configurations...` (or right-click the project and choose `Debug As`).

2. Double-click `Android Application`.

3. Name your configuration `MyFirstAndroidAppDebugConfig`.

4. Choose the project by clicking the `Browse` button and choosing the `MyFirstAndroidApp` project.

5. Switch to the `Target` tab and set the `Deployment Target Selection Mode` to `Always prompt to pick device`.

6. Click `Apply` and then click `Close`.

You now have a `Debug` configuration for your application.

Running Your Android Application in the Emulator

Now you can run the `MyFirstAndroidApp` application using the following steps:

1. Choose the `Run As` icon drop-down menu on the toolbar (🔍).

2. Pull the drop-down menu and choose the `Run` configuration you created. (If you do not see it listed, choose the `Run Configurations...` item and select the appropriate configuration. The `Run` configuration shows up on this drop-down list the next time you run the configuration.)

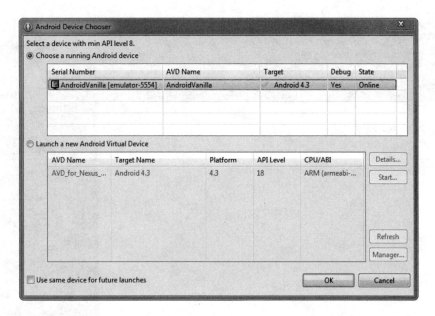

Figure 3.21   Manually choosing a deployment target selection mode.

3. Because you chose the `Always prompt to pick device` selection mode, you are now prompted for your emulator instance. Change the selection to `Launch a New Android Virtual Device` and then select the AVD you created. Here, you can choose from an already-running emulator or launch a new instance with an AVD that is compatible with the application settings, as shown in Figure 3.21.

4. The Android emulator starts up, which might take a moment.

5. Click the `Menu` button or push the slider to the right to unlock the emulator.

6. The application starts, as shown in Figure 3.22.

7. Click the `Back` button in the emulator to end the application, or click `Home` to suspend it.

8. Click the `All Apps` button (see Figure 3.23) found in the `Favorites tray` to browse all installed applications from the `All Apps` screen.

9. Your screen should now look something like Figure 3.24. Click the `My First Android App` icon to launch the application again.

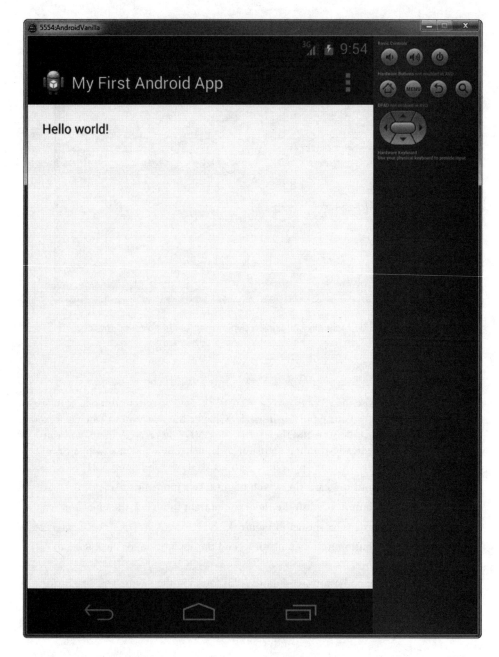

Figure 3.22 My First Android App running in the emulator.

Figure 3.23   The `All Apps` button.

Figure 3.24   The `My First Android App` icon
shown in the `All Apps` screen.

Debugging Your Android Application in the Emulator

Before going any further, you need to become familiar with debugging in the emulator. To illustrate some useful debugging tools, let's manufacture an error in the My First Android App.

In your project, edit the source file called MyFirstAndroidAppActivity.java. Create a new method called forceError() in your class and make a call to this method in your Activity class's onCreate() method. The forceError() method forces a new unhandled error in your application.

The forceError() method should look something like this:

```
public void forceError() {
    if(true) {
        throw new Error("Whoops");
    }
}
```

It's probably helpful at this point to run the application and watch what happens. Do this using the Run configuration first. In the emulator, you see that the application has stopped unexpectedly. You are prompted by a dialog that enables you to force the application to close, as shown in Figure 3.25.

Shut down the application but keep the emulator running. Now it's time to debug. You can debug the MyFirstAndroidApp application using the following steps:

1. Choose the Debug As icon drop-down menu on the toolbar.
2. Pull the drop-down menu and choose the Debug configuration you created. (If you do not see it listed, choose the Debug Configurations... item and select the appropriate configuration. The Debug configuration shows up on this drop-down list the next time you run the configuration.)
3. Continue as you did with the Run configuration and choose the appropriate AVD, and then launch the emulator again, unlocking it if needed.

It takes a moment for the debugger to attach. If this is the first time you've debugged an Android application, you may need to click through some dialogs, such as the one shown in Figure 3.26, the first time your application attaches to the debugger.

In the Android IDE, use the Debug perspective to set breakpoints, step through code, and watch the LogCat logging information about your application. This time, when the application fails, you can determine the cause using the debugger. You might need to click through several dialogs as you set up to debug within the Android IDE. If you allow the application to continue after throwing the exception, you can examine the results in the Debug perspective of the Android IDE. If you examine the LogCat logging pane, you see that your application was forced to exit due to an unhandled exception (see Figure 3.27).

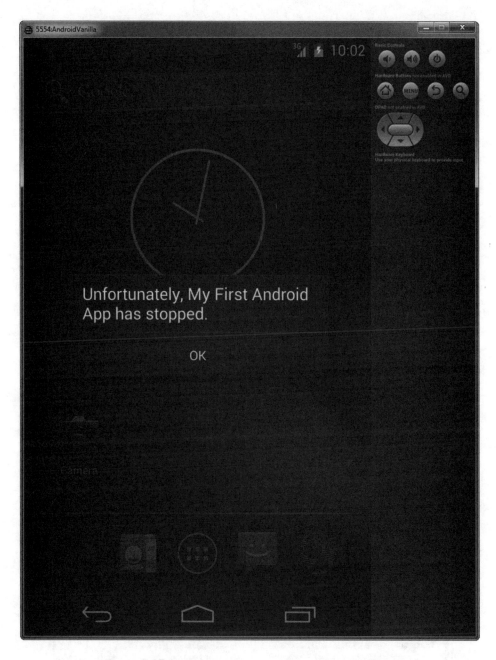

Figure 3.25 `My First Android App` crashing gracefully.

Figure 3.26   Switching to Debug perspective
for Android emulator debugging.

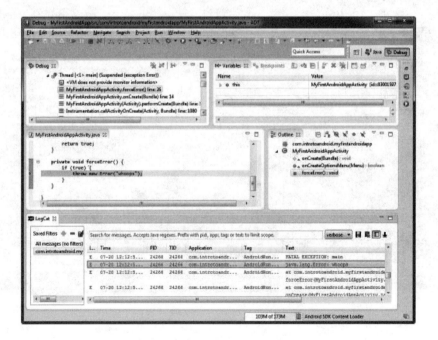

Figure 3.27   Debugging MyFirstAndroidApp in the Android IDE.

Specifically, there's a red `AndroidRuntime` error: `java.lang.Error: whoops`. Back in the emulator, click the `Force Close` button. Now set a breakpoint on the `forceError()` method by right-clicking the left side of the line of code and choosing `Toggle Breakpoint` (or double-clicking).

Tip

In the Android IDE, you can step through code using `Step Into` (F5), `Step Over` (F6), `Step Return` (F7), or `Resume` (F8). On Mac OS X, you might find that the F8 key is mapped globally. If you want to use the keyboard convenience command, you might want to change the keyboard mapping in the Android IDE by choosing `Window`, `Preferences`, `General`, `Keys` and then finding the entry for `Resume` and changing it to something else. Alternatively, you can change the Mac OS X global mapping by going to `System Preferences`, `Keyboard & Mouse`, `Keyboard Shortcuts` and then changing the mapping for F8 to something else.

In the emulator, restart your application and step through your code. You see that your application has thrown the exception, and then the exception shows up in the `Variable Browser` pane of the `Debug` perspective. Expanding its contents shows that it is the "Whoops" error.

This is a great time to crash your application repeatedly and get used to the controls. While you're at it, switch over to the DDMS perspective. Note that the emulator has a list of processes running on the device, such as `system_process` and `com.android.phone`. If you launch `MyFirstAndroidApp`, you see `com.introtoandroid.myfirstandroidapp` show up as a process on the emulator listing. Force the app to close because it crashes, and note that it disappears from the process list. You can use DDMS to kill processes, inspect threads and the heap, and access the phone file system.

Adding Logging Support to Your Android Application

Before you start diving into the various features of the Android SDK, you should familiarize yourself with logging, a valuable resource for debugging and learning Android. Android logging features are in the `Log` class of the `android.util` package. See Table 3.1 for some helpful methods in the `android.util.Log` class.

Table 3.1 **Commonly Used Logging Methods**

Method	Purpose
`Log.e()`	Log errors
`Log.w()`	Log warnings
`Log.i()`	Log informational messages
`Log.d()`	Log debug messages
`Log.v()`	Log verbose messages

To add logging support to `MyFirstAndroidApp`, edit the file `MyFirstAndroidApp`
`.java`. First, you must add the appropriate import statement for the `Log` class:

```
import android.util.Log;
```

Tip

To save time in the Android IDE, you can use the imported classes in your code and add the
imports needed by hovering over the imported class name and choosing the `Add Imported`
`Class QuickFix` option.

You can also use the `Organize Imports` command (`Ctrl+Shift+O` in Windows or
`Command+Shift+O` on a Mac) to have the Android IDE automatically organize your imports.
This removes unused imports and adds new ones for packages used but not imported. If a
naming conflict arises, as it often does with the `Log` class, you can choose the package you
intended to use.

Next, within the `MyFirstAndroidApp` class, declare a constant string that you use to
tag all logging messages from this class. You can use the `LogCat` utility within the Android IDE to filter your logging messages to this `DEBUG_TAG` tag string:

```
private static final String DEBUG_TAG= "MyFirstAppLogging";
```

Now, within the `onCreate()` method, you can log something informational:

```
Log.i(DEBUG_TAG,

    "In the onCreate() method of the MyFirstAndroidAppActivity Class");
```

While you're here, you must comment out your previous `forceError()` call so that
your application doesn't fail. Now you're ready to run `MyFirstAndroidApp`. Save your
work and debug it in the emulator. Notice that your logging messages appear in the
`LogCat` listing, with the `Tag` field `MyFirstAppLogging` (see Figure 3.28).

Adding Some Media Support to Your Application

Next, let's add some pizzazz to `MyFirstAndroidApp` by having the application play an
MP3 music file. Android media player features are found in the `MediaPlayer` class of the
`android.media` package.

You can create `MediaPlayer` objects from existing application resources or by specifying a target file using a URI. For simplicity, we begin by accessing an MP3 using the `Uri`
class from the `android.net` package.

Table 3.2 shows some methods used in the `android.media.MediaPlayer` and
`android.net.Uri` classes.

To add MP3 playback support to `MyFirstAndroidApp`, edit the file `MyFirst`
`AndroidApp.java`. First, you must add the appropriate import statements for the
`MediaPlayer` class:

```
import android.media.MediaPlayer;

import android.net.Uri;
```

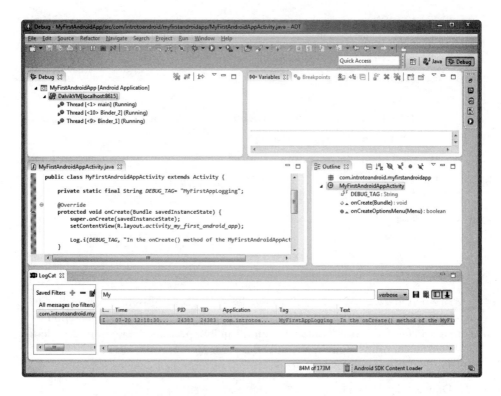

Figure 3.28 A LogCat log for MyFirstAndroidApp.

Table 3.2 **Commonly Used MediaPlayer and Uri Parsing Methods**

Method	Purpose
MediaPlayer.create()	Creates a new media player with a given target to play
MediaPlayer.start()	Starts media playback
MediaPlayer.stop()	Stops media playback
MediaPlayer.release()	Releases the media player resources
Uri.parse()	Instantiates a Uri object from an appropriately formatted URI address

Next, within the MyFirstAndroidApp class, declare a member variable for your MediaPlayer object:

```
private MediaPlayer mp;
```

Now, create a new method called playMusicFromWeb() in your class and make a call to this method in your onCreate() method. The playMusicFromWeb() method creates a

valid `Uri` object, creates a `MediaPlayer` object, and starts the MP3 playing. If the operation should fail for some reason, the method logs a custom error with your logging tag.
The `playMusicFromWeb()` method should look something like this:

```
public void playMusicFromWeb() {

    try {

        Uri file = Uri.parse("http://www.perlgurl.org/podcast/archives"

            + "/podcasts/PerlgurlPromo.mp3");

        mp = MediaPlayer.create(this, file);

        mp.start();

    }

    catch (Exception e) {

        Log.e(DEBUG_TAG, "Player failed", e);

    }

}
```

As of Android 4.2.2 (API Level 17), using the `MediaPlayer` class to access media content on the Web requires the `INTERNET` permission to be registered in the application's
Android manifest file. Finally, your application requires special permissions to access location-based functionality. You must register this permission in your `AndroidManifest`
`.xml` file. To add permissions to your application, perform the following steps:

1. Double-click the `AndroidManifest.xml` file.
2. Switch to the `Permissions` tab.
3. Click the `Add` button and choose `Uses Permission`.
4. In the right pane, select `android.permission.INTERNET` (see Figure 3.29).
5. Save the file.

Later on, you'll learn all about the various `Activity` states and callbacks that could
contain portions of the `playMusicFromWeb()` method. For now, know that the
`onCreate()` method is called every time the user navigates to the `Activity` (forward or
backward) and whenever he or she rotates the screen or causes other device configuration
changes. This doesn't cover all cases but will work well enough for this example.

And finally, you want to cleanly exit when the application shuts down. To do
this, you need to override the `onStop()` method of your `Activity` class and stop the
`MediaPlayer` object and release its resources. The `onStop()` method should look something like this:

```
protected void onStop() {

    if (mp != null) {

        mp.stop();
```

```
            mp.release();

        }

        super.onStop();

    }
```

Tip

In the Android IDE, you can right-click within the class and choose `Source` (or press
`Alt+Shift+S`). Choose the option `Override/Implement Methods` and select the
`onStop()` method.

Now, if you run `MyFirstAndroidApp` in the emulator (and you have an Internet
connection to grab the data found at the URI location), your application plays the
MP3. When you shut down the application, the `MediaPlayer` is stopped and released
appropriately.

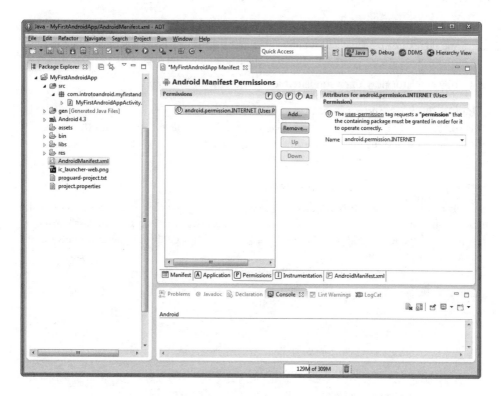

Figure 3.29   Adding the `INTERNET` permission in the manifest.

Adding Location-Based Services to Your Application

Your application knows how to say "Hello" and play some music, but it doesn't know where it's located. Now is a good time to become familiar with some simple location-based calls to get the GPS coordinates. To have some fun with location-based services and map integration, you will use some of the Google applications available on typical Android devices—specifically, the Maps application. You do not need to create another AVD, because you included the Google APIs as part of the target for the AVD you already created.

Configuring the Location of the Emulator

The emulator does not have location sensors, so the first thing you need to do is seed your emulator with some GPS coordinates. You can find the exact steps for how to do this in Appendix B, "Quick-Start Guide: The Android Emulator," in the section "Configuring the GPS Location of the Emulator." After you have configured the location of your emulator, the Maps application should display your simulated location, as shown in Figure 3.30. Make sure that the location icon (🔘) is showing, which is indicative that the location settings have been enabled on the AVD.

> **Warning**
>
> If you do not see the location icon presented in the `status bar`, this means that the location is not yet activated and requires configuring within the AVD.

Your emulator now has a simulated location: Yosemite Valley!

Finding the Last Known Location

To add location support to `MyFirstAndroidApp`, edit the file `MyFirstAndroidApp.java`. First, you must add the appropriate import statements:

```
import android.location.Location;

import android.location.LocationManager;
```

Now, create a new method called `getLocation()` in your class and make a call to this method in your `onCreate()` method. The `getLocation()` method gets the last known location on the device and logs it as an informational message. If the operation fails for some reason, the method logs an error.

The `getLocation()` method should look something like this:

```
public void getLocation() {

    try {

        LocationManager locMgr = (LocationManager)

            this.getSystemService(LOCATION_SERVICE);

        Location recentLoc = locMgr.

            getLastKnownLocation(LocationManager.GPS_PROVIDER);

        Log.i(DEBUG_TAG, "loc: " + recentLoc.toString());
```

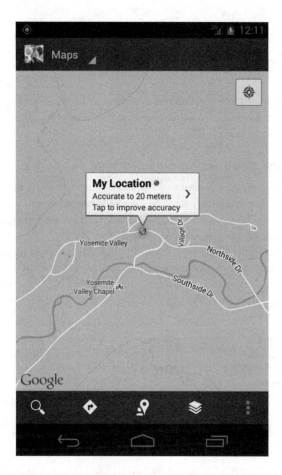

Figure 3.30   Setting the location of the emulator to Yosemite Valley.

```
    }
    catch (Exception e) {
        Log.e(DEBUG_TAG, "Location failed", e);
    }
}
```

Finally, your application requires special permission to access location-based functionality. You must register this permission in your AndroidManifest.xml file. To add location-based service permissions to your application, perform the following steps:

1. Double-click the AndroidManifest.xml file.
2. Switch to the Permissions tab.

3. Click the Add button and choose Uses Permission.

4. In the right pane, select android.permission.ACCESS_FINE_LOCATION.

5. Save the file.

Now, if you run My First Android App in the emulator, your application logs the GPS coordinates you provided to the emulator as an informational message, viewable in the LogCat pane of the Android IDE.

Debugging Your Application on Hardware

You have mastered running applications in the emulator. Now let's put the application on real hardware. This section discusses how to install the application on a Nexus 4 device with Android 4.3. To learn how to install on a different device or different Android version, read *http://d.android.com/tools/device.html*.

Connect an Android device to your computer via USB and relaunch the Debug configuration of the application. Because you chose the Always prompt to pick device Deployment Target Selection Mode for the configuration, you should now see a real Android device listed as an option in the Android Device Chooser (see Figure 3.31).

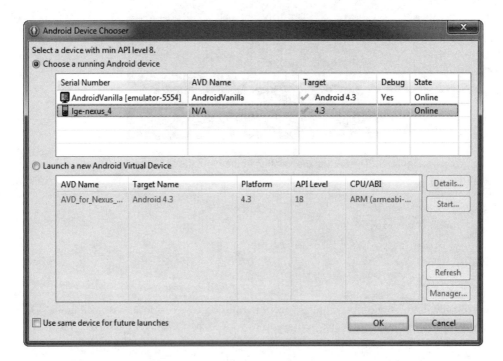

Figure 3.31 Android Device Chooser
with USB-connected Android device.

Choose the Android device as your target, and you see that the `My First Android App` application gets loaded onto the Android device and launched, just as before. Provided you have enabled the development debugging options on the device, you can debug the application here as well. To allow USB debugging, go to `Settings`, `Developer Options`, and under `Debugging`, choose `USB debugging`. A dialog prompt will appear (see Figure 3.32) requesting that USB debugging be allowed. Click `OK` to allow debugging.

Once the USB-connected Android device is recognized, you may be prompted with another dialog asking you to confirm the development computer's RSA key fingerprint. If so, select the option `Always allow from this computer` and click `OK` (see Figure 3.33).

Once enabled, you can tell that the device is actively using a USB debugging connection because a little Android bug-like icon appears in the `status bar` (). Figure 3.34 shows a screenshot of the application running on a real device (in this case, a smartphone running Android 4.3).

Figure 3.32   Allowing USB debugging.

Figure 3.33   Remembering the computer's RSA key fingerprint.

Debugging on the device is much the same as debugging on the emulator, but with a couple of exceptions. You cannot use the emulator controls to do things such as send an SMS or configure the location to the device, but you can perform real actions (true SMS, actual location data) instead.

Summary

This chapter showed you how to add, build, run, and debug Android projects using the Android IDE. You started by installing the sample applications from within the Android IDE. You then began testing your development environment using a sample application from the Android SDK, and then you created a new Android application from scratch using the Android IDE. You also learned how to make some quick modifications to the application, demonstrating some exciting Android features you will learn about in future chapters.

Figure 3.34 `My First Android App` running
on Android device hardware.

In the next few chapters, you will learn about the tools available for use in developing Android applications and then focus on the finer points about defining your Android application using the application manifest file. You will also learn how to organize your application resources, such as images and strings, for use within your application.

Quiz Questions

1. What are the benefits of choosing the `Snapshot` feature listed under the Emulation Options section of the AVD creation wizard?

2. What do the `e`, `w`, `i`, `v`, `d` letters stand for in relation to the `android.util.Log` class, for example, `Log.e()`?

3. What are the `Debug` breakpoint keyboard shortcuts for `Step Into`, `Step Over`, `Step Return`, and `Resume`?

4. What is the keyboard shortcut for organizing imports?

5. What is the keyboard shortcut for toggling a breakpoint in the Android IDE?

6. What is the keyboard shortcut for `Override/Implement Methods` in the Android IDE?

Exercises

1. Create a Nexus 7 AVD using the preconfigured device definitions.

2. Describe the purpose of the `Minimum Required SDK`, `Target SDK`, and `Compile With` options listed in the `Android Application Project` creation wizard.

3. Found in the `Android Application Project` creation wizard, describe the difference between a `Blank Activity` and a `Fullscreen Activity`.

4. Perform the steps for configuring the `Run` or `Debug` configurations of the `MyFirstAndroidApp` to launch the application on all compatible devices/AVDs when running or debugging. Write down each of the steps taken in order.

5. Create a new `Android Application Project` with a new `Launcher Icon`. For the `Launcher Icon`, increase the padding to 50%, change the `Foreground Scaling` to `Center`, give it a shape of `Circle`, and change the icon's background color to blue. Perform any other necessary steps required in order to create the application.

6. There are three `Navigation Types` available when creating a `Blank Activity`. Create a new `Android Application Project` for each `Navigation Type` available to see what each option provides. Perform any other necessary steps required in order to create the application.

References and More Information

Android SDK Reference regarding the application `Activity` class:
   http://d.android.com/reference/android/app/Activity.html
Android SDK Reference regarding the application `Log` class:
   http://d.android.com/reference/android/util/Log.html
Android SDK Reference regarding the application `MediaPlayer` class:
   http://d.android.com/reference/android/media/MediaPlayer.html
Android SDK Reference regarding the application `Uri` class:
   http://d.android.com/reference/android/net/Uri.html
Android SDK Reference regarding the application `LocationManager` class:
   http://d.android.com/reference/android/location/LocationManager.html
Android Tools: "Using Hardware Devices":
   http://d.android.com/tools/device.html
Android Resources: "Common Tasks and How to Do Them in Android":
   http://d.android.com/guide/faq/commontasks.html
Android sample code:
   http://d.android.com/tools/samples/index.html

II

Android Application Basics

4

Understanding the Anatomy of an Android Application

Classical computer science classes often define a program in terms of functionality and data, and Android applications are no different. They perform tasks, display information to the screen, and act upon data from a variety of sources.

Developing Android applications for mobile devices with limited resources requires a thorough understanding of the application lifecycle. Android uses its own terminology for these application building blocks—terms such as *context*, *activity*, and *intent*. This chapter familiarizes you with the most important terms, and their related Java class components, used by Android applications.

Mastering Important Android Terminology

This chapter introduces you to the terminology used in Android application development and provides you with a more thorough understanding of how Android applications function and interact with one another. Here are some of the important terms covered in this chapter:

- **Context:** The context is the central command center for an Android application. Most application-specific functionality can be accessed or referenced through the context. The Context class (`android.content.Context`) is a fundamental building block of any Android application and provides access to application-wide features such as the application's private files and device resources as well as system-wide services. The application-wide Context object is instantiated as an Application object (`android.app.Application`).

- **Activity:** An Android application is a collection of tasks, each of which is called an activity. Each activity within an application has a unique task or purpose. The Activity class (`android.app.Activity`) is a fundamental building block of any Android application, and most applications are made up of several activities. Typically, the purpose is to handle the display of a single screen, but thinking only in terms of "an activity is a screen" is too simplistic. An Activity class extends the Context class, so it also has all of the functionality of the Context class.

- **Fragment:** An activity has a unique task or purpose, but it can be further componentized; each component is called a fragment. Each fragment within an application has a unique task or purpose within its parent activity. The Fragment class (android .app.Fragment) is often used to organize activity functionality in such a way as to allow a more flexible user experience across various screen sizes, orientations, and aspect ratios. A fragment is commonly used to hold the code and screen logic for placing the same user interface component in multiple screens, which are represented by multiple Activity classes.

- **Intent:** The Android operating system uses an asynchronous messaging mechanism to match task requests with the appropriate activity. Each request is packaged as an intent. You can think of each such request as a message stating an intent to do something. Using the Intent class (android.content.Intent) is the primary method by which application components such as activities and services communicate with one another.

- **Service:** Tasks that do not require user interaction can be encapsulated in a service. A service is most useful when the operations are lengthy (offloading time-consuming processing) or need to be done regularly (such as checking a server for new mail). Whereas activities run in the foreground and generally have a user interface, the Service class (android.app.Service) is used to handle background operations related to an Android application. The Service class extends the Context class.

The Application Context

The application Context is the central location for all top-level application functionality. The Context class can be used to manage application-specific configuration details as well as application-wide operations and data. Use the application Context to access settings and resources shared across multiple Activity instances.

Retrieving the Application Context

You can retrieve the Context for the current process using the getApplication Context() method, found in common classes such as Activity and Service, like this:

```
Context context = getApplicationContext();
```

Using the Application Context

After you have retrieved a valid application Context object, it can be used to access application-wide features and services, including the following:

- Retrieving application resources such as strings, graphics, and XML files
- Accessing application preferences
- Managing private application files and directories

- Retrieving uncompiled application assets
- Accessing system services
- Managing a private application database (SQLite)
- Working with application permissions

Warning

Because the `Activity` class is derived from the `Context` class, you can sometimes use this instead of retrieving the application `Context` explicitly. However, don't be tempted to just use your `Activity Context` in all cases, because doing so can lead to memory leaks. You can find a great article on this topic at *http://android-developers.blogspot .com/2009/01/avoiding-memory-leaks.html.*

Retrieving Application Resources

You can retrieve application resources using the `getResources()` method of the application `Context`. The most straightforward way to retrieve a resource is by using its resource identifier, a unique number automatically generated within the `R.java` class. The following example retrieves a `String` instance from the application resources by its resource ID:

```
String greeting = getResources().getString(R.string.hello);
```

We talk more about different types of application resources in Chapter 6, "Managing Application Resources."

Accessing Application Preferences

You can retrieve shared application preferences using the `getSharedPreferences()` method of the application `Context`. The `SharedPreferences` class can be used to save simple application data, such as configuration settings or persistent application state information. We talk more about application preferences in Chapter 11, "Using Android Preferences."

Accessing Application Files and Directories

You can use the application `Context` to access, create, and manage application files and directories private to the application as well as those on external storage. We talk more about application file management in Chapter 12, "Working with Files and Directories."

Retrieving Application Assets

You can retrieve application resources using the `getAssets()` method of the application `Context`. This returns an `AssetManager` (`android.content.res.AssetManager`) instance that can then be used to open a specific asset by its name.

Performing Application Tasks with Activities

The Android `Activity` class (`android.app.Activity`) is core to any Android application. Much of the time, you define and implement an `Activity` class for each screen in

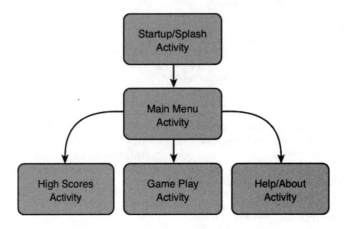

Figure 4.1   A simple game with five activities.

your application. For example, a simple game application might have the following five activities, as shown in Figure 4.1:

- **A startup or splash screen:** This activity serves as the primary entry point to the application. It displays the application name and version information and transitions to the main menu after a short interval.

- **A main menu screen:** This activity acts as a switch to drive the user to the core activities of the application. Here, the users must choose what they want to do within the application.

- **A game play screen:** This activity is where the core game play occurs.

- **A high scores screen:** This activity might display game scores or settings.

- **A Help/About screen:** This activity might display the information the user might need to play the game.

The Lifecycle of an Android `Activity`

Android applications can be multiprocess, and the Android operating system allows multiple applications to run concurrently, provided memory and processing power are available. Applications can have background behavior, and applications can be interrupted and paused when events such as phone calls occur. Only one active application can be visible to the user at a time—specifically, a single application `Activity` is in the foreground at any given time.

The Android operating system keeps track of all `Activity` objects running by placing them on an `Activity` stack (see Figure 4.2). This `Activity` stack is referred to as the "back stack." When a new `Activity` starts, the `Activity` on the top of the stack (the

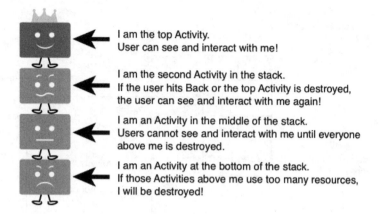

I am the top Activity.
User can see and interact with me!

I am the second Activity in the stack.
If the user hits Back or the top Activity is destroyed,
the user can see and interact with me again!

I am an Activity in the middle of the stack.
Users cannot see and interact with me until everyone
above me is destroyed.

I am an Activity at the bottom of the stack.
If those Activities above me use too many resources,
I will be destroyed!

Figure 4.2   The Activity stack.

current foreground Activity) pauses, and the new Activity pushes onto the top of the stack. When that Activity finishes, it is removed from the Activity stack, and the previous Activity in the stack resumes.

Android applications are responsible for managing their state and their memory, resources, and data. They must pause and resume seamlessly. Understanding the different states within the Activity lifecycle is the first step in designing and developing robust Android applications.

Using Activity Callbacks to Manage Application State and Resources

Different important state changes within the Activity lifecycle are punctuated by a series of important method callbacks. These callbacks are shown in Figure 4.3.

Here are the method stubs for the most important callbacks of the Activity class:

```
public class MyActivity extends Activity {
    protected void onCreate(Bundle savedInstanceState);
    protected void onStart();
    protected void onRestart();
    protected void onResume();
    protected void onPause();
    protected void onStop();
    protected void onDestroy();
}
```

Now let's look at each of these callback methods, when they are called, and what they are used for.

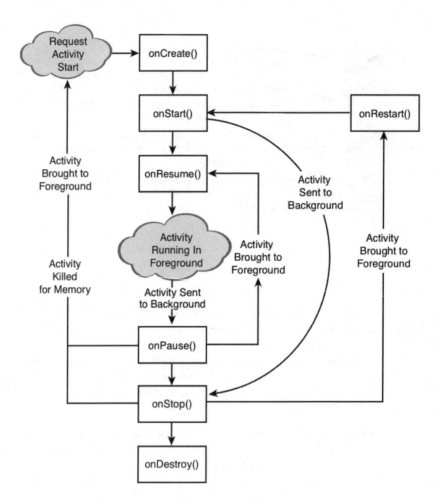

Figure 4.3   The lifecycle of an Android Activity.

Initializing Static **Activity** Data in **onCreate()**

When an Activity first starts, the onCreate() method is called. The onCreate()
method has a single parameter, a Bundle, which is null if this is a newly started Activity.
If this Activity was killed for memory reasons and is now restarted, the Bundle contains
the previous state information for this Activity so that it can reinitiate. It is appropriate
to perform any setup, such as layout and data binding, in the onCreate() method. This
includes calls to the setContentView() method.

Initializing and Retrieving Activity Data in `onResume()`

When the `Activity` reaches the top of the `Activity` stack and becomes the foreground process, the onResume() method is called. Although the `Activity` might not be visible yet to the user, this is the most appropriate place to retrieve any instances of resources (exclusive or otherwise) that the `Activity` needs to run. Often, these resources are the most process intensive, so we keep them around only while the `Activity` is in the foreground.

Tip

The onResume() method is often the appropriate place to start audio, video, and animations.

Stopping, Saving, and Releasing `Activity` Data in `onPause()`

When another `Activity` moves to the top of the `Activity` stack, the current `Activity` is informed that it is being pushed down the `Activity` stack by way of the onPause() method.

Here, the `Activity` should stop any audio, video, and animations it started in the onResume() method. This is also where you must deactivate resources such as database Cursor objects or other objects that should be cleaned up should your `Activity` be terminated. The onPause() method may be the last chance for the `Activity` to clean up and release any resources it does not need while in the background. You need to save any uncommitted data here, in case your application does not resume. The system reserves the right to kill an `Activity` without further notice after the call on onPause().

The `Activity` can also save state information to `Activity`-specific preferences or application-wide preferences. We talk more about preferences in Chapter 11, "Using Android Preferences."

The `Activity` needs to perform anything in the onPause() method in a timely fashion, because the new foreground `Activity` is not started until the onPause() method returns.

Warning

Generally speaking, any resources and data retrieved in the onResume() method should be released in the onPause() method. If they aren't, there is a chance that these resources can't be cleanly released if the process is terminated.

Avoiding Activities Being Killed

Under low-memory conditions, the Android operating system can kill the process for any `Activity` that has been paused, stopped, or destroyed. This essentially means that any `Activity` not in the foreground is subject to a possible shutdown.

If the `Activity` is killed after onPause(), the onStop() and onDestroy() methods will not be called. The more resources released by an `Activity` in the onPause()

method, the less likely the `Activity` is to be killed while in the background without further state methods being called.

The act of killing an `Activity` does not remove it from the `Activity` stack. Instead, the `Activity` state is saved into a `Bundle` object, assuming the `Activity` implements and uses `onSaveInstanceState()` for custom data, although some `View` data is automatically saved. When the user returns to the `Activity` later, the `onCreate()` method is called again, this time with a valid `Bundle` object as the parameter.

Tip

So why does it matter if your application is killed when it is straightforward to resume? Well, it's primarily about responsiveness. The application designer must maintain the data and resources the application needs to resume quickly without degrading the CPU and system resources while paused in the background.

Saving `Activity` State into a `Bundle` with `onSaveInstanceState()`

If an `Activity` is vulnerable to being killed by the Android operating system due to low memory, or in response to state changes like a keyboard opening, the `Activity` can save state information to a `Bundle` object using the `onSaveInstanceState()` callback method. This call is not guaranteed under all circumstances, so use the `onPause()` method for essential data commits. What we recommend doing is saving important data to persistent storage in `onPause()`, but using `onSaveInstanceState()` to start any data that can be used to rapidly restore the current screen to the state it was in (as the name of the method might imply).

Tip

You might want to use the `onSaveInstanceState()` method to store nonessential information such as uncommitted form field data or any other state information that might make the user's experience with your application less cumbersome.

When this `Activity` is returned to later, this `Bundle` is passed in to the `onCreate()` method, allowing the `Activity` to return to the exact state it was in when the `Activity` paused. You can also read `Bundle` information after the `onStart()` callback method using the `onRestoreInstanceState()` callback. Thus, when the `Bundle` information is there, restoring the previous state will be faster and more efficient than starting from scratch.

Destroying Static `Activity` Data in `onDestroy()`

When an `Activity` is being destroyed in the normal course of operation, the `onDestroy()` method is called. The `onDestroy()` method is called for one of two reasons: the `Activity` has completed its lifecycle voluntarily, or the `Activity` is being killed by the Android operating system because it needs the resources but still has the time to gracefully destroy the `Activity` (as opposed to terminating it without calling the `onDestroy()` method).

Tip

The isFinishing() method returns false if the Activity has been killed by the Android operating system. This method can also be helpful in the onPause() method to know if the Activity is not going to resume right away. However, the Activity might still be killed in the onStop() method at a later time, regardless. You may be able to use this as a hint as to how much instance state information to save or permanently persist.

Organizing Activity Components with Fragments

Until Version 3.0 (API Level 11) of the Android SDK, usually a one-to-one relationship existed between an Activity class and an application screen. In other words, for each screen in your app, you defined an Activity to manage its user interface. This worked well enough for small-screen devices such as smartphones, but when the Android SDK started adding support for other types of devices such as tablets and televisions, this relationship did not prove flexible enough. There were times when screen functionality needed to be componentized at a lower level than the Activity class.

Therefore, Android 3.0 introduced a new concept called fragments. A fragment is a chunk of screen functionality or user interface with its own lifecycle that can exist within an activity and is represented by the Fragment class (android.app.Fragment) and several supporting classes. A Fragment class instance must exist within an Activity instance (and its lifecycle), but fragments need not be paired with the same Activity class each time they are instantiated.

Tip

Even though fragments were not introduced until API Level 11, the Android SDK includes a Compatibility Package (also called the Support Package) that enables Fragment library usage on all currently used Android platform versions (as far back as API Level 4). Fragment-based application design is considered a best practice when designing applications for maximum device compatibility. Fragments do make application design more involved, but your user interfaces will be much more flexible when designing for different-size screens.

Fragments, and how they make applications more flexible, are best illustrated by example. Consider a simple MP3 music player application that allows the user to view a list of artists, drill down to a list of their albums, and drill down further to see each track in an album. When the user chooses to play a song at any point, that track's album art is displayed along with the track information and progress (with "Next," "Previous," "Pause," and so on).

Now, if you were using the simple one-screen-to-one-activity rule of thumb, you'd count four screens here, which could be called List Artists, List Artist Albums, List Album Tracks, and Show Track. You could implement four activities, one for each screen. This would likely work just fine for a small-screen device such as a smartphone. But on a tablet or a television, you're wasting a whole lot of space. Or, thought of another way, you have the opportunity to provide a much richer user experience on a device with more screen real estate. Indeed, on a large enough screen, you might want to implement a standard music library interface:

- Column 1 displays a list of artists. Selecting an artist filters the second column.
- Column 2 displays a list of that artist's albums. Selecting an album filters the third column.
- Column 3 displays a list of that album's tracks.
- The bottom half of the screen, below the columns, always displays the artist, album, or track art and details, depending on what is selected in the columns above. If the user ever chooses the "Play" function, the application can display the track information and progress in this area of the screen as well.

This sort of application design requires only a single screen, and thus a single `Activity` class, as shown in Figure 4.4.

But then you're stuck with having to develop basically two separate applications: one to work on smaller screens, and another to work on larger ones. This is where fragments come in. If you componentize your features and make four fragments (List Artists, List Artist Albums, List Album Tracks, Show Track), you can mix and match them on the fly, while still having only one code base to maintain.

We discuss fragments in detail in Chapter 9, "Partitioning the User Interface with Fragments."

Managing `Activity` Transitions with Intents

In the course of the lifetime of an Android application, the user might transition between a number of different `Activity` instances. At times, there might be multiple `Activity` instances on the `Activity` stack. Developers need to pay attention to the lifecycle of each `Activity` during these transitions.

Some `Activity` instances—such as the application splash/startup screen—are shown and then permanently discarded when the main menu screen `Activity` takes over. The user cannot return to the splash screen `Activity` without relaunching the application. In this case, use the `startActivity()` and appropriate `finish()` methods.

Other `Activity` transitions are temporary, such as a child `Activity` displaying a dialog and then returning to the original `Activity` (which was paused on the `Activity` stack and now resumes). In this case, the parent `Activity` launches the child `Activity` and expects a result. For this, use the `startActivityForResult()` and `onActivityResult()` methods.

Transitioning between Activities with Intents

Android applications can have multiple entry points. A specific `Activity` can be designated as the main `Activity` to launch by default within the `AndroidManifest.xml` file;

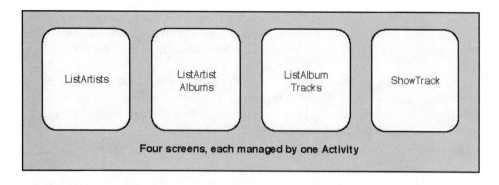

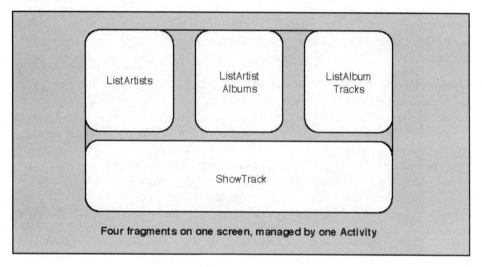

Figure 4.4   How fragments can improve application workflow flexibility.

we talk more about this file in Chapter 5, "Defining Your Application Using the Android Manifest File."

Other activities might be designated to launch under specific circumstances. For example, a music application might designate a generic `Activity` to launch by default from the `Application` menu but also define specific alternative entry-point activities for accessing specific music playlists by playlist ID or artists by name.

Launching a New `Activity` by Class Name

You can start activities in several ways. The simplest method is to use the application `Context` object to call the `startActivity()` method, which takes a single parameter, an `Intent`.

An `Intent` (`android.content.Intent`) is an asynchronous message mechanism used by the Android operating system to match task requests with the appropriate `Activity` or `Service` (launching it, if necessary) and to dispatch broadcast `Intent` events to the system at large.

For now, though, we focus on the `Intent` object and how it is used with activities. The following line of code calls the `startActivity()` method with an explicit `Intent`. This `Intent` requests the launch of the target `Activity` named `MyDrawActivity` by its class. This class is implemented elsewhere within the package.

```
startActivity(new Intent(getApplicationContext(),
    MyDrawActivity.class));
```

This line of code might be sufficient for some applications, which simply transition from one `Activity` to the next. However, you can use the `Intent` mechanism in a much more robust manner. For example, you can use the `Intent` structure to pass data between activities.

Creating Intents with Action and Data

You've seen the simplest case of using an `Intent` to launch a class by name. Intents need not specify the component or class they want to launch explicitly. Instead, you can create an intent filter and register it within the Android manifest file. An intent filter is used by activities, services, and broadcast receivers to specify which intents each is interested in receiving (and filter out the rest). The Android operating system attempts to resolve the `Intent` requirements and launch the appropriate `Activity` based on the filter criteria.

The guts of the `Intent` object are composed of two main parts: the action to be performed and, optionally, the data to be acted upon. You can also specify action/data pairs using `Intent` action types and `Uri` objects. As you saw in Chapter 3, "Writing Your First Android Application," a `Uri` object represents a string that gives the location and name of an object. Therefore, an `Intent` is basically saying "do this" (the action) to "that" (the URI describing to what resource to do the action).

The most common action types are defined in the `Intent` class, including `ACTION_MAIN` (describes the main entry point of an `Activity`) and `ACTION_EDIT` (used in conjunction with a URI to the data edited). You also find action types that generate integration points with activities in other applications, such as the browser or Phone Dialer.

Launching an `Activity` Belonging to Another Application

Initially, your application might be starting only activities defined within its own package. However, with the appropriate permissions, applications might also launch external activities within other applications. For example, a customer relationship management (CRM) application might launch the Contacts application to browse the Contacts database, choose a specific contact, and return that contact's unique identifier to the CRM application for use.

Here is an example of how to create a simple `Intent` with a predefined action
(`ACTION_DIAL`) to launch the Phone Dialer with a specific phone number to dial in the
form of a simple `Uri` object:

```
Uri number = Uri.parse("tel:5555551212");
Intent dial = new Intent(Intent.ACTION_DIAL, number);
startActivity(dial);
```

You can find a list of commonly used Google application intents at *http://d.android
.com/guide/appendix/g-app-intents.html*. Also available is the developer-managed Reg-
istry of Intents protocols at OpenIntents, found at *http://openintents.org/en/intentstable*.
A growing list of intents is available from third-party applications and those within the
Android SDK.

Passing Additional Information Using Intents

You can also include additional data in an `Intent`. The `Extras` property of an `Intent` is
stored in a `Bundle` object. The `Intent` class also has a number of helper methods for getting and setting name/value pairs for many common data types.

For example, the following `Intent` includes two extra pieces of information—a string
value and a `boolean`:

```
Intent intent = new Intent(this, MyActivity.class);
intent.putExtra("SomeStringData","Foo");
intent.putExtra("SomeBooleanData",false);
startActivity(intent);
```

Then in the `onCreate()` method of the `MyActivity` class, you can retrieve the extra
data sent as follows:

```
Bundle extras = getIntent().getExtras();
if (extras != null) {
    String myStr = extras.getString("SomeStringData");
    Boolean myBool = extras.getBoolean("SomeBooleanData");
}
```

Tip

The strings you use to identify your `Intent` object extras can be whatever you want. However, the Android convention for the key name for "extra" data is to include a package
prefix—for example, `com.introtoandroid.Multimedia.SomeStringData`. We also recommend defining the extra string names in the `Activity` for which they are used. (We've
skipped doing this in the preceding example to keep it short.)

Organizing Application Navigation with Activities and Intents

As previously mentioned, your application likely has a number of screens, each with its own `Activity`. There is a close relationship between activities and intents, and application navigation. You often see a kind of menu paradigm used in several different ways for application navigation:

- **Main menu or list-style screen:** acts as a switch in which each menu item launches a different `Activity` in an application, for instance, menu items for launching the Play Game `Activity`, the High Scores `Activity`, and the Help `Activity`.

- **Drill-down-list-style screen:** acts as a directory in which each menu item launches the same `Activity`, but each item passes in different data as part of the `Intent` (for example, a menu of all database records). Choosing a specific item might launch the Edit Record `Activity`, passing in that particular item's unique identifier.

- **Click actions:** Sometimes you want to navigate between screens in the form of a wizard. You might set the click handler for a user interface control, such as a "Next" button, to trigger a new `Activity` to start and the current one to finish.

- **Options menus:** Some applications like to hide their navigational options until the user needs them. The user can then click the `Menu` button on the device and launch an options menu, where each option listed corresponds to an `Intent` to launch a different `Activity`. Options menus are no longer recommended for use, as action bars are now the preferred method for presenting options.

- **Action-bar-style navigation:** Action bars are functional title bars with navigational button options, each of which spawns an `Intent` and launches a specific `Activity`. To support action bars on devices running Android versions all the way back to 2.1 (API Level 7), you should use the `android-support-v7-appcompat` Support Library that comes packaged with the SDK.

We talk more about application navigation in Chapter 17, "Planning the Android Application Experience."

Working with Services

Trying to wrap your head around activities and intents when you start with Android development can be daunting. We have tried to distill everything you need to know to start writing Android applications with multiple `Activity` classes, but we'd be remiss if we didn't mention that there's a lot more here, much of which is discussed throughout this book using practical examples. However, we need to give you a "heads up" about some of these topics now because we begin to touch on them in the next chapter when we cover configuring the Android manifest file for your application.

One application component we have briefly discussed is the service. An Android `Service` (`android.app.Service`) can be thought of as a developer-created component that has no user interface of its own. An Android `Service` can be one of two things, or both. It can be used to perform lengthy operations that may go beyond the scope of a single `Activity`. Additionally, a `Service` can be the server of a client/server for providing functionality through remote invocation via inter-process communication (IPC). Although often used to control long-running server operations, the processing could be whatever the developer wants. Any `Service` classes exposed by an Android application must be registered in the Android manifest file.

You can use services for different purposes. Generally, you use a `Service` when no input is required from the user. Here are some circumstances in which you might want to implement or use an Android `Service`:

- A weather, email, or social network app might implement a service to routinely check for updates on the network. (Note: There are other implementations for polling, but this is a common use of services.)

- A game might create a service to download and process the content for the next level in advance of when the user needs it.

- A photo or media app that keeps its data in sync online might implement a service to package and upload new content in the background when the device is idle.

- A video-editing app might offload heavy processing to a queue on its service in order to avoid affecting overall system performance for nonessential tasks.

- A news application might implement a service to "preload" content by downloading news stories in advance of when the user launches the application, to improve performance and responsiveness.

A good rule of thumb is that if the task requires the use of a worker thread, might affect application responsiveness and performance, and is not time sensitive to the application, consider implementing a service to handle the task outside the main application and any individual activity lifecycles.

Receiving and Broadcasting Intents

Intents serve yet another purpose. You can broadcast an `Intent` (via a call to `send Broadcast()`) to the Android system at large, allowing any interested application (called a `BroadcastReceiver`) to receive that broadcast and act upon it. Your application might send off as well as listen for `Intent` broadcasts. Broadcasts are generally used to inform the system that something interesting has happened. For example, a commonly listened-for broadcast `Intent` is `ACTION_BATTERY_LOW`, which is broadcast as a warning when the battery is low. If your application has a battery-hogging service of some kind, or might lose data in the event of an abrupt shutdown, it might want to listen for this kind of broadcast and act accordingly. There are also broadcast events for other interesting system events, such as SD card state changes, applications being installed or removed, and the wallpaper being changed.

Your application can also share information using this same broadcast mechanism. For example, an email application might broadcast an `Intent` whenever a new email arrives so that other applications (such as spam filters or antivirus apps) that might be interested in this type of event can react to it.

Summary

We have tried to strike a balance between providing a thorough reference and overwhelming you with details you won't need to know when developing a typical Android application. We have focused on the details you need to know to move forward with developing Android applications and to understand every example provided within this book.

The `Activity` class is the core building block of any Android application. Each `Activity` performs a specific task within the application, generally represented by a single screen. Each `Activity` is responsible for managing its own resources and data through a series of lifecycle callbacks. Meanwhile, you can break your `Activity` class into functional components using the `Fragment` class. This allows more than one `Activity` to display similar components of a screen without duplicating code across multiple `Activity` classes. The transition from one `Activity` to the next is achieved through the `Intent` mechanism. An `Intent` object acts as an asynchronous message that the Android operating system processes and responds to by launching the appropriate `Activity` or `Service`. You can also use `Intent` objects to broadcast system-wide events to any interested applications listening.

Quiz Questions

1. Which class does the `Activity` class extend?
2. What is the method for retrieving the application `Context` discussed in this chapter?
3. What is the method for retrieving application resources discussed in this chapter?
4. What is the method for accessing application preferences discussed in this chapter?
5. What is the method for retrieving application assets discussed in this chapter?
6. What is another name for the `Activity` stack?
7. What is the method for saving `Activity` state discussed in this chapter?
8. What is the method for broadcasting an `Intent` discussed in this chapter?

Exercises

1. For each of the `Activity` callback methods, describe the method's overall purpose during the `Activity` lifecycle.
2. Using the online documentation, determine the method names responsible for the lifecycle of a `Fragment`.

3. Create a list of ten `Activity` action intents using the online documentation, where an `Activity` is the target component of the `Intent` action.

4. Using the online documentation, determine the method names responsible for the lifecycle of a `Service`.

References and More Information

Android SDK Reference regarding the application `Context` class:
http://d.android.com/reference/android/content/Context.html
Android SDK Reference regarding the `Activity` class:
http://d.android.com/reference/android/app/Activity.html
Android SDK Reference regarding the `Fragment` class:
http://d.android.com/reference/android/app/Fragment.html
Android API Guides: "Fragments":
http://d.android.com/guide/components/fragments.html
Android Tools: Support Library:
http://d.android.com/tools/extras/support-library.html
Android API Guides: "Intents and Intent Filters":
http://d.android.com/guide/components/intents-filters.html

Defining Your Application Using the Android Manifest File

Android projects use a special configuration file called the Android manifest file to determine application settings—settings such as the application name and version, as well as what permissions the application requires to run and what application components it is composed of. In this chapter, you explore the Android manifest file in detail and learn how applications use it to define and describe application behavior.

Configuring Android Applications Using the Android Manifest File

The Android application manifest file is a specially formatted XML file that must accompany each Android application. This file contains important information about the application's identity. Here, you define the application's name and version information as well as what application components the application relies upon, what permissions the application requires to run, and other application configuration information.

The Android manifest file is named `AndroidManifest.xml` and must be included at the top level of any Android project. The information in this file is used by the Android system to

- Install and upgrade the application package
- Display the application details, such as the application name, description, and icon, to users
- Specify application system requirements, including which Android SDKs are supported, what device configurations are required (for example, D-pad navigation), and which platform features the application relies upon (for example, multitouch capabilities)
- Specify what features are required by the application for market-filtering purposes
- Register application activities and when they should be launched

- Manage application permissions
- Configure other advanced application component configuration details, including defining services, broadcast receivers, and content providers
- Specify intent filters for your activities, services, and broadcast receivers
- Enable application settings such as debugging and configuring instrumentation for application testing

Tip

When you use the Android IDE, the Android Project Wizard creates the initial `Android Manifest.xml` file for you. If you are not using the Android IDE, the `android` command-line tool creates the Android manifest file for you as well.

Editing the Android Manifest File

The manifest resides at the top level of your Android project. You can edit the Android manifest file by using the Android IDE manifest file resource editor, which is a feature of the ADT Bundle, or by manually editing the XML.

Tip

For simple configuration changes, we recommend using the editor. However, if we are adding a bunch of `Activity` registrations, or something more complex, we usually edit the XML directly because the resource editor can be somewhat confusing and no support documentation is available. We've found that when a more complex configuration results in nested XML (such as an intent filter, for example), it's too easy for users to end up with manifest settings at the wrong level in the XML tag hierarchy. Therefore, if you use the editor, you should always spot-check the resulting XML to make sure it looks correct.

Editing the Manifest File Using the Android IDE

You can use the Android IDE manifest file resource editor to edit the project manifest file. The Android IDE manifest file resource editor organizes the manifest information into categories:

- The `Manifest` tab
- The `Application` tab
- The `Permissions` tab
- The `Instrumentation` tab
- The `AndroidManifest.xml` tab

Let's take a closer look at a sample Android manifest file. We've chosen a more complex sample project to illustrate a number of different characteristics of the Android manifest file, as opposed to the very simple default manifest file you configured for the

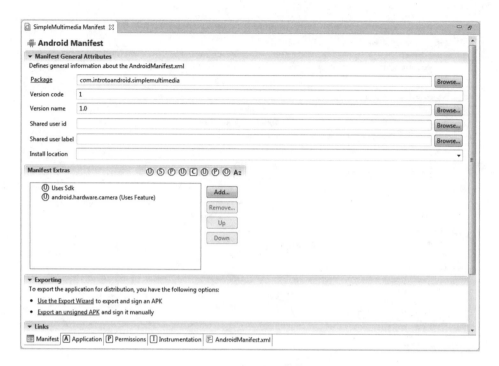

Figure 5.1   The `Manifest` tab of the Android IDE
manifest file resource editor.

`MyFirstAndroidApp` project. The application manifest we will be discussing is for an application named `SimpleMultimedia`.

Configuring Package-Wide Settings Using the `Manifest` Tab

The `Manifest` tab (see Figure 5.1) contains package-wide settings, including the package name, version information, and supported Android SDK information. You can also set any hardware or feature requirements here.

Managing Application and `Activity` Settings Using the `Application` Tab

The `Application` tab (see Figure 5.2) contains application-wide settings, including the application label and icon, as well as information about the application components, such as activities, and other application components, including configuration for services, intent filters, and content providers.

Enforcing Application Permissions Using the `Permissions` Tab

The `Permissions` tab (see Figure 5.3) contains any permission rules required by your application. This tab can also be used to enforce custom permissions created for the application.

Figure 5.2   The `Application` tab of the Android IDE
manifest file resource editor.

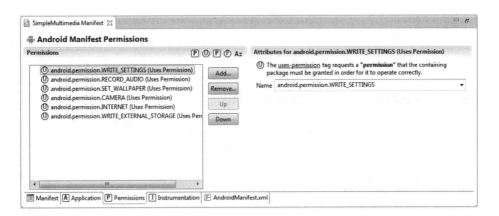

Figure 5.3   The `Permissions` tab of the Android IDE
manifest file resource editor.

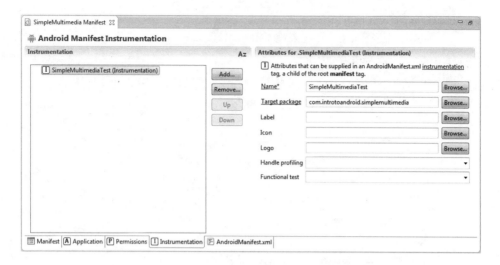

Figure 5.4   The `Instrumentation` tab of the Android IDE manifest file resource editor.

Warning

Do not confuse the application Permission field (a drop-down list on the `Application` tab) with the `Permissions` tab features. Use the `Permissions` tab to define the permissions required by the application.

Managing Test Instrumentation Using the `Instrumentation` Tab

The `Instrumentation` tab (seen in Figure 5.4) allows the developer to declare any instrumentation classes for monitoring the application. We talk more about instrumentation and testing in Chapter 18, "Testing Android Applications."

Editing the Manifest File Manually

The Android manifest file is a specially formatted XML file. You can edit the XML manually by clicking the `AndroidManifest.xml` tab.

Android manifest files generally include a single `<manifest>` tag with a single `<application>` tag. The following is a sample `AndroidManifest.xml` file for an application called `SimpleMultimedia`:

```
<?xml version="1.0" encoding="utf-8"?>

<manifest xmlns:android="http://schemas.android.com/apk/res/android"

    package="com.introtoandroid.simplemultimedia"

    android:versionCode="1"

    android:versionName="1.0">
```

```xml
    <application android:icon="@drawable/ic_launcher"
        android:label="@string/app_name"
        android:debuggable="true">
        <activity android:name=".SimpleMultimediaActivity"
            android:label="@string/app_name">
            <intent-filter>
                <action
                    android:name="android.intent.action.MAIN" />
                <category
                    android:name="android.intent.category.LAUNCHER" />
            </intent-filter>
        </activity>
        <activity android:name="AudioActivity" />
        <activity android:name="StillImageActivity" />
        <activity android:name="VideoPlayActivity" />
    </application>
    <uses-sdk
        android:minSdkVersion="10"
        android:targetSdkVersion="18" />
    <uses-permission
        android:name="android.permission.WRITE_SETTINGS" />
    <uses-permission
        android:name="android.permission.RECORD_AUDIO" />
    <uses-permission
        android:name="android.permission.SET_WALLPAPER" />
    <uses-permission
        android:name="android.permission.CAMERA" />
    <uses-permission
        android:name="android.permission.INTERNET" />
    <uses-permission
        android:name="android.permission.WRITE_EXTERNAL_STORAGE" />
    <uses-feature
        android:name="android.hardware.camera" />
</manifest>
```

Here is a summary of what this file tells us about the `SimpleMultimedia` application:

- The application uses the package name `com.introtoandroid.simplemultimedia`.
- The application version name is 1.0.
- The application version code is 1.
- The application name and label are stored in the resource string called `@string/app_name` within the `/res/values/strings.xml` resource file.
- The application is `debuggable` on an Android device.
- The application icon is the graphics file called `ic_launcher` (which could be a PNG, JPG, or GIF) stored within the `/res/drawable-*` directory (there are actually multiple versions for different pixel densities).
- The application has four activities (`SimpleMultimediaActivity`, `AudioActivity`, `StillImageActivity`, and `VideoPlayActivity`).
- `SimpleMultimediaActivity` is the primary entry point for the application because it handles the action `android.intent.action.MAIN`. This `Activity` shows in the application launcher, because its category is `android.intent.category.LAUNCHER`.
- The application requires the following permissions to run: the ability to write settings, the ability to record audio, the ability to set the wallpaper on the device, the ability to access the built-in camera, the ability to communicate over the Internet, and the ability to write to external storage.
- The application works from any API level from 10 to 18; in other words, Android SDK 2.3.3 is the lowest supported platform version, and the application was written to target Jelly Bean MR2 (for example, Android 4.3).
- Finally, the application requests to use the camera with the `<uses-feature>` tag.

Tip

When using the `<uses-feature>` tag, you can specify an optional attribute of `android:required` and set the value to `true` or `false`. This is used for configuring Google Play store filtering. If this attribute were set to `true`, Google Play would show your application listing only to users with devices that have that particular hardware or software feature, in this case, a camera. To learn more about Google Play store filtering, visit *http://d.android.com/google/play/filters.html*.

Now let's talk about some of these important configurations in detail.

Note

Within the previous manifest code listing, you may be wondering why there is a dot (`.`) in front of the `SimpleMultimedia` name attribute of the `<activity>` tag. The dot is used as shorthand to specify that the `SimpleMultimedia` class belongs to the package name specified in the manifest. We could have specified the entire package name path, but we have used the shorthand to save on typing the extra characters.

Managing Your Application's Identity

Your application's Android manifest file defines the application properties. The package name must be defined in the Android manifest file within the `<manifest>` tag using the package attribute:

```
<manifest

    xmlns:android="http://schemas.android.com/apk/res/android"

    package="com.introtoandroid.simplemultimedia"

    android:versionCode="1"

    android:versionName="1.0">
```

Versioning Your Application

Versioning your application appropriately is vital to maintaining your application in the field. Intelligent versioning can help reduce confusion and make product support and upgrades simpler. Two different version attributes are defined within the `<manifest>` tag: the version name and the version code.

The version name (`android:versionName`) is a user-friendly, developer-defined version attribute. This information is displayed to users when they manage applications on their devices and when they download the application from marketplaces. Developers use this version information to keep track of their application versions in the field. We discuss appropriate versioning for mobile applications in detail in Chapter 15, "Learning the Android Software Development Process."

Warning

Although you can use an `@string` resource reference for some manifest file settings, such as the `android:versionName`, some publishing systems don't support this.

The Android operating system uses the version code (`android:versionCode`), which is a numeric attribute, to manage application upgrades. We talk more about publishing and upgrade support in Chapter 19, "Publishing Your Android Application."

Setting the Application Name and Icon

Overall application settings are configured with the `<application>` tag of the Android manifest file. Here, you set information such as the application icon (`android:icon`) and friendly name (`android:label`). These settings are attributes of the `<application>` tag.

For example, here we set the application icon to an image resource provided with the application package, and the application label to a string resource:

```
<application android:icon="@drawable/ic_launcher"

    android:label="@string/app_name">
```

You can also set optional application settings as attributes in the `<application>` tag, such as the application description (`android:description`) and the setting to enable the application for debugging on devices (`android:debuggable="true"`).

Enforcing Application System Requirements

In addition to configuring your application's identity, the Android manifest file is used to specify any system requirements necessary for the application to run properly. For example, an augmented reality application might require that the device have GPS, a compass, and a camera. Similarly, an application that relies on the Bluetooth APIs available within the Android SDK requires a device with an SDK version of API Level 5 or higher (Android 2.0), because that's where those APIs were introduced.

These types of system requirements can be defined and enforced in the Android manifest file. When an application is installed on a device, the Android platform checks these requirements and will error out if necessary. Similarly, the Google Play store uses information in the Android manifest file to filter which applications to offer to which devices so that users install applications that should work on their devices.

Some of the application system requirements that developers can configure through the Android manifest file include

- The Android SDK versions supported by the application
- The Android platform features used by the application
- The Android hardware configurations required by the application
- The screen sizes and pixel densities supported by the application
- Any external libraries that the application links to

Targeting Specific SDK Versions

Different Android devices run different versions of the Android platform. Often, you see old, less powerful, or even less expensive devices running older versions of the Android platform, whereas newer, more powerful devices that show up on the market often run the latest Android software.

There are now hundreds of different Android devices in users' hands. Developers must decide who their target audience is for a given application. Are they trying to support the largest population of users and therefore want to support as many different versions of the platform as possible? Or are they developing a bleeding-edge game that requires the latest device hardware?

Tip

You can expand the range of target SDKs that your application supports by using the Android Support Package, or by using Java reflection to check for SDK features before using them.

> You can read more about using the Support Package at *http://d.android.com/tools/extras/*
> *support-library.html* and more about backward compatibility at *http://android-developers*
> *.blogspot.com/2009/04/backward-compatibility-for-android.html* and *http://android-*
> *developers.blogspot.com/2010/07/how-to-have-your-cupcake-and-eat-it-too.html*. There
> are multiple revisions of the Support Package, and three different versions—v4, v7, and
> v13—which provide support libraries for adding newer API features to older Android ver-
> sions, for API Level 4 and up, API Level 7 and up, or API Level 13 and up.

Developers can specify which versions of the Android platform an application supports within
its Android manifest file using the `<uses-sdk>` tag. This tag has three important attributes:

- **The `minSdkVersion` attribute:** This attribute specifies the lowest API level that the
  application supports.
- **The `targetSdkVersion` attribute:** This attribute specifies the optimum API level
  that the application supports.
- **The `maxSdkVersion` attribute:** This attribute specifies the highest API level that
  the application supports.

> **Tip**
>
> The Google Play store filters applications available to a given user based on settings such
> as the `<uses-sdk>` tag within an application's manifest file. This is a required tag for ap-
> plications that are to be published on Google Play. Neglecting to use this tag results in a
> warning in the build environment. To learn more about the `<uses-sdk>` tag, please read
> *http://d.android.com/guide/topics/manifest/uses-sdk-element.html*.

Each attribute of the `<uses-sdk>` tag is an integer that represents the API level associated with a given Android SDK. This value does not directly correspond to the SDK version. Instead, it is the revision of the API level associated with that SDK. The API level is
set by the developers of the Android SDK. You need to check the SDK documentation
to determine the API level value for each version. Table 5.1 shows the Android SDK
versions available for shipping applications.

Specifying the Minimum SDK Version

You should always specify the `minSdkVersion` attribute for your application. This value
represents the lowest Android SDK version your application supports.

For example, if your application requires APIs introduced in Android SDK 1.6,
you would check that SDK's documentation and find that this release is defined as
API Level 4. Therefore, add the following to your Android manifest file within the
`<manifest>` tag block:

```
<uses-sdk android:minSdkVersion="4" />
```

It's that simple. You should use the lowest API level possible if you want your application to be compatible with the largest number of Android devices. However, you must
ensure that your application is tested sufficiently on any non-target platforms (any API
level supported below your target SDK, as described in the next section).

Table 5.1 **Android SDK Versions and Their API Levels**

Android SDK Version	API Level	Code Name/Version Code
Android 1.0	1	BASE
Android 1.1	2	BASE_1_1
Android 1.5	3	CUPCAKE
Android 1.6	4	DONUT
Android 2.0	5	ECLAIR
Android 2.0.1	6	ECLAIR_0_1
Android 2.1.X	7	ECLAIR_MR1
Android 2.2.X	8	FROYO
Android 2.3, 2.3.1, 2.3.2	9	GINGERBREAD
Android 2.3.3, 2.3.4	10	GINGERBREAD_MR1
Android 3.0.X	11	HONEYCOMB
Android 3.1.X	12	HONEYCOMB_MR1
Android 3.2	13	HONEYCOMB_MR2
Android 4.0, 4.0.1, 4.0.2	14	ICE_CREAM_SANDWICH
Android 4.0.3, 4.0.4	15	ICE_CREAM_SANDWICH_MR1
Android 4.1, 4.1.1	16	JELLY_BEAN
Android 4.2, 4.2.2	17	JELLY_BEAN_MR1
Android 4.3	18	JELLY_BEAN_MR2

Specifying the Target SDK Version

You should always specify the targetSdkVersion attribute for your application. This value represents the Android SDK version your application was built for and tested against.

For example, if your application was built using APIs that are backward compatible to Android 2.3.3 (API Level 10), but targeted and tested using Android 4.3 SDK (API Level 18), you would want to specify the targetSdkVersion attribute as 18. Therefore, add the following to your Android manifest file within the <manifest> tag block:

```
<uses-sdk android:minSdkVersion="10" android:targetSdkVersion="18" />
```

Why should you specify the target SDK version you used? Well, the Android platform has built-in functionality for backward compatibility (to a point). Think of it like this: A specific method of a given API might have been around since API Level 1. However, the internals of that method—its behavior—might have changed slightly from SDK to SDK. When you specify the target SDK version for your application, the Android operating system attempts to match your application with the exact version of the SDK (and the behavior as you tested it within the application), even when running a different (newer) version of the platform. This means that the application should continue to behave in "the old way" despite any changes or "improvements" to the SDK that might cause unintended consequences in the application.

Specifying the Maximum SDK Version

You will rarely want to specify the maxSdkVersion attribute for your application. This value represents the highest Android SDK version your application supports, in terms of API level. It restricts forward compatibility of your application.

One reason you might want to set this attribute is if you want to limit who can install the application to exclude devices with the newest SDKs. For example, you might develop a free beta version of your application with plans for a paid version for the newest SDK. By setting the maxSdkVersion attribute of the manifest file for your free application, you disallow anyone with the newest SDK to install it. The downside of this idea? If your users have devices that receive over-the-air SDK updates, your application would cease to work (and appear) on devices where it had previously functioned perfectly, which might upset your users and result in bad ratings on your market of choice. In short, use maxSdkVersion only when absolutely necessary and when you understand the risks associated with its use.

Enforcing Application Platform Requirements

Android devices have different hardware and software configurations. Some devices have built-in keyboards and others rely on the software keyboard. Similarly, certain Android devices support the latest 3D graphics libraries and others provide little or no graphics support. The Android manifest file has several informational tags for flagging the system features and hardware configurations supported or required by an Android application.

Specifying Supported Input Methods

The <uses-configuration> tag can be used to specify which hardware and software input methods the application supports. There are different configuration attributes for five-way navigation: the hardware keyboard and keyboard types; navigation devices such as the directional pad, trackball, and wheel; and touchscreen settings.

There is no "OR" support within a given attribute. If an application supports multiple input configurations, there must be multiple <uses-configuration> tags defined in your Android manifest file—one for each configuration supported.

For example, if your application requires a physical keyboard and touchscreen input using a finger or a stylus, you need to define two separate <uses-configuration> tags in your manifest file, as follows:

```
<uses-configuration android:reqHardKeyboard="true"

    android:reqTouchScreen="finger" />

<uses-configuration android:reqHardKeyboard="true"

    android:reqTouchScreen="stylus" />
```

For more information about the `<uses-configuration>` tag of the Android manifest file, see the Android SDK Reference at *http://d.android.com/guide/topics/manifest/uses-configuration-element.html.*

Warning

Make sure to test your application with all of the available types of input methods, as not all devices support all types. For example, Google TVs do not have touchscreens, and if you design your application for touchscreen inputs, your app will not work properly on Google TV devices.

Specifying Required Device Features

Not all Android devices support every Android feature. Put another way: there are a number of APIs (and related hardware) that Android device manufacturers and carriers may optionally include. For example, not all Android devices have multitouch capability or a camera flash.

The `<uses-feature>` tag is used to specify which Android features your application uses to run properly. These settings are for informational purposes only—the Android operating system does not enforce these settings, but publication channels such as the Google Play store use this information to filter the applications available to a given user. Other applications might check this information as well.

If your application requires multiple features, you must create a `<uses-feature>` tag for each feature. For example, an application that requires both a light and a proximity sensor requires two tags:

```
<uses-feature android:name="android.hardware.sensor.light" />

<uses-feature android:name="android.hardware.sensor.proximity" />
```

One common reason to use the `<uses-feature>` tag is for specifying the OpenGL ES versions supported by your application. By default, all applications function with OpenGL ES 1.0 (which is a required feature of all Android devices). However, if your application requires features available only in later versions of OpenGL ES, such as 2.0 or 3.0, you must specify this feature in the Android manifest file. This is done using the `android:glEsVersion` attribute of the `<uses-feature>` tag. Specify the lowest version of OpenGL ES that the application requires. If the application works with 1.0, 2.0, and 3.0, specify the lowest version (so that the Google Play store allows more users to install your application).

Tip

OpenGL ES 3.0 support has been added to Android Jelly Bean 4.3. The value for specifying the `android:glEsVersion` for OpenGL ES 3.0 support is `0x00030000`. To learn more about this new addition to Android 4.3, see *http://d.android.com/about/versions/android-4.3.html#Graphics.*

For more information about the <uses-feature> tag of the Android manifest file, see the Android SDK Reference at *http://d.android.com/guide/topics/manifest/uses-feature-element.html*.

Tip

If a certain feature is not required for your application to function properly, rather than providing filters for the Google Play store to limit access to specific devices, you could check for certain device features at runtime and allow specific application functionality only if those particular features are present on the user's device. That way, you maximize the number of users who can install and use your application. To check for specific features at runtime, use the hasSystemFeature() method. For example, to see if the device your application is running on has touchscreen capabilities and returns a Boolean value: getPackage Manager().hasSystemFeature("android.hardware.touchscreen");

Specifying Supported Screen Sizes

Android devices come in many shapes and sizes. Screen sizes and pixel densities vary tremendously across the wide range of Android devices available on the market today. The <supports-screens> tag can be used to specify which Android types of screens the application supports. The Android platform categorizes screen types in terms of sizes (small, normal, large, and xlarge) and pixel density (LDPI, MDPI, HDPI, XHDPI, and XXHDPI, representing low-, medium-, high-, extra-high-, and extra-extra-high-density displays). These characteristics effectively cover the variety of screen types available within the Android platform.

For example, if the application supports QVGA screens (small) and HVGA, WQVGA, and WVGA screens (normal) regardless of pixel density, the application's <supports-screens> tag is configured as follows:

```
<supports-screens android:resizable="false"
                  android:smallScreens="true"
                  android:normalScreens="true"
                  android:largeScreens="false"
                  android:compatibleWidthLimitDp="320"
                  android:anyDensity="true"/>
```

For more information about the <supports-screens> tag of the Android manifest file, see the Android SDK Reference at *http://d.android.com/guide/topics/manifest/supports-screens-element.html* as well as the Android Developers Guide on screen support at *http://d.android.com/guide/practices/screens_support.html#DensityConsiderations*.

Working with External Libraries

You can register any shared libraries your application links to within the Android manifest file. By default, every application is linked to the standard Android packages (such as android.app) and is aware of its own package. However, if your application links to additional packages, they should be registered within the <application> tag of the Android manifest file using the <uses-library> tag. For example:

```
<uses-library android:name="com.sharedlibrary.sharedStuff" />
```

This feature is often used for linking to optional Google APIs. For more information about the <uses-library> tag of the Android manifest file, see the Android SDK Reference at *http://d.android.com/guide/topics/manifest/uses-library-element.html.*

Other Application Configuration Settings and Filters

You'll want to be aware of several other lesser-used manifest file settings because they are also used by the Google Play store for application filtering:

- The <supports-gl-texture> tag is used to specify the GL texture compression format supported by the application. This tag is used by applications that use the graphics libraries and are intended to be compatible only with devices that support a specific compression format. For more information about this manifest file tag, see the Android SDK documentation at *http://d.android.com/guide/topics/manifest/supports-gl-texture-element.html.*

- The <compatible-screens> tag is used solely by the Google Play store to restrict installation of your application to devices with specific screen sizes. This tag is not checked by the Android operating system, and usage is discouraged unless you absolutely need to restrict the installation of your application on certain devices. For more information about this manifest file tag, see the Android SDK documentation at *http://d.android.com/guide/topics/manifest/compatible-screens-element.html.*

Registering Activities in the Android Manifest

Each Activity within the application must be defined within the Android manifest file with an <activity> tag. For example, the following XML excerpt registers an Activity class called AudioActivity:

```
<activity android:name="AudioActivity" />
```

This Activity must be defined as a class within the com.introtoandroid.simple multimedia package—that is, the package specified in the <manifest> element of the Android manifest file. You can also enforce the scope of the Activity class by using the dot as a prefix in the Activity class name:

```
<activity android:name=".AudioActivity" />
```

Or you can specify the complete class name:

```
<activity android:name="com.introtoandroid.simplemultimedia.AudioActivity" />
```

Warning

You must define the `<activity>` tag for each `Activity` or it will not run as part of your application. It is quite common for developers to implement an `Activity` and then forget to do this. They then spend a lot of time troubleshooting why it isn't running properly, only to realize they forgot to register it in the Android manifest file.

Designating a Primary Entry Point `Activity` for Your Application Using an Intent Filter

You designate an `Activity` class as the primary entry point by configuring an intent filter using the Android manifest tag `<intent-filter>` in the Android manifest file with the MAIN action type and the LAUNCHER category.

For example, the following XML configures an `Activity` called `SimpleMultimedia Activity` as the primary launching point of the application:

```
<activity android:name=".SimpleMultimediaActivity"

    android:label="@string/app_name">

    <intent-filter>

        <action android:name="android.intent.action.MAIN" />

        <category android:name="android.intent.category.LAUNCHER" />

    </intent-filter>

</activity>
```

Configuring Other Intent Filters

The Android operating system uses intent filters to resolve implicit intents—that is, intents that do not specify a specific activity or other component type to launch. Intent filters can be applied to activities, services, and broadcast receivers. An intent filter declares that this application component is capable of handling or processing a specific type of intent when it matches the filter's criteria.

Different applications have the same sorts of intent filters and are able to process the same sorts of requests. In fact, this is how the "share" features and the flexible application launch system of the Android operating system work. For example, you can have several different Web browsers installed on a device, all of which can handle "browse the Web" intents by setting up the appropriate filters.

Intent filters are defined using the `<intent-filter>` tag and must contain at least one `<action>` tag but can also contain other information, such as `<category>` and `<data>` blocks. Here, we have a sample intent filter block that might be found within an `<activity>` block:

```
<intent-filter>

    <action android:name="android.intent.action.VIEW" />

    <category android:name="android.intent.category.BROWSABLE" />
```

```
    <category android:name="android.intent.category.DEFAULT" />

    <data android:scheme="geoname"/>

</intent-filter>
```

This intent filter definition uses a predefined action called VIEW, the action for viewing particular content. It also handles Intent objects in the BROWSABLE or DEFAULT category and uses a scheme of geoname so that when a URI starts with geoname://, the Activity with this intent filter can be launched to view the content.

> **Tip**
>
> You can define custom actions unique to your application. If you do so, be sure to document these actions if you want them to be used by third parties. You can document these however you want: your SDK documentation could be provided on your website, or confidential documents could be given directly to a client. For the most visibility, consider using an online registry, such as that at OpenIntents (*http://openintents.org*).

Registering Other Application Components

All application components must be defined within the Android manifest file. In addition to activities, all services and broadcast receivers must be registered within the Android manifest file.

- Services are registered using the <service> tag.
- Broadcast receivers are registered using the <receiver> tag.
- Content providers are registered using the <provider> tag.

Both services and broadcast receivers use intent filters. If your application acts as a content provider, effectively exposing a shared data service for use by other applications, it must declare this capability within the Android manifest file using the <provider> tag. Configuring a content provider involves determining what subsets of data are shared and what permissions are required to access them, if any. We begin our discussion of content providers in Chapter 13, "Leveraging Content Providers."

Working with Permissions

The Android operating system has been locked down so that applications have limited capability to adversely affect operations outside their process space. Instead, Android applications run within the bubble of their own virtual machine, with their own Linux user account (and related permissions).

Registering Permissions Your Application Requires

Android applications have no permissions by default. Instead, any permissions for shared resources or privileged access—whether it's shared data, such as the Contacts database, or access to underlying hardware, such as the built-in camera—must be explicitly registered within the Android manifest file. These permissions are granted when the application is installed.

The following XML excerpt for the preceding Android manifest file defines a permission using the `<uses-permission>` tag to gain access to the built-in camera:

```
<uses-permission android:name="android.permission.CAMERA" />
```

A complete list of the permissions can be found in the `android.Manifest.permission` class. Your application manifest should include only the permissions required to run. The user is informed what permissions each Android application requires at install time.

Tip

You might find that, in certain cases, permissions are not enforced (you can operate without the permission) by one device or another. In these cases, it is prudent to request the permission anyway for two reasons. First, the user is informed that the application is performing those sensitive actions, and second, that permission could be enforced in a later device update. Also be aware that in early SDK versions, not all permissions were necessarily enforced at the platform level.

Warning

Be aware that users will see these permissions before they install your application. If the application description or type of application you are providing does not clearly justify the permissions requested, you may get low ratings simply for asking for unnecessary permissions. We see many applications requesting permissions they do not need or have no reason to ask for. Many people who realize this will not follow through and install the application. Privacy is a big concern for many users, so be sure to respect it.

Registering Permissions Your Application Enforces

Applications can also define and enforce their own permissions via the `<permission>` tag to be used by other applications. Permissions must be described and then applied to specific application components, such as activities, using the `android:permission` attribute.

Tip

Use Java-style scoping for unique naming of application permissions (for example, `com.introtoandroid.SimpleMultimedia.ViewMatureMaterial`).

Permissions can be enforced at several points:

- When starting an `Activity` or `Service`
- When accessing data provided by a content provider
- At the method call level
- When sending or receiving broadcasts by an `Intent`

Permissions can have three primary protection levels: normal, dangerous, and signature. The normal protection level is a good default for fine-grained permission enforcement within the application. The dangerous protection level is used for higher-risk activities, which might adversely affect the device. Finally, the signature protection level permits any application signed with the same certificate to use that component for controlled application interoperability. You will learn more about application signing in Chapter 19, "Publishing Your Android Application."

Permissions can be broken down into categories, called permission groups, which describe or warn why specific activities require permission. For example, permissions might be applied for activities that expose sensitive user data such as location and personal information (`android.permission-group.LOCATION` and `android.permission-group.PERSONAL_INFO`), access underlying hardware (`android.permission-group.HARDWARE_CONTROLS`), or perform operations that might incur fees to the user (`android.permission-group.COST_MONEY`). A complete list of permission groups is available within the `Manifest.permission_group` class.

For more information about applications and how they can enforce their own permissions, check out the `<permission>` manifest tag SDK documentation at *http://d.android.com/guide/topics/manifest/permission-element.html.*

Exploring Other Manifest File Settings

We have now covered the basics of the Android manifest file, but many other settings are configurable within the Android manifest file using different tag blocks, not to mention attributes within each tag we have already discussed.

Some other features you can configure within the Android manifest file include

- Setting application-wide themes within the `<application>` tag attributes
- Configuring unit-testing features using the `<instrumentation>` tag
- Aliasing activities using the `<activity-alias>` tag
- Creating broadcast receivers using the `<receiver>` tag
- Creating content providers using the `<provider>` tag, along with managing content provider permissions using the `<grant-uri-permission>` and `<path-permission>` tags
- Including other data within your activity, service, or receiver component registrations with the `<meta-data>` tag

For more detailed descriptions of each tag and attribute available in the Android SDK (and there are many), please review the Android SDK Reference on the Android manifest file at *http://d.android.com/guide/topics/manifest/manifest-intro.html.*

Summary

Each Android application has a specially formatted XML configuration file called `AndroidManifest.xml`. This file describes the application's identity in great detail. Some information that you must define within the Android manifest file includes the application's name and version information, what application components it contains, which device configurations it requires, and what permissions it needs to run. The Android manifest file is by the Android operating system to install, upgrade, and run the application package. Some details of the Android manifest file are also used by third parties, including the Google Play publication channel.

Quiz Questions

1. What are the names of the five tabs of the Android IDE manifest file resource editor?

2. What are the two different attributes for defining version within the `<manifest>` tag?

3. What is the manifest XML tag for specifying which versions of the Android SDK your application supports?

4. What is the manifest XML tag for specifying the input methods your application supports?

5. What is the manifest XML tag for specifying the required device features for your application?

6. What is the manifest XML tag for specifying screen sizes supported by your application?

7. What is the manifest XML tag for working with external libraries?

8. What is the manifest XML tag for registering permissions your application enforces?

Exercises

1. Define a fictitious `<application>` manifest XML tag; include the `icon`, `label`, `allowBackup`, `enabled`, `debuggable`, and `testOnly` attributes; and include values for each.

2. Describe why it is important to choose a target SDK.

3. Using the Android documentation, list all the potential string values available for defining the `reqNavigation` attribute of the `<uses-configuration>` tag.

4. Using the Android documentation, create a list of five hardware features of the `name` attribute of the `<uses-feature>` tag.

5. Using the Android documentation, name all of the possible attributes and their value types of the `<supports-screens>` manifest XML tag.

6. Using the Android documentation, create a list of ten different values that could be used for defining the `name` attribute of the `<uses-permission>` manifest XML tag.

References and More Information

Android Developers Guide: "The `AndroidManifest.xml` File":
  http://d.android.com/guide/topics/manifest/manifest-intro.html
Android Developers Guide: "What Is API Level":
  http://d.android.com/guide/topics/manifest/uses-sdk-element.html#ApiLevels
Android Developers Guide: "Supporting Multiple Screens":
  http://d.android.com/guide/practices/screens_support.html
Android Developers Guide: "Security Tips":
  http://d.android.com/training/articles/security-tips.html
Android Google Services: "Filters on Google Play":
  http://d.android.com/google/play/filters.html

Managing Application Resources

The well-written application accesses its resources programmatically instead of the developer hard-coding them into the source code. This is done for a variety of reasons. Storing application resources in a single place is a more organized approach to development and makes the code more readable and maintainable. Externalizing resources such as strings makes it easier to localize applications for different languages and geographic regions. Finally, different resources may be necessary for different devices.

In this chapter, you learn how Android applications store and access important resources such as strings, graphics, and other data. You also learn how to organize Android resources within the project files for localization and different device configurations.

What Are Resources?

All Android applications are composed of two things: functionality (code instructions) and data (resources). The functionality is the code that determines how your application behaves. This includes any algorithms that make the application run. Resources include text strings, styles and themes, dimensions, images and icons, audio files, videos, and other data used by the application.

> **Tip**
>
> Many of the code examples provided in this chapter are taken from the
> `SimpleResourceView`, `ResourceRoundup`, and `ParisView` applications. The
> source code for these applications is provided for download on the book's website.

Storing Application Resources

Android resource files are stored separately from the `.java` class files in the Android project. Most common resource types are stored in XML. You can also store raw data files and graphics as resources. Resources are organized in a strict directory hierarchy. All resources must be stored under the `/res` project directory in specially named subdirectories whose names must be lowercase.

Table 6.1 **Default Android Resource Directories**

Resource Subdirectory	Purpose
/res/drawable-*/	Graphics resources
/res/layout/	User interface resources
/res/menu/	Menu resources for showing options or actions in activities
/res/values/	Simple data such as strings, styles and themes, and dimensions
/res/values-sw*/	Dimension resources for overriding defaults
/res/values-v*/	Style and theme resources for newer API customizations

Different resource types are stored in different directories. The resource subdirectories generated when you create an Android project are shown in Table 6.1.

Each resource type corresponds to a specific resource subdirectory name. For example, all graphics are stored under the /res/drawable directory structure. Resources can be further organized in a variety of ways using even more specially named directory qualifiers. For example, the /res/drawable-hdpi directory stores graphics for high-density screens, the /res/drawable-ldpi directory stores graphics for low-density screens, the /res/drawable-mdpi directory stores graphics for medium-density screens, the /res/drawable-xhdpi directory stores graphics for extra-high-density screens, and the /res/drawable-xxhdpi directory stores graphics for extra-extra-high-density screens. If you had a graphics resource that was shared by all screens, you would simply store that resource in the /res/drawable directory. We talk more about resource directory qualifiers later in this chapter.

If you use the Android IDE, you will find that adding resources to your project is simple. The Android IDE automatically detects new resources when you add them to the appropriate project resource subdirectory under /res. These resources are compiled, resulting in the generation of the R.java source file, which enables you to access your resources programmatically.

Resource Value Types

Android applications rely on many different types of resources—such as text strings, graphics, and color schemes—for user interface design.

These resources are stored in the /res directory of your Android project in a strict (but reasonably flexible) set of directories and files. All resource filenames must be lowercase and simple (letters, numbers, and underscores only).

The resource types supported by the Android SDK and how they are stored within the project are shown in Table 6.2.

Table 6.2 **How Common Resource Types Are Stored in the Project File Hierarchy**

Resource Type	Required Directory	Suggested Filenames	XML Tag
Strings	`/res/values/`	`strings.xml`	`<string>`
String pluralization	`/res/values/`	`strings.xml`	`<plurals>`, `<item>`
Arrays of strings	`/res/values/`	`strings.xml` or `arrays.xml`	`<string-array>`, `<item>`
Booleans	`/res/values/`	`bools.xml`	`<bool>`
Colors	`/res/values/`	`colors.xml`	`<color>`
Color state lists	`/res/color/`	Examples include `buttonstates.xml`, `indicators.xml`	`<selector>`, `<item>`
Dimensions	`/res/values/`	`dimens.xml`	`<dimen>`
IDs	`/res/values/`	`ids.xml`	`<item>`
Integers	`/res/values/`	`integers.xml`	`<integer>`
Arrays of integers	`/res/values/`	`integers.xml`	`<integer-array>`
Mixed-type arrays	`/res/values/`	`arrays.xml`	`<array>`, `<item>`
Simple drawables (paintables)	`/res/values/`	`drawables.xml`	`<drawable>`
Graphics definition XML files such as shapes	`/res/drawable/`	Examples include `icon.png`, `logo.jpg`	Supported graphics files or drawables
Tweened animations	`/res/anim/`	Examples include `fadesequence.xml`, `spinsequence.xml`	`<set>`, `<alpha>`, `<scale>`, `<translate>`, `<rotate>`
Property animations	`/res/animator/`	`mypropanims.xml`	`<set>`, `<objectAnimator>`, `<valueAnimator>`
Frame-by-frame animations	`/res/drawable/`	Examples include `sequence1.xml`, `sequence2.xml`	`<animation-list>`, `<item>`
Menus	`/res/menu/`	Examples include `mainmenu.xml`, `helpmenu.xml`	`<menu>`
XML files	`/res/xml/`	Examples include `data.xml`, `data2.xml`	Defined by the developer

(continues)

Table 6.2 **Continued**

Resource Type	Required Directory	Suggested Filenames	XML Tag
Raw files	`/res/raw/`	Examples include `jingle.mp3`, `somevideo.mp4`, `helptext.txt`	Defined by the developer
Layouts	`/res/layout/`	Examples include `main.xml`, `help.xml`	Varies; must be a layout control
Styles and themes	`/res/values/`	`styles.xml`, `themes.xml`	`<style>`

Tip

Some resource files, such as animation files and graphics, are referenced by variables named from their filenames (regardless of file suffix), so name your files appropriately. Check the Android Developer website at *http://d.android.com/guide/topics/resources/ available-resources.html* for more details.

Storing Primitive Resource Types

Simple resource value types, such as strings, colors, dimensions, and other primitives, are stored under the `/res/values` project directory in XML files. Each resource file under the `/res/values` directory should begin with the following XML header:

```
<?xml version="1.0" encoding="utf-8"?>
```

Next comes the root node `<resources>` followed by the specific resource element types such as `<string>` or `<color>`. Each resource is defined using a different element name. Primitive resource types simply have a unique name and a value, like this color resource:

```
<color name="myFavoriteShadeOfRed">#800000</color>
```

Tip

Although the XML filenames are arbitrary, the best practice is to store your resources in separate files to reflect their types, such as `strings.xml`, `colors.xml`, and so on. However, there is nothing stopping developers from creating multiple resource files for a given type, such as two separate XML files called `bright_colors.xml` and `muted_colors.xml`, if they so choose. You will learn later in Chapter 14, "Designing Compatible Applications," about alternative resources, too, that influence how the files may be named and subdivided.

Storing Graphics and Files

In addition to simple resource types stored in the `/res/values` directory, you can also store numerous other types of resources, such as graphics, arbitrary XML files, and raw files. These types of resources are not stored in the `/res/values` directory but instead are stored in specially named directories according to their type. For example, graphics are stored as files in the `/res/drawable` directory structure. XML files can be stored in the `/res/xml` directory, and raw files can be stored in the `/res/raw` directory.

Make sure you name resource files appropriately because the resource name for graphics and files is derived from the filename of the specific resource. For example, a file called `flag.png` in the `/res/drawable` directory is given the name `R.drawable.flag`.

Storing Other Resource Types

All other resource types—be they tweened animation sequences, color state lists, or menus—are stored in special XML formats in various directories, as shown in Table 6.2. Again, each resource must be uniquely named.

Understanding How Resources Are Resolved

The Android platform has a very robust mechanism for loading the appropriate resources at runtime. You can organize Android project resources based on more than a dozen different criteria. It can be useful to think of the resources stored in the directory hierarchy discussed in this chapter as the application's *default resources*. You can also supply special versions of your resources to load instead of the defaults under certain conditions. These specialized resources are called *alternative resources*.

Two common reasons that developers use alternative resources are for internationalization and localization purposes and to design an application that runs smoothly on different device screens and orientations. We focus on default resources in this chapter and discuss alternative resources in Chapter 14, "Designing Compatible Applications."

Default and alternative resources are best illustrated by example. Let's presume that we have a simple application with its requisite string, graphics, and layout resources. In this application, the resources are stored in the top-level resource directories (for example, `/res/values/strings.xml`, `/res/drawable/mylogo.png`, and `/res/layout/main.xml`). No matter what Android device (huge hi-def screen, postage-stamp-size screen, portrait or landscape orientation, and so on) you run this application on, the same resource data is loaded and used. This application uses only default resources.

But what if we want our application to use different graphics sizes based on the screen density? We could use alternative graphics resources to do this. For example, we could provide different logos for different device screen densities by providing five versions of `mylogo.png`:

- `/res/drawable-ldpi/mylogo.png` (low-density screens)
- `/res/drawable-mdpi/mylogo.png` (medium-density screens)

- `/res/drawable-hdpi/mylogo.png` (high-density screens)

- `/res/drawable-xhdpi/mylogo.png` (extra-high-density screens)

- `/res/drawable-xxhdpi/mylogo.png` (extra-extra-high-density screens)

Let's look at another example. Let's say we find that the application would look much better if the layout were fully customized for portrait versus landscape orientations. We could change the layout, moving controls around, in order to achieve a more pleasant user experience and provide two layouts:

- `/res/layout-port/main.xml` (layout loaded in portrait mode)

- `/res/layout-land/main.xml` (layout loaded in landscape mode)

We are introducing the concept of alternative resources now because they are hard to avoid completely, but we will work primarily with default resources for most of this book, simply in order to focus on specific programming tasks without the clutter that results from trying to customize an application to run beautifully on every device configuration one might use.

Accessing Resources Programmatically

Developers access specific application resources using the `R.java` class file and its sub-classes, which are automatically generated when you add resources to your project (if you use the Android IDE). You can refer to any resource identifier in your project by its name (which is why it must be unique). For example, a `String` named `strHello` defined within the resource file called `/res/values/strings.xml` is accessed in the code as follows:

```
R.string.strHello
```

This variable is not the actual data associated with the `String` named `hello`. Instead, you use this resource identifier to retrieve the resource of that type (which happens to be `String`) from the project resources associated with the application.

First, you retrieve the `Resources` instance for your application `Context` (`android.content.Context`), which is, in this case, `this` because the `Activity` class extends `Context`. Then you use the `Resources` instance to get the appropriate kind of resource you want. You find that the `Resources` class (`android.content.res.Resources`) has helper methods for handling every kind of resource.

For example, a simple way to retrieve the `String` text is to call the `getString()` method of the `Resources` class, like this:

```
String myString = getResources().getString(R.string.strHello);
```

Before we go any further, we find it can be helpful to dig in and create some resources, so let's create a simple example.

Setting Simple Resource Values Using the Android IDE

To illustrate how to set resources using the Android IDE, let's look at an example. Create a new Android project and navigate to the `/res/values/strings.xml` file in the Android IDE and double-click the file to edit it. Alternatively, you can use the Android project included with the book called `ResourceRoundup` to follow along. Your `strings.xml` resource file opens in the right pane and should look something like Figure 6.1, but with fewer strings.

There are two tabs at the bottom of this pane. The `Resources` tab provides a friendly method to easily insert primitive resource types such as strings, colors, and dimension resources. The `strings.xml` tab shows the raw XML resource file you are creating. Sometimes, editing the XML file manually is much faster, especially if you add a number of new resources. Click the `strings.xml` tab, and your pane should look something like Figure 6.2.

Now add some resources using the `Add` button on the `Resources` tab. Specifically, create the following resources:

- A color resource named `prettyTextColor` with a value of `#ff0000`

- A dimension resource named `textPointSize` with a value of `14pt`

- A drawable resource named `redDrawable` with a value of `#F00`

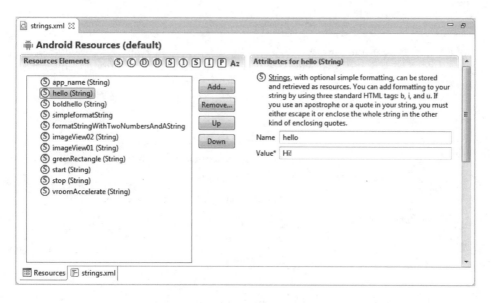

Figure 6.1   A sample string resource file in the Android IDE resource editor (Editor view).

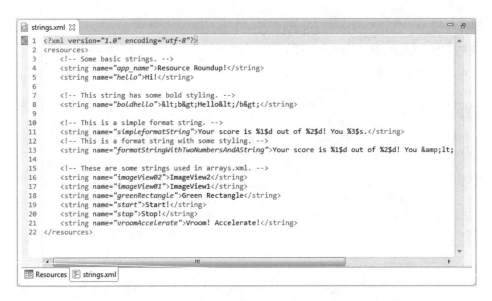

Figure 6.2   A sample string resource file in the Android IDE
resource editor (XML view).

Now you have several resources of various types in your `strings.xml` resource file.
If you switch back to the XML view, you see that the Android IDE resource editor has
added the appropriate XML elements to your file, which now should look something
like this:

```
<?xml version="1.0" encoding="utf-8"?>

<resources>

    <string name="app_name">ResourceRoundup</string>

    <string

        name="hello">Hello World, ResourceRoundupActivity</string>

    <color name="prettyTextColor">#ff0000</color>

    <dimen name="textPointSize">14pt</dimen>

    <drawable name="redDrawable">#F00</drawable>

</resources>
```

Save the `strings.xml` resource file. The Android IDE automatically generates the
`R.java` file in your project, with the appropriate resource IDs, which enables you to
programmatically access your resources after they are compiled into the project. If you

navigate to your R.java file, which is located under the /src directory in your package, it will look something like this:

```
package com.introtoandroid.resourceroundup;
public final class R {
   public static final class attr {
     }
   public static final class color {
       public static final int prettyTextColor=0x7f050000;
     }
   public static final class dimen {
       public static final int textPointSize=0x7f060000;
     }
   public static final class drawable {
       public static final int icon=0x7f020000;
       public static final int redDrawable=0x7f020001;
     }
   public static final class layout {
       public static final int main=0x7f030000;
     }
   public static final class string {
       public static final int app_name=0x7f040000;
       public static final int hello=0x7f040001;
     }
}
```

Now you are free to use these resources in your code. If you navigate to your ResourceRoundupActivity.java source file, you can add some lines to retrieve your resources and work with them, like this:

```
String myString = getResources().getString(R.string.hello);
int myColor =
    getResources().getColor(R.color.prettyTextColor);
float myDimen =
    getResources().getDimension(R.dimen.textPointSize);
ColorDrawable myDraw = (ColorDrawable)getResources().
    getDrawable(R.drawable.redDrawable);
```

Some resource types, such as string arrays, are more easily added to resource files by editing the XML by hand. For example, if we go back to the `strings.xml` file and choose the `strings.xml` tab, we can add a string array to our resource listing by adding the following XML element:

```xml
<?xml version="1.0" encoding="utf-8"?>

<resources>

    <string name="app_name">Use Some Resources</string>

    <string
        name="hello">Hello World, UseSomeResources</string>

    <color name="prettyTextColor">#ff0000</color>

    <dimen name="textPointSize">14pt</dimen>

    <drawable name="redDrawable">#F00</drawable>

    <string-array name="flavors">

        <item>Vanilla</item>

        <item>Chocolate</item>

        <item>Strawberry</item>

    </string-array>

</resources>
```

Save the `strings.xml` file, and now the string array named `flavors` is available in your source file `R.java`, so you can use it programmatically in `ResourceRoundup Activity.java`, like this:

```java
String[] aFlavors =

    getResources().getStringArray(R.array.flavors);
```

You now have a general idea of how to add simple resources using the Android IDE, but there are quite a few different types of data available to add as resources. It is a common practice to store different types of resources in different files. For example, you might store the strings in `/res/values/strings.xml` but store the `prettyTextColor` color resource in `/res/values/colors.xml` and the `textPointSize` dimension resource in `/res/values/dimens.xml`. Reorganizing where you keep your resources in the resource directory hierarchy does not change the names of the resources or the code used earlier to access the resources programmatically.

Now let's take a closer look at how to add some of the most common types of resources to your Android applications.

Working with Different Types of Resources

In this section, we look at the specific types of resources available for Android applications, how they are defined in the project files, and how you can access this resource data programmatically.

Table 6.3 **String Resource Formatting Examples**

String Resource Value	Displays As
Hello, World	Hello, World
"User's Full Name:"	User's Full Name:
User\'s Full Name:	User's Full Name:
She said, \"Hi.\"	She said, "Hi."
She\'s busy but she did say, \"Hi.\"	She's busy but she did say, "Hi."

For each type of resource, you learn what types of values can be stored and in what format. Some resource types (such as string and color) are well supported with the Android IDE resource editor, whereas others (such as Animation sequences) are more easily managed by editing the XML files directly.

Working with String Resources

String resources are among the simplest resource types available to the developer. String resources might be used to show text labels on form views and for help text. The application name is also stored as a string resource, by default.

String resources are defined in XML under the /res/values project directory and compiled into the application package at build time. All strings with apostrophes or single straight quotes need to be escaped or wrapped in double straight quotes. Some examples of well-formatted string values are shown in Table 6.3.

You can edit the strings.xml file using the Resources tab, or you can edit the XML directly by clicking the file and choosing the strings.xml tab. After you save the file, the resource identifiers are automatically added to your R.java class file.

String values are appropriately tagged with the <string> tag and represent a name/value pair. The name attribute is how you refer to the specific string programmatically, so name these resources wisely.

Here is an example of the string resource file /res/values/strings.xml:

```
<?xml version="1.0" encoding="utf-8"?>

<resources>

    <string name="app_name">Resource Viewer</string>

    <string name="test_string">Testing 1,2,3</string>

    <string name="test_string2">Testing 4,5,6</string>

</resources>
```

Bold, Italic, and Underlined Strings

You can also add three HTML-style attributes to string resources: bold, italic, and underlining. You specify the styling using the <b>, <i>, and <u> tags, respectively, for example:

```
<string
    name="txt"><b>Bold</b>,<i>Italic</i>,<u>Line</u></string>
```

Using String Resources as Format Strings

You can create format strings, but you need to escape all bold, italic, and underlining tags if you do so. For example, this text shows a score and the "win" or "lose" string:

```
<string
    name="winLose">Score: %1$d of %2$d! You %3$s.</string>
```

If you want to include bold, italic, or underlining in this format string, you need to escape the format tags. For example, if you want to italicize the "win" or "lose" string at the end, your resource would look like this:

```
<string name="winLoseStyled">
    Score: %1$d of %2$d! You &lt;i&gt;%3$s&lt;/i&gt;.</string>
```

> **Note**
>
> Those of you who are familiar with XML will recognize this as standard XML escaping. Indeed, that's all it is. After the standard set of XML escape characters is parsed, the string is then interpreted with the formatting tags. As with any XML document, you'd also need to escape single quotes (' is `&apos;`), double quotes (" is `&quot;`), and ampersands (& is `&amp;`).

Using String Resources Programmatically

As shown earlier in this chapter, accessing string resources in code is straightforward. There are two primary ways in which you can access a string resource.

The following code accesses your application's string resource named `hello`, returning only the `String`. All HTML-style attributes (bold, italic, and underlining) are stripped from the `String`.

```
String myStrHello =
    getResources().getString(R.string.hello);
```

You can also access the `String` and preserve the formatting by using this other method:

```
CharSequence myBoldStr =
    getResources().getText(R.string.boldhello);
```

To load a format `String`, you need to make sure any format variables are properly escaped. One way you can do this is by using the `htmlEncode()` method of the `TextUtils` (`android.text.TextUtils`) class:

```
String mySimpleWinString;

mySimpleWinString =
    getResources().getString(R.string.winLose);

String escapedWin = TextUtils.htmlEncode(mySimpleWinString);

String resultText = String.format(mySimpleWinString, 5, 5, escapedWin);
```

The resulting text in the `resultText` variable is

```
Score: 5 of 5! You Won.
```

Now if you have styling in this format `String` like the preceding string resource `winLoseStyled`, you need to take a few more steps to handle the escaped italic tags. For this, you might want to use the `fromHtml()` method of the `Html` class (`android.text.Html`), as shown here:

```
String myStyledWinString;

myStyledWinString =

    getResources().getString(R.string.winLoseStyled);

String escapedWin = TextUtils.htmlEncode(myStyledWinString);

String resultText =

    String.format(myStyledWinString, 5, 5, escapedWin);

CharSequence styledResults = Html.fromHtml(resultText);
```

The resulting text in the `styledResults` variable is

```
Score: 5 of 5! You <i>Won</i>.
```

This variable, `styledResults`, can then be used in user interface controls such as `TextView` objects, where styled text is displayed correctly.

Working with Quantity Strings

A special resource type called `<plurals>` can be used to define strings that are useful for changing a word's grammatical quantity form. Here is an example string resource file with the resource path of `res/values/strings.xml` that defines two different quantity forms of a particular animal name that changes based on the context of the quantity:

```
<resources>

    <plurals name="quantityOfGeese">

        <item quantity="one">You caught a goose!</item>

        <item quantity="other">You caught %d geese!</item>

    </plurals>

</resources>
```

The singular form for this particular animal is `goose`, and the plural form is `geese`. The `%d` value is used so we can display the exact quantity of geese to the user. To work with pluralized resources in your code, the method `getQuantityString()` can be used to retrieve a plural string resource like so:

```
int quantity = getQuantityOfGeese();

Resources plurals = getResources();
```

Table 6.4 **String `quantity` Values**

Value	Description
zero	Used for languages that have words with a zero `quantity` form
one	Used for languages that have words with a singular `quantity` form
two	Used for languages that have words for specifying two
few	Used for languages that have words for specifying a small `quantity` batch
many	Used for languages that have words for specifying a large `quantity` batch
other	Used for languages that have words that do not have a `quantity` form

```
String geeseFound = plurals.getQuantityString(
        R.plurals.quantityOfGeese, quantity, quantity);
```

getQuantityString() takes three variables. The first is the plural resource; the second is the `quantity` value, which is used to tell the application which grammatical form of the word to display; and the third value is defined only when the actual `quantity` is to be displayed to the user, substituting `%d` with the actual integer value.

When internationalizing your application, managing the translation of words properly and accounting for `quantity` in a particular language is very important. Not all languages follow the same rules for `quantity`, so in order to make this process manageable, using plural string resource files will definitely help.

For a particular word, you are able to define many different grammatical forms. To define more than one quantity form of a given word in your string resource file, you simply specify more than one `<item>` element and provide a value for the `quantity` attribute for that particular `<item>` denoting the word's `quantity`. The values that you can use to specify the `<item>`'s quantity are shown in Table 6.4.

Working with String Arrays

You can specify lists of strings in resource files. This can be a good way to store menu options and drop-down list values. String arrays are defined in XML under the `/res/values` project directory and compiled into the application package at build time.

String arrays are appropriately tagged with the `<string-array>` tag and a number of `<item>` child tags, one for each `String` in the array. Here is an example of a simple array resource file, `/res/values/arrays.xml`:

```
<?xml version="1.0" encoding="utf-8"?>
<resources>
    <string-array name="flavors">
        <item>Vanilla</item>
        <item>Chocolate</item>
```

```
        <item>Strawberry</item>
        <item>Coffee</item>
        <item>Sherbet</item>
    </string-array>
    <string-array name="soups">
        <item>Vegetable minestrone</item>
        <item>New England clam chowder</item>
        <item>Organic chicken noodle</item>
    </string-array>
</resources>
```

As shown earlier in this chapter, accessing string array resources is easy. The method `getStringArray()` retrieves a string array from a resource file, in this case, one named `flavors`:

```
String[] aFlavors =
    getResources().getStringArray(R.array.flavors);
```

Working with Boolean Resources

Other primitive types are supported by the Android resource hierarchy as well. Boolean resources can be used to store information about application game preferences and default values. Boolean resources are defined in XML under the `/res/values` project directory and compiled into the application package at build time.

Defining Boolean Resources in XML

Boolean values are appropriately tagged with the `<bool>` tag and represent a name/value pair. The `name` attribute is how you refer to the specific Boolean value programmatically, so name these resources wisely.

Here is an example of the Boolean resource file `/res/values/bools.xml`:

```
<?xml version="1.0" encoding="utf-8"?>

<resources>
    <bool name="onePlusOneEqualsTwo">true</bool>
    <bool name="isAdvancedFeaturesEnabled">false</bool>
</resources>
```

Using Boolean Resources Programmatically

To use a Boolean resource in code, you can load it using the `getBoolean()` method of the `Resources` class. The following code accesses your application's Boolean resource named `bAdvancedFeaturesEnabled`:

```
boolean isAdvancedMode =
    getResources().getBoolean(R.bool.isAdvancedFeaturesEnabled);
```

Working with Integer Resources

In addition to strings and Boolean values, you can also store integers as resources. Integer resources are defined in XML under the `/res/values` project directory and compiled into the application package at build time.

Defining Integer Resources in XML

Integer values are appropriately tagged with the `<integer>` tag and represent a name/value pair. The `name` attribute is how you refer to the specific integer programmatically, so name these resources wisely.

Here is an example of the integer resource file `/res/values/nums.xml`:

```xml
<?xml version="1.0" encoding="utf-8"?>

<resources>

    <integer name="numTimesToRepeat">25</integer>

    <integer name="startingAgeOfCharacter">3</integer>

</resources>
```

Using Integer Resources Programmatically

To use the integer resource, you must load it using the `Resources` class. The following code accesses your application's integer resource named `numTimesToRepeat`:

```java
int repTimes = getResources().getInteger(R.integer.numTimesToRepeat);
```

> **Tip**
>
> Much as with string arrays, you can create integer arrays as resources using the `<integer-array>` tag with child `<item>` tags, defining one for each item in the array. You can then load the integer array using the `getIntArray()` method of the `Resources` class.

Working with Colors

Android applications can store RGB color values, which can then be applied to other screen elements. You can use these values to set the color of text or other elements, such as the screen background. Color resources are defined in XML under the `/res/values` project directory and compiled into the application package at build time.

Defining Color Resources in XML

RGB color values always start with the hash symbol (#). The alpha value can be given for transparency control. The following color formats are supported:

- #RGB (for example, `#F00` is 12-bit color, red)
- #ARGB (for example, `#8F00` is 12-bit color, red with alpha 50%)
- #RRGGBB (for example, `#FF00FF` is 24-bit color, magenta)
- #AARRGGBB (for example, `#80FF00FF` is 24-bit color, magenta, with alpha 50%)

Color values are appropriately tagged with the <color> tag and represent a name/value pair. Here is an example of a simple color resource file, /res/values/colors.xml:

```xml
<?xml version="1.0" encoding="utf-8"?>
<resources>
    <color name="background_color">#006400</color>
    <color name="text_color">#FFE4C4</color>
</resources>
```

Using Color Resources Programmatically

The example at the beginning of the chapter accessed a color resource. Color resources are simply integers. The following example shows the method getColor() retrieving a color resource called prettyTextColor:

```
int myResourceColor =
    getResources().getColor(R.color.prettyTextColor);
```

Working with Dimensions

Many user interface layout controls, such as text controls and buttons, are drawn to specific dimensions. These dimensions can be stored as resources. Dimension values always end with a unit of measurement tag.

Defining Dimension Resources in XML

Dimension values are tagged with the <dimen> tag and represent a name/value pair. Dimension resources are defined in XML under the /res/values project directory and compiled into the application package at build time.

The dimension units supported are shown in Table 6.5.

Table 6.5 **Dimension Unit Measurements Supported**

Unit of Measurement	Description	Resource Tag Required	Example
Pixels	Actual screen pixels	px	20px
Inches	Physical measurement	in	1in
Millimeters	Physical measurement	mm	1mm
Points	Common font measurement unit	pt	14pt
Screen density—independent pixels	Pixels relative to 160dpi screen (preferable for dimension screen compatibility)	dp	1dp
Scale-independent pixels	Best for scalable font display	sp	14sp

Here is an example of a simple dimension resource file called /res/values/dimens.xml:

```
<?xml version="1.0" encoding="utf-8"?>

<resources>

    <dimen name="FourteenPt">14pt</dimen>

    <dimen name="OneInch">1in</dimen>

    <dimen name="TenMillimeters">10mm</dimen>

    <dimen name="TenPixels">10px</dimen>

</resources>
```

Note

Generally, dp is used for layouts and graphics, whereas sp is used for text. A device's default settings will usually result in dp and sp being the same. However, because the user can control the size of text when it's in sp units, you would not use sp for text where the font layout size was important, such as with a title. Instead, it's good for content text where the user's settings might be important (such as a really large font for the vision impaired).

Using Dimension Resources Programmatically

Dimension resources are simply floating-point values. The getDimension() method retrieves a dimension resource called textPointSize:

```
float myDimension =

    getResources().getDimension(R.dimen.textPointSize);
```

Warning

Be cautious when choosing dimension units for your applications. If you are planning to target multiple devices, with different screen sizes and resolutions, you need to rely heavily on the more scalable dimension units, such as dp and sp, as opposed to pixels, points, inches, and millimeters.

Drawable Resources

The Android SDK supports many different types of drawable resources for managing the different types of graphics files that your project requires. These resource types are also useful for managing the presentation of your project's drawable files. Table 6.6 presents some of the different types of drawable resources that you can define.

Working with Simple Drawables

You can specify simple colored rectangles by using the drawable resource type, which can then be applied to other screen elements. These drawable resource types are defined in specific paint colors, much as the color resources are defined.

Table 6.6 **Different Drawable Resources**

Drawable Class	Description
ShapeDrawable	A geometric shape such as a circle or rectangle
ScaleDrawable	Defines the scaling of a Drawable
TransitionDrawable	Used to cross-fade between drawables
ClipDrawable	Drawable used to clip a region of a Drawable
StateListDrawable	Used to define different states of a Drawable such as pressed or selected
LayerDrawable	An array of drawables
BitmapDrawable	Bitmap graphics file
NinePatchDrawable	Stretchable PNG file

Defining Simple Drawable Resources in XML

Simple paintable drawable resources are defined in XML under the /res/values project directory and compiled into the application package at build time. Paintable drawable resources use the <drawable> tag and represent a name/value pair. Here is an example of a simple drawable resource file called /res/values/drawables.xml:

```
<?xml version="1.0" encoding="utf-8"?>

<resources>

    <drawable name="red_rect">#F00</drawable>

</resources>
```

Although it might seem a tad confusing, you can also create XML files that describe other Drawable subclasses, such as ShapeDrawable. Drawable XML definition files are stored in the /res/drawable directory within your project, along with image files. This is not the same as storing <drawable> resources, which are paintable drawables. ShapeDrawable resources are stored in the /res/values directory, as explained previously.

Here is a simple ShapeDrawable described in the file /res/drawable/red_oval.xml:

```
<?xml version="1.0" encoding="utf-8"?>

<shape

    xmlns:android=

        "http://schemas.android.com/apk/res/android"

    android:shape="oval">

        <solid android:color="#f00"/>

</shape>
```

Of course, we don't need to specify the size because it will scale automatically to the layout it's placed in, much like any vector graphics format.

Using Simple Drawable Resources Programmatically

Drawable resources defined with `<drawable>` are simply rectangles of a given color, which is represented by the `Drawable` subclass `ColorDrawable`. The following code retrieves a `ColorDrawable` resource called `redDrawable`:

```
ColorDrawable myDraw = (ColorDrawable)getResources().
    getDrawable(R.drawable.redDrawable);
```

> **Tip**
>
> To learn how to define XML resources for a particular type of drawable and to learn how to access the different types of drawable resources in your code, see the Android documentation at *http://d.android.com/guide/topics/resources/drawable-resource.html*.

Working with Images

Applications often include visual elements such as icons and graphics. Android supports several image formats that can be directly included as resources for your application. These image formats are shown in Table 6.7.

These image formats are all well supported by popular graphics editors such as Adobe Photoshop, GIMP, and Microsoft Paint. Adding image resources to your project is easy. Simply drag the image asset into the `/res/drawable` resource directory hierarchy and it will automatically be included in the application package.

> **Warning**
>
> All resource filenames must be lowercase and simple (letters, numbers, and underscores only). This rule applies to all files, including graphics.

Table 6.7 **Image Formats Supported in Android**

Supported Image Format	Description	Required Extension
Portable Network Graphics (PNG)	Preferred format (lossless)	`.png`
Nine-Patch Stretchable Graphics	Preferred format (lossless)	`.9.png`
Joint Photographic Experts Group (JPEG)	Acceptable format (lossy)	`.jpg`, `.jpeg`
Graphics Interchange Format (GIF)	Discouraged format	`.gif`
WebP (WEBP)	Android 4.0+	`.webp`

Working with Nine-Patch Stretchable Graphics

Android device screens, be they smartphones, tablets, or TVs, come in various dimensions. It can be handy to use stretchable graphics to allow a single graphic that can scale appropriately for different screen sizes and orientations or different lengths of text. This can save you or your designer a lot of time in creating graphics for many different screen sizes.

Android supports Nine-Patch Stretchable Graphics for this purpose. Nine-Patch graphics are simply PNG graphics that have patches, or areas of the image, defined to scale appropriately, instead of the entire image scaling as one unit. Often the center segment is transparent or a solid color for a background because it's the stretched part. As such, a common use for Nine-Patch graphics is to create frames and borders. Little more than the corners are needed, so a very small graphics file can be used to frame any size image or `View` control.

Nine-Patch Stretchable Graphics can be created from PNG files using the `draw9patch` tool included with the `/tools` directory of the Android SDK. We talk more about compatibility and using Nine-Patch graphics in Chapter 14, "Designing Compatible Applications."

Using Image Resources Programmatically

Image resources are simply another kind of `Drawable` called a `BitmapDrawable`. Most of the time, you need only the resource ID of the image to set as an attribute on a user interface control.

For example, if we drop the graphics file `flag.png` into the `/res/drawable` directory and add an `ImageView` control to the main layout, we can interact with that control programmatically in the layout by first using the `findViewById()` method to retrieve a control by its identifier and then casting it to the proper type of control—in this case, an `ImageView` (`android.widget.ImageView`) object:

```
ImageView flagImageView =
    (ImageView)findViewById(R.id.ImageView01);

flagImageView.setImageResource(R.drawable.flag);
```

Similarly, if you want to access the `BitmapDrawable` (`android.graphics.drawable`
`.BitmapDrawable`) object directly, you can request that resource directly using the `getDrawable()` method, as follows:

```
BitmapDrawable bitmapFlag = (BitmapDrawable)
    getResources().getDrawable(R.drawable.flag);

int iBitmapHeightInPixels =
    bitmapFlag.getIntrinsicHeight();

int iBitmapWidthInPixels = bitmapFlag.getIntrinsicWidth();
```

Finally, if you work with Nine-Patch graphics, the call to `getDrawable()` will return a `NinePatchDrawable` (`android.graphics.drawable.NinePatchDrawable`) object instead of a `BitmapDrawable` object:

```
NinePatchDrawable stretchy = (NinePatchDrawable)

    getResources().getDrawable(R.drawable.pyramid);

int iStretchyHeightInPixels =

    stretchy.getIntrinsicHeight();

int iStretchyWidthInPixels = stretchy.getIntrinsicWidth();
```

Working with Color State Lists

A special resource type called `<selector>` can be used to define different colors or drawables to be used depending on a control's state. For example, you could define a color state list for a `Button` control: gray when the button is disabled, green when it is enabled, and yellow when it is being pressed. Similarly, you could provide different drawables based on the state of an `ImageButton` control.

The `<selector>` element can have one or more child `<item>` elements that define different colors for different states. There are quite a few attributes that you are able to define for the `<item>` element, and you can define one or more for supporting many different states for your `View` objects. Table 6.8 shows many of the attributes that you are able to define for the `<item>` element.

Table 6.8 **Color State List `<item>` Attributes**

Attribute	Values
color	Required attribute for specifying a hexadecimal color in one of the following formats: #RGB, #ARGB, #RRGGBB, or #AARRGGBB, where A is alpha, R is red, G is green, and B is blue
state_enabled	Boolean value denoting whether this object is capable of receiving touch or click events, true or false
state_checked	Boolean value denoting whether this object is checked or unchecked, true or false
state_checkable	Boolean value denoting whether this object is checkable or not checkable, true or false
state_selected	Boolean value denoting whether this object is selected or not selected, true or false
state_focused	Boolean value denoting whether this object is focused or not focused, true or false
state_pressed	Boolean value denoting whether this object is pressed or not pressed, true or false

Defining a Color State List Resource

You first must create a resource file defining the various states that you want to apply to your `View` object. To do so, you define a color resource that contains the `<selector>` element and the various `<item>`s and their attributes that you want to apply. Following is an example file named `text_color.xml` that resides under the color resource directory, `res/color/text_color.xml`:

```
<selector xmlns:android="http://schemas.android.com/apk/res/android">

    <item android:state_disabled="true"

        android:color="#C0C0C0"/>

    <item android:state_enabled="true"

        android:color="#00FF00"/>

    <item android:state_pressed="true"

        android:color="#FFFF00"/>

    <item android:color="#000000"/>

</selector>
```

We have defined four different state values in this file: disabled, enabled, pressed, and a default value, provided by just defining an `<item>` element with only a `color` attribute.

Defining a `Button` for Applying the State List Resource

Now that we have a color state list resource, we can apply this value to one of our `View` objects. Here, we define a `Button` and set the `textColor` attribute to the state list resource file `text_color.xml` that we defined previously:

```
<Button

    android:layout_width="match_parent"

    android:layout_height="wrap_content"

    android:text="@string/text"

    android:textColor="@color/text_color" />
```

When a user interacts with our `Button` view, the disabled state is gray, the enabled state is green, the pressed state is yellow, and the default state is black.

Working with Animation

Android provides two categories of animations. The first category, property animation, allows you to animate an object's properties. The second category of animation is view animation. There are two different types of view animations: *frame-by-frame* animation and *tween* animations.

Frame-by-frame animation involves the display of a sequence of images in rapid succession. Tweened animation involves applying standard graphical transformations such as rotations and fades to a single image.

The Android SDK provides some helper utilities for loading and using animation resources. These utilities are found in the `android.view.animation.AnimationUtils` class. Let's look at how you define the different view animations in terms of resources.

Defining and Using Frame-by-Frame Animation Resources

Frame-by-frame animation is often used when the content changes from frame to frame. This type of animation can be used for complex frame transitions—much like a kid's flip book.

To define frame-by-frame resources, take the following steps:

1. Save each frame graphic as an individual drawable resource. It may help to name your graphics sequentially, in the order in which they are displayed—for example, `frame1.png`, `frame2.png`, and so on.

2. Define the animation set resource in an XML file within the `/res/drawable/` resource directory hierarchy.

3. Load, start, and stop the animation programmatically.

Here is an example of a simple frame-by-frame animation resource file called `/res/drawable/juggle.xml` that defines a simple three-frame animation that takes 1.5 seconds to complete a single loop:

```xml
<?xml version="1.0" encoding="utf-8" ?>
<animation-list
    xmlns:android="http://schemas.android.com/apk/res/android"
    android:oneshot="false">
    <item
        android:drawable="@drawable/splash1"
        android:duration="500" />
    <item
        android:drawable="@drawable/splash2"
        android:duration="500" />
    <item
        android:drawable="@drawable/splash3"
        android:duration="500" />
</animation-list>
```

Frame-by-frame animation set resources defined with `<animation-list>` are represented by the `Drawable` subclass `AnimationDrawable`. The following code retrieves an `AnimationDrawable` resource called `juggle`:

```java
AnimationDrawable jugglerAnimation = (AnimationDrawable)getResources().
    getDrawable(R.drawable.juggle);
```

After you have a valid `AnimationDrawable` (`android.graphics.drawable.Animation Drawable`), you can assign it to a `View` control on the screen and start and stop animation.

Defining and Using Tweened Animation Resources

Tweened animation features include scaling, fading, rotation, and translation. These actions can be applied simultaneously or sequentially and might use different interpolators.

Tweened animation sequences are not tied to a specific graphics file, so you can write one sequence and then use it for a variety of different graphics. For example, you can make moon, star, and diamond graphics all pulse using a single scaling sequence, or you can make them spin using a rotate sequence.

Defining Tweened Animation Sequence Resources in XML

Graphics animation sequences can be stored as specially formatted XML files in the `/res/anim` directory and are compiled into the application binary at build time.

Here is an example of a simple animation resource file called `/res/anim/spin.xml` that defines a simple rotate operation—rotating the target graphic counterclockwise four times in place, taking 10 seconds to complete:

```xml
<?xml version="1.0" encoding="utf-8" ?>

<set xmlns:android="http://schemas.android.com/apk/res/android"

    android:shareInterpolator="false">

    <rotate

        android:fromDegrees="0"

        android:toDegrees="-1440"

        android:pivotX="50%"

        android:pivotY="50%"

        android:duration="10000" />

</set>
```

Using Tweened Animation Sequence Resources Programmatically

If we go back to the earlier example of a `BitmapDrawable`, we can now include some animation simply by adding the following code to load the animation resource file `spin.xml` and set the animation in motion:

```java
ImageView flagImageView =

    (ImageView)findViewById(R.id.ImageView01);

flagImageView.setImageResource(R.drawable.flag);

...

Animation an =

    AnimationUtils.loadAnimation(this, R.anim.spin);

flagImageView.startAnimation(an);
```

Now you have your graphic spinning. Notice that we loaded the animation using the base class object `Animation`. You can also extract specific animation types using the subclasses that match: `RotateAnimation`, `ScaleAnimation`, `TranslateAnimation`, and `AlphaAnimation` (found in the `android.view.animation` package).

There are a number of different interpolators you can use with your tweened animation sequences.

Working with Menus

You can also include menu resources in your project files. Like animation resources, menu resources are not tied to a specific control but can be reused in any menu control.

Defining Menu Resources in XML

Each menu resource (which is a set of individual menu items) is stored as a specially formatted XML file in the `/res/menu` directory and is compiled into the application package at build time.

Here is an example of a simple menu resource file called `/res/menu/speed.xml` that defines a short menu with four items in a specific order:

```
<menu xmlns:android="http://schemas.android.com/apk/res/android">
    <item
        android:id="@+id/start"
        android:title="Start!"
        android:orderInCategory="1"></item>
    <item
        android:id="@+id/stop"
        android:title="Stop!"
        android:orderInCategory="4"></item>
    <item
        android:id="@+id/accel"
        android:title="Vroom! Accelerate!"
        android:orderInCategory="2"></item>
    <item
        android:id="@+id/decel"
        android:title="Decelerate!"
        android:orderInCategory="3"></item>
</menu>
```

You can create menus using the Android IDE, which can access the various configuration attributes for each menu item. In the previous case, we set the title (label) of each menu item and the order in which the items display. Now, you can use string resources for those titles instead of typing in the strings. For example:

```
<menu xmlns:android=

    "http://schemas.android.com/apk/res/android">

    <item

        android:id="@+id/start"

        android:title="@string/start"

        android:orderInCategory="1"></item>

    <item

        android:id="@+id/stop"

        android:title="@string/stop"

        android:orderInCategory="2"></item>

</menu>
```

Using Menu Resources Programmatically

To access the preceding menu resource called /res/menu/speed.xml, simply override the method onCreateOptionsMenu() in your Activity class, returning true to cause the menu to be displayed:

```
public boolean onCreateOptionsMenu(Menu menu) {

    getMenuInflater().inflate(R.menu.speed, menu);

    return true;

}
```

That's it. Now if you run your application and press the Menu button, you see the menu. A number of other XML attributes can be assigned to menu items. For a complete list of these attributes, see the Android SDK Reference for menu resources at the website *http://d.android.com/guide/topics/resources/menu-resource.html*. You will learn a lot more about menus and menu event handling in Chapter 7, "Exploring User Interface Building Blocks."

Working with XML Files

You can include arbitrary XML resource files to your project. You should store these XML files in the /res/xml directory, and they are compiled into the application package at build time.

The Android SDK has a variety of packages and classes available for XML manipulation. You will learn more about XML handling in Chapter 12, "Working with Files and Directories." For now, we create an XML resource file and access it through code.

Defining Raw XML Resources

First, put a simple XML file in the `/res/xml` directory. In this case, the file `my_pets.xml` with the following contents can be created:

```
<?xml version="1.0" encoding="utf-8"?>

<pets>

    <pet name="Bit" type="Bunny" />

    <pet name="Nibble" type="Bunny" />

    <pet name="Stack" type="Bunny" />

    <pet name="Queue" type="Bunny" />

    <pet name="Heap" type="Bunny" />

    <pet name="Null" type="Bunny" />

    <pet name="Nigiri" type="Fish" />

    <pet name="Sashimi II" type="Fish" />

    <pet name="Kiwi" type="Lovebird" />

</pets>
```

Using XML Resources Programmatically

Now you can access this XML file as a resource programmatically in the following manner:

```
XmlResourceParser myPets =
    getResources().getXml(R.xml.my_pets);
```

You can then use the parser of your choice to parse the XML. We discuss working with files, including XML files, in Chapter 12, "Working with Files and Directories."

Working with Raw Files

Your application can also include raw files as part of its resources. For example, your application might use raw files such as audio files, video files, and other file formats not supported by the `Android Asset Packaging Tool` (aapt).

Tip

For a full list of supported media formats, have a look at the following Android documentation: *http://d.android.com/guide/appendix/media-formats.html*.

Defining Raw File Resources

All raw resource files are included in the `/res/raw` directory and are added to your package without further processing.

Warning

All resource filenames must be lowercase and simple (letters, numbers, and underscores only). This also applies to raw file filenames even though the tools do not process these files other than to include them in your application package.

The resource filename must be unique to the directory and should be descriptive because the filename (without the extension) becomes the name by which the resource is accessed.

Using Raw File Resources Programmatically

You can access raw file resources from the `/res/raw` resource directory and any resource from the `/res/drawable` directory (bitmap graphics files, anything not using the `<resource>` XML definition method). Here is one way to open a file called `the_help.txt`:

```
InputStream iFile =
    getResources().openRawResource(R.raw.the_help);
```

References to Resources

You can reference resources instead of duplicating them. For example, your application might need to reference a single string resource in multiple string arrays.

The most common use of resource references is in layout XML files, where layouts can reference any number of resources to specify attributes for layout colors, dimensions, strings, and graphics. Another common use is within style and theme resources.

Resources are referenced using the following format:

```
@resource_type/variable_name
```

Recall that earlier we had a string array of soup names. If we want to localize the soup listing, a better way to create the array is to create individual string resources for each soup name and then store the references to those string resources in the string array (instead of the text).

To do this, we define the string resources in the `/res/strings.xml` file like this:

```
<?xml version="1.0" encoding="utf-8"?>

<resources>

    <string name="app_name">Application Name</string>

    <string name="chicken_soup">Organic chicken noodle</string>

    <string name="minestrone_soup">Veggie minestrone</string>

    <string name="chowder_soup">New England clam chowder</string>

</resources>
```

Then we can define a localizable string array that references the string resources by name in the `/res/arrays.xml` file like this:

```
<?xml version="1.0" encoding="utf-8"?>

<resources>
```

```
<string-array name="soups">

    <item>@string/minestrone_soup</item>

    <item>@string/chowder_soup</item>

    <item>@string/chicken_soup</item>

</string-array>

</resources>
```

Tip

Save the `strings.xml` file first so that the string resources (which are picked up by the aapt and included in the `R.java` class) are defined prior to trying to save the `arrays.xml` file, which references those particular string resources. Otherwise, you might get the following error:

```
Error: No resource found that matches the given name.
```

You can also use references to make aliases to other resources. For example, you can alias the system resource for the OK String to an application resource name by including the following in your `strings.xml` resource file:

```
<?xml version="1.0" encoding="utf-8"?>

<resources>

    <string id="app_ok">@android:string/ok</string>

</resources>
```

You learn more about all the different system resources available later in this chapter.

Tip

Much as with string and integer arrays, you can create arrays of any type of resource by using the `<array>` tag with child `<item>` tags, defining one item for each resource in the array. You can then load the array of miscellaneous resources using the `obtainTyped Array()` method of the `Resources` class. The typed array resource is commonly used for grouping and loading a bunch of drawable resources with a single call. For more information, see the Android SDK documentation on typed array resources.

Working with Layouts

Much as Web designers use HTML, user interface designers can use XML to define Android application screen elements and layout. A layout XML resource is where many different resources come together to form the definition of an Android application screen. Layout resource files are included in the `/res/layout/` directory and are compiled into the application package at build time. Layout files might include many user interface controls and define the layout for an entire screen or describe custom controls used in other layouts.

Figure 6.3   How the `activity_simple_resource_view.xml` layout file displays in the emulator.

Following is a simple example of a layout file (`/res/layout/activity_simple_resource_view.xml`) that sets the screen's background color and displays some text in the middle of the screen (see Figure 6.3).

The `activity_simple_resource_view.xml` layout file that displays this screen references a number of other resources, including colors, strings, and dimension values, all of which were defined in the `strings.xml`, `styles.xml`, `colors.xml`, and `dimens.xml` resource files. The color resource for the screen background color and resources for a `TextView` control's color, string, and text size follow:

```
<?xml version="1.0" encoding="utf-8"?>

<LinearLayout xmlns:android=

    "http://schemas.android.com/apk/res/android"
```

```
        android:orientation="vertical"
        android:layout_width="match_parent"
        android:layout_height="match_parent"
        android:background="@color/background_color">
        <TextView
            android:id="@+id/TextView01"
            android:layout_width="match_parent"
            android:layout_height="match_parent"
            android:text="@string/test_string"
            android:textColor="@color/text_color"
            android:gravity="center"
            android:textSize="@dimen/text_size" />
</LinearLayout>
```

The preceding layout describes all the visual elements on a screen. In this example, a LinearLayout control is used as a container for other user interface controls—here, a single TextView that displays a line of text.

Tip

You can encapsulate common layout definitions in their own XML files and then include those layouts within other layout files using the <include> tag. For example, you can use the following <include> tag to include another layout file called /res/layout/ mygreenrect.xml within the activity_resource_roundup.xml layout definition:

```
<include layout="@layout/mygreenrect"/>
```

Designing Layouts in the Android IDE

Layouts can be designed and previewed in the Android IDE by using the resource editor functionality (see Figure 6.4). If you click the project file /res/layout/activity_ simple_resource_view.xml, you see the Layout tab, which shows a preview of the Graphical Layout, and the activity_simple_resource_view.xml tab, which shows the raw XML of the layout file.

As with most user interface editors, the Android IDE works well for your basic layout needs, enables you to create user interface controls such as TextView and Button controls easily, and enables setting the controls' properties in the Properties pane.

Tip

Moving the Properties pane to the far right of the workspace in the Android IDE makes it easier to browse and set control properties when designing layouts.

Now is a great time to get to know the layout resource editor, also known as the layout designer. Try creating a new Android project called ParisView (available as a

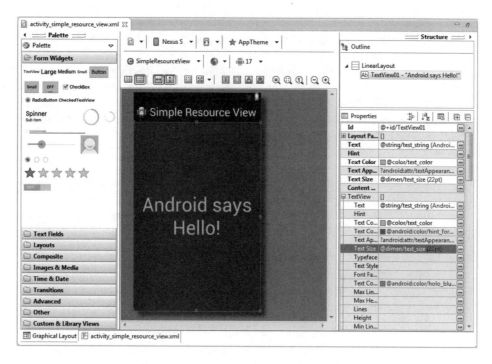

Figure 6.4   Designing a layout file using the Android IDE.

sample project). Navigate to the `/res/layout/activity_paris_view.xml` layout file and double-click it to open it in the editor. It's quite simple by default, with only a black (empty) rectangle and a `String` of text.

Below in the `Resource` pane of the Android IDE perspective, you notice the `Outline` tab. This outline is the XML hierarchy of this layout file. By default, you see a `LinearLayout`. If you expand it, you see it contains one `TextView` control. Click the `TextView` control. You see that the `Properties` pane of the Android IDE perspective now has all the properties available for that object. If you scroll down to the property called `text`, you see that it's set to the string resource variable `@string/hello_world`.

Tip

You can also select specific controls by clicking them in the layout designer's preview area. The currently selected control is highlighted in red. We prefer to use the `Outline` view, so we can be sure we are clicking what we expect.

You can use the layout designer to set and preview layout control properties. For example, you can modify the `TextView` property called `textSize` by typing `18pt` (a dimension). You see the results of your change to the property immediately in the preview area.

Take a moment to switch to the `activity_paris_view.xml` tab. Notice that the properties you set are now in the XML. If you save and run your project in the emulator now, you will see similar results to what you see in the designer preview.

Now select `Images & Media` within the `Palette`. Drag and drop the `ImageView` object within the preview editor. Now you have a new control in your layout.

Drag two PNG (or JPG) graphics files into your `/res/drawable` project directory, naming them `flag.png` and `background.png`. Now go to the `Outline` view, browse the properties of your `ImageView` control, and then set the `src` property manually by typing `@drawable/flag`.

Now, you see that the graphic shows up in your preview. While we're at it, select the `LinearLayout` object and set its `background` property to the background drawable you added.

If you save the layout file and run the application in the emulator (as shown in Figure 6.5) or on the phone, you will see results much like those in the resource designer preview pane.

Using Layout Resources Programmatically

Objects within layouts, whether they are `Button` or `ImageView` controls, are all derived from the `View` class. Here is how you would retrieve a `TextView` object named `TextView01`, called in an `Activity` class after the call to `setContentView()`:

```
TextView txt = (TextView)findViewById(R.id.TextView01);
```

You can also access the underlying XML of a layout resource much as you would any XML file. The following code retrieves the `main.xml` layout file for XML parsing:

```
XmlResourceParser myMainXml =

    getResources().getLayout(R.layout.activity_paris_view);
```

Developers can also define custom layouts with unique attributes. We talk much more about layout files and designing Android user interfaces in Chapter 8, "Designing with Layouts."

Warning

The Java code associated with your project is pretty much unaware of which version of a resource is loaded—whether it's the default or some alternative version. Take special care when providing alternative layout resources. Layout resources tend to be more complicated; the child controls within them are often referred to in code by name. Therefore, if you begin to create alternative layout resources, make sure each named child control that is referenced in code exists in each alternative layout. For example, if you have a user interface with a `Button` control, make sure the `Button` control's identifier (`android:id`) is the same in the landscape, portrait, and other alternative layout resources. You may include different controls and properties in each layout and rearrange them as you like, but those controls that are referred to and interacted with programmatically should exist in all layouts so that your code runs smoothly, regardless of the layout loaded. If they don't, you'll need to code conditionally, or you may even want to consider whether the screen is so different it should be represented by a different `Activity` class.

Figure 6.5   A layout with a `LinearLayout`, `TextView`, and `ImageView`, shown in the Android emulator.

Referencing System Resources

In addition to the resources included in your project, you can also take advantage of the generic resources provided as part of the Android SDK. You can access system resources much as you would your own resources. The `android` package contains all kinds of resources, which you can browse by looking in the `android.R` subclasses. Here, you find system resources for

- Animation sequences for fading in and out
- Arrays of email/phone types (home, work, and such)
- Standard system colors
- Dimensions for application thumbnails and icons

- Many commonly used drawable and layout types
- Error strings and standard button text
- System styles and themes

You can reference system resources in other resources such as layout files by specifying the @android package name before the resource. For example, to set the background to the system color for darker gray, you set the appropriate background `color` attribute to @android:color/darker_gray.

You can access system resources programmatically through the android.R class. If we go back to our animation example, we could have used a system animation instead of defining our own. Here is the same animation example again, except it uses a system animation to fade in:

```
ImageView flagImageView =

    (ImageView)findViewById(R.id.ImageView01);

flagImageView.setImageResource(R.drawable.flag);

Animation an = AnimationUtils.

    loadAnimation(this, android.R.anim.fade_in);

flagImageView.startAnimation(an);
```

Warning

Although referencing system resources can be useful to give your application a look that is more consistent with the rest of a particular device's user interface (something users will appreciate), you still need to be cautious when doing so. If a particular device has system resources that are dramatically different or fails to include specific resources your application relies upon, your application may not look right or behave as expected. An installable application, called rs:ResEnum (*https://play.google.com/store/apps/details?id=com .risesoftware.rsresourceenumerator*), can be used to enumerate and display the various system resources available on a given device. Thus, you can quickly verify system resource availability across your target devices.

Summary

Android applications rely on various types of resources, including strings, string arrays, colors, dimensions, drawable objects, graphics, animation sequences, layouts, and more. Resources can also be raw files. Many of these resources are defined with XML and organized into specially named project directories. Both default and alternative resources can be defined using this resource hierarchy.

Resources are compiled and accessed using the R.java class file, which is automatically generated by the Android IDE when the application resources are saved, allowing developers to access the resources programmatically.

Quiz Questions

1. True or false: All graphics are stored under the `/res/graphics` directory structure.
2. What are the various resource types supported by the Android SDK?
3. What `Resource` method would you use to retrieve a string resource?
4. What `Resource` method would you use to retrieve a string array resource?
5. What image formats does the Android SDK support?
6. What is the format for referencing resources?

Exercises

1. Using the Android documentation, create a list of the different types of drawable resources.
2. Using the Android documentation, create a list of the available keyword values for the `quantity` attribute of the `<item>` element for quantity strings (`<plurals>`).
3. Provide an example of `TypedArray` defined in XML.

References and More Information

Android API Guides: "App Resources":
   http://d.android.com/guide/topics/resources/index.html
Android API Guides: "Resource Types":
   http://d.android.com/guide/topics/resources/available-resources.html

III

Android User Interface Design Essentials

7

Exploring User Interface Building Blocks

Most Android applications inevitably need some form of user interface. In this chapter, we discuss the user interface elements available within the Android SDK. Some of these elements display information to the user, whereas others are input controls that can be used to gather information from the user. In this chapter, you learn how to use a variety of common user interface controls to build different types of screens.

Introducing Android Views and Layouts

Before we go any further, we need to define a few terms to give you a better understanding of certain capabilities provided by the Android SDK before they are fully introduced. First, let's talk about the `View` and what it is to the Android SDK.

The Android `View`

The Android SDK has a Java package named `android.view`. This package contains a number of interfaces and classes related to drawing on the screen. However, when we refer to the `View` object, we actually refer to only one of the classes within this package: the `android.view.View` class.

The `View` class is the basic user interface building block within Android. It represents a rectangular portion of the screen. The `View` class serves as the base class for nearly all the user interface controls and layouts within the Android SDK.

The Android Controls

The Android SDK contains a Java package named `android.widget`. When we refer to controls, we are typically referring to a class within this package. The Android SDK includes classes to draw most common objects, including `ImageView`, `FrameLayout`, `EditText`, and `Button` classes. As mentioned previously, all controls are typically derived from the `View` class.

This chapter is primarily about controls that display and collect data from the user. We cover many of these basic controls in detail.

Your layout resource files are composed of different user interface controls. Some are static, and you don't need to work with them programmatically. Others you'll want to be able to access and modify in your Java code. Each control you want to be able to access programmatically must have a unique identifier specified using the `android:id` attribute. You use this identifier to access the control with the `findViewById()` method in your `Activity` class. Most of the time, you'll want to cast the `View` returned to the appropriate control type. For example, the following code illustrates how to access a `TextView` control using its unique identifier:

```
TextView tv = (TextView)findViewById(R.id.TextView01);
```

Note

Do not confuse the user interface controls in the `android.widget` package with App Widgets. An `AppWidget` (`android.appwidget`) is an application extension, often displayed on the Android `Home` screen.

The Android Layout

One special type of control found within the `android.widget` package is called a layout. A layout control is still a `View` object, but it doesn't actually draw anything specific on the screen. Instead, it is a parent container for organizing other controls (children). Layout controls determine how and where on the screen child controls are drawn. Each type of layout control draws its children using particular rules. For instance, the `LinearLayout` control draws its child controls in a single horizontal row or a single vertical column. Similarly, a `TableLayout` control displays each child control in tabular format (in cells within specific rows and columns).

In Chapter 8, "Designing with Layouts," we organize various controls within layouts and other containers. These special `View` controls, which are derived from the `android .view.ViewGroup` class, are useful only after you understand the various display controls these containers can hold. By necessity, we use some of the layout `View` objects within this chapter to illustrate how to use the controls previously mentioned. However, we don't go into the details of the various layout types available as part of the Android SDK until the next chapter.

Note

Many of the code examples provided in this chapter are taken from the `ViewSamples` application. The source code for the `ViewSamples` application is provided for download on the book's website.

Displaying Text to Users with **TextView**

One of the most basic user interface elements, or controls, in the Android SDK is the `TextView` control. You use it to draw text on the screen. You primarily use it to display fixed text strings or labels.

Frequently, the `TextView` control is a child control within other screen elements and controls. As with most of the user interface elements, it is derived from `View` and is within the `android.widget` package. Because it is a `View`, all the standard attributes such as width, height, padding, and visibility can be applied to the object. However, because this is a text-displaying control, you can apply many other `TextView` attributes to control behavior and how the text is viewed in a variety of situations.

First, though, let's see how to put some quick text up on the screen. `<TextView>` is the XML layout file tag used to display text on the screen. You can set the `android:text` property of the `TextView` to be either a raw text string in the layout file or a reference to a string resource.

Here are examples of both methods you can use to set the `android:text` attribute of a `TextView`. The first method sets the text attribute to a raw string; the second method uses a string resource called `sample_text`, which must be defined in the `strings.xml` resource file.

```
<TextView

    android:id="@+id/TextView01"

    android:layout_width="wrap_content"

    android:layout_height="wrap_content"

    android:text="Some sample text here" />

<TextView

    android:id="@+id/TextView02"

    android:layout_width="wrap_content"

    android:layout_height="wrap_content"

    android:text="@string/sample_text" />
```

To display this `TextView` on the screen, all your `Activity` needs to do is call the `setContentView()` method with the layout resource identifier where you defined the preceding XML shown. You can change the text displayed programmatically by calling the `setText()` method on the `TextView` object. Retrieving the text is done with the `getText()` method.

Now let's talk about some of the more common attributes of `TextView` objects.

Configuring Layout and Sizing

The `TextView` control has some special attributes that dictate how the text is drawn and flows. You can, for instance, set the `TextView` to be a single line high and a fixed width.

If, however, a string of text is too long to fit, the text truncates abruptly. Luckily, there are some attributes that can handle this problem.

> **Tip**
>
> When looking through the attributes available to `TextView` objects, you should be aware that the `TextView` class contains all the functionality needed by editable controls. This means that many of the attributes apply only to input fields, which are used primarily by the subclass `EditText` object. For example, the `autoText` attribute, which helps the user by fixing common spelling mistakes, is most appropriately set on editable text fields (`EditText`). There is no need to use this attribute normally when you are simply displaying text.

The width of a `TextView` can be controlled in terms of the `ems` measurement rather than in pixels. An *em* is a term used in typography that is defined in terms of the point size of a particular font. (For example, the measure of an em in a 12-point font is 12 points.) This measurement provides better control over how much text is viewed, regardless of the font size. Through the `ems` attribute, you can set the width of the `TextView`. Additionally, you can use the `maxEms` and `minEms` attributes to set the maximum width and minimum width, respectively, of the `TextView` in terms of ems.

The height of a `TextView` can be set in terms of lines of text rather than pixels. Again, this is useful for controlling how much text can be viewed regardless of the font size. The `lines` attribute sets the number of lines that the `TextView` can display. You can also use `maxLines` and `minLines` to control the maximum height and minimum height, respectively, that the `TextView` displays.

Here is an example that combines these two types of sizing attributes. This `TextView` is two lines of text high and 12 ems of text wide. The layout width and height are specified to the size of the `TextView` and are required attributes in the XML schema:

```
<TextView
    android:id="@+id/TextView04"
    android:layout_width="wrap_content"
    android:layout_height="wrap_content"
    android:lines="2"
    android:ems="12"
    android:text="@string/autolink_test" />
```

Instead of having the text only truncate at the end, as happens in the preceding example, we can enable the `ellipsize` attribute to replace the last couple of characters with an ellipsis (. . .) so the user knows that not all text is displayed.

Creating Contextual Links in Text

If your text contains references to email addresses, Web pages, phone numbers, or even street addresses, you might want to consider using the attribute `autoLink` (see Figure 7.1). The `autoLink` attribute has six values that you can use. When enabled, these `autoLink` attribute

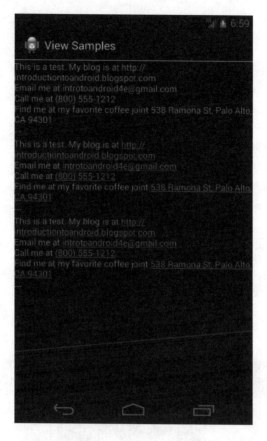

Figure 7.1   Three `TextView` types: `Simple`, `autoLink all`
(not clickable), and `autoLink all` (clickable).

values create standard Web-style links to the application that can act on that data type. For instance, setting the attribute to web automatically finds and links any URLs to Web pages.

Your text can contain the following values for the `autoLink` attribute:

- **none:** disables all linking
- **web:** enables linking of URLs to Web pages
- **email:** enables linking of email addresses to the mail client with the recipient filled in
- **phone:** enables linking of phone numbers to the dialer application with the phone number filled in, ready to be dialed
- **map:** enables linking of street addresses to the map application to show the location
- **all:** enables all types of linking

Turning on the autoLink feature relies on the detection of the various types within the Android SDK. In some cases, the linking might not be correct or might be misleading.

Here is an example that links email and Web pages, which, in our opinion, are the most reliable and predictable:

```
<TextView
    android:id="@+id/TextView02"
    android:layout_width="wrap_content"
    android:layout_height="wrap_content"
    android:text="@string/autolink_test"
    android:autoLink="web|email" />
```

Two helper values are available for this attribute as well. You can set it to none to make sure no type of data is linked. You can also set it to all to have all known types linked. Figure 7.2 illustrates what happens when you click these links. The default for a TextView is not to link any types. If you want the user to see the various data types highlighted but you don't want the user to click them, you can set the linksClickable attribute to false.

Figure 7.2 Clickable autoLinks: a URL launches the browser, a phone number launches the dialer, and a street address launches Google Maps.

Retrieving Data from Users with Text Fields

The Android SDK provides a number of controls for retrieving data from users. One of the most common types of data that applications often need to collect from users is text. One frequently used text field control to handle this type of job is the `EditText` control.

Retrieving Text Input Using `EditText` Controls

The Android SDK provides a convenient control called `EditText` to handle text input from a user. The `EditText` class is derived from `TextView`. In fact, most of its functionality is contained within `TextView` but is enabled when created as an `EditText`. The `EditText` object has a number of useful features enabled by default, many of which are shown in Figure 7.3.

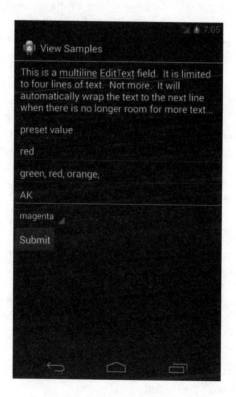

Figure 7.3   Various styles of `EditText`, `Spinner`, and `Button` controls.

First, though, let's see how to define an `EditText` control in an XML layout file:

```
<EditText
    android:id="@+id/EditText01"
    android:layout_height="wrap_content"
    android:hint="type here"
    android:lines="4"
    android:layout_width="match_parent" />
```

This layout code shows a basic `EditText` element. There are a couple of interesting things to note. First, the `hint` attribute puts some text in the edit box that goes away when the user starts entering text (run the sample code to see an example of a `hint` in action). Essentially, this gives a hint to the user as to what should go there. Next is the `lines` attribute, which defines how many lines tall the input box is. If this is not set, the entry field grows as the user enters text. However, setting a size allows the user to scroll within a fixed size to edit the text. This also applies to the width of the entry.

By default, the user can perform a long press to bring up a context menu. This provides some basic copy, cut, and paste operations to the user as well as the ability to change the input method and add a word to the user's dictionary of frequently used words (shown in Figure 7.4). You do not need to provide any additional code for this useful behavior to benefit your users. You can also highlight a portion of the text from code. A call to `setSelection()` does this, and a call to `selectAll()` highlights the entire text entry field.

The `EditText` object is essentially an editable `TextView`. This means that you can read text from it in the same way as you did with `TextView`: by using the `getText()` method. You can also set initial text to draw in the text entry area using the `setText()` method.

Constraining User Input with Input Filters

There are times when you don't want the user to type just anything. Validating input after the user has entered something is one way to do this. However, a better way to avoid wasting the user's time is to filter the input. The `EditText` control provides a way to set an `InputFilter` that does only this.

The Android SDK provides some `InputFilter` objects for use. `InputFilter` objects enforce such rules as allowing only uppercase text and limiting the length of the text entered. You can create custom filters by implementing the `InputFilter` interface, which contains the single method called `filter()`. Here is an example of an `EditText` control with two built-in filters that might be appropriate for a two-letter state abbreviation:

```
final EditText text_filtered =
    (EditText) findViewById(R.id.input_filtered);
text_filtered.setFilters(new InputFilter[] {
    new InputFilter.AllCaps(),
```

```
      new InputFilter.LengthFilter(2)
});
```

The `setFilters()` method call takes an array of `InputFilter` objects. This is useful for combining multiple filters, as shown. In this case, we convert all input to uppercase. Additionally, we set the maximum length to two characters long. The `EditText` control looks the same as any other, but if you try to type in lowercase, the text is converted to uppercase, and the string is limited to two characters. This does not mean that all possible inputs are valid, but it does help users to not concern themselves with making the input too long or bother with the case of the input. This also helps your application by guaranteeing that any text from this input is a length of two characters. It does not constrain the input to only letters, though.

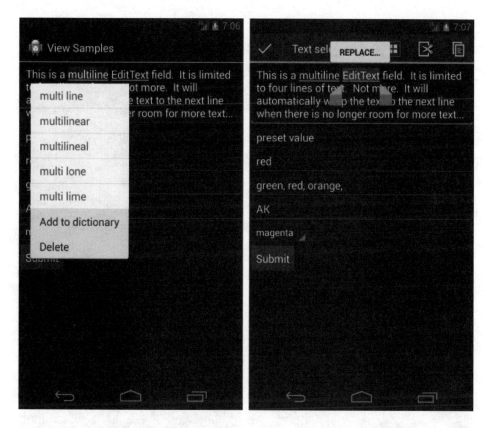

Figure 7.4   A long press on an `EditText` control typically launches a context menu for selections, cutting, and copying. (The `Paste` option appears when you have copied text.)

Helping the User with Autocompletion

In addition to providing a basic text editor with the EditText control, the Android SDK provides a way to help the user with entering commonly used data into forms. This functionality is provided through the autocomplete feature.

There are two forms of autocomplete. One is the more standard style of filling in the entire text entry based on what the user types. If the user begins typing a string that matches a word in a developer-provided list, the user can choose to complete the word with just a tap. This is done through the AutoCompleteTextView control (see Figure 7.5, left). The second method allows the user to enter a list of items, each of which has autocomplete functionality (see Figure 7.5, right). These items must be separated in some way by providing a Tokenizer to the MultiAutoCompleteTextView object that handles this method. A common Tokenizer implementation is provided for comma-separated

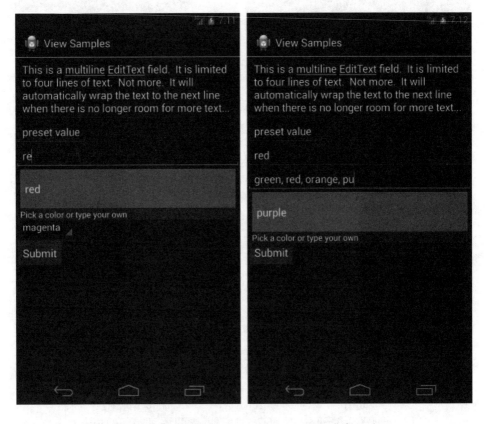

Figure 7.5   Using AutoCompleteTextView (left) and
MultiAutoCompleteTextView (right).

lists and is used by specifying the `MultiAutoCompleteTextView.CommaTokenizer` object. This can be helpful for lists of specifying common tags and the like.

Both of the autocomplete text editors use an `Adapter` to get the list of text they use to provide completions to the user. This example shows how to provide an `AutoComplete TextView` that can help users type some of the basic colors from an array in the code:

```
final String[] COLORS = {
    "red", "green", "orange", "blue", "purple",
    "black", "yellow", "cyan", "magenta" };
ArrayAdapter<String> adapter =
    new ArrayAdapter<String>(this,
        android.R.layout.simple_dropdown_item_1line,
        COLORS);
AutoCompleteTextView text = (AutoCompleteTextView)
    findViewById(R.id.AutoCompleteTextView01);
text.setAdapter(adapter);
```

In this example, when the user starts typing in the field, if he or she starts with one of the letters in the `COLORS` array, a drop-down list shows all the available completions. Note that this does not limit what the user can enter. The user is still free to enter any text (such as "puce"). The `Adapter` controls the look of the drop-down list. In this case, we use a built-in layout made for such things. Here is the layout resource definition for this `AutoCompleteTextView` control:

```
<AutoCompleteTextView
    android:id="@+id/AutoCompleteTextView01"
    android:layout_width="match_parent"
    android:layout_height="wrap_content"
    android:completionHint="Pick a color or type your own"
    android:completionThreshold="1" />
```

There are a couple more things to notice here. First, you can choose when the completion drop-down list shows by filling in a value for the `completionThreshold` attribute. In this case, we set it to a single character, so it displays immediately if there is a match. The default value is two characters of typing before it displays autocompletion options. Second, you can set some text in the `completionHint` attribute. This displays at the bottom of the drop-down list to help users. Finally, the drop-down list for completions is sized to the `TextView`. This means that it should be wide enough to show the completions and the text for the `completionHint` attribute.

The `MultiAutoCompleteTextView` is essentially the same as the regular autocomplete, except that you must assign a `Tokenizer` to it so that the control knows where each autocompletion should begin. The following is an example that uses the same `Adapter` as the previous example but includes a `Tokenizer` for a list of user color responses, each separated by a comma:

```
MultiAutoCompleteTextView mtext =
    (MultiAutoCompleteTextView) findViewById(R.id.MultiAutoCompleteTextView01);
mtext.setAdapter(adapter);
mtext.setTokenizer(new MultiAutoCompleteTextView.CommaTokenizer());
```

As you can see, the only change is setting the `Tokenizer`. Here, we use the built-in comma `Tokenizer` provided by the Android SDK. In this case, whenever a user chooses a color from the list, the name of the color is completed, and a comma is automatically added so that the user can immediately start typing in the next color. As before, this does not limit what the user can enter. If the user enters "maroon" and places a comma after it, the autocompletion starts again as the user types another color, regardless of the fact that it didn't help the user type in the color maroon. You can create your own `Tokenizer` by implementing the `MultiAutoCompleteTextView.Tokenizer` interface. You can do this if you prefer entries separated by a semicolon or some other more complex separator.

Giving Users Choices Using `Spinner` Controls

Sometimes you want to limit the choices available for users to type. For instance, if users are going to enter the name of a state, you might as well limit them to only the valid states, because this is a known set. Although you could do this by letting them type something and then blocking invalid entries, you can also provide similar functionality with a `Spinner` control. As with the autocomplete method, the possible choices for a spinner can come from an `Adapter`. You can also set the available choices in the layout definition by using the `entries` attribute with an array resource (specifically a string array that is referenced as something such as `@array/state-list`). The `Spinner` control isn't actually an `EditText`, although it is frequently used in a similar fashion. Here is an example of the XML layout definition for a `Spinner` control for choosing a color:

```
<Spinner
    android:id="@+id/Spinner01"
    android:layout_width="wrap_content"
    android:layout_height="wrap_content"
    android:entries="@array/colors"
    android:prompt="@string/spin_prompt" />
```

This places a `Spinner` control on the screen. A closed `Spinner` control is shown in Figure 7.5, with just the first choice, red, displayed. An open `Spinner` control is shown in Figure 7.6, which shows all the color selections available. When the user selects this control, a pop-up shows the prompt text followed by a list of the possible choices. This list allows only a single item to be selected at a time, and when one is selected, the pop-up goes away.

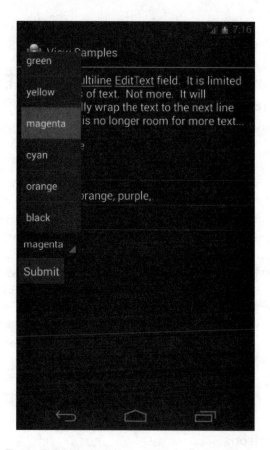

Figure 7.6   Filtering choices with a `Spinner` control.

There are a couple of things to notice here. First, the `entries` attribute is set to the value of a string array resource, referred to here as `@array/colors`. Second, the `prompt` attribute is defined as a string resource. Unlike some other string attributes, this one is required to be a string resource. The `prompt` displays when the `Spinner` control is opened and all selections are displayed. The `prompt` can be used to tell the user what kinds of values can be selected.

Because the `Spinner` control is not a `TextView`, but a list of `TextView` objects, you can't directly request the selected text from it. Instead, you have to retrieve the specific selected option (each of which is a `TextView` control) and extract the text directly from it:

```
final Spinner spin = (Spinner) findViewById(R.id.Spinner01);

TextView text_sel = (TextView)spin.getSelectedView();

String selected_text = text_sel.getText().toString();
```

Alternatively, we could have called the `getSelectedItem()` or `getSelectedItemId()` method to deal with other forms of selection.

Allowing Simple User Selections with Buttons and Switches

Other common user interface elements are buttons and switches. In this section, you learn about different kinds of buttons and switches provided by the Android SDK. These include the basic `Button`, `CheckBox`, `ToggleButton`, and `RadioButton`.

- A basic `Button` is often used to perform some sort of action, such as submitting a form or confirming a selection. A basic `Button` control can contain a text or image label.

- A `CheckBox` is a button with two states—checked and unchecked. You often use `CheckBox` controls to turn a feature on or off or to pick multiple items from a list.

- A `ToggleButton` is similar to a `CheckBox`, but you use it to visually show the state. The default behavior of a toggle is like that of a power on/off button.

- A `Switch` is similar to a `CheckBox`, in that it is a two-state control. The default behavior of a control is like a slider switch that can be moved between "on" and "off" positions. This control was introduced in API Level 14 (Android 4.0).

- A `RadioButton` provides selection of an item. Grouping `RadioButton` controls together in a container called a `RadioGroup` enables the developer to enforce that only one `RadioButton` is selected at a time.

You can find examples of each type of control in Figure 7.7.

Using Basic Buttons

The `android.widget.Button` class provides a basic `Button` implementation in the Android SDK. Within the XML layout resources, buttons are specified using the `Button` element. The primary attribute for a basic `Button` is the text field. This is the label that appears on the middle of the button's face. You often use basic `Button` controls for buttons with text such as "OK," "Cancel," or "Submit."

Tip

You can find many common application string values in the Android system resource strings, exposed in `android.R.string`. There are strings for common button text such as "Yes," "No," "OK," "Cancel," and "Copy." For more information on system resources, see Chapter 6, "Managing Application Resources."

The following XML layout resource file shows a typical `Button` control definition:

```
<Button
    android:id="@+id/basic_button"
    android:layout_width="wrap_content"
```

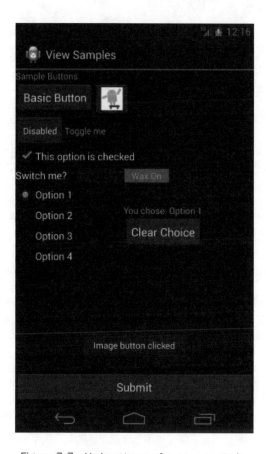

Figure 7.7   Various types of `Button` controls.

```
android:layout_height="wrap_content"

android:text="Basic Button" />
```

Tip

One popular styling method for buttons is the borderless button. To create a button without borders, all you need to do is set the `style` attribute of your `Button` in your layout file to `style: "?android:attr/borderlessButtonStyle"`. To learn more about styling your buttons, see *http://d.android.com/guide/topics/ui/controls/button.html#Style*.

A `Button` control won't do anything, other than animate, without some code to handle the click event. Here is an example of some code that handles a click for a basic `Button` and displays a `Toast` message on the screen:

```
setContentView(R.layout.buttons);

final Button basic_button = (Button) findViewById(R.id.basic_button);
```

```
basic_button.setOnClickListener(new View.OnClickListener() {
    public void onClick(View v) {
        Toast.makeText(ButtonsActivity.this,
            "Button clicked", Toast.LENGTH_SHORT).show();
    }
});
```

Tip

A Toast (`android.widget.Toast`) is a simple dialog-like message that displays for a second or so and then disappears. Toast messages are useful for providing the user with nonessential confirmation messages; they are also quite handy for debugging. Figure 7.7 shows an example of a Toast message that displays the text "Image button clicked."

To handle the click event for when a `Button` control is pressed, we first get a reference to the `Button` by its resource identifier. Next, the `setOnClickListener()` method is called. It requires a valid instance of the class `View.OnClickListener`. A simple way to provide this is to define the instance right in the method call. This requires implementing the `onClick()` method. Within the `onClick()` method, you are free to carry out whatever actions you need. Here, we simply display a message to the users telling them that the button was, in fact, clicked.

A `Button`-like control whose primary label is an image is an `ImageButton`. An `ImageButton` is, for most purposes, almost exactly like a basic `Button`. Click actions are handled in the same way. The primary difference is that you can set its `src` attribute to be an image. Here is an example of an `ImageButton` definition in an XML layout resource file:

```xml
<ImageButton
    android:layout_width="wrap_content"
    android:layout_height="wrap_content"
    android:id="@+id/image_button"
    android:src="@drawable/droid"
    android:contentDescription="@string/droidSkater" />
```

In this case, a small drawable resource is referenced. Refer to Figure 7.7 to see what this "Android" button looks like. (It's to the right of the basic `Button`.)

Tip

You can also use the `onClick` XML attribute to set the name of your click method within your `Activity` class and implement it that way. Simply specify the name of your `Activity` class's click method name using this attribute like so—`android:onClick="myMethod"`— and define a public void method that takes a single `View` parameter and implement your click handling.

Using `CheckBox` and `ToggleButton` Controls

The `CheckBox` button is often used in lists of items where the user can select multiple items. The Android `CheckBox` contains a `text` attribute that appears to the side of the check box. Because the `CheckBox` class is derived from the `TextView` and `Button` classes, most of the attributes and methods behave in a similar fashion.

Here is an XML layout resource definition for a simple `CheckBox` control with some default text displayed:

```
<CheckBox
    android:id="@+id/checkbox"
    android:layout_width="wrap_content"
    android:layout_height="wrap_content"
    android:text="Check me?" />
```

The following example shows how to check for the state of the button programmatically and how to change the text label to reflect the change:

```
final CheckBox check_button = (CheckBox) findViewById(R.id.checkbox);
check_button.setOnClickListener(new View.OnClickListener() {
    public void onClick (View v) {
        CheckBox cb = (CheckBox)findViewById(R.id.checkbox);
        cb.setText(check_button.isChecked() ?
            "This option is checked" :
            "This option is not checked");
    }
});
```

This is similar to the basic `Button` control. A `CheckBox` control automatically shows the state as checked or unchecked. This enables us to deal with behavior in our application rather than worrying about how the button should behave. The layout shows that the text starts out one way, but after the user clicks the button, the text changes to one of two different things, depending on the checked state. You can see how this `CheckBox` is displayed once it has been clicked (and the text has been updated) in Figure 7.7 (center).

A `ToggleButton` is similar to a `CheckBox` in behavior but is usually used to show or alter the "on" or "off" state of something. Like the `CheckBox`, it has a state (checked or not). Also like the `CheckBox`, the act of changing what displays on the `ToggleButton` is handled for us. Unlike the `CheckBox`, it does not show text next to it. Instead, it has two text fields. The first attribute is `textOn`, which is the text that displays on the `ToggleButton` when its checked state is on. The second attribute is `textOff`, which is the text that displays on the `ToggleButton` when its checked state is off. The default text for these is "ON" and "OFF," respectively.

The following layout code shows a definition for a `ToggleButton` control that shows "Enabled" or "Disabled" based on the state of the button:

```
<ToggleButton

    android:id="@+id/toggle_button"

    android:layout_width="wrap_content"

    android:layout_height="wrap_content"

    android:text="Toggle"

    android:textOff="Disabled"

    android:textOn="Enabled" />
```

This type of button does not actually display the value for the text attribute, even though it's a valid attribute to set. Here, the only purpose it serves is to demonstrate that it doesn't display. You can see what this `ToggleButton` looks like in Figure 7.7 ("Enabled").

The `Switch` control (`android.widget.Switch`), which was introduced in API Level 14, provides two-state behavior similar to that of the `ToggleButton` control, only instead of the control being clicked to toggle between the states, it looks more like a slider. The following layout code shows a definition for a `Switch` control with a prompt ("Switch Me?") and two states: "Wax On" and "Wax Off":

```
<Switch android:id="@+id/switch1"

    android:layout_width="wrap_content"

    android:layout_height="wrap_content"

    android:text="Switch me?"

    android:textOn="Wax On"

    android:textOff="Wax Off" />
```

Using `RadioGroup` and `RadioButton`

You often use radio buttons when a user should be allowed to select only one item from a small group of items. For instance, a question asking for gender can give three options: male, female, and unspecified. Only one of these options should be checked at a time. The `RadioButton` objects are similar to `CheckBox` objects. They have a text label next to them, set via the `text` attribute, and they have a state (checked or unchecked). However, you can group `RadioButton` objects inside a `RadioGroup` that handles enforcing their combined states so that only one `RadioButton` can be checked at a time. If the user selects a `RadioButton` that is already checked, it does not become unchecked. However, you can provide the user with an action to clear the state of the entire `RadioGroup` so that none of the buttons are checked.

Here, we have an XML layout resource with a `RadioGroup` containing four `RadioButton` objects (shown in Figure 7.7, toward the bottom of the screen). The

RadioButton objects have text labels: "Option 1," "Option 2," and so on. The XML layout resource definition is shown here:

```
<RadioGroup

    android:id="@+id/RadioGroup01"

    android:layout_width="wrap_content"

    android:layout_height="wrap_content">

    <RadioButton

        android:id="@+id/RadioButton01"

        android:layout_width="wrap_content"

        android:layout_height="wrap_content"

        android:text="Option 1" />

    <RadioButton

        android:id="@+id/RadioButton02"

        android:layout_width="wrap_content"

        android:layout_height="wrap_content"

        android:text="Option 2" />

    <RadioButton

        android:id="@+id/RadioButton03"

        android:layout_width="wrap_content"

        android:layout_height="wrap_content"

        android:text="Option 3" />

    <RadioButton

        android:id="@+id/RadioButton04"

        android:layout_width="wrap_content"

        android:layout_height="wrap_content"

        android:text="Option 4" />

</RadioGroup>
```

You can handle actions on these RadioButton objects through the RadioGroup object. The following example shows registering for clicks on the RadioButton objects within the RadioGroup and setting the text of a TextView called TextView01, which is defined elsewhere in the layout file:

```
final RadioGroup group = (RadioGroup)findViewById(R.id.RadioGroup01);

final TextView tv = (TextView)

    findViewById(R.id.TextView01);

group.setOnCheckedChangeListener(new
```

```
RadioGroup.OnCheckedChangeListener() {
    public void onCheckedChanged(
        RadioGroup group, int checkedId) {
        if (checkedId != -1) {
            RadioButton rb = (RadioButton)
                findViewById(checkedId);
            if (rb != null) {
                tv.setText("You chose: " + rb.getText());
            }
        } else {
            tv.setText("Choose 1");
        }
    }
});
```

As this layout example demonstrates, there is nothing special you need to do to make the RadioGroup and internal RadioButton objects work properly. The preceding code illustrates how to register to receive a notification whenever the RadioButton selection changes.

The code demonstrates that the notification contains the resource identifier for the specific RadioButton chosen by the user, as defined in the layout resource file. To do something interesting with this, you need to provide a mapping between this resource identifier (or the text label) and the corresponding functionality in your code. In the example, we query for the button that was selected, get its text, and assign its text to another TextView control that we have on the screen.

As mentioned, the entire RadioGroup can be cleared so that none of the RadioButton objects are selected. The following example demonstrates how to do this in response to a button click outside the RadioGroup:

```
final Button clear_choice = (Button) findViewById(R.id.Button01);

clear_choice.setOnClickListener(new View.OnClickListener() {
    public void onClick(View v) {
        RadioGroup group = (RadioGroup)
            findViewById(R.id.RadioGroup01);
        if (group != null) {
            group.clearCheck();
        }
    }
}
```

The action of calling the `clearCheck()` method triggers a call to the `onChecked ChangedListener()` callback method. This is why we have to make sure that the resource identifier we received is valid. Right after a call to the `clearCheck()` method, it is not a valid identifier but instead is set to the value -1 to indicate that no `RadioButton` is currently checked.

Tip

You can also handle `RadioButton` clicks using specific click handlers on individual `RadioButtons` within a `RadioGroup`. The implementation mirrors that of a regular `Button` control.

Retrieving Dates, Times, and Numbers from Users with Pickers

The Android SDK provides a couple of controls for getting date, time, and number input from the user. The first is the `DatePicker` control (see Figure 7.8, top). It can be used to get a month, day, and year from the user.

The basic XML layout resource definition for a `DatePicker` follows:

```
<DatePicker
    android:id="@+id/DatePicker01"
    android:layout_width="wrap_content"
    android:layout_height="wrap_content"
    android:calendarViewShown="false"
    android:spinnersShown="true" />
```

Tip

If you want to control the minimum or maximum date that a user can choose from a `DatePicker`, you can set the `android:minDate` or `android:maxDate` values in your layout file, or you can set these values programmatically using `setMinDate()` or `setMaxDate()`.

As you can see from this example, a couple of attributes help control the look of the picker. Setting the `calenderViewShown` attribute to `true`, when using API Level 11 and up, will show a full calendar, including week numbers, but may take up more space than you can allow. Try it in the sample code, though, to see what it looks like. As with many of the other controls, your code can register to receive a method call when the date changes. You do this by implementing the `onDateChanged()` method:

```
final DatePicker date = (DatePicker)findViewById(R.id.DatePicker01);
date.init(2013, 4, 8,
    new DatePicker.OnDateChangedListener() {
        public void onDateChanged(DatePicker view, int year,
```

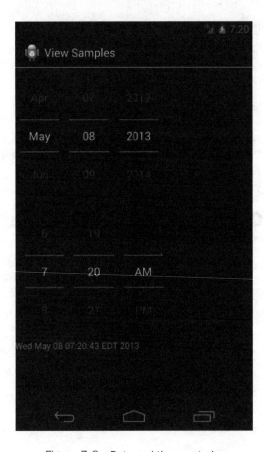

Figure 7.8   Date and time controls.

```
int monthOfYear, int dayOfMonth) {
Calendar calendar = Calendar.getInstance();
calendar.set(year,
       monthOfYear,
       dayOfMonth,
       time.getCurrentHour(),
       time.getCurrentMinute());
text.setText(calendar.getTime().toString());
  }
});
```

The preceding code sets the DatePicker.OnDateChangedListener via a call to the
DatePicker.init() method. The DatePicker control is initialized to a specific date

(note that the month field is zero based, so May is month number 4, not 5). In our example, a `TextView` control is set with the date value that the user entered into the `DatePicker` control.

A `TimePicker` control (also shown in Figure 7.8, bottom) is similar to the `DatePicker` control. It also doesn't have any unique attributes. However, to register for a method call when the values change, you call the more traditional method of `TimePicker.set` `OnTimeChangedListener()`, as shown here:

```
time.setOnTimeChangedListener(new TimePicker.OnTimeChangedListener() {
    public void onTimeChanged(TimePicker view,
            int hourOfDay, int minute) {
        Calendar calendar = Calendar.getInstance();
        calendar.set(calendar.get(Calendar.YEAR),
                calendar.get(Calendar.MONTH),
                calendar.get(Calendar.DAY_OF_MONTH),
                hourOfDay,
                minute);
        text.setText(calendar.getTime().toString());
    }
});
```

As in the previous example, this code also sets a `TextView` to a string displaying the time value that the user entered. When you use the `DatePicker` control and the `TimePicker` control together, the user can set both a date and a time.

Android also provides a `NumberPicker` widget, which is very similar to the `TimePicker` widget. You can use a `NumberPicker` to present to users a selection mechanism for choosing a number from a predefined range. There are two different types of `NumberPickers` you can present, both of which are entirely based on the theme your application is using. To learn more about the `NumberPicker`, see *http://d.android.com/ reference/android/widget/NumberPicker.html*.

Using Indicators to Display Progress and Activity to Users

The Android SDK provides a number of controls that can be used to visually show some form of information to the user. These indicator controls include the `ProgressBar`, activity bars, activity circles, clocks, and other similar controls.

Indicating Progress with `ProgressBar`

Applications commonly perform actions that can take a while. A good practice during this time is to show the user some sort of progress indicator to indicate that the application is off "doing something." Applications can also show how far a user is through some operation, such as playing a song or watching a video. The Android SDK provides several types of ProgressBar.

The standard ProgressBar is a circular indicator that only animates. It does not show how complete an action is. It can, however, show that something is taking place. This is useful when an action is indeterminate in length. There are three sizes of this type of progress indicator (see Figure 7.9).

The second type is a horizontal ProgressBar that shows the completeness of an action. (For example, you can see how much of a file has downloaded.) This horizontal ProgressBar can also have a secondary progress indicator on it. This can be used, for instance, to show the completion of a downloading media file while that file plays.

Figure 7.9   Various types of progress and rating indicators.

Here is an XML layout resource definition for a basic indeterminate `ProgressBar`:

```
<ProgressBar
    android:id="@+id/progress_bar"
    android:layout_width="wrap_content"
    android:layout_height="wrap_content" />
```

The default style is for a medium-size circular progress indicator—not a "bar" at all. The other two styles for an indeterminate `ProgressBar` are `progressBarStyleLarge` and `progressBarStyleSmall`. This style animates automatically. The next example shows the layout definition for a horizontal progress indicator:

```
<ProgressBar
    android:id="@+id/progress_bar"
    style="?android:attr/progressBarStyleHorizontal"
    android:layout_width="match_parent"
    android:layout_height="wrap_content"
    android:max="100" />
```

We have also set the attribute for `max` in this example to `100`. This can help mimic a percentage `ProgressBar`—that is, setting the progress to `75` shows the indicator at 75% complete.

We can set the indicator progress status programmatically as follows:

```
mProgress = (ProgressBar) findViewById(R.id.progress_bar);
mProgress.setProgress(75);
```

You can also put a `ProgressBar` in your application's title bar (as shown in Figure 7.9). This can save screen real estate and can also make it easy to turn on and off an indeterminate progress indicator without changing the look of the screen. Indeterminate progress indicators are commonly used to display progress on pages where items need to be loaded before the page can finish drawing. This is often employed on Web browser screens. The following code demonstrates how to place this type of indeterminate progress indicator on your `Activity` screen:

```
requestWindowFeature(Window.FEATURE_INDETERMINATE_PROGRESS);
requestWindowFeature(Window.FEATURE_PROGRESS);
setContentView(R.layout.indicators);
setProgressBarIndeterminateVisibility(true);
setProgressBarVisibility(true);
setProgress(5000);
```

To use the indeterminate indicator on your `Activity` object's title bar, you need to request the feature `Window.FEATURE_INDETERMINATE_PROGRESS`, as previously shown.

This shows a small circular indicator in the right side of the title bar. For a horizontal `ProgressBar` style that shows behind the title, you need to enable `Window.FEATURE_PROGRESS`. These features must be enabled before your application calls the `setContentView()` method, as shown in the preceding example.

You need to know about a couple of important default behaviors. First, the indicators are visible by default. Calling the visibility methods shown in the preceding example can set visibility on or off. Second, the horizontal `ProgressBar` defaults to a maximum progress value of `10000`. In the preceding example, we set it to `5000`, which is equivalent to 50%. When the value reaches the maximum value, the indicators fade away so that they aren't visible. This happens for both indicators.

Indicating Activity with Activity Bars and Activity Circles

When there is no telling how long an operation will take to complete, but you need a way to indicate to the user that an operation is taking place, you should use an activity bar or an activity circle. You define an activity bar or circle exactly like you define a `ProgressBar`, with one small change: you need to tell Android that the operation running will continue for an indeterminate amount of time by either setting the attribute within your layout file using `android:indeterminate`, or from within your code by setting the `ProgressBar`'s visibility to indeterminate using the `setProgressBarIndeterminateVisibility()` method.

Tip

When using an activity circle, there is no need to display any text to users to let them know that an operation is taking place. The activity circle alone is enough for users to understand that an operation is taking place. To learn more about activity bars and activity circles, see *http://d.android.com/design/building-blocks/progress.html#activity*.

Adjusting Progress with Seek Bars

You have seen how to display progress to the user. What if, however, you want to give the user some ability to move the indicator—for example, to set the current cursor position in a playing media file or to tweak a volume setting? You accomplish this by using the `SeekBar` control provided by the Android SDK. It's like the regular horizontal `ProgressBar` but includes a thumb, or selector, that can be dragged by the user. A default thumb selector is provided, but you can use any drawable item as a thumb. In Figure 7.9 (center), we replaced the default thumb with a little Android graphic.

Here, we have an example of an XML layout resource definition for a simple `SeekBar`:

```
<SeekBar
    android:id="@+id/seekbar1"
    android:layout_height="wrap_content"
```

```
android:layout_width="240dp"

android:max="500"

android:thumb="@drawable/droidsk1" />
```

With this sample `SeekBar`, the user can drag the thumb named `droidsk1` to any value between `0` and `500`. Although this is shown visually, it might be useful to show the user the exact value selected. To do this, you can provide an implementation of the `onProgressChanged()` method, as shown here:

```
SeekBar seek = (SeekBar) findViewById(R.id.seekbar1);

seek.setOnSeekBarChangeListener(

    new SeekBar.OnSeekBarChangeListener() {

        public void onProgressChanged(

            SeekBar seekBar, int progress,boolean fromTouch) {

            ((TextView)findViewById(R.id.seek_text))

                .setText("Value: "+progress);

            seekBar.setSecondaryProgress(

                (progress+seekBar.getMax())/2);

        }

});
```

There are two interesting things to notice in this example. The first is that the `fromTouch` parameter tells the code if the change came from the user input or if, instead, it came from a programmatic change as demonstrated with the regular `ProgressBar` controls. The second interesting thing is that the `SeekBar` still enables you to set a secondary progress value. In this example, we set the secondary indicator to be halfway between the user's selected value and the maximum value of the `ProgressBar`. You might use this feature to show the progress of a video and the buffer stream.

Note

If you want to create your own activity indicator, you can define a custom indicator. For most situations, the default indicators that Android provides should be enough. If you need to display a custom indicator, you should read more about how to do so here: *http://d.android .com/design/building-blocks/progress.html#custom-indicators*.

Other Valuable User Interface Controls

Android has a number of other ready-to-use user interface controls to incorporate into your applications. This section is dedicated to introducing the `RatingBar` and various time controls, such as the `Chronometer`, `DigitalClock`, `TextClock`, and `AnalogClock`.

Displaying Rating Data with `RatingBar`

Although the `SeekBar` is useful for allowing a user to set a value, such as the volume, the `RatingBar` has a more specific purpose: showing ratings or getting a rating from a user. By default, this `ProgressBar` uses the star paradigm, with five stars by default. A user can drag across this horizontally to set a rating. A program can set the value as well. However, the secondary indicator cannot be used because it is used internally by this particular control.

Here is an example of an XML layout resource definition for a `RatingBar` with four stars:

```
<RatingBar

    android:id="@+id/ratebar1"

    android:layout_width="wrap_content"

    android:layout_height="wrap_content"

    android:numStars="4"

    android:stepSize="0.25" />
```

This layout definition for a `RatingBar` demonstrates setting both the number of stars and the increment between each rating value. Figure 7.9 (center) illustrates how the `RatingBar` behaves. In this layout definition, a user can choose any rating value between 0 and 4.0, in increments of 0.25, the `stepSize` value. For instance, users could set a value of 2.25. This is visualized to the users, by default, with the stars partially filled.

Although the value is indicated to the user visually, you might still want to show its numeric representation. You can do this by implementing the `onRatingChanged()` method of the `RatingBar.OnRatingBarChangeListener` class, as shown here:

```
RatingBar rate = (RatingBar) findViewById(R.id.ratebar1);

rate.setOnRatingBarChangeListener(new

    RatingBar.OnRatingBarChangeListener() {

    public void onRatingChanged(RatingBar ratingBar,

        float rating, boolean fromTouch) {

        ((TextView)findViewById(R.id.rating_text))

            .setText("Rating: "+ rating);

    }

});
```

The preceding example shows how to register the listener. When the user selects a rating using the control, a `TextView` is set to the numeric rating the user entered. One interesting thing to note is that, unlike the `SeekBar`, the implementation of the `onRatingChange()` method is called after the change is complete, usually when the user lifts a finger—that is, while the user is dragging across the stars to make a rating, this method isn't called. It is called when the user stops pressing the control.

Showing Time Passage with the `Chronometer`

Sometimes you want to show time passing instead of incremental progress. In this case, you can use the `Chronometer` control as a timer (see Figure 7.9, near the bottom). This might be useful if it's the user who is taking time doing some task or playing a game where some action needs to be timed. The `Chronometer` control can be formatted with text, as shown in this XML layout resource definition:

```
<Chronometer
    android:id="@+id/Chronometer01"
    android:layout_width="wrap_content"
    android:layout_height="wrap_content"
    android:format="Timer: %s" />
```

You can use the `Chronometer` object's `format` attribute to put text around the time that displays. A `Chronometer` won't show the passage of time until its `start()` method is called. To stop it, simply call its `stop()` method. Finally, you can change the time from which the timer is counting—that is, you can set it to count from a particular time in the past instead of from the time it was started. You call the `setBase()` method to do this.

Tip

The `Chronometer` uses the `elapsedRealtime()` method's time base. Passing `android .os.SystemClock.elapsedRealtime()` in to the `setBase()` method starts the Chronometer control at `0`.

In this next code example, the timer is retrieved from the `View` by its resource identifier. We then check its base value and reset it to `0`. Finally, we start the timer counting up from there.

```
final Chronometer timer =
    (Chronometer)findViewById(R.id.Chronometer01);
long base =  timer.getBase();
Log.d(ViewsMenu.debugTag, "base = "+ base);
timer.setBase(0);
timer.start();
```

Tip

You can listen for changes to the `Chronometer` by implementing the `Chronometer .OnChronometerTickListener` interface.

Displaying the Time

Displaying the time in an application is often not necessary because Android devices have a `status bar` to display the current time. However, two clock controls are available to display this information: the `DigitalClock` and `AnalogClock` controls.

Using the `DigitalClock`

The `DigitalClock` control (Figure 7.9, bottom) is a compact text display of the current time in standard numeric format based on the user's settings. It is a `TextView`, so anything you can do with a `TextView` you can do with this control, except change its text. You can change the color and style of the text, for example.

By default, the `DigitalClock` control shows the seconds and automatically updates as each second ticks by. Here is an example of an XML layout resource definition for a `DigitalClock` control:

```
<DigitalClock

    android:id="@+id/DigitalClock01"

    android:layout_width="wrap_content"

    android:layout_height="wrap_content" />
```

Using the `TextClock`

The `TextClock` control was recently added in API Level 17 and is meant to be a replacement for the `DigitalClock`, which was deprecated in API Level 17. The `TextClock` has many more features than the `DigitalClock` and allows you to format the display of the date and/or time. In addition, the `TextClock` allows you to display the time in 12-hour mode or 24-hour mode and even allows you to set the time zone.

By default, the `TextClock` control does not show the seconds. Here is an example of an XML layout resource definition for a `TextClock` control:

```
<TextClock

    android:id="@+id/TextClock01"

    android:layout_width="wrap_content"

    android:layout_height="wrap_content" />
```

Using the `AnalogClock`

The `AnalogClock` control (Figure 7.9, bottom) is a dial-based clock with a basic clock face with two hands. It updates automatically as each minute passes. The image of the clock scales appropriately with the size of its `View`.

Here is an example of an XML layout resource definition for an `AnalogClock` control:

```
<AnalogClock

    android:id="@+id/AnalogClock01"
```

```
android:layout_width="wrap_content"

android:layout_height="wrap_content" />
```

The `AnalogClock` control's clock face is simple. However, you can set its minute and hour hands. You can also set the clock face to specific drawable resources, if you want to jazz it up. Neither of these clock controls accepts a different time or a static time to display. They can show only the current time in the current time zone of the device, so they are not particularly useful.

Summary

The Android SDK provides many useful user interface components that developers can use to create compelling and easy-to-use applications. This chapter introduced you to many of the most useful controls and discussed how each behaves, how to style them, and how to handle input events from the user.

You learned how controls can be combined to create user entry forms. Important controls for forms include `EditText`, `Spinner`, and various `Button` controls. You also learned about controls that can indicate progress or the passage of time to users. We talked about many common user interface controls in this chapter; however, there are many others. In the next chapter, you will learn how to use various layout and container controls to organize a variety of controls on the screen easily and accurately.

Quiz Questions

1. What `Activity` method would you use to retrieve a `TextView` object?

2. What `TextView` method would you use to retrieve the text of that particular object?

3. What user interface control is used for retrieving text input from users?

4. What are the two different types of autocompletion controls?

5. True or false: A `Switch` control has three or more possible states.

6. True or false: The `DateView` control is used for retrieving dates from users.

Exercises

1. Create a simple application that accepts text input from a user with an `EditText` object and, when the user clicks an update `Button`, displays the text within a `TextView` control.

2. Create a simple application that has an integer defined in an integer resource file and, when the application is launched, displays the integer within a `TextView` control.

3. Create a simple application with a red color value defined in a color resource file. Define a Button control in the layout with a default blue textColor attribute. When the application is launched, have the default blue textColor value change to the red color value you defined in the color resource file.

References and More Information

Android Design:

http://d.android.com/design/index.html

Android Design: "Building Blocks":

http://d.android.com/design/building-blocks/index.html

Android SDK Reference regarding the application View class:

http://d.android.com/reference/android/view/View.html

Android SDK Reference regarding the application TextView class:

http://d.android.com/reference/android/widget/TextView.html

Android SDK Reference regarding the application EditText class:

http://d.android.com/reference/android/widget/EditText.html

Android SDK Reference regarding the application Button class:

http://d.android.com/reference/android/widget/Button.html

Android SDK Reference regarding the application CheckBox class:

http://d.android.com/reference/android/widget/CheckBox.html

Android SDK Reference regarding the application Switch class:

http://d.android.com/reference/android/widget/Switch.html

Android SDK Reference regarding the application RadioGroup class:

http://d.android.com/reference/android/widget/RadioGroup.html

Android API Guides: "User Interface":

http://d.android.com/guide/topics/ui/index.html

8

Designing with Layouts

In this chapter, we discuss how to design user interfaces for Android applications. Here, we focus on the various layout controls you can use to organize screen elements in different ways. We also cover some of the more complex `View` controls we call container views. These are `View` controls that can contain other `View` controls.

Creating User Interfaces in Android

Application user interfaces can be simple or complex, involving many different screens or only a few. Layouts and user interface controls can be defined as application resources or created programmatically at runtime.

Although it's a bit confusing, the term *layout* is used for two different but related purposes in Android user interface design:

- In terms of resources, the `/res/layout` directory contains XML resource definitions often called layout resource files. These XML files provide a template for how to draw controls on the screen; layout resource files may contain any number of controls.

- The term is also used to refer to a set of `ViewGroup` classes, such as `LinearLayout`, `FrameLayout`, `TableLayout`, `RelativeLayout`, and `GridLayout`. These controls are used to organize other `View` controls. We talk more about these classes later in this chapter.

Creating Layouts Using XML Resources

As discussed in previous chapters, Android provides a simple way to create layout resource files in XML. These resources are stored in the `/res/layout` project directory hierarchy. This is the most common and convenient way to build Android user interfaces and is especially useful for defining screen elements and default control properties that you know about at compile time. These layout resources are then used much like templates. They are loaded with default attributes that you can modify programmatically at runtime.

You can configure almost any `ViewGroup` or `View` (or `View` subclass) attribute using the XML layout resource files. This method greatly simplifies the user interface design process, moving much of the static creation and layout of user interface controls, and basic definition of control attributes, to the XML instead of littering the code. Developers reserve the ability to alter these layouts programmatically as necessary, but they should set all the defaults in the XML template whenever possible.

You'll recognize the following as a simple layout file with a `LinearLayout` and a single `TextView` control. Here is the default layout file provided with any new Android project in the Android IDE, referred to as /res/layout/activity_main.xml:

```
<?xml version="1.0" encoding="utf-8"?>

<LinearLayout xmlns:android=

    "http://schemas.android.com/apk/res/android"

    android:orientation="vertical"

    android:layout_width="match_parent"

    android:layout_height="match_parent" >

<TextView

    android:layout_width="match_parent"

    android:layout_height="wrap_content"

    android:text="@string/hello" />

</LinearLayout>
```

This block of XML shows a basic layout with a single `TextView` control. The first line, which you might recognize from most XML files, is required with the `android` layout namespace, as shown. Because it's common across all the files, we do not show it in any other examples.

Next, we have the `LinearLayout` element. `LinearLayout` is a `ViewGroup` that shows each child `View` either in a single column or in a single row. When applied to a full screen, it merely means that each child `View` is drawn under the previous `View` if the orientation is set to vertical or to the right of the previous `View` if the orientation is set to horizontal.

Finally, there is a single child `View`—in this case, a `TextView`. A `TextView` is a control that is also a `View`. A `TextView` draws text on the screen. In this case, it draws the text defined in the "`@string/hello`" string resource.

Creating only an XML file, though, won't actually draw anything on the screen. A particular layout is usually associated with a particular `Activity`. In your default Android project, there is only one `Activity`, which sets the `activity_main.xml` layout by default. To associate the `activity_main.xml` layout with the `Activity`, use the method call `setContentView()` with the identifier of the `activity_main.xml` layout. The ID of the layout matches the XML filename without the extension. In this case, the preceding example came from `activity_main.xml`, so the identifier of this layout is simply `activity_main`:

```
setContentView(R.layout.activity_main);
```

Warning

The Android tools team has made every effort to make the Android IDE graphical layout designer feature complete, and this tool can be helpful for designing and previewing how layout resources will look on a variety of different devices. However, the preview can't replicate exactly how the layout appears to end users. For this, you must test your application on a properly configured emulator and, more important, on your target devices.

Creating Layouts Programmatically

You can create user interface components such as layouts at runtime programmatically, but for organization and maintainability, it's best to leave this for the odd case rather than the norm. The main reason is that the creation of layouts programmatically is onerous and difficult to maintain, whereas the XML resources are visual and more organized and could be used by a separate designer with no Java skills.

Tip

The code examples provided in this section are taken from the SameLayout application. The source code for the SameLayout application is provided for download on the book's website.

The following example shows how to programmatically have an `Activity` instantiate a `LinearLayout` and place two `TextView` controls within it as child controls. The same two string resources are used for the contents of the controls; these actions are done at runtime instead.

```
public void onCreate(Bundle savedInstanceState) {

    super.onCreate(savedInstanceState);

    TextView text1 = new TextView(this);
    text1.setText(R.string.string1);

    TextView text2 = new TextView(this);
    text2.setText(R.string.string2);
    text2.setTextSize(TypedValue.COMPLEX_UNIT_SP, 60);

    LinearLayout l1 = new LinearLayout(this);
    l1.setOrientation(LinearLayout.VERTICAL);
    l1.addView(text1);
    l1.addView(text2);

    setContentView(l1);
}
```

The onCreate() method is called when the Activity is created. The first thing this method does is some normal housekeeping by calling the constructor for the base class.

Next, two TextView controls are instantiated. The Text property of each TextView is set using the setText() method. All TextView attributes, such as TextSize, are set by making method calls on the TextView control. These actions perform the same function of setting the properties Text and TextSize as when using the Android IDE layout resource designer, except these properties are set at runtime instead of defined in the layout files compiled into your application package.

> **Tip**
>
> The XML property name is usually similar to the method calls for getting and setting that same control property programmatically. For instance, android:visibility maps to the methods setVisibility() and getVisibility(). In the preceding sample TextView, the methods for getting and setting the TextSize property are getTextSize() and setTextSize().

To display the TextView controls appropriately, we need to encapsulate them within a container of some sort (a layout). In this case, we use a LinearLayout with the orientation set to VERTICAL so that the second TextView begins beneath the first, each aligned to the left of the screen. The two TextView controls are added to the LinearLayout in the order we want them to display.

Finally, we call the setContentView() method, part of the Activity class, to draw the LinearLayout and its contents on the screen.

As you can see, the code can rapidly grow in size as you add more View controls and you need more attributes for each View. Here is that same layout, now in an XML layout file:

```xml
<?xml version="1.0" encoding="utf-8"?>

<LinearLayout

    xmlns:android="http://schemas.android.com/apk/res/android"

    android:orientation="vertical"

    android:layout_width="match_parent"

    android:layout_height="match_parent">

    <TextView

        android:id="@+id/TextView1"

        android:layout_width="match_parent"

        android:layout_height="wrap_content"

        android:text="@string/string1" />

    <TextView

        android:id="@+id/TextView2"

        android:layout_width="match_parent"
```

```
        android:layout_height="wrap_content"

        android:textSize="60sp"

        android:text="@string/string2" />

</LinearLayout>
```

You might notice that this isn't a literal translation of the code example from the previous section, although the output is identical, as shown in Figure 8.1.

First, in the XML layout files, `layout_width` and `layout_height` are required attributes. Next, you see that each `TextView` control has a unique `id` property assigned so that it can be accessed programmatically at runtime. Finally, the `textSize` property needs to have its units defined. The XML attribute takes a `dimension` type.

The end result differs only slightly from the programmatic method. However, it's far easier to read and maintain. Now you need only one line of code to display this

Figure 8.1   Two different methods of creating
a screen have the same result.

layout view. Again, the layout resource is stored in the `/res/layout/resource_based_layout.xml` file:

```
setContentView(R.layout.resource_based_layout);
```

Organizing Your User Interface

In Chapter 7, "Exploring User Interface Building Blocks," we talked about how the class `View` is the building block for user interfaces in Android. All user interface controls, such as `Button`, `Spinner`, and `EditText`, derive from the `View` class.

Now we talk about a special kind of `View` called a `ViewGroup`. The classes derived from `ViewGroup` enable developers to display `View` controls such as `TextView` and `Button` controls on the screen in an organized fashion.

It's important to understand the difference between `View` and `ViewGroup`. Like other `View` controls, including the controls from the previous chapter, `ViewGroup` controls represent a rectangle of screen space. What makes a `ViewGroup` different from a typical control is that `ViewGroup` objects contain other `View` controls. A `View` that contains other `View` controls is called a *parent view*. The parent `View` contains `View` controls called *child views,* or *children.*

You add child `View` controls to a `ViewGroup` programmatically using the method `addView()`. In XML, you add child objects to a `ViewGroup` by defining the child `View` control as a child node in the XML (within the parent XML element, as we've seen various times using the `LinearLayout` `ViewGroup`).

`ViewGroup` subclasses are broken down into two categories:

- Layout classes
- `View` container controls

Using `ViewGroup` Subclasses for Layout Design

Many of the most important subclasses of `ViewGroup` used for screen design end with "Layout." For example, the most common layout classes are `LinearLayout`, `RelativeLayout`, `TableLayout`, `FrameLayout`, and `GridLayout`. You can use each of these classes to position other `View` controls on the screen in different ways. For example, we've been using the `LinearLayout` to arrange various `TextView` and `EditText` controls on the screen in a single vertical column. Users do not generally interact with the layouts directly. Instead, they interact with the `View` controls they contain.

Using `ViewGroup` Subclasses as `View` Containers

The second category of `ViewGroup` subclasses is the indirect "subclasses"—some formal, and some informal. These special `View` controls act as `View` containers like `Layout` objects do, but they also provide some kind of active functionality that enables users to interact with them like other controls. Unfortunately, these classes are not known by any handy names; instead, they are named for the kind of functionality they provide.

Some of the classes that fall into this category include `GridView`, `ImageSwitcher`, `ScrollView`, and `ListView`. It can be helpful to consider these objects as different kinds of `View` browsers, or container classes. A `ListView` displays each `View` control as a list item, and the user can browse the individual controls using vertical scrolling capability.

Using Built-in Layout Classes

We have talked a lot about the `LinearLayout` layout, but there are several other types of layouts. Each layout has a different purpose and order in which it displays its child `View` controls on the screen. Layouts are derived from `android.view` `.ViewGroup`.

The types of layouts built into the Android SDK framework include the following:

- `LinearLayout`
- `RelativeLayout`
- `FrameLayout`
- `TableLayout`
- `GridLayout`

Tip

Many of the code examples provided in this section are taken from the `SimpleLayout` application. The source code for the `SimpleLayout` application is provided for download on the book's website.

All layouts, regardless of their type, have basic layout attributes. Layout attributes apply to any child `View` control within that layout. You can set layout attributes at runtime programmatically, but ideally you set them in the XML layout files using the following syntax:

```
android:layout_attribute_name="value"
```

There are several layout attributes that all `ViewGroup` objects share. These include size attributes and margin attributes. You can find basic layout attributes in the `ViewGroup` `.LayoutParams` class. The margin attributes enable each child `View` within a layout to have padding on each side. Find these attributes in the `ViewGroup.MarginLayoutParams` class. There are also a number of `ViewGroup` attributes for handling child `View` drawing bounds and animation settings.

Some of the important attributes shared by all `ViewGroup` subtypes are shown in Table 8.1.

Table 8.1 Important **ViewGroup** Attributes

Attribute Name (all begin with android:)	Applies to	Description	Value
layout_height	Parent View Child View	Height of the View. Used on attribute for child View controls within layouts. Required in some layouts, optional in others.	Dimension value or match_parent or wrap_content.
layout_width	Parent View Child View	Width of the View. Used on attribute for child View controls within layouts. Required in some layouts, optional in others.	Dimension value or match_parent or wrap_content.
layout_margin	Parent View Child View	Extra space around all sides of the View.	Dimension value. Use more specific margin attributes to control individual margin sides, if necessary.

Here is an XML layout resource example of a LinearLayout set to the size of the screen, containing one TextView that is set to its full height and the width of the LinearLayout (and therefore the screen):

```
<LinearLayout xmlns:android=
    "http://schemas.android.com/apk/res/android"
    android:layout_width="match_parent"
    android:layout_height="match_parent">
    <TextView
        android:id="@+id/TextView01"
        android:layout_height="match_parent"
        android:layout_width="match_parent" />
</LinearLayout>
```

Here is an example of a Button object with some margins set via XML used in a layout resource file:

```
<Button
    android:id="@+id/Button01"
    android:layout_width="wrap_content"
```

```
android:layout_height="wrap_content"

android:text="Press Me"

android:layout_marginRight="20dp"

android:layout_marginTop="60dp" />
```

Remember that a layout element can cover any rectangular space on the screen; it doesn't need to fill the entire screen. Layouts can be nested within one another. This provides great flexibility when developers need to organize screen elements. It is common to start with a FrameLayout or LinearLayout as the parent layout for the entire screen and then organize individual screen elements inside the parent layout using whichever layout type is most appropriate.

Now let's talk about each of the common layout types individually and how they differ from one another.

Using LinearLayout

A LinearLayout view organizes its child View controls in a single row, as shown in Figure 8.2, or a single column, depending on whether its orientation attribute is set to horizontal or vertical. This is a very handy layout method for creating forms.

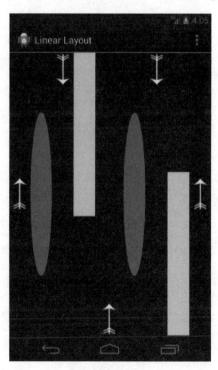

Figure 8.2   An example of LinearLayout (horizontal orientation).

You can find the layout attributes available for `LinearLayout` child `View` controls in `android.widget.LinearLayout.LayoutParams`. Table 8.2 describes some of the important attributes specific to `LinearLayout` views.

Table 8.2 **Important `LinearLayout` View Attributes**

Attribute Name (all begin with `android:`)	Applies to	Description	Value
`orientation`	Parent `View`	The layout is a single row (horizontal) or single column (vertical) of controls.	Either `horizontal` or `vertical`.
`gravity`	Parent `View`	The gravity of child views within a layout.	One or more constants separated by "`|`". The constants available are `top`, `bottom`, `left`, `right`, `center_vertical`, `fill_vertical`, `center_horizontal`, `fill_horizontal`, `center`, `fill`, `clip_vertical`, `clip_horizontal`, `start`, and `end`.
`weightSum`	Parent `View`	The sum of all child control weights.	A number that defines the sum of all child control weights. Default is `1`.
`layout_gravity`	Child `View`	The gravity for a specific child `View`. Used for positioning of views.	One or more constants separated by "`|`". The constants available are `top`, `bottom`, `left`, `right`, `center_vertical`, `fill_vertical`, `center_horizontal`, `fill_horizontal`, `center`, `fill`, `clip_vertical`, `clip_horizontal`, `start`, and `end`.
`layout_weight`	Child `View`	The weight for a specific child `View`. Used to provide the ratio of screen space used within the parent control.	The sum of values across all child views in a parent `View` must equal the `weightSum` attribute of the parent `LinearLayout` control. For example, one child control might have a value of `.3` and another a value of `.7`.

Note

To learn more about `LinearLayout`, see the Android API Guides discussion at *http:// d.android.com/guide/topics/ui/layout/linear.html*.

Using `RelativeLayout`

The `RelativeLayout` view enables you to specify where the child `View` controls are in relation to each other. For instance, you can set a child `View` to be positioned "above" or "below" or "to the left of" or "to the right of" another `View`, referred to by its unique identifier. You can also align child `View` controls relative to one another or to the parent layout edges. Combining `RelativeLayout` attributes can simplify creating interesting user interfaces without resorting to multiple layout groups to achieve a desired effect. Figure 8.3 shows where the `Button` controls are relative to each other.

You can find the layout attributes available for `RelativeLayout` child `View` controls in `android.widget.RelativeLayout.LayoutParams`. Table 8.3 describes some of the important attributes specific to `RelativeLayout` views.

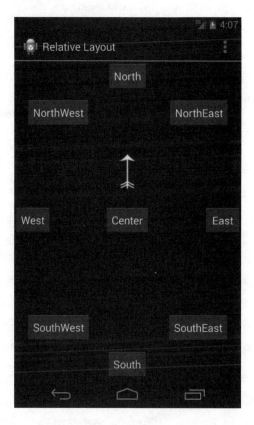

Figure 8.3   An example of `RelativeLayout` usage.

Table 8.3 **Important `RelativeLayout` View Attributes**

Attribute Name (all begin with `android:`)	Applies to	Description	Value
`gravity`	Parent `View`	The gravity of child views within a layout.	One or more constants separated by " `|` ". The constants available are `top`, `bottom`, `left`, `right`, `center_vertical`, `fill_vertical`, `center_horizontal`, `fill_horizontal`, `center`, `fill`, `clip_vertical`, `clip_horizontal`, `start`, and `end`.
`layout_centerInParent`	Child `View`	Centers the child `View` horizontally and vertically within the parent `View`.	True or false.
`layout_centerHorizontal`	Child `View`	Centers the child `View` horizontally within the parent `View`.	True or false.
`layout_centerVertical`	Child `View`	Centers the child `View` vertically within the parent `View`.	True or false.
`layout_alignParentTop`	Child `View`	Aligns the child `View` with the top edge of the parent `View`.	True or false.
`layout_alignParentBottom`	Child `View`	Aligns the child `View` with the bottom edge of the parent `View`.	True or false.
`layout_alignParentLeft`	Child `View`	Aligns the child `View` with the left edge of the parent `View`.	True or false.
`layout_alignParentRight`	Child `View`	Aligns the child `View` with the right edge of the parent `View`.	True or false.
`layout_alignRight`	Child `View`	Aligns the right edge of the child `View` with the right edge of another child `View`, specified by ID.	A `View` ID; for example, `@id/Button1`.

Table 8.3 **Continued**

Attribute Name (all begin with `android:`)	Applies to	Description	Value
`layout_alignLeft`	Child `View`	Aligns the left edge of the child `View` with the left edge of another child `View`, specified by ID.	A `View` ID; for example, `@id/Button1`.
`layout_alignTop`	Child `View`	Aligns the top edge of the child `View` with the top edge of another child `View`, specified by ID.	A `View` ID; for example, `@id/Button1`.
`layout_alignBottom`	Child `View`	Aligns the bottom edge of the child `View` with the bottom edge of another child `View`, specified by ID.	A `View` ID; for example, `@id/Button1`.
`layout_above`	Child `View`	Positions the bottom edge of the child `View` above another child `View`, specified by ID.	A `View` ID; for example, `@id/Button1`.
`layout_below`	Child `View`	Positions the top edge of the child `View` below another child `View`, specified by ID.	A `View` ID; for example, `@id/Button1`.
`layout_toLeftOf`	Child `View`	Positions the right edge of the child `View` to the left of another child `View`, specified by ID.	A `View` ID; for example, `@id/Button1`.
`layout_toRightOf`	Child `View`	Positions the left edge of the child `View` to the right of another child `View`, specified by ID.	A `View` ID; for example, `@id/Button1`.

Here is an example of an XML layout resource with a `RelativeLayout` and two child `View` controls—a `Button` object aligned relative to its parent, and an `ImageView` aligned and positioned relative to the `Button` (and the parent):

```xml
<?xml version="1.0" encoding="utf-8"?>
<RelativeLayout xmlns:android=
    "http://schemas.android.com/apk/res/android"
    android:id="@+id/RelativeLayout01"
    android:layout_height="match_parent"
    android:layout_width="match_parent">
    <Button
        android:id="@+id/ButtonCenter"
        android:text="Center"
        android:layout_width="wrap_content"
        android:layout_height="wrap_content"
        android:layout_centerInParent="true" />
    <ImageView
        android:id="@+id/ImageView01"
        android:layout_width="wrap_content"
        android:layout_height="wrap_content"
        android:layout_above="@id/ButtonCenter"
        android:layout_centerHorizontal="true"
        android:src="@drawable/arrow" />
</RelativeLayout>
```

Note

To learn more about `RelativeLayout`, see the Android API Guides discussion at *http://d.android.com/guide/topics/ui/layout/relative.html*.

Using `FrameLayout`

A `FrameLayout` view is designed to display a stack of child `View` items. You can add multiple views to this layout, but each `View` is drawn from the top-left corner of the layout. You can use this to show multiple images within the same region, as shown in Figure 8.4 on page 223, and the layout is sized to the largest child `View` in the stack.

You can find the layout attributes available for `FrameLayout` child `View` controls in `android.widget.FrameLayout.LayoutParams`. Table 8.4 on page 225, describes some of the important attributes specific to `FrameLayout` views.

Figure 8.4   An example of `FrameLayout` usage.

Here is an example of an XML layout resource with a `FrameLayout` and two child `View` controls, both `ImageView` controls. The green rectangle is drawn first and the red oval is drawn on top of it. The green rectangle is larger, so it defines the bounds of the `FrameLayout`:

```
<FrameLayout xmlns:android=
    "http://schemas.android.com/apk/res/android"
    android:id="@+id/FrameLayout01"
    android:layout_width="wrap_content"
    android:layout_height="wrap_content"
    android:layout_gravity="center">
```

```
    <ImageView
        android:id="@+id/ImageView01"
        android:layout_width="wrap_content"
        android:layout_height="wrap_content"
        android:src="@drawable/green_rect"
        android:contentDescription="@string/green_rect"
        android:minHeight="200dp"
        android:minWidth="200dp" />
    <ImageView
        android:id="@+id/ImageView02"
        android:layout_width="wrap_content"
        android:layout_height="wrap_content"
        android:src="@drawable/red_oval"
        android:contentDescription="@string/red_oval"
        android:minHeight="100dp"
        android:minWidth="100dp"
        android:layout_gravity="center" />
</FrameLayout>
```

Using `TableLayout`

A `TableLayout` view organizes children into rows, as shown in Figure 8.5. You add individual `View` controls within each row of the table using a `TableRow` layout `View` (which is basically a horizontally oriented `LinearLayout`) for each row of the table. Each column of the `TableRow` can contain one `View` (or layout with child `View` controls). You place `View` items added to a `TableRow` in columns in the order they are added. You can specify the column number (zero based) to skip columns as necessary (the bottom row shown in Figure 8.5 demonstrates this); otherwise, the `View` control is put in the next column to the right. Columns scale to the size of the largest `View` of that column. You can also include normal `View` controls instead of `TableRow` elements, if you want the `View` to take up an entire row.

Table 8.4 Important **FrameLayout** View Attributes

Attribute Name (all begin with android:)	Applies to	Description	Value
foreground	Parent View	Drawable to draw over the content.	Drawable resource.
foregroundGravity	Parent View	The gravity of the foreground drawable.	One or more constants separated by "|". The constants available are top, bottom, left, right, center_vertical, fill_vertical, center_horizontal, fill_horizontal, center, fill, clip_vertical, and clip_horizontal.
measureAllChildren	Parent View	Restricts the size of the layout to all child views or just the child views set to VISIBLE (and not those set to INVISIBLE).	True or false.
layout_gravity	Child View	A gravity constant that describes the child View within the parent.	One or more constants separated by "|". The constants available are top, bottom, left, right, center_vertical, fill_vertical, center_horizontal, fill_horizontal, center, fill, clip_vertical, clip_horizontal, start, and end.

Figure 8.5   An example of TableLayout usage.

You can find the layout attributes available for TableLayout child View controls in android.widget.TableLayout.LayoutParams. You can find the layout attributes available for TableRow child View controls in android.widget.TableRow.LayoutParams. Table 8.5 describes some of the important attributes specific to TableLayout controls.

Here is an example of an XML layout resource with a TableLayout with two rows (two TableRow child objects). The TableLayout is set to stretch the columns to the size of the screen width. The first TableRow has three columns; each cell has a Button object. The second TableRow puts only one Button control into the second column explicitly:

```
<TableLayout xmlns:android=
    "http://schemas.android.com/apk/res/android"
    android:id="@+id/TableLayout01"
    android:layout_width="match_parent"
    android:layout_height="match_parent"
    android:stretchColumns="*">
    <TableRow
        android:id="@+id/TableRow01">
        <Button
```

Table 8.5 Important **TableLayout** and **TableRow** View Attributes

Attribute Name (all begin with **android:**)	Applies to	Description	Value
collapseColumns	TableLayout	A comma-delimited list of column indices to collapse (zero based).	String or string resource; for example, "0,1,3,5".
shrinkColumns	TableLayout	A comma-delimited list of column indices to shrink (zero based).	String or string resource. Use "*" for all columns; for example, "0,1,3,5".
stretchColumns	TableLayout	A comma-delimited list of column indices to stretch (zero based).	String or string resource. Use "*" for all columns; for example, "0,1,3,5".
layout_column	TableRow child View	Index of the column this child View should be displayed in (zero based).	Integer or integer resource; for example, 1.
layout_span	TableRow child View	Number of columns this child View should span across.	Integer or integer resource greater than or equal to 1; for example, 3.

```
        android:id="@+id/ButtonLeft"

        android:text="Left Door" />

    <Button

        android:id="@+id/ButtonMiddle"

        android:text="Middle Door" />

    <Button

        android:id="@+id/ButtonRight"

        android:text="Right Door" />

    </TableRow>

    <TableRow

        android:id="@+id/TableRow02">

        <Button

        android:id="@+id/ButtonBack"

        android:text="Go Back"

        android:layout_column="1" />

    </TableRow>

</TableLayout>
```

Using `GridLayout`

Introduced in Android 4.0 (API Level 14), the `GridLayout` organizes its children inside a grid. But don't confuse it with `GridView`; this layout grid is dynamically created. Unlike a `TableLayout`, child `View` controls in a `GridLayout` can span rows and columns and are flatter and more efficient in terms of layout rendering. In fact, it is the child `View` controls of a `GridLayout` that tell the layout where they are to be placed. Figure 8.6 shows an example of a `GridLayout` with five child controls.

You can find the layout attributes available for `GridLayout` child `View` controls in `android.widget.GridLayout.LayoutParams`. Table 8.6 describes some of the important attributes specific to `GridLayout` controls.

The following is an example of an XML layout resource with a `GridLayout` view resulting in four rows and four columns. Each child control occupies a certain number of rows and columns. Because the default span attribute value is 1, we only specify when the element will take up more than one row or column. For instance, the first `TextView` is one row high and three columns wide. The height and width of each of the `View` controls are specified to control the look of the result; otherwise, the `GridLayout` control will automatically assign sizing.

```xml
<?xml version="1.0" encoding="utf-8"?>
<GridLayout xmlns:android="http://schemas.android.com/apk/res/android"
    android:id="@+id/gridLayout1"
    android:layout_width="match_parent"
    android:layout_height="match_parent"
    android:columnCount="4"
    android:rowCount="4" >
    <TextView
        android:layout_width="150dp"
        android:layout_height="50dp"
        android:layout_column="0"
        android:layout_columnSpan="3"
        android:layout_row="0"
        android:background="#ff0000"
        android:gravity="center"
        android:text="one" />
    <TextView
        android:layout_width="100dp"
        android:layout_height="100dp"
        android:layout_column="1"
        android:layout_columnSpan="2"
```

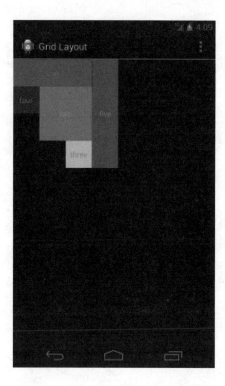

Figure 8.6   An example of `GridLayout` usage.

```
    android:layout_row="1"

    android:layout_rowSpan="2"

    android:background="#ff7700"

    android:gravity="center"

    android:text="two" />

<TextView

    android:layout_width="50dp"

    android:layout_height="50dp"

    android:layout_column="2"

    android:layout_row="3"

    android:background="#00ff00"

    android:gravity="center"

    android:text="three" />
```

```
    <TextView
        android:layout_width="50dp"
        android:layout_height="50dp"
        android:layout_column="0"
        android:layout_row="1"
        android:background="#0000ff"
        android:gravity="center"
        android:text="four" />
    <TextView
        android:layout_width="50dp"
        android:layout_height="200dp"
        android:layout_column="3"
        android:layout_row="0"
        android:layout_rowSpan="4"
        android:background="#0077ff"
        android:gravity="center"
        android:text="five" />
</GridLayout>
```

Tip

You may add a `GridLayout` to legacy applications all the way back to Android 2.1 (API Level 7) using the v7 Support Library (Revision 13+). To learn more about the support version of this layout, see the following: *http://d.android.com/reference/android/support/v7/widget/GridLayout.html.*

Using Multiple Layouts on a Screen

Combining different layout methods on a single screen can create complex layouts. Remember that because a layout contains `View` controls and is, itself, a `View` control, it can contain other layouts.

Tip

Want to create a certain amount of space between `View` controls without using a nested layout? Check out the `Space` view (`android.widget.Space`).

Figure 8.7 demonstrates a combination of layout views used in conjunction to create a more complex and interesting screen.

Warning

Keep in mind that individual screens of mobile applications should remain sleek and relatively simple. This is not just because this design results in a more positive user experience; cluttering your screens with complex (and deep) `View` hierarchies can lead to performance problems. Use the Hierarchy Viewer to inspect your application layouts; you can also use the `lint` tool to

Table 8.6 **Important `GridLayout` View Attributes**

Attribute Name (all begin with `android:`)	Applies to	Description	Value
`columnCount`	`GridLayout`	Defines a fixed number of columns for the grid.	A whole number; for example, 4.
`rowCount`	`GridLayout`	Defines a fixed number of rows for the grid.	A whole number; for example, 3.
`orientation`	`GridLayout`	When a row or column value is not specified on a child, this is used to determine whether the next child is down a row or over a column.	Can be vertical (down a row) or horizontal (over a column).
`layout_column`	Child `View` of `GridLayout`	Index of the column this child `View` should be displayed in (zero based).	Integer or integer resource; for example, 1.
`layout_columnSpan`	Child `View` of `GridLayout`	Number of columns this child `View` should span across.	Integer or integer resource greater than or equal to 1; for example, 3.
`layout_row`	Child `View` of `GridLayout`	Index of the row this child `View` should be displayed in (zero based).	Integer or integer resource; for example, 1.
`layout_rowSpan`	Child `View` of `GridLayout`	Number of rows this child `View` should span down.	Integer or integer resource greater than or equal to 1; for example, 3.
`layout_gravity`	Child `View` of `GridLayout`	Specifies the "direction" in which the `View` should be placed within the grid cells it will occupy.	One or more constants separated by "`|`". The constants available are `baseline`, `top`, `bottom`, `left`, `right`, `center_vertical`, `fill_vertical`, `center_horizontal`, `fill_horizontal`, `center`, `fill`, `clip_vertical`, `clip_horizontal`, `start`, and `end`. Defaults to `LEFT|BASELINE`.

Figure 8.7   An example of multiple layouts used together.

help optimize your layouts and identify unnecessary components. You can also use `<merge>` and `<include>` tags in your layouts for creating a common set of reusable components instead of duplicating them. `ViewStub` can be used to add more complex views to your layouts during runtime as they are needed, rather than building them directly into your layouts.

Using Container Control Classes

Layouts are not the only controls that can contain other `View` controls. Although layouts are useful for positioning other `View` controls on the screen, they aren't interactive. Now let's talk about the other kind of `ViewGroup`: the containers. These `View` controls encapsulate other, simpler `View` types and give the user the ability to interactively browse the child `View` controls in a standard fashion. Much like layouts, each of these controls has a special, well-defined purpose.

The types of `ViewGroup` containers built into the Android SDK framework include

- Lists and grids
- `ScrollView` and `HorizontalScrollView` for scrolling
- `ViewFlipper`, `ImageSwitcher`, and `TextSwitcher` for switching

Tip

Many of the code examples provided in this chapter are taken from the `AdvancedLayouts` application. The source code for the `AdvancedLayouts` application is provided for download on the book's website.

Using Data-Driven Containers

Some of the `View` container controls are designed for displaying repetitive `View` controls in a particular way. Examples of this type of `View` container control include `ListView` and `GridView`:

- **ListView:** contains a vertically scrolling, horizontally filled list of `View` controls, each of which typically contains a row of data. The user can choose an item to perform some action upon.
- **GridView:** contains a grid of `View` controls, with a specific number of columns. This container is often used with image icons; the user can choose an item to perform some action upon.

These containers are all types of `AdapterView` controls. An `AdapterView` control contains a set of child `View` controls to display data from some data source. An `Adapter` generates these child `View` controls from a data source. Because this is an important part of all these container controls, we talk about the `Adapter` objects first.

In this section, you learn how to bind data to `View` controls using `Adapter` objects. In the Android SDK, an `Adapter` reads data from some data source and generates the data for a `View` control based on some rules, depending on the type of `Adapter` used. This `View` is used to populate the child `View` controls of a particular `AdapterView`.

The most common `Adapter` classes are the `CursorAdapter` and the `ArrayAdapter`. The `CursorAdapter` gathers data from a `Cursor`, whereas the `ArrayAdapter` gathers data from an array. A `CursorAdapter` is a good choice when using data from a database. The `ArrayAdapter` is a good choice when there is only a single column of data or when the data comes from a resource array.

You should know some common elements of `Adapter` objects. When creating an `Adapter`, you provide a layout identifier. This layout is the template for filling in each row of data. The template you create contains identifiers for particular controls to which the `Adapter` assigns data. A simple layout can contain as little as a single `TextView` control. When making an `Adapter`, refer to both the layout resource and the identifier of the `TextView` control. The Android SDK provides some common layout resources for use in your application.

Using `ArrayAdapter`

An `ArrayAdapter` binds each element of the array to a single `View` control within the layout resource. Here is an example of creating an `ArrayAdapter`:

```
private String[] items = {
    "Item 1", "Item 2", "Item 3" };
ArrayAdapter adapt =
    new ArrayAdapter<String>
        (this, R.layout.textview, items);
```

In this example, we have a string array called `items`. This is the array used by the `ArrayAdapter` as the source data. We also use a layout resource, which is the `View` that is repeated for each item in the array. This is defined as follows:

```
<TextView xmlns:android=
    "http://schemas.android.com/apk/res/android"
    android:layout_width="match_parent"
    android:layout_height="wrap_content"
    android:textSize="20sp" />
```

This layout resource contains only a single `TextView`. However, you can use a more complex layout with constructors that also take the resource identifier of a `TextView` within the layout. Each child `View` within the `AdapterView` that uses this `Adapter` gets one `TextView` instance with one of the strings from the string array.

If you have an array resource defined, you can also directly set the `entries` attribute for an `AdapterView` to the resource identifier of the array to automatically provide the `ArrayAdapter`.

Using `CursorAdapter`

A `CursorAdapter` binds one or more columns of data to one or more `View` controls within the layout resource provided. This is best shown with an example. We also discuss `Cursor` objects in Chapter 13, "Leveraging Content Providers," where we provide a more in-depth discussion of content providers.

The following example demonstrates creating a `CursorAdapter` by querying the `Contacts` content provider. The `CursorAdapter` requires the use of a `Cursor`.

```
CursorLoader loader = new CursorLoader(
    this, ContactsContract.CommonDataKinds.Phone.CONTENT_URI,
    null, null, null, null);
Cursor contacts = loader.loadInBackground();
```

```
ListAdapter adapter = new SimpleCursorAdapter(
    this, R.layout.scratch_layout,
    contacts, new String[] {
        ContactsContract.CommonDataKinds.Phone.DISPLAY_NAME,
        ContactsContract.CommonDataKinds.Phone.NUMBER
    }, new int[] {
        R.id.scratch_text1,
        R.id.scratch_text2
    }, 0);
```

In this example, we present a couple of new concepts. First, you need to know that the Cursor must contain a field named _id. In this case, we know that the ContactsContract content provider does have this field. This field is used later when we handle the user selecting a particular item.

Note

The CursorLoader class was introduced in Android 3.0 (API Level 11). If you need to support applications prior to Android 3.0, you can use the Android Support Library to add the CursorLoader class (android.support.v4.content.CursorLoader) to your application. We talk more about the Android Support Library in Chapter 14, "Designing Compatible Applications."

We instantiate a new CursorLoader to get the Cursor. Then, we instantiate a SimpleCursorAdapter as a ListAdapter. Our layout, R.layout.scratch_layout, has two TextView controls in it, which are used in the last parameter. SimpleCursorAdapter enables us to match up columns in the database with particular controls in our layout. For each row returned from the query, we get one instance of the layout within our AdapterView.

Binding Data to the AdapterView

Now that you have an Adapter object, you can apply this to one of the AdapterView controls. Either of them will work. Here is an example of this with a ListView, continuing from the previous sample code:

```
((ListView)findViewById(R.id.scratch_adapter_view)).setAdapter(adapter);
```

The call to the setAdapter() method of the AdapterView, a ListView in this case, should come after your call to setContentView(). This is all that is required to bind data to your AdapterView. Figure 8.8 shows the same data in a GridView and ListView.

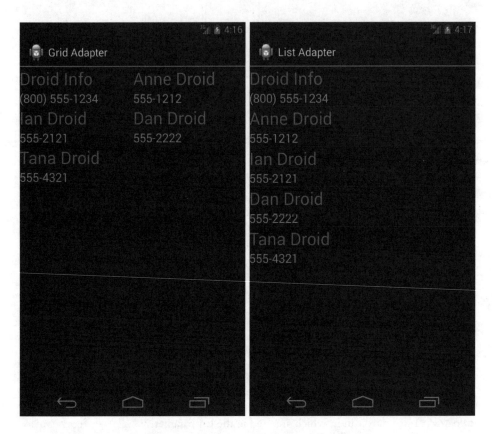

Figure 8.8 `GridView` and `ListView`: same data,
same list item, different layout views.

Handling Selection Events

You often use `AdapterView` controls to present data from which the user should select.
Both of the discussed controls—`ListView` and `GridView`—enable your application to
monitor for click events in the same way. You need to call `setOnItemClickListener()`
on your `AdapterView` and pass in an implementation of the `AdapterView.OnItemClick`
`Listener` class. Here is a sample implementation of this class:

```
av.setOnItemClickListener(
    new AdapterView.OnItemClickListener() {
    @Override
    public void onItemClick(
        AdapterView<?> parent, View view,
        int position, long id) {
```

```
    Toast.makeText(Scratch.this, "Clicked _id="+id,

        Toast.LENGTH_SHORT).show();

    }

});
```

In the preceding example, av is our `AdapterView`. The implementation of the `onItemClick()` method is where all the interesting work happens. The `parent` parameter is the `AdapterView` where the item was clicked. This is useful if your screen has more than one `AdapterView` on it. The `View` parameter is the specific `View` within the item that was clicked. The position is the zero-based position within the list of items that the user selects. Finally, the `id` parameter is the value of the `_id` column for the particular item that the user selects. This is useful for querying for further information about the particular row of data that the item represents.

Your application can also listen for long-click events on particular items. Additionally, your application can listen for selected items. Although the parameters are the same, your application receives a call as the highlighted item changes. This can be in response to the user scrolling with the arrow keys and not selecting an item for action.

Using `ListActivity`

The `ListView` control is commonly used for full-screen menus or lists of items from which a user selects. Thus, you might consider using `ListActivity` as the base class for such screens. Using the `ListActivity` can simplify these types of screens.

First, to handle item events, you now need to provide an implementation in your `ListActivity`. For instance, the equivalent of `onListItemClickListener` is to implement the `onListItemClick()` method within your `ListActivity`.

Second, to assign an `Adapter`, you need a call to the `setListAdapter()` method. You do this after the call to the `setContentView()` method. However, this hints at some of the limitations of using `ListActivity`.

To use `ListActivity`, the layout that is set with the `setContentView()` method must contain a `ListView` with the identifier set to `android:list`; this cannot be changed. Second, you can also have a `View` with an identifier set to `android:empty` to have a `View` display when no data is returned from the `Adapter`. Finally, this works only with `ListView` controls, so it has limited use. However, when it does work for your application, it can save some coding.

Tip

You can create `ListView` headers and footers using `ListView.FixedViewInfo` with the `ListView` methods `addHeaderView()` and `addFooterView()`.

If you need a two-level list, you should use an `ExpandableListActivity`. You then use an `ExpandableListView` for presenting your `View` data. `ExpandableListActivity` allows an item within your list to expand and present a sublist of items. To create a sublist of items, you need to create an `ExpandableListAdapter` to associate with your `ExpandableListView`.

Adding Scrolling Support

One of the easiest ways to provide vertical scrolling for a screen is by using the `Scroll View` (vertical scrolling) and `HorizontalScrollView` (horizontal scrolling) controls. Either control can be used as a wrapper container, causing all child `View` controls to have one continuous scroll bar. The `ScrollView` and `HorizontalScrollView` controls can have only one child, though, so it's customary to have that child be a layout, such as a `Linear Layout`, which then contains all the "real" child controls to be scrolled through.

Tip

The code examples of scrolling in this section are provided in the `SimpleScrolling` application. The source code for the `SimpleScrolling` application is available for download on the book's website.

Figure 8.9 shows a screen with and without a `ScrollView` control.

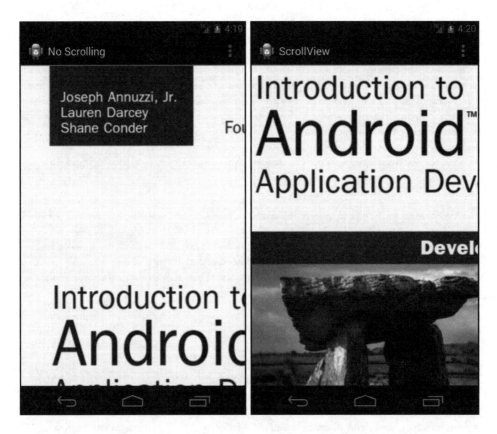

Figure 8.9   A screen without (left) and with (right) a `ScrollView` control.

Exploring Other `View` Containers

Many other user interface controls are available within the Android SDK. Some of these controls are listed here:

- **Switchers:** A `ViewSwitcher` control contains only two child `View` controls, and only one of those is shown at a time. It switches between the two, animating as it does so. Primarily, the `ImageSwitcher` and `TextSwitcher` objects are used. Each one provides a way to set a new child `View`, either a `Drawable` resource or a text string, and then animates from what is displayed to the new contents.

- **`ViewPager`:** A `ViewPager` is a useful `View` container for when your application has many different pages of data and you need to support swiping left and right through that data. To use a `ViewPager`, you must create a `PagerAdapter` that provides the data for the `ViewPager`. Fragments are typically used for paging data with `View Pager`; we talk about fragments more in Chapter 9, "Partitioning the User Interface with Fragments."

- **`DrawerLayout`:** A new layout pattern that has been embraced by the Android team is the `DrawerLayout`. This layout is especially useful for providing a list of navigation items that are hidden off the screen but presented when users swipe from the left or the right, or when they press the `Home` button from the action bar if the `Drawer Layout` resides to the left. `DrawerLayout` should really be used only for navigation and only when there are more than three top-level views within your application.

Summary

The Android SDK provides a number of powerful methods for designing usable and great-looking screens. This chapter introduced you to many of these. You first learned about many of the Android layout controls that can manage the placement of your controls on the screen. `LinearLayout` and `RelativeLayout` are two of the most common, but others such as `FrameLayout`, `GridLayout`, and `TableLayout` provide great flexibility for your layouts. In many cases, these enable you to have a single screen design that works on most screen sizes and aspect ratios.

You then learned about other objects that contain views and how to group or place them on the screen in a particular way. These included a variety of different controls for placing data on the screen in a readable and browsable way. In addition, you have learned how to use `ListView` and `GridView` as data-driven containers for displaying repetitive content. You now have all the tools you need to develop applications with usable and exciting user interfaces.

Quiz Questions

1. True or false: `LinearLayout`, `FrameLayout`, `TableLayout`, `RelativeLayout`, and `GridLayout` refer to a set of `ViewControl` classes.

2. True or false: A `LinearLayout` is used for showing each child `View` either in a single column or in a single row.

3. What is the method name for associating an XML layout resource file with an `Activity`?

4. True or false: The only way to create an Android user interface is by defining one in a layout resource XML file.

5. What is the syntax for assigning values to attributes within a layout resource XML file?

6. True or false: A `FrameLayout` is used for wrapping images within a picture frame.

7. True or false: The `android.widget.SlidingDrawer` class was added in API Level 17.

8. What is the name of the control for adding horizontal or vertical scrolling?

Exercises

1. Use the Android documentation to determine the difference between a `Cursor Adapter` and a `SimpleCursorAdapter`, and provide an explanation of that difference.

2. Use the Android documentation to determine the difference between a `GridView` and a `GridLayout`, and provide an explanation of that difference.

3. Create a simple Android application demonstrating how to use the `ViewSwitcher` control. In the `ViewSwitcher`, define two layouts. The first is a `GridLayout` defining a login form with a `Login` button; when the `Login` button is clicked, switch to a `LinearLayout` displaying a welcome message. The second layout has a `Logout` button; when the `Logout` button is clicked, switch back to the `GridLayout`.

References and More Information

Android SDK Reference regarding the application `ViewGroup` class:
   http://d.android.com/reference/android/view/ViewGroup.html
Android SDK Reference regarding the application `LinearLayout` class:
   http://d.android.com/reference/android/widget/LinearLayout.html
Android SDK Reference regarding the application `RelativeLayout` class:
   http://d.android.com/reference/android/widget/RelativeLayout.html
Android SDK Reference regarding the application `FrameLayout` class:
   http://d.android.com/reference/android/widget/FrameLayout.html
Android SDK Reference regarding the application `TableLayout` class:
   http://d.android.com/reference/android/widget/TableLayout.html
Android SDK Reference regarding the application `GridLayout` class:
   http://d.android.com/reference/android/widget/GridLayout.html

Android SDK Reference regarding the application `ListView` class:
  http://d.android.com/reference/android/widget/ListView.html
Android SDK Reference regarding the application `ListActivity` class:
  http://d.android.com/reference/android/app/ListActivity.html
Android SDK Reference regarding the application `ExpandableListActivity` class:
  http://d.android.com/reference/android/app/ExpandableListActivity.html
Android SDK Reference regarding the application `ExpandableListView` class:
  http://d.android.com/reference/android/widget/ExpandableListView.html
Android SDK Reference regarding the application `ExpandableListAdapter` class:
  http://d.android.com/reference/android/widget/ExpandableListAdapter.html
Android SDK Reference regarding the application `GridView` class:
  http://d.android.com/reference/android/widget/GridView.html
Android SDK Reference regarding the application `ViewPager` class:
  http://d.android.com/reference/android/support/v4/view/ViewPager.html
Android SDK Reference regarding the application `PagerAdapter` class:
  http://d.android.com/reference/android/support/v4/view/PagerAdapter.html
Android SDK Reference regarding the application `DrawerLayout` class:
  http://d.android.com/reference/android/support/v4/widget/DrawerLayout.html
Android Design: "Navigation Drawer":
  http://d.android.com/design/patterns/navigation-drawer.html
Android Training: "Creating a Navigation Drawer":
  http://d.android.com/training/implementing-navigation/nav-drawer.html
Android API Guides: "Layouts":
  http://d.android.com/guide/topics/ui/declaring-layout.html

9

Partitioning the User Interface with Fragments

Traditionally, each screen within an Android application was tied to a specific `Activity` class. However, in Android 3.0 (Honeycomb), the concept of a user interface component called a `Fragment` was introduced. Fragments were then included in the Android Support Library for use with Android 1.6 (API Level 4) and up. Fragments decouple user interface behavior from a specific `Activity` lifecycle. Instead, `Activity` classes can mix and match user interface components to create more flexible user interfaces for the Android devices of the future. This chapter explains what fragments are and how you can use them. In this chapter, we also introduce the concept of nested fragments, which have been added to Android 4.2.

Understanding Fragments

Fragments were added to the Android SDK at a crucial time when consumers were experiencing an explosion in the variety of Android devices coming to market. We now see not just smartphones but other larger-screen devices such as tablets and televisions that run the platform. These larger devices come with substantially more screen real estate for developers to take advantage of. Your typical streamlined and elegant smartphone user interface often looks oversimplified on a tablet, for example. By incorporating `Fragment` components into your user interface design, you can write one application that can be tailored to these different screen characteristics and orientations instead of different applications tailored for different types of devices. This greatly improves code reuse, simplifies application testing needs, and makes publication and application package management much less cumbersome.

As we stated in the introduction to this chapter, the basic rule of thumb for developing Android applications used to be to have one `Activity` per screen of an application. This ties the underlying "task" functionality of an `Activity` class very directly to the user interface. However, as bigger device screens came along, this technique faced some issues. When you had more room on a single screen to do more, you had to implement separate `Activity` classes, with very similar functionality, to handle the cases where you wanted to provide more functionality on a given screen. Fragments help manage this problem

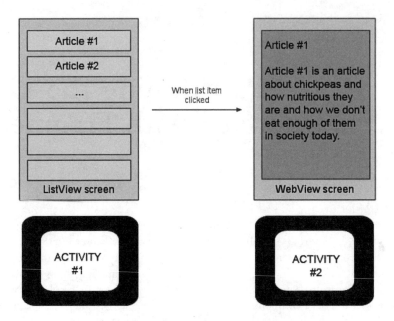

Figure 9.1   Traditional screen workflow without fragments.

by encapsulating screen functionality into reusable components that can be mixed and matched within `Activity` classes.

Let's look at a theoretical example. Let's say you have a traditional smartphone application with two screens. Perhaps it's an online news journal application. The first screen contains a `ListActivity` with a `ListView` control. Each item in the `ListView` represents an article available from the journal that you might want to read. When you click a specific article, since this is an online news journal application, you are sent to a new screen that displays the article contents in a `WebView` control. This traditional screen workflow is illustrated in Figure 9.1.

This workflow works fine for small-screen smartphones, but it's a waste of all the space on a tablet or a television. Here, you might want to be able to peruse the article list and preview or read the article on the same screen. If we organize the `ListView` and the `WebView` screen functionality into two standalone `Fragment` components, we can easily create a layout that includes both on the same screen when screen real estate allows, as shown in Figure 9.2.

Understanding the `Fragment` Lifecycle

We discussed the `Activity` lifecycle back in Chapter 4, "Understanding the Anatomy of an Android Application." Now let's look at how a `Fragment` fits into the mix. First of all,

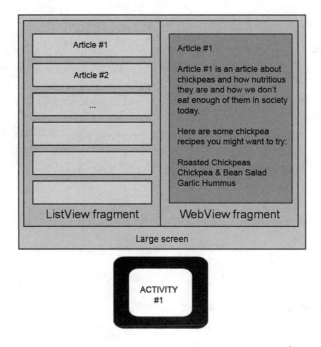

Figure 9.2 Improved screen workflow with fragments.

a Fragment must be hosted within an Activity class. It has its own lifecycle, but it is not a standalone component that can exist outside the context of an Activity.

The responsibilities of Activity class management are greatly simplified when the entire user interface state is moved off into individual fragments. Activity classes with only fragments in their layouts no longer need to spend a lot of time saving and restoring their state because the Activity object now keeps track of any Fragment that is currently attached automatically. The Fragment components themselves keep track of their own state using their own lifecycle. Naturally, you can mix fragments with View controls directly in an Activity class. The Activity class will be responsible for managing the View controls, as normal.

Instead, the Activity must focus on managing its Fragment classes. Coordination between an Activity and its Fragment components is facilitated by the FragmentManager (android.app.FragmentManager). The FragmentManager is acquired from the getFragmentManager() method, which is available within the Activity and Fragment classes.

Defining Fragments

Fragment implementations that have been defined as regular classes within your application can be added to your layout resource files by using the <fragment> XML tag and then loaded into your `Activity` using the standard `setContentView()` method, which is normally called in the `onCreate()` method of your `Activity`.

When you reference a `Fragment` class that you have defined in your application package in an XML layout file, use the `<fragment>` tag. This tag has a few important attributes. Specifically, you will need to set the `android:name` attribute of the fragment to the fully qualified `Fragment` class name. You will also need to give the item a unique identifier using the `android:id` attribute so that you can access that component programmatically, if needed. You still need to set the component's `layout_width` and `layout_height` attributes as you would for any other control in your layout. Here is a simple example of a `<fragment>` layout reference that refers to a class called `FieldNoteListFragment`, which is defined as a `.java` class in the package:

```
<fragment
    android:name="com.introtoandroid.simplefragments.FieldNoteListFragment"
    android:id="@+id/list"
    android:layout_width="match_parent"
    android:layout_height="match_parent" />
```

Managing `Fragment` Modifications

As you can see, when you have multiple `Fragment` components on a single screen, within a single `Activity`, user interaction on one `Fragment` (such as our news `ListView` Fragment) often causes the `Activity` to update another `Fragment` (such as our article `WebView` Fragment). An update or modification to a `Fragment` is performed using a `FragmentTransaction` (`android.app.FragmentTransaction`). A number of different actions can be applied to a `Fragment` using a `FragmentTransaction` operation, such as the following:

- A `Fragment` can be attached or reattached to the parent `Activity`.
- A `Fragment` can be hidden and unhidden from view.

Perhaps at this point you are wondering how the `Back` button fits into the `Fragment`-based user interface design. Well, now the parent `Activity` class has its own back stack. As the developer, you can decide which `FragmentTransaction` operations are worth storing in the back stack and which are not by using the `addToBackStack()` method of the `FragmentTransaction` object. For example, in our news application example, we might want each of the articles displayed in the `WebView` Fragment to be added to the parent `Activity` class's back stack so that if the user hits the `Back` button, he or she traverses the articles already read before backing out of the `Activity` entirely.

Attaching and Detaching Fragments with Activities

After you have a `Fragment` that you want to include within your `Activity` class, the lifecycle of the `Fragment` comes into play. The following callback methods are important to managing the lifecycle of a Fragment, as it is created and then destroyed when it is no longer used. Many of these lifecycle events mirror those in the Activity lifecycle:

- The onAttach() callback method is called when a Fragment is first attached to a specific Activity class.

- The onCreate() callback method is called when a Fragment is first being created.

- The onCreateView() callback method is called when the user interface layout, or View hierarchy, associated with the Fragment should be created.

- The onActivityCreated() callback method will inform the Fragment when its parent Activity class's onCreate() method has completed.

- The onStart() callback method is called when the Fragment's user interface becomes visible but is not yet active.

- The onResume() callback method makes the Fragment's user interface active for interaction after the Activity has resumed or the Fragment was updated using a FragmentTransaction.

- The onPause() callback method is called when the parent Activity is paused, or the Fragment is being updated by a FragmentTransaction. It indicates that the Fragment is no longer active or in the foreground.

- The onStop() callback method is called when the parent Activity is stopped, or the Fragment is being updated by a FragmentTransaction. It indicates the Fragment is no longer visible.

- The onDestroyView() callback method is called to clean up any user interface layout, or View hierarchy resources, associated with the Fragment.

- The onDestroy() callback method is called to clean up any other resources associated with the Fragment.

- The onDetach() callback method is called just before the Fragment is detached from the Activity class.

Working with Special Types of Fragments

Recall from Chapter 8, "Designing with Layouts," that there are a number of special Activity classes for managing certain common types of user interfaces. For example, the ListActivity class simplifies the creation of an Activity that manages a ListView control. Similarly, the PreferenceActivity class simplifies the creation of an Activity to manage shared preferences. And as we saw in our news reader application example, we often want to use user interface controls such as ListView and WebView within our Fragment components.

Because fragments are meant to decouple this user interface functionality from the Activity class, you'll now find equivalent Fragment subclasses that perform this functionality instead. Some of the specialty `Fragment` classes you'll want to familiarize yourself with include the following:

- **`ListFragment` (`android.app.ListFragment`)**: Much like a `ListActivity`, this `Fragment` class hosts a `ListView` control.

- **`PreferenceFragment` (`android.preference.PreferenceFragment`)**: Much like a `PreferenceActivity`, this `Fragment` class lets you easily manage user preferences.

- **`WebViewFragment` (`android.webkit.WebViewFragment`)**: This type of `Fragment` hosts a `WebView` control to easily render Web content. Your application will still need the `android.permission.INTERNET` permission to access the Internet.

- **`DialogFragment` (`android.app.DialogFragment`)**: Decoupling user interface functionality from your `Activity` classes means you won't want your dialogs managed by the `Activity` either. Instead, you can use this class to host and manage `Dialog` controls as fragments. Dialogs can be traditional pop-ups or embedded. We discuss dialogs in detail in Chapter 10, "Displaying Dialogs."

Note

You may have noticed that `TabActivity`, the helper class for working with the `TabHost` control, is not listed as a `Fragment` class. If you are simply using `TabHost` without the `TabActivity` helper class, you can easily move this into a `Fragment`. However, if you are using `TabActivity`, when you move to a `Fragment`-based application design, you'll want to look over how the action bars work, which allow you to add tabs. For more information, see the Android SDK documentation for the `TabActivity` (`android.app.TabActivity`), `ActionBar` (`android.app.ActionBar`), and `ActionBar.Tab` (`android.app.ActionBar.Tab`) classes.

Designing `Fragment`-Based Applications

At the end of the day, `Fragment`-based applications are best learned by example. Therefore, let's work through a fairly straightforward example to help nail down the many concepts we have discussed thus far in the chapter. To keep things simple, we will target a specific version of the Android platform: Android 4.3. However, you will soon find that you can also create `Fragment`-based applications for almost any device by using the Android Support Package.

Tip

Many of the code examples provided in this section are taken from the `SimpleFragments` application. The source code for the `SimpleFragments` application is provided for download on the book's website.

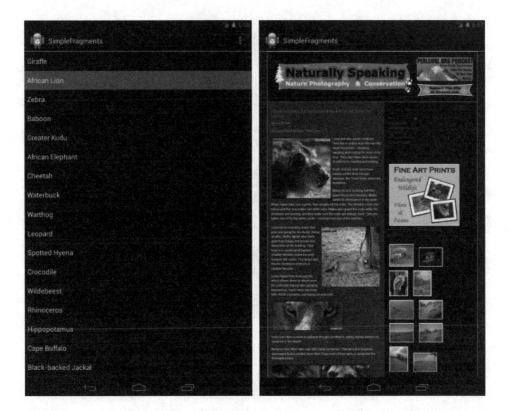

Figure 9.3   One fragment per `Activity`/screen.

Shane and Lauren (two of the authors) are big travelers. When they went to Africa, they took tons of pictures and wrote up a bunch of information about the different animals they saw in the wild on their blog. They called it their "African Field Notes" (*http://www.perlgurl.org/archives/photography/special_assignments/african_field_notes/*). Let's make a simple application with a `ListView` of wild animal names. Clicking a `ListView` item will load a `WebView` control and display the specific blog post associated with that animal. To keep things simple, we'll store our list of animals and blog URLs in string array resources. (See the sample code for a complete implementation.)

So how will our fragments work? We will use a `ListFragment` for the list of animals and a `WebViewFragment` to display each blog post. In portrait mode, we will display one fragment per screen, requiring two `Activity` classes, as shown in Figure 9.3.

In landscape mode, we will display both fragments on the same screen within the same `Activity` class, as shown in Figure 9.4.

Figure 9.4   Both fragments in a single `Activity`/screen.

Implementing a `ListFragment`

Let's begin by defining a custom `ListFragment` class called `FieldNoteListFragment` to host our wild animal names. This class will need to determine whether the second `Fragment`, the `FieldNoteWebViewFragment`, should be loaded or if `ListView` clicks should simply cause the `FieldNoteViewActivity` to be launched:

```
public class FieldNoteListFragment extends ListFragment implements
        FragmentManager.OnBackStackChangedListener {

    private static final String DEBUG_TAG = "FieldNoteListFragment";
    int mCurPosition = -1;
    boolean mShowTwoFragments;

    @Override
    public void onActivityCreated(Bundle savedInstanceState) {
        super.onActivityCreated(savedInstanceState);

        getListView().setChoiceMode(ListView.CHOICE_MODE_SINGLE);
```

```
        String[] fieldNotes = getResources().getStringArray(
                R.array.fieldnotes_array);
        setListAdapter(new ArrayAdapter<String>(getActivity(),
                android.R.layout.simple_list_item_activated_1, fieldNotes));


        View detailsFrame = getActivity().findViewById(R.id.fieldentry);
        mShowTwoFragments = detailsFrame != null
                && detailsFrame.getVisibility() == View.VISIBLE;


        if (savedInstanceState != null) {
            mCurPosition = savedInstanceState.getInt("curChoice", 0);
        }


        if (mShowTwoFragments == true || mCurPosition != -1) {
            viewAnimalInfo(mCurPosition);
        }


        getFragmentManager().addOnBackStackChangedListener(this);
    }


    @Override
    public void onBackStackChanged() {
        FieldNoteWebViewFragment details =
            (FieldNoteWebViewFragment) getFragmentManager()
                .findFragmentById(R.id.fieldentry);
        if (details != null) {
            mCurPosition = details.getShownIndex();
            getListView().setItemChecked(mCurPosition, true);

            if (!mShowTwoFragments) {
                viewAnimalInfo(mCurPosition);
            }
        }
    }
```

```java
@Override
public void onSaveInstanceState(Bundle outState) {
    super.onSaveInstanceState(outState);
    outState.putInt("curChoice", mCurPosition);
}


@Override
public void onListItemClick(ListView l, View v, int position, long id) {
    viewAnimalInfo(position);
}


void viewAnimalInfo(int index) {
    mCurPosition = index;
    if (mShowTwoFragments == true) {
        // Check what fragment is currently shown, replace if needed.
        FieldNoteWebViewFragment details =
            (FieldNoteWebViewFragment) getFragmentManager()
                .findFragmentById(R.id.fieldentry);
        if (details == null || details.getShownIndex() != index) {

            FieldNoteWebViewFragment newDetails = FieldNoteWebViewFragment
                    .newInstance(index);

            FragmentManager fm = getFragmentManager();
            FragmentTransaction ft = fm.beginTransaction();
            ft.replace(R.id.fieldentry, newDetails);
            if (index != -1) {
                String[] fieldNotes = getResources().getStringArray(
                        R.array.fieldnotes_array);
                String strBackStackTagName = fieldNotes[index];
                ft.addToBackStack(strBackStackTagName);
            }
```

```
            ft.setTransition(FragmentTransaction.TRANSIT_FRAGMENT_FADE);
            ft.commit();

        }

    } else {
        Intent intent = new Intent();
        intent.setClass(getActivity(), FieldNoteViewActivity.class);
        intent.putExtra("index", index);
        startActivity(intent);
    }

    }

}
```

Most of the `Fragment` control's initialization happens in the `onActivityCreated()` callback method so that we initialize the `ListView` only once. We then check to see which display mode we want to be in by checking to see if our second component is defined in the layout. Finally, we leave the display details to the helper method called `viewAnimalInfo()`, which is also called whenever an item in the `ListView` control is clicked.

The logic for the `viewAnimalInfo()` method takes into account both display modes. If the device is in portrait mode, the `FieldNoteViewActivity` is launched via an `Intent`. However, if the device is in landscape mode, we have some `Fragment` finagling to do.

Specifically, the `FragmentManager` is used to find the existing `FieldNoteWebView` `Fragment` by its unique identifier (`R.id.fieldentry`, as defined in the layout resource file). Then, a new `FieldNoteWebViewFragment` instance is created for the new animal blog post being requested. Next, a `FragmentTransaction` is started, in which the existing `FieldNoteWebViewFragment` is replaced with the new one. We put the old one on the back stack so that the `Back` button works nicely, set the transition animation to fade between the blog entries, and commit the transaction, thus causing the screen to update asynchronously.

Finally, we can monitor the back stack with a call to the `addOnBackStack` `ChangedListener()` method. The callback `onBackStackChanged()` updates the list to the current selected item. This provides a robust way to keep the `ListView` item selection synchronized with the currently displayed `Fragment` both when adding a new `Fragment` to the back stack and when removing one, such as when the user presses the `Back` button.

Implementing a `WebViewFragment`

Next, we create a custom `WebViewFragment` class called `FieldNoteWebViewFragment`
to host the blog entries related to each wild animal. This `Fragment` class does little more
than determine which blog entry URL to load and then load it in the `WebView` control.

```
public class FieldNoteWebViewFragment extends WebViewFragment {

    private static final String DEBUG_TAG = "FieldNoteWebViewFragment";

    public static FieldNoteWebViewFragment newInstance(int index) {
        Log.v(DEBUG_TAG, "Creating new instance: " + index);
        FieldNoteWebViewFragment fragment =
                    new FieldNoteWebViewFragment();

        Bundle args = new Bundle();
        args.putInt("index", index);
        fragment.setArguments(args);
        return fragment;
    }


    public int getShownIndex() {
        int index = -1;
        Bundle args = getArguments();
        if (args != null) {
            index = args.getInt("index", -1);
        }
        if (index == -1) {
            Log.e(DEBUG_TAG, "Not an array index.");
        }

        return index;
    }


    @Override
    public void onActivityCreated(Bundle savedInstanceState) {
        super.onActivityCreated(savedInstanceState);
```

```
String[] fieldNoteUrls = getResources().getStringArray(
        R.array.fieldnoteurls_array);
int fieldNoteUrlIndex = getShownIndex();

WebView webview = getWebView();
webview.setPadding(0, 0, 0, 0);
webview.getSettings().setLoadWithOverviewMode(true);
webview.getSettings().setUseWideViewPort(true);

if (fieldNoteUrlIndex != -1) {
    String fieldNoteUrl = fieldNoteUrls[fieldNoteUrlIndex];
    webview.loadUrl(fieldNoteUrl);
}
else
{
    String fieldNoteUrl = "http://www.perlgurl.org/archives/" +
                          "photography/special_assignments/" +
                          "african_field_notes/";
    webview.loadUrl(fieldNoteUrl);
}
}
}
```

Most of the `Fragment` control's initialization happens in the `onActivityCreated()` callback method so that we initialize the `WebView` only once. The default configuration of the `WebView` control doesn't look so pretty, so we make some configuration changes, remove the padding around the control, and set some settings to make the browser fit nicely in the screen area provided. If we've received a request for a specific animal to load, we look up the URL and load it; otherwise, we load the "default" front page of the field notes blog.

Defining the Layout Files

Now that you've implemented your `Fragment` classes, you can place them in the appropriate layout resource files. You'll need to create two layout files. In landscape mode, you'll want a single `simple_fragments_layout.xml` layout file to host both `Fragment` components. In portrait mode, you'll want a comparable layout file that hosts only the `ListFragment` you implemented. The user interface of the `WebViewFragment` you implemented will be generated at runtime.

Let's start with the landscape mode layout resource, called /res/layout-land/ simple_fragments_layout.xml. Note that we store this simple_fragments_ layout.xml resource file in a special resource directory for landscape mode use only. We discuss how to store alternative resources in this way in depth in Chapter 14, "Designing Compatible Applications." For now, suffice it to say that this layout will be automatically loaded whenever the device is in landscape mode.

```xml
<?xml version="1.0" encoding="utf-8"?>

<LinearLayout

    xmlns:android="http://schemas.android.com/apk/res/android"

    android:orientation="horizontal"

    android:layout_width="match_parent"

    android:layout_height="match_parent">

    <fragment

android:name="com.introtoandroid.simplefragments.FieldNoteListFragment"

        android:id="@+id/list"

        android:layout_weight="1"

        android:layout_width="0dp"

        android:layout_height="match_parent" />

    <FrameLayout

        android:id="@+id/fieldentry"

        android:layout_weight="4"

        android:layout_width="0dp"

        android:layout_height="match_parent" />

</LinearLayout>
```

Here, we have a fairly straightforward LinearLayout control with two child controls. One is a static Fragment component that references the custom ListFragment class you implemented. For the second region where we want to put the WebViewFragment, we include a FrameLayout region that we will replace with our specific FieldNoteWebView Fragment instance programmatically at runtime.

Tip

When dealing with Fragment components that will be updated via add or replace (dynamic), do not mix them with Fragment components instantiated via the layout (static). Instead, use a placeholder element such as a FrameLayout, as in the sample code. Dynamic Fragment components and the static ones defined using <fragment> from the layout do not mix well with the fragment transaction manager or with the back stack.

The resources stored in the normal layout directory will be used whenever the device is not in landscape mode (in other words, portrait mode). Here, we need to define two layout files. First, let's define our static `ListFragment` in its own `/res/layout/simple_fragments_layout.xml` file. It looks much like the previous version, without the second `FrameLayout` control:

```
<?xml version="1.0" encoding="utf-8"?>
<LinearLayout
    xmlns:android="http://schemas.android.com/apk/res/android"
    android:orientation="horizontal"
    android:layout_width="match_parent"
    android:layout_height="match_parent">
    <fragment
android:name="com.introtoandroid.simplefragments.FieldNoteListFragment"
        android:id="@+id/list"
        android:layout_weight="1"
        android:layout_width="0dp"
        android:layout_height="match_parent" />
</LinearLayout>
```

Defining the `Activity` Classes

You're almost done. Now you need to define your `Activity` classes to host your `Fragment` components. You'll need two `Activity` classes: a primary class and a secondary one that is used only to display the `FieldNoteWebViewFragment` when in portrait mode. Let's call the primary `Activity` class `SimpleFragmentsActivity` and the secondary `Activity` class `FieldNoteViewActivity`.

As mentioned earlier, moving all your user interface logic to `Fragment` components greatly simplifies your `Activity` class implementation. For example, here is the complete implementation for the `SimpleFragmentsActivity` class:

```
public class SimpleFragmentsActivity extends Activity {
    @Override
    public void onCreate(Bundle savedInstanceState) {
        super.onCreate(savedInstanceState);
        setContentView(R.layout.simple_fragments_layout);
    }
}
```

Yup. That's it. The `FieldNoteViewActivity` class is only slightly more interesting:

```
public class FieldNoteViewActivity extends Activity {
    @Override
    public void onCreate(Bundle savedInstanceState) {
        super.onCreate(savedInstanceState);

        if (getResources().getConfiguration().orientation ==
            Configuration.ORIENTATION_LANDSCAPE) {
            finish();
            return;
        }

        if (savedInstanceState == null) {
            FieldNoteWebViewFragment details = new FieldNoteWebViewFragment();
            details.setArguments(getIntent().getExtras());

            FragmentManager fm = getFragmentManager();
            FragmentTransaction ft = fm.beginTransaction();
            ft.add(android.R.id.content, details);
            ft.commit();
        }
    }
}
```

Here, we check that we're in the appropriate orientation to be using this `Activity`. Then we create an instance of the `FieldNoteWebViewFragment` and programmatically add it to the `Activity`, generating its user interface at runtime by adding it to the `android.R.id.content` view, which is the root view of any `Activity` class. That's all that's needed to implement this simple sample application with `Fragment` components.

Using the Android Support Package

Fragments are so important to the future of the Android platform that the Android team provided a compatibility library so that developers can update their legacy applications as far back as Android 1.6, if they so choose. This library was originally called the Compatibility Package and is now called the Android Support Package.

Adding `Fragment` Support to Legacy Applications

The choice of whether or not to update older applications is a personal one for the development team. Non-`Fragment` applications should continue to function for the foreseeable future without error, mostly due to the Android team's continued policy of supporting legacy applications as much as possible when new platform versions are released. Here are some considerations for developers with legacy applications who are considering whether or not to revise their existing code:

- Leave your legacy application as is, and the ramifications are not catastrophic. Your application will not be using the latest and greatest features that the Android platform has to offer (and users will notice this), but it should continue to run as well as it always has without any additional work on your part. If you have no plans to update or upgrade your old applications, this may very well be a reasonable choice. The potentially inefficient use of screen space may be problematic but should not create new errors.

- If your application has a lot of market traction and you've continued to update it as the Android platform has matured, you're more likely to want to consider the Android Support Package. Your users may demand it. You can certainly continue to support your legacy application and create a separate new-and-improved version that uses the new platform features, but this means organizing and managing different source code branches and different application packages, and it complicates application publication and reporting, not to mention maintenance. Better to revise your existing application to use the Android Support Package and do your best to keep your single code base manageable. The size and resources of your organization may be contributing factors to the decision here.

- Just because you start using the Android Support Package in your applications does not mean you have to implement every new feature (fragments, loaders, and so on) immediately. You can simply pick and choose the features that make the most sense for your application and add others over time via application updates when your team has the resources and inclination.

- Choosing to not update your code to new controls could leave your legacy application looking dated compared to other applications. If your application is already completely customized and isn't using stock controls—often the case with games and other highly graphical apps—it may not need updating. If, however, you conform to stock system controls, look, and feel, it may be more important for your application to get a fresh look.

Using Fragments in New Applications Targeting Older Platforms

If you're just starting to develop a new application and plan to target some of the older platform versions, incorporating fragments into your design is a much easier decision. If you're just starting a project, there's little reason not to use them and quite a few reasons why you should:

- Regardless of what devices and platforms you are targeting now, there will be new ones in the future that you cannot foresee. Fragments give you the flexibility to easily adjust your user interface screen workflows without rewriting or retesting all your application code.

- Incorporating the Android Support Package into your applications early means that if other important platform features are added later, you'll easily be able to update the libraries and start using them.

- By using the Android Support Package, your application will not show its age nearly as quickly since you will be incorporating the newer features of the platform and providing them to users on older platforms.

Linking the Android Support Package to Your Project

The Android Support Package is simply a set of static support libraries (available as a .jar file) that you can link to your Android application and use. You can download the Android Support Package using the Android SDK Manager and then add it to the projects of your choice. It is an optional package and not linked by default. Android Support Packages are versioned like everything else, and they are updated occasionally with new features—and more important, bug fixes.

Tip

You can find out more about the latest version package at the Android Developer website: *http://d.android.com/tools/extras/support-library.html*.

There are actually three Android Support Packages: v4, v7, and v13. The v4 package aims to provide new classes introduced in Honeycomb and beyond to platform versions as far back as API Level 4 (Android 1.6). This is the package you want to use when supporting your legacy applications. The v7 package provides additional APIs that are not found within the v4 package and is for supporting newer features all the way back to API Level 7 (Android 2.1). The v13 package provides more efficient implementations of some items, such as the `FragmentPagerAdapter`, when running on API Level 13 and later. If you're targeting API Level 13 or later, use this package instead. Be aware that parts of the package that are part of the platform are not available in this package; they aren't needed.

To use the Android Support Package with your application, take the following steps:

1. Use the Android SDK Manager to download the Android Support Package.

2. Find your project in the `Package Explorer` or `Project Explorer`.

3. Right-click the project and choose `Android Tools`, `Add Compatibility Library...`. The most updated library will be downloaded, and your project settings will be modified to use the newest library.

4. Begin using the APIs available as part of the Android Support Package. For example, to create a class extending `FragmentActivity`, you need to import `android .support.v4.app.FragmentActivity`.

Note

A few differences exist between the APIs used by the Android Support Package and those found in the later versions of the Android SDK. However, there are some renamed classes to avoid name collisions, and not all classes and features are currently incorporated into the Android Support Package.

Exploring Nested Fragments

A recent addition to Android 4.2 (API Level 17) is the ability to nest fragments within fragments. Nested fragments have also been added to the Android Support Library, making this API capability available all the way back to Android 1.6 (API Level 4). In order to add a `Fragment` within another `Fragment`, you must invoke the `Fragment` method `getChildFragmentManager()`, which returns a `FragmentManager`. Once you have the `FragmentManager`, you can start a `FragmentTransaction` by calling `begin Transaction()` and then invoking the `add()` method, including the `Fragment` to add and its layout, followed by the `commit()` method. You can even use the `getParentFragment()` method from within a child `Fragment` to get the parent `Fragment` for manipulation.

This opens many possibilities for creating dynamic and reusable nested components. Some examples include tabbed fragments within tabbed fragments, paging from one `Fragment` item/`Fragment` detail screen to the next `Fragment` item/`Fragment` detail screen with `ViewPager`, paging fragments with `ViewPager` within tabbed fragments, along with a host of many other use cases.

Summary

Fragments were introduced into the Android SDK to help address the different types of device screens that application developers need to target now and in the future. A `Fragment` is simply a self-contained chunk of a user interface, with its own lifecycle, that can be independent of a specific `Activity` class. Fragments must be hosted within `Activity` classes, but they give the developer a lot more flexibility when it comes to breaking screen workflow into components that can be mixed and matched in different ways, depending on the screen real estate available on the device. Fragments were introduced in Android 3.0, but legacy applications can use them if they take advantage of the Android Support Package, which allows applications that target API Level 4 (Android 1.6) and higher to use these more recent additions to the Android SDK. In addition, the nested fragments APIs provide even greater flexibility for creating reusable components for your applications.

Quiz Questions

1. What class facilitates coordination between an `Activity` and its `Fragment` components?

2. What method call is used for acquiring the class that facilitates coordination between an `Activity` and its `Fragment` components?

3. To what value should the `android:name` attribute of the `<fragment>` XML tag be set?

4. True or false: The `onActivityAttach()` callback method is called when a `Fragment` is first attached to a specific `Activity` class.

5. What are the subclasses of the `Fragment` (`android.app.Fragment`) class?

6. What type of control does a `ListFragment` (`android.app.ListFragment`) host?

7. Fragments were introduced in API Level 11 (Android 3.0). How would you add `Fragment` support to your application to support devices running versions of Android older than API Level 11?

Exercises

1. Using the Android documentation, review how to add a `Fragment` to the back stack. Create a simple application with a layout consisting of one `Fragment` for inserting a number (start with 1 in the first `Fragment`) and a button below it. Upon clicking the button, replace the first `Fragment` with a second `Fragment` and insert the number 2 in that `Fragment`. Continue this capability all the way up to 10, and while doing so, add each `Fragment` to the back stack to support back navigation.

2. Using the Android IDE, create a new Android Application Project, and on the `Create Activity` page, select the `Master/Detail Flow` option, then select `Finish`. Launch this application on both a handset and a tablet-size screen to see what it does, and then analyze the code to get a feel for how fragments have been used.

3. Create a two-pane `Fragment` layout where both fragments are generated and inserted into a layout programmatically at runtime. Have each `Fragment` take up 50% of the screen space, and use different colors for each `Fragment`.

References and More Information

Android SDK Reference regarding the application `Fragment` class:
   http://d.android.com/reference/android/app/Fragment.html
Android SDK Reference regarding the application `ListFragment` class:
   http://d.android.com/reference/android/app/ListFragment.html
Android SDK Reference regarding the application `PreferenceFragment` class:
   http://d.android.com/reference/android/preference/PreferenceFragment.html
Android SDK Reference regarding the application `WebViewFragment` class:
   http://d.android.com/reference/android/webkit/WebViewFragment.html
Android SDK Reference regarding the application `DialogFragment` class:
   http://d.android.com/reference/android/app/DialogFragment.html
Android API Guides: "Fragments":
   http://d.android.com/guide/components/fragments.html
Android Developers Blog: "The Android 3.0 Fragments API":
   http://android-developers.blogspot.com/2011/02/android-30-fragments-api.html

10

Displaying Dialogs

Android application user interfaces need to be elegant and easy to use. One important technique developers can use is to implement dialogs to inform the user or allow the user to perform actions such as edits without redrawing the main screen. In this chapter, we discuss how to incorporate dialogs into your applications.

Choosing Your `Dialog` Implementation

The Android platform is growing and changing quickly. New revisions of the Android SDK are released on a frequent basis. This means that developers are always struggling to keep up with the latest that Android has to offer. The Android platform has been in a period of transition from a traditional smartphone platform to a "smart device" platform that will support a much wider variety of devices, such as tablets, TVs, and toasters. To this end, one of the most important additions to the platform is the concept of the `Fragment`. We discussed fragments in detail in the previous chapter, but they have wide ramifications in terms of Android application user interface design. One area of application design that has received an overhaul during this transition is the way in which dialogs are implemented.

There are two methods for incorporating dialogs into your application—the legacy method and the method recommended for developers moving forward:

- Using the legacy method, which has existed since the first Android SDK was released, an `Activity` class manages its dialogs in a dialog pool. Dialogs are created, initialized, updated, and destroyed using `Activity` class callback methods. Dialogs are not shared among activities. This type of dialog implementation works for all versions of the Android platform; however, many of the methods used in this type of solution have been deprecated as of API Level 13 (Android 3.2). The Android API guides no longer discuss using this legacy method for adding dialogs to an application. Continuing to use the deprecated `Activity` dialog methods is not recommended and will not be discussed in this book.

- Using the `Fragment`-based method, which was introduced in API Level 11 (Android 3.0), dialogs are managed using the `FragmentManager` class (`android.app .FragmentManager`). A `Dialog` becomes a special type of `Fragment` that must still be used within the scope of an `Activity` class, but its lifecycle is managed like that of any other `Fragment`. This type of `Dialog` implementation works with the newest versions of the Android platform and is backward compatible with older devices as long as you incorporate the latest Android Support Package into your application to gain access to these new classes for use with older Android SDKs. `Fragment`-based dialogs are the recommended choice for moving forward with the Android platform.

Note

Unlike with some other platforms, which routinely remove deprecated methods after a few releases, deprecated methods within the Android SDK can normally be used safely for the foreseeable future, as necessary. That said, developers should understand the ramifications of using deprecated methods and techniques, which may include difficulty in upgrading application functionality to use the latest SDK features later on, slower performance as newer features are streamlined and legacy ones are left as is, and the possibility of the application "showing its age." Deprecated methods are also unlikely to receive any sort of fixes or updates.

We will cover the `Fragment`-based methods in this chapter. If you are developing new applications or updating existing applications to use the latest technologies the Android SDK has to offer, we highly recommend implementing the `Fragment`-based method and using the Android Support Package to support older versions of the Android platform.

Exploring the Different Types of Dialogs

Regardless of which way you implement them, a number of different `Dialog` types are available within the Android SDK. Each type has a special function that most users should be somewhat familiar with. The `Dialog` types available as part of the Android SDK include the following:

- **Dialog**: the basic class for all `Dialog` types. A basic `Dialog` (`android.app.Dialog`) is shown in the top left of Figure 10.1.
- **AlertDialog**: a `Dialog` with one, two, or three `Button` controls. An `AlertDialog` (`android.app.AlertDialog`) is shown in the top center of Figure 10.1.
- **CharacterPickerDialog**: a `Dialog` for choosing an accented character associated with a base character. A `CharacterPickerDialog` (`android.text.method` `.CharacterPickerDialog`) is shown in the top right of Figure 10.1.
- **DatePickerDialog**: a `Dialog` with a `DatePicker` control. A `DatePickerDialog` (`android.app.DatePickerDialog`) is shown in the bottom left of Figure 10.1.
- **ProgressDialog**: a `Dialog` with a determinate or indeterminate `ProgressBar` control. An indeterminate `ProgressDialog` (`android.app.ProgressDialog`) is shown in the bottom center of Figure 10.1.

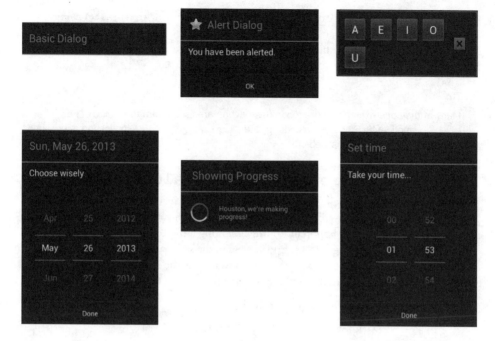

Figure 10.1   A sample of different Dialog types available in Android.

- **TimePickerDialog**: a Dialog with a TimePicker control. A TimePickerDialog (android.app.TimePickerDialog) is shown in the bottom right of Figure 10.1.
- **Presentation**: Added in API Level 17, a Presentation (android.app .Presentation) dialog is a type of Dialog used for presenting content to a secondary display.

If none of the existing Dialog types is adequate, you can create custom Dialog windows, with your specific layout requirements.

Working with Dialogs and Dialog Fragments

An Activity can use dialogs to organize information and react to user-driven events. For example, an Activity might display a dialog informing the user of a problem or asking the user to confirm an action such as deleting a data record. Using dialogs for simple tasks helps keep the number of application activities manageable.

Moving forward, most Activity classes should be "Fragment aware." In most cases dialogs should be coupled with user-driven events within specific fragments. There is a special subclass of Fragment called a DialogFragment (android.app.DialogFragment) that can be used for this purpose.

A DialogFragment is the best way to define and manage dialogs for use within your user interface.

Tip

Many of the code examples provided in this section are taken from the SimpleFrag Dialogs application. The source code for the SimpleFragDialogs application is provided for download on the book's website.

Tracing the Lifecycle of a Dialog and DialogFragment

Each Dialog must be defined within the DialogFragment in which it is used. A Dialog may be launched once or used repeatedly. Understanding how a DialogFragment manages the Dialog lifecycle is important to implementing a Dialog correctly.

The Android SDK manages a DialogFragment in the same way that fragments are managed. We can be sure that a DialogFragment follows nearly the same lifecycle as a Fragment. Let's look at the key methods that a DialogFragment must use to manage a Dialog:

- The show() method is used to display the Dialog.
- The dismiss() method is used to stop showing the Dialog.

Adding a DialogFragment with a Dialog to an Activity involves several steps:

1. Define a class that extends DialogFragment. You can define this class within your Activity, but if you plan to reuse this DialogFragment in other activities, define this class in a separate file. This class must define a new DialogFragment class method that instantiates and returns a new instance of itself.

2. Define a Dialog within the DialogFragment class. Override the onCreate Dialog() method and define your Dialog here. Simply return the Dialog from this method. You are able to define various Dialog attributes for your Dialog using methods such as setTitle(), setMessage(), or setIcon().

3. In your Activity class, instantiate a new DialogFragment instance, and once you have the DialogFragment instance, show the Dialog using the show() method.

Defining a DialogFragment

A DialogFragment class can be defined within an Activity or within a Fragment. The type of Dialog you are creating will determine the type of data that you must supply to the Dialog definition inside the DialogFragment class.

Setting Dialog Attributes

A Dialog is not too useful without setting the contextual elements. One way of doing this is by defining one or more of the attributes made available by the Dialog class. The base Dialog class and all of the Dialog subclasses define a setTitle() method. Setting the title usually helps a user determine what the `Dialog` is used for. The particular type of `Dialog` you are implementing determines the other methods that are made available to you for setting different `Dialog` attributes. In addition, setting attributes is also important for accessibility purposes, for example, to translate text to speech.

Showing a `Dialog`

You can display any `Dialog` within an `Activity` by calling the `show()` method of the `DialogFragment` class on a valid `DialogFragment` object identifier.

Dismissing a `Dialog`

Most types of dialogs have automatic dismissal circumstances. However, if you want to force a `Dialog` to be dismissed, simply call the `dismiss()` method on the `Dialog` identifier.

Here's an example of a simple class called `SimpleFragDialogActivity` that illustrates how to implement a simple `DialogFragment` with a `Dialog` control that is launched when a `Button` called `Button_AlertDialog` (defined in a layout resource) is clicked:

```
public class SimpleFragDialogActivity extends Activity {

    @Override
    public void onCreate(Bundle savedInstanceState) {
        super.onCreate(savedInstanceState);
        setContentView(R.layout.main);
        // Handle Alert Dialog Button
        Button launchAlertDialog = (Button) findViewById(
            R.id.Button_AlertDialog);
        launchAlertDialog.setOnClickListener(new View.OnClickListener() {
            @Override
            public void onClick(View v) {
                DialogFragment newFragment =
                    AlertDialogFragment.newInstance();
                showDialogFragment(newFragment);
            }
        });
    }

    public static class AlertDialogFragment extends DialogFragment {
        public static AlertDialogFragment newInstance() {
            AlertDialogFragment newInstance = new AlertDialogFragment();
            return newInstance;
        }
    }
}
```

```
@Override
public Dialog onCreateDialog(Bundle savedInstanceState) {

    AlertDialog.Builder alertDialog =
            new AlertDialog.Builder(getActivity());
    alertDialog.setTitle("Alert Dialog");
    alertDialog.setMessage("You have been alerted.");
    alertDialog.setIcon(android.R.drawable.btn_star);
    alertDialog.setPositiveButton(android.R.string.ok,
            new DialogInterface.OnClickListener() {
        @Override
        public void onClick(DialogInterface dialog, int which) {
            Toast.makeText(getActivity(),
                    "Clicked OK!", Toast.LENGTH_SHORT).show();
            return;
        }
    });
    return alertDialog.create();
    }

}


void showDialogFragment(DialogFragment newFragment) {
    newFragment.show(getFragmentManager(), null);
}

}
```

The full implementation of this `AlertDialog`, as well as many other types of dialogs, can be found in the sample code provided on the book's website.

Working with Custom Dialogs

When the `Dialog` types do not suit your purpose exactly, you can create a custom `Dialog`. One easy way to create a custom `Dialog` is to begin with an `AlertDialog` and use an `AlertDialog.Builder` class to override its default layout. In order to create a custom `Dialog` this way, the following steps must be performed:

1. Design a custom layout resource to display in the `AlertDialog`.
2. Define the custom `Dialog` identifier in the `Activity` or `Fragment`.

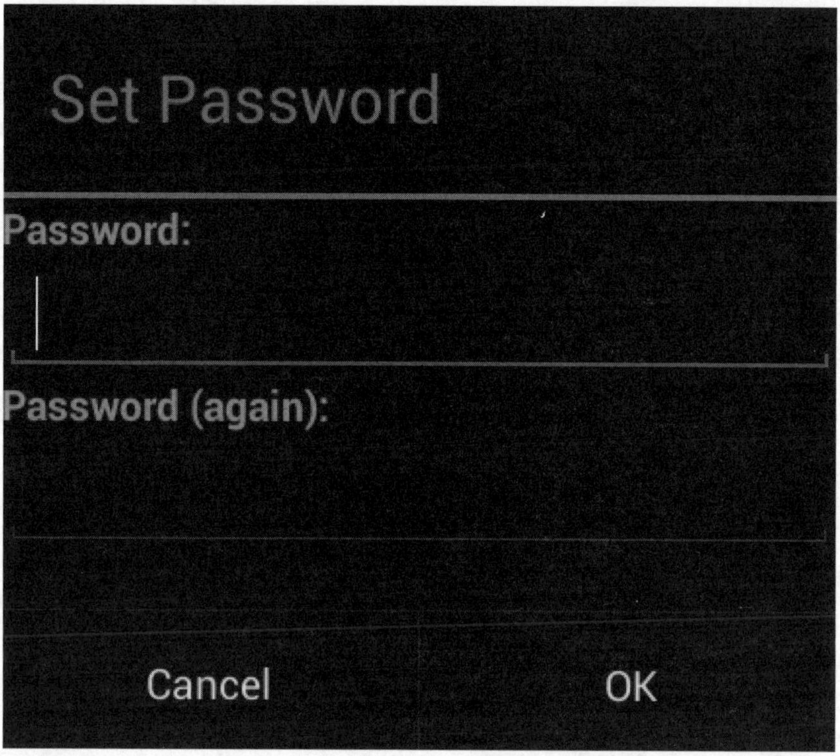

Figure 10.2   A custom Dialog implementation.

3. Use a LayoutInflater to inflate the custom layout resource for the Dialog.
4. Launch the Dialog using the show() method.

Figure 10.2 shows a custom Dialog implementation that accepts values into two EditText controls and, when OK is clicked, displays whether the two input values are equal.

Working with Support Package Dialog Fragments

The previous example will work only on devices that are running Android 3.0 (API Level 11) or newer. If you want your DialogFragment implementation to work on devices running older versions of Android, you must make a few small changes to the code. Doing so will allow your DialogFragment to work on devices all the way back to Android 1.6 (API Level 4).

Tip

Many of the code examples provided in this section are taken from the `SupportFrag Dialog` application. The source code for the `SupportFragDialog` application is provided for download on the book's website.

Let's look at a quick example of how you might implement a simple `AlertDialog`. In order to show an advantage of using the `Fragment`-based `Dialog` technique, we pass some data to the `Dialog` that demonstrates multiple instances of the `DialogFragment` class running within a single `Activity`.

First, import the support version of the `DialogFragment` class (`android.support .v4.app.DialogFragment`) that is part of the Support Library. Then, just as before, you need to implement your own `DialogFragment` class. This class simply needs to be able to return an instance of the object that is fully configured and needs to implement the `onCreateDialog` method, which returns the fully configured `AlertDialog`, much as it did using the legacy method. The following code is a full implementation of a simple `DialogFragment` that manages an `AlertDialog`:

```
public class MyAlertDialogFragment extends DialogFragment {


    public static MyAlertDialogFragment

        newInstance(String fragmentNumber) {

        MyAlertDialogFragment newInstance = new MyAlertDialogFragment();

        Bundle args = new Bundle();

        args.putString("fragnum", fragmentNumber);

        newInstance.setArguments(args);

        return newInstance;

    }


    @Override

    public Dialog onCreateDialog(Bundle savedInstanceState) {

        final String fragNum = getArguments().getString("fragnum");


        AlertDialog.Builder alertDialog = new AlertDialog.Builder(

            getActivity());

        alertDialog.setTitle("Alert Dialog");

        alertDialog.setMessage("This alert brought to you by "

            + fragNum );

        alertDialog.setIcon(android.R.drawable.btn_star);
```

```
alertDialog.setPositiveButton(android.R.string.ok,
    new DialogInterface.OnClickListener() {
@Override
public void onClick(DialogInterface dialog, int which) {
    ((SimpleFragDialogActivity) getActivity())
        .doPositiveClick(fragNum);
    return;
}
});
return alertDialog.create();
}
}
```

Now that you have defined your `DialogFragment`, you can use it within your `Activity` much as you would any `Fragment`—but this time, you must use the support version of the `FragmentManager` class, by calling the `getSupportFragmentManager()` method.

In your `Activity`, you need to import two support classes for this implementation to work: `android.support.v4.app.DialogFragment` and `android.support.v4.app.FragmentActivity`. Be sure to extend your `Activity` class from `FragmentActivity`, and not `Activity` as in the previous example, or your code will not work. The `FragmentActivity` class is a special class that makes fragments available with the Support Package.

The following `FragmentActivity` class, called `SupportFragDialogActivity`, has a layout resource that contains two `Button` controls, each of which triggers a new instance of the `MyAlertDialogFragment` to be generated and shown. The `show()` method of the `DialogFragment` is used to display the `Dialog`, adding the `Fragment` to the support version of the `FragmentManager`, and passing in a little bit of information to configure the specific instance of the `DialogFragment` and its internal `AlertDialog`.

```
public class SupportFragDialogActivity extends FragmentActivity {
    @Override
    public void onCreate(Bundle savedInstanceState) {
        super.onCreate(savedInstanceState);
        setContentView(R.layout.main);

        // Handle Alert Dialog Button
        Button launchAlertDialog = (Button) findViewById(
            R.id.Button_AlertDialog);
```

```
        launchAlertDialog.setOnClickListener(new View.OnClickListener() {
            public void onClick(View v) {
                String strFragmentNumber = "Fragment Instance One";
                DialogFragment newFragment = MyAlertDialogFragment
                    .newInstance(strFragmentNumber);
                showDialogFragment(newFragment, strFragmentNumber);
            }
        });


        // Handle Alert Dialog 2 Button
        Button launchAlertDialog2 = (Button) findViewById(
            R.id.Button_AlertDialog2);
        launchAlertDialog2.setOnClickListener(new View.OnClickListener() {
            public void onClick(View v) {
                String strFragmentNumber = "Fragment Instance Two";
                DialogFragment newFragment = MyAlertDialogFragment
                    .newInstance(strFragmentNumber);
                showDialogFragment(newFragment, strFragmentNumber);
            }
        });
    }


    void showDialogFragment(DialogFragment newFragment,
            String strFragmentNumber) {
        newFragment.show(getSupportFragmentManager(), strFragmentNumber);
    }


    public void doPositiveClick(String strFragmentNumber) {
        Toast.makeText(getApplicationContext(),
            "Clicked OK! (" + strFragmentNumber + ")",
            Toast.LENGTH_SHORT).show();
    }
}
```

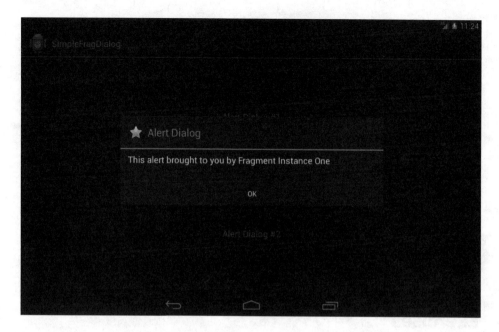

Figure 10.3   Using `DialogFragment` instances in an `Activity`.

Figure 10.3 shows a `FragmentActivity` using a `DialogFragment` to display a `Dialog` to the user with the Support Package.

`DialogFragment` instances can be traditional pop-ups (as shown in the example provided) or they can be embedded like any other `Fragment`. Why might you want to embed a `Dialog`? Consider the following example: You've created a picture gallery application and implemented a custom `Dialog` that displays a larger image when you click a thumbnail. On small-screen devices, you might want this to be a pop-up `Dialog`, but on a tablet or TV, you might have the screen space to show the larger graphic off to the right or below the thumbnails. This would be a good opportunity to take advantage of code reuse and simply embed your `Dialog`.

Summary

Dialogs are useful controls for keeping your Android application user interfaces clean and user-friendly. Many types of `Dialog` controls are defined in the Android SDK, and you can create custom `Dialog` controls if none of the canned controls suit your purposes.

Developers should be aware that there are two different but similar approaches to implementing `DialogFragment` components within applications. The first approach is not backward compatible, but it does work well with devices that use Honeycomb and beyond. The second approach involves using a special type of `DialogFragment` and `FragmentActivity`. This method is backward compatible and provides the `Dialog Fragment` class for legacy applications that you may be maintaining.

Quiz Questions

1. What are the different types of dialogs available within the Android SDK?

2. True or false: When using a `DialogFragment`, you define the `Dialog` in the `Activity onCreateDialog()` method.

3. What is the method used to stop showing a `Dialog`?

4. What `Dialog` type should you use when creating a custom `Dialog`?

5. True or false: To display a backward-compatible `DialogFragment`, your `Activity` class must extend from the `FragmentActivity` Support Package class.

6. What is the method call for retrieving the `FragmentManager` when using the Support Package?

Exercises

1. Using the Android documentation, determine what interface classes the `DialogFragment` class implements.

2. Create an application that displays an `AlertDialog` and implement the `DialogInterface.OnCancelListener` to display a cancel message set with `setCancelMessage`, saying that the `Dialog` has been canceled when the user cancels the `Dialog`.

3. Create an application that is single-pane on small devices and two-pane on large devices. Implement a simple `DialogFragment` with text that displays as a `Dialog` on small devices, but on large devices, embed the `Fragment` into the right pane of the two-pane layout.

References and More Information

Android SDK Reference regarding the application `Dialog` class:
   http://d.android.com/reference/android/app/Dialog.html
Android SDK Reference regarding the application `AlertDialog` class:
   http://d.android.com/reference/android/app/AlertDialog.html
Android SDK Reference regarding the application `DatePickerDialog` class:
   http://d.android.com/reference/android/app/DatePickerDialog.html

Android SDK Reference regarding the application `TimePickerDialog` class:
   http://d.android.com/reference/android/app/TimePickerDialog.html
Android SDK Reference regarding the application `ProgressDialog` class:
   http://d.android.com/reference/android/app/ProgressDialog.html
Android SDK Reference regarding the application `CharacterPickerDialog` class:
   http://d.android.com/reference/android/text/method/CharacterPickerDialog.html
Android SDK Reference regarding the application `DialogFragment` class:
   http://d.android.com/reference/android/app/DialogFragment.html
Android API Guides: "Dialogs":
   http://d.android.com/guide/topics/ui/dialogs.html
Android `DialogFragment` Reference: "Selecting Between `Dialog` or Embedding":
   http://d.android.com/reference/android/app/DialogFragment.html#DialogOrEmbed

IV

Android Application Design Essentials

11

Using Android Preferences

Applications are about functionality and data. In this chapter, we explore the simplest way to store, manage, and share application data persistently within Android applications: by using shared preferences. The Android SDK includes a number of helpful APIs for storing and retrieving application preferences in different ways. Preferences are stored as groups of key/value pairs that can be used by the application. Shared preferences are most appropriate for storing simple kinds of data, such as application state and user settings, in a persistent fashion.

Working with Application Preferences

Many applications need a lightweight data storage mechanism called shared preferences for storing application state, simple user information, configuration options, and other such information. The Android SDK provides a simple preferences system for storing primitive application data at the `Activity` level and preferences shared across all of an application's activities.

> **Tip**
>
> Many of the code examples provided in this section are taken from the `Simple Preferences` application. The source code for the `SimplePreferences` application is provided for download on the book's website.

Determining When Preferences Are Appropriate

Application preferences are sets of data values that are stored *persistently*, meaning that the preference data persists across application lifecycle events. In other words, the application or device can be started and stopped, turned on and off, without losing the data.

Many simple data values can be stored as application preferences. For example, your application might want to store the username of the application user. The application could use a single preference to store this information:

- The data type of the preference is a `String`.
- The key for the stored value is a `String` called "UserName".
- The value for the data is the username "HarperLee1926".

Storing Different Types of Preference Values

Preferences are stored as groups of key/value pairs. The following data types are supported as preference setting values:

- `Boolean` values
- `Float` values
- `Integer` values
- `Long` values
- `String` values
- A `Set` of multiple `String` values (new as of API Level 11)

Preference functionality can be found in the `SharedPreferences` interface of the `android.content` package. To add preferences support to your application, you must take the following steps:

1. Retrieve an instance of a `SharedPreferences` object.
2. Create a `SharedPreferences.Editor` to modify the preference content.
3. Make changes to the preferences using the `Editor`.
4. Commit your changes.

Creating Private Preferences for Use by a Single `Activity`

Individual activities can have their own private preferences, though they are still represented by the `SharedPreferences` class. These preferences are for the specific `Activity` only and are not shared with other activities within the application. The `Activity` gets only one group of private preferences, which are simply named after the `Activity` class. The following code retrieves an `Activity` class's private preferences, called from within the `Activity`:

```
import android.content.SharedPreferences;

...

SharedPreferences settingsActivity = getPreferences(MODE_PRIVATE);
```

You have now retrieved the private preferences for that specific `Activity` class. Because the underlying name is based on the `Activity` class, any change to the `Activity` class will change what preferences are read.

Creating Shared Preferences for Use by Multiple Activities

Creating shared preferences is similar. The only two differences are that we must name our preference set and use a different call to get the preference instance:

```
import android.content.SharedPreferences;

...

SharedPreferences settings =
    getSharedPreferences("MyCustomSharedPreferences", MODE_PRIVATE);
```

You have now retrieved the shared preferences for the application. You can access these shared preferences by name from any `Activity` in the application. There is no limit to the number of different shared preferences you can create. For example, you could have some shared preferences called "UserNetworkPreferences" and others called "AppDisplayPreferences." How you organize shared preferences is up to you. However, you should declare the name of your preferences as a variable so that you can reuse the name across multiple activities consistently. Here is an example:

```
public static final String PREFERENCE_FILENAME = "AppPrefs";
```

Searching and Reading Preferences

Reading preferences is straightforward. Simply retrieve the `SharedPreferences` instance you want to read. You can check for a preference by name, retrieve strongly typed preferences, and register to listen for changes to the preferences. Table 11.1 describes some helpful methods in the `SharedPreferences` interface.

Table 11.1 **Important `android.content.SharedPreferences` Methods**

Method	Purpose
`SharedPreferences.contains()`	Sees whether a specific preference exists by name
`SharedPreferences.edit()`	Retrieves the `Editor` to change these preferences
`SharedPreferences.getAll()`	Retrieves a map of all preference key/value pairs
`SharedPreferences.getBoolean()`	Retrieves a specific `Boolean`-type preference by name
`SharedPreferences.getFloat()`	Retrieves a specific `Float`-type preference by name
`SharedPreferences.getInt()`	Retrieves a specific `Integer`-type preference by name
`SharedPreferences.getLong()`	Retrieves a specific `Long`-type preference by name
`SharedPreferences.getString()`	Retrieves a specific `String`-type preference by name
`SharedPreferences.getStringSet()`	Retrieves a specific `Set` of `String` preferences by name (method added in API Level 11)

Adding, Updating, and Deleting Preferences

To change preferences, you need to open the preference Editor, make your changes, and commit them. Table 11.2 describes some helpful methods in the Shared Preferences.Editor interface.

Table 11.2 Important **android.content.SharedPreferences.Editor** Methods

Method	Purpose
SharedPreferences.Editor.clear()	Removes all preferences. This operation happens before any put operation, regardless of when it is called within an editing session; then all other changes are made and committed.
SharedPreferences.Editor.remove()	Removes a specific preference by name. This operation happens before any put operation, regardless of when it is called within an editing session; then all other changes are made and committed.
SharedPreferences.Editor.putBoolean()	Sets a specific Boolean-type preference by name.
SharedPreferences.Editor.putFloat()	Sets a specific Float-type preference by name.
SharedPreferences.Editor.putInt()	Sets a specific Integer-type preference by name.
SharedPreferences.Editor.putLong()	Sets a specific Long-type preference by name.
SharedPreferences.Editor.putString()	Sets a specific String-type preference by name.
SharedPreferences.Editor.putStringSet()	Sets a specific Set of String-type preferences by name (method added in API Level 11).
SharedPreferences.Editor.commit()	Commits all changes from this editing session.
SharedPreferences.Editor.apply()	Much like the commit() method, this method commits all preference changes from this editing session. However, this method commits the changes to in-memory SharedPreferences immediately but commits the changes to disk asynchronously within the application lifecycle (method added in API Level 9).

The following block of code retrieves an `Activity` class's private preferences, opens the preference `Editor`, adds a `Long`-type preference called `SomeLong`, and saves the change:

```
import android.content.SharedPreferences;

...

SharedPreferences settingsActivity = getPreferences(MODE_PRIVATE);

SharedPreferences.Editor prefEditor = settingsActivity.edit();

prefEditor.putLong("SomeLong", java.lang.Long.MIN_VALUE);

prefEditor.commit();
```

Tip

If you're targeting devices that run at least API Level 9 (Android 2.3 and higher), you would benefit from using the `apply()` method instead of the `commit()` method in the preceding code. However, if you need to support legacy versions of Android, you'll want to stick with the `commit()` method, or check at runtime before calling the most appropriate method. Even when you are writing as little as one preference, using `apply()` could smooth out the operation because any call to the file system may block for a noticeable (and therefore unacceptable) length of time.

Reacting to Preference Changes

Your application can listen for, and react to, changes to shared preferences by implementing a listener and registering it with the specific `SharedPreferences` object using the `registerOnSharedPreferenceChangeListener()` and `unregisterOnSharedPreference ChangeListener()` methods. This interface class has just one callback, which passes your code the shared preferences object that changed and which specific preference key name changed.

Finding Preferences Data on the Android File System

Internally, application preferences are stored as XML files. You can access the preferences file using the `File Explorer` via `Dalvik Debug Monitor Server` (DDMS). You find these files on the Android file system in the following directory:

```
/data/data/<package name>/shared_prefs/<preferences filename>.xml
```

The preferences filename is the `Activity` class name for private preferences or the specific name you give for the shared preferences. Here is an example of the XML file contents of a preferences file with some simple values:

```
<?xml version="1.0" encoding="utf-8" standalone="yes" ?>

<map>

    <string name="String_Pref">Test String</string>

    <int name="Int_Pref" value="-2147483648" />
```

```
<float name="Float_Pref" value="-Infinity" />

<long name="Long_Pref" value="9223372036854775807" />

<boolean name="Boolean_Pref" value="false" />
</map>
```

Understanding the application preferences file format can be helpful for testing purposes. You can use DDMS to copy the preferences files to and from the device. Since the shared preferences are just a file, regular file permissions apply. When creating the file, you specify the mode (permissions) for the file. This determines if the file is readable outside the existing package.

Note

For more information about using DDMS and the `File Explorer`, please see Appendix C, "Quick-Start Guide: Android DDMS."

Creating Manageable User Preferences

You now understand how to store and retrieve shared preferences programmatically. This works very well for keeping application state and such, but what if you have a set of user settings and you want to create a simple, consistent, and platform-standard way in which the user can edit them? Good news! You can use the handy `PreferenceActivity` class (`android.preference.PreferenceActivity`) to easily achieve this goal.

Tip

Many of the code examples provided in this section are taken from the `SimpleUserPrefs` application. The source code for the `SimpleUserPrefs` application is provided for download on the book's website.

Implementing a `PreferenceActivity`-based solution requires the following steps:

1. Define the preference set in a preference resource file.

2. Implement a `PreferenceFragment` class and tie it to the preference resource file. Note that `PreferenceFragment` will work only on Android 3.0 and above. In the interest of backward compatibility, a `PreferenceActivity` without the `PreferenceFragment` can be used to support legacy platform versions as needed.

3. Implement a `PreferenceActivity` class and add the `PreferenceFragment` you just created.

4. Hook up the `Activity` within your application as you normally would. For example, register it in the manifest file, start the `Activity` as normal, and so on.

Now let's look at these steps in more detail.

Creating a Preference Resource File

First, you create an XML resource file to define the preferences your users are allowed to edit. A preference resource file contains a root-level <PreferenceScreen> tag, followed by various preference types. These preference types are based on the Preference class (android.preference.Preference) and its subclasses, such as CheckBoxPreference, EditTextPreference, ListPreference, MultiSelectListPreference, and more. Some preferences have been around since the Android SDK was first released, whereas others, such as the MultiSelectListPreference class, were introduced in Android API Level 11 and are not backward compatible with older devices.

Each preference should have some metadata, such as a title and some summary text that will be displayed to the user. You can also specify default values and, for those preferences that launch dialogs, the dialog prompt. For the specific metadata associated with a given preference type, see its subclass attributes in the Android SDK documentation. Here are some common Preference attributes that most preferences should set:

- The android:key attribute is used to specify the key name for the shared preference.

- The android:title attribute is used to specify the friendly name of the preference, as shown on the editing screen.

- The android:summary attribute is used to give more details about the preference, as shown on the editing screen.

- The android:defaultValue attribute is used to specify a default value of the preference.

Like any resource files, preference resource files can use raw strings or reference string resources. The following preference resource file example does a bit of both (the string array resources are defined elsewhere in the strings.xml resource file):

```xml
<?xml version="1.0" encoding="utf-8"?>
<PreferenceScreen
    xmlns:android="http://schemas.android.com/apk/res/android">
    <EditTextPreference
        android:key="username"
        android:title="Username"
        android:summary="This is your ACME Service username"
        android:defaultValue=""
        android:dialogTitle="Enter your ACME Service username:" />
```

```
<EditTextPreference
    android:key="email"
    android:title="Configure Email"
    android:summary="Enter your email address"
    android:defaultValue="your@email.com" />
<PreferenceCategory
    android:title="Game Settings">
    <CheckBoxPreference
        android:key="bSoundOn"
        android:title="Enable Sound"
        android:summary="Turn sound on and off in the game"
        android:defaultValue="true" />
    <CheckBoxPreference
        android:key="bAllowCheats"
        android:title="Enable Cheating"
        android:summary="Turn the ability to cheat on and off in the game"
        android:defaultValue="false" />
</PreferenceCategory>
<PreferenceCategory
    android:title="Game Character Settings">
    <ListPreference
        android:key="gender"
        android:title="Game Character Gender"
        android:summary="This is the gender of your game character"
        android:entries="@array/char_gender_types"
        android:entryValues="@array/char_genders"
        android:dialogTitle="Choose a gender for your character:" />
    <ListPreference
        android:key="race"
        android:title="Game Character Race"
        android:summary="This is the race of your game character"
        android:entries="@array/char_race_types"
```

```
        android:entryValues="@array/char_races"

        android:dialogTitle="Choose a race for your character:" />

   </PreferenceCategory>

</PreferenceScreen>
```

This XML preference file is organized into two categories and defines fields for collecting several pieces of information, including a username (`String`), sound setting (`boolean`), cheat setting (`boolean`), character gender (fixed `String`), and character race (fixed `String`).

For instance, this example uses the `CheckBoxPreference` type to manage `boolean` shared preference values, for example, game settings such as whether or not sound is enabled or whether cheating is allowed. Boolean values are checked on and off straight from the screen. The example uses the `EditTextPreference` type to manage the username, and it uses `ListPreference` types to allow the user to choose from a list of options. Finally, the settings are organized into categories using `<PreferenceCategory>` tags.

Next, you need to wire up your `PreferenceActivity` class and tell it about your preference resource file.

Using the `PreferenceActivity` Class

The `PreferenceActivity` class (`android.preference.PreferenceActivity`) is a helper class that is capable of displaying a `PreferenceFragment`. This `Preference Fragment` loads up your XML preference resource file and transforms it into a standard settings screen, much as you see in the Android device settings. Figure 11.1 shows what the screen for the preference resource file discussed in the previous section looks like when loaded into a `PreferenceActivity` class.

To wire up your new preference resource file, create a new class that extends the `PreferenceActivity` class within your application. Next, override the `onCreate()` method of your class. Retrieve the `FragmentManager` for the `Activity`, start a `FragmentTransaction`, insert your `PreferenceFragment` into the `Activity`, and then call `commit()`. Tie the preference resource file to the `PreferenceFragment` class using the `addPreferencesFromResource()` method. You will also want to retrieve an instance of the `PreferenceManager` (`android.preference.PreferenceManager`) and set the name of these preferences for use in the rest of your application at this time, if you're using a name other than the default. Here is the complete implementation of the `SimpleUserPrefsActivity` class, which encapsulates these steps:

```java
public class SimpleUserPrefsActivity extends PreferenceActivity {

    @Override
    public void onCreate(Bundle savedInstanceState) {

        super.onCreate(savedInstanceState);

        FragmentManager manager = getFragmentManager();

        FragmentTransaction transaction = manager.beginTransaction();
```

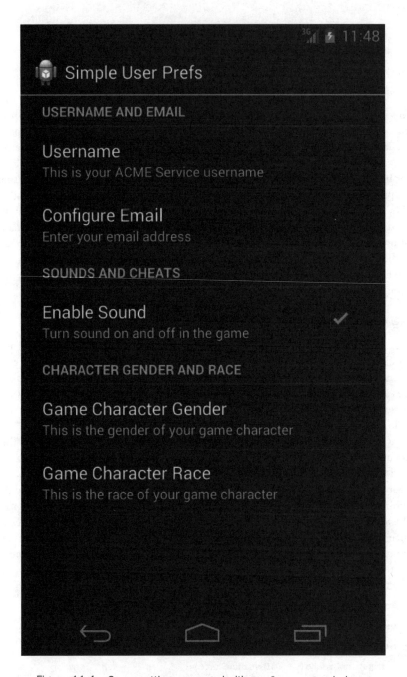

Figure 11.1   Game settings managed with PreferenceActivity.

```
        transaction.replace(android.R.id.content,
            new SimpleUserPrefsFragment());
        transaction.commit();
    }


    public static class SimpleUserPrefsFragment extends PreferenceFragment {
        @Override
        public void onCreate(Bundle savedInstanceState) {
            super.onCreate(savedInstanceState);
            PreferenceManager manager = getPreferenceManager();
            manager.setSharedPreferencesName("user_prefs");
            addPreferencesFromResource(R.xml.userprefs);
        }

    }

}
```

Now you can simply wire up the `Activity` as you normally would. Don't forget to register it within your application's Android manifest file. When you run the application and start the `UserPrefsActivity`, you should see a screen that looks like Figure 11.1. Trying to edit all other preferences will launch a dialog with the appropriate type of prompt (`EditText` or `Spinner` control), as shown in Figures 11.2 and 11.3.

Use the `EditTextPreference` type to manage `String` shared preference values, such as username, as shown in Figure 11.2.

Use the `ListPreference` type to force the user to choose from a list of options, as shown in Figure 11.3.

Organizing Preferences with Headers

The concept of `Preference` headers was added in Android 3.0 (API Level 11). The headers feature allows your application to present a list of options for navigating to setting subscreens. A very good example of a system application that uses the headers feature is the Android system Settings application. On large-screen devices, the left pane displays the setting list items and, depending on which setting item is selected, determines what setting options are displayed in the right pane. There are a few setup steps for making your application ready for incorporating the preference headers feature:

1. Create individual `PreferenceFragment` classes for each setting collection.

2. Define the header list using the `<preference-headers>` tag in a new XML file.

3. Create a new `PreferenceActivity` class that calls the method `onBuildHeaders` for loading the headers resource file.

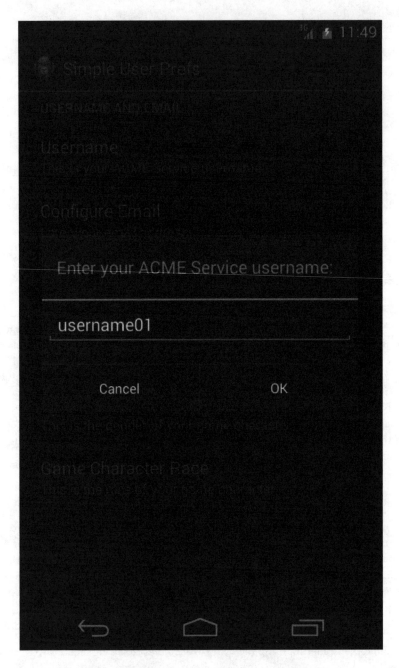

Figure 11.2   Editing an EditText (String) preference.

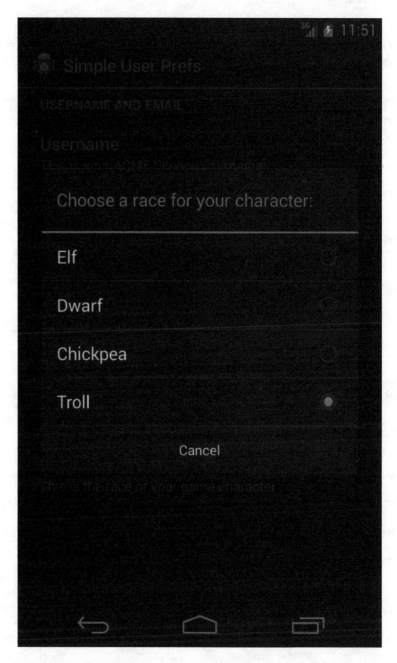

Figure 11.3   Editing a `ListPreference` (`String` array) preference.

Tip

Many of the code examples provided in this section are taken from the `UserPrefsHeaders` application. The source code for the `UserPrefsHeaders` application is provided for download on the book's website.

An example headers file follows, which groups settings into separate header entries:

```
<preference-headers xmlns:android="http://schemas.android.com/apk/res/android">

    <header
android:fragment="com.introtoandroid.userprefs.UserPrefsActivity$UserNameFrag"
            android:title="Personal Settings"
            android:summary="Configure your personal settings" />
    <header
android:fragment="com.introtoandroid.userprefs.UserPrefsActivity$GameSettingsFrag"
            android:title="Game Settings"
            android:summary="Configure your game settings" />
    <header
android:fragment="com.introtoandroid.userprefs.UserPrefsActivity$CharSettingsFrag"
            android:title="Character Settings"
            android:summary="Configure your character settings" />
</preference-headers>
```

Here, we have defined some `<header>` entries within a `<preference-headers>` node. Each `<header>` defines just three attributes: `android:fragment`, `android:title`, and `android:summary`. Here is how our new `UserPrefsActivity` class should look:

```
public class UserPrefsActivity extends PreferenceActivity {
    /** Called when the activity is first created. */
    @Override
    public void onCreate(Bundle savedInstanceState) {
        super.onCreate(savedInstanceState);
    }
```

```java
@Override
public void onBuildHeaders(List<Header> target) {
    loadHeadersFromResource(R.xml.preference_headers, target);
}


public static class UserNameFrag extends PreferenceFragment {
    @Override
    public void onCreate(Bundle savedInstanceState) {
        super.onCreate(savedInstanceState);
        PreferenceManager manager = getPreferenceManager();
        manager.setSharedPreferencesName("user_prefs");
        addPreferencesFromResource(R.xml.personal_settings);
    }
}


public static class GameSettingsFrag extends PreferenceFragment {
    @Override
    public void onCreate(Bundle savedInstanceState) {
        super.onCreate(savedInstanceState);
        PreferenceManager manager = getPreferenceManager();
        manager.setSharedPreferencesName("user_prefs");
        addPreferencesFromResource(R.xml.game_settings);
    }
}


public static class CharSettingsFrag extends PreferenceFragment {
    @Override
    public void onCreate(Bundle savedInstanceState) {
        super.onCreate(savedInstanceState);
        PreferenceManager manager = getPreferenceManager();
```

```
        manager.setSharedPreferencesName("user_prefs");

        addPreferencesFromResource(R.xml.character_settings);

    }

  }

}
```

For the sake of clarity, we will show just one of the `<PreferenceScreen>` files:

```
<PreferenceScreen xmlns:android="http://schemas.android.com/apk/res/android">

    <PreferenceCategory

        android:title="Username and Email">

    <EditTextPreference

        android:key="username"

        android:title="Username"

        android:summary="This is your ACME Service username"

        android:defaultValue="username01"

        android:dialogTitle="Enter your ACME Service username:" />

        <EditTextPreference

            android:key="email"

            android:title="Configure Email"

            android:summary="Enter your email address"

            android:defaultValue="your@email.com" />

    </PreferenceCategory>

</PreferenceScreen>
```

Now that we have implemented our application, we are able to see the differences in how the settings are displayed on single-pane and two-pane screens as shown in Figure 11.4 and Figure 11.5.

Tip

A headers list displayed on small-screen devices in single-pane mode can be cumbersome to navigate. Instead, it is usually better for smaller-screen devices to present the settings page directly, rather than showing the headers list grouping individual `PreferenceScreen` items.

Learning about Cloud Save for Android Applications

Google Play Game Services now includes a feature called Cloud Save. This service allows you to save user application state information to the cloud easily, much like a set of

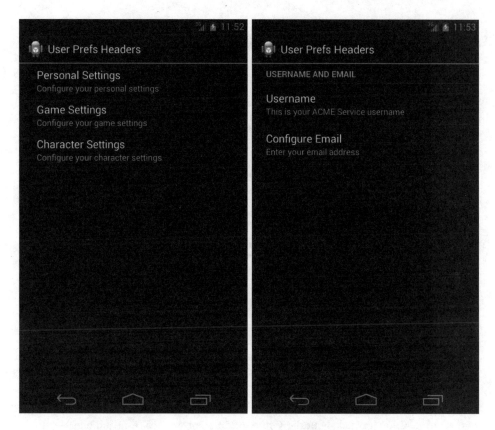

Figure 11.4 `Preference` headers showing on a small screen as a single-pane layout: the headers layout (left) and the settings layout (right).

preferences. The difference is that this data will persist across a user's different devices. For example, a game application might use Cloud Save to store a user's game level and sync the game level across the user's devices, so he or she doesn't have to start all over again when playing the same application on a different device. In the case that a user loses a device, or needs to reinstall the game for some reason, the proper information can be restored easily without any loss of data. You can think of Cloud Save as a set of remote preferences. Application developers can save a reasonable amount of data (currently 128KB) for their users with Cloud Save. Just to be clear, this service is not meant to replace a back-end data storage mechanism. To learn more about the Cloud Save service, see *https://developers.google.com/games/services/android/cloudsave*.

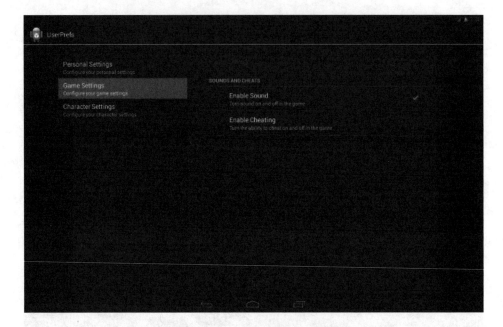

Figure 11.5 `Preference` headers and settings shown on a
large screen as a two-pane layout.

Summary

In this chapter, you learned about the variety of different ways to store and manage application data that are available on the Android platform. The method you use depends on what kind of data you need to store. With these skills, you are well on your way to leveraging one of the more powerful and unique features of Android. Use shared preferences to store simple application data, such as strings and numbers, in a persistent manner. You can also use the `PreferenceActivity` or `PreferenceFragment` class to simplify the creation of user preference screens within your application that use the standard look and feel of the platform on which your application is running. You learned how to use `Preference` headers for displaying your application preferences in either single-pane or two-pane layout. In addition, you learned that you can store and sync information such as preferences for your users with Cloud Save.

Quiz Questions

1. What are the different data types supported as preference setting values?

2. True or false: You use the `getPreferences()` method to retrieve the private preferences of a specific `Activity`.

3. What is the directory on the Android file system that stores application `Preference` XML files?

4. What are the common `Preference` attributes that most preferences should set?

5. What is the method call for accessing the `Preference` resource file from within a `PreferenceFragment`?

Exercises

1. Using information gathered from the Android documentation, write a simple code snippet demonstrating how you would configure a preference item to launch an `Activity` instead of a setting screen.

2. Using the Android documentation, determine the `SharedPreferences` method call for listening for preference changes.

3. Using the `SimpleUserPrefs` and `UserPrefsHeaders` applications, modify the code to only display the `<preference-headers>` list on large screens in two-pane mode.

References and More Information

Android SDK Reference regarding the `SharedPreferences` interface:
   http://d.android.com/reference/android/content/SharedPreferences.html
Android SDK Reference regarding the `SharedPreferences.Editor` interface:
   http://d.android.com/reference/android/content/SharedPreferences.Editor.html
Android SDK Reference regarding the `PreferenceActivity` class:
   http://d.android.com/reference/android/preference/PreferenceActivity.html
Android SDK Reference regarding the `PreferenceScreen` class:
   http://d.android.com/reference/android/preference/PreferenceScreen.html
Android SDK Reference regarding the `PreferenceCategory` class:
   http://d.android.com/reference/android/preference/PreferenceCategory.html
Android SDK Reference regarding the `Preference` class:
   http://d.android.com/reference/android/preference/Preference.html
Android SDK Reference regarding the `CheckBoxPreference` class:
   http://d.android.com/reference/android/preference/CheckBoxPreference.html
Android SDK Reference regarding the `EditTextPreference` class:
   http://d.android.com/reference/android/preference/EditTextPreference.html
Android SDK Reference regarding the `ListPreference` class:
   http://d.android.com/reference/android/preference/ListPreference.html

12

Working with Files and Directories

Android applications can store raw files on a device using a variety of methods. The Android SDK includes a number of helpful APIs for working with private application and cache files as well as for accessing external files on removable storage such as SD cards. Developers who need to store information safely and persistently will find the available file management APIs familiar and easy to use. In this chapter, we show you how to use the Android file system to read, write, and delete application data.

Working with Application Data on a Device

As discussed in the previous chapter, shared preferences provide a simple mechanism for storing simple application data persistently. However, many applications require a more robust solution that allows for any type of data to be stored and accessed in a persistent fashion. Some types of data that an application might want to store include the following:

- **Multimedia content such as images, sounds, video, and other complex information:** These types of data structures are not supported as shared preferences. You may, however, store a shared preference that includes the file path or URI to the multimedia and store the multimedia on the device file system or download it just when needed.

- **Content downloaded from a network:** As mobile devices, Android devices are not guaranteed to have persistent network connections. Ideally, an application will download content from the network once and keep it as long as necessary. Sometimes data should be kept indefinitely, whereas other circumstances simply require data to be cached for a certain amount of time.

- **Complex content generated by the application:** Android devices function under stricter memory and storage constraints than desktop computers and servers do. Therefore, if your application has taken a long time to process data and come up with a result, that result should be stored for reuse, as opposed to re-creating it on demand.

Android applications can create and use directories and files to store their data in a variety of ways. The most common ways include the following:

- Storing private application data under the application directory
- Caching data under the application's cache directory
- Storing shared application data on external storage devices or shared device directory areas

Note

You can use `Dalvik Debug Monitor Service` (DDMS) to copy files to and from a device. For more information about using DDMS and the `File Explorer`, please see Appendix C, "Quick-Start Guide: Android DDMS."

Practicing Good File Management

You should follow a number of best practices when working with files on the Android file system. Here are a few of the most important ones:

- Anytime you read or write data to disk, you are performing intensive blocking operations and using valuable device resources. Therefore, in most cases, file access functionality of your applications should not be performed on the main UI thread of the application. Instead, these operations should be handled asynchronously using threads, `AsyncTask` objects, or other asynchronous methods. Even working with small files can slow down the UI thread due to the nature of the underlying file system and hardware.
- Android devices have limited storage capacity. Therefore, store only what you need to store, and clean up old data when it is no longer needed to free up space on the device. Use external storage whenever it is appropriate to give the user more flexibility.
- Be a good citizen: be sure to check for availability of resources such as disk space and external storage opportunities prior to using them and causing errors or crashes. Also, don't forget to set appropriate file permissions for new files, and to release resources when you're not using them (in other words, if you open them, close them, and so on).
- Implement efficient file access algorithms for reading, writing, and parsing file contents. Use the many profiling tools available as part of the Android SDK to identify and improve the performance of your code. A good place to start is with the `StrictMode` API (`android.os.StrictMode`).
- If the data the application needs to store is well structured, you may want to consider using a SQLite database to store application data.
- Test your application on real devices. Different devices have different processor speeds. Do not assume that because your application runs smoothly on the emulator

it will run as such on real devices. If you're using external storage, test when external storage is not available.

Let's explore how file management is achieved on the Android platform.

Understanding Android File Permissions

Remember from Chapter 1, "Introducing Android," that each Android application is its own user on the underlying Linux operating system. It has its own application directory and files. Files created in the application's directory are private to that application by default.

Files can be created on the Android file system with different permissions. These permissions specify how a file is accessed. Permission modes are most commonly used when creating files. These permission modes are defined in the Context class (`android .content.Context`):

- `MODE_PRIVATE` (the default) is used to create a file that can be accessed only by the "owner" application itself. From a Linux perspective, this means the specific user identifier. The constant value of `MODE_PRIVATE` is 0, so you may see this used in legacy code.
- `MODE_APPEND` is used to append data to the end of an existing file. The constant value of `MODE_APPEND` is `32768`.

Warning

Up until API Level 17, `MODE_WORLD_READABLE` and `MODE_WORLD_WRITEABLE` constants were viable options for exposing data to other applications, but they have now been deprecated. Using these constants in your applications may present security vulnerabilities when exposing data to other applications. Exposing your application's data using these two file permission settings is now discouraged. The new and recommended approach is to use API components specifically designed for exposing application data for reading and writing by others, which include using the `Service`, `ContentProvider`, and/or `BroadcastReceiver` APIs.

An application does not need any special Android manifest file permissions to access its own private file system area. However, in order for your application to access external storage, it will need to register for the `WRITE_EXTERNAL_STORAGE` permission.

Working with Files and Directories

Within the Android SDK, you can also find a variety of standard Java file utility classes (such as `java.io`) for handling different types of files, such as text files, binary files, and XML files. In Chapter 6, "Managing Application Resources," you learned that Android applications can also include raw and XML files as resources. Retrieving the file handle to a resource file is performed slightly differently from accessing files on the device file system, but once you have a file handle, either method allows you to perform read operations and the like in the same fashion. After all, a file is a file.

Clearly, Android application file resources are part of the application package and are therefore accessible only to the application itself. But what about file system files? Android application files are stored in a standard directory hierarchy on the Android file system.

Generally speaking, applications access the Android device file system using methods within the Context class (android.content.Context). The application, or any Activity class, can use the application Context to access its private application file directory or cache directory. From there, you can add, remove, and access files associated with your application. By default, these files are private to the application and cannot be accessed by other applications or by the user.

Tip

Many of the code examples provided in this section are taken from the SimpleFiles and FileStreamOfConsciousness applications. The SimpleFiles application demonstrates basic file and directory operations; it has no user interface (just LogCat output). The FileStreamOfConsciousness application demonstrates how to log strings to a file as a chat stream; this application is multithreaded. The source code for these applications is provided for download on the book's website.

Exploring with the Android Application Directories

Android application data is stored on the Android file system in the following top-level directory:

```
/data/data/<package name>/
```

Several default subdirectories are created for storing databases, preferences, and files as necessary. The actual location of these directories varies by device. You can also create other custom directories as needed. All file operations begin by interacting with the application Context object. Table 12.1 lists some important methods available for application file management. You can use all the standard java.io package utilities to work with FileStream objects and such.

Creating and Writing to Files in the Default Application Directory

Android applications that require only the occasional file to be created should rely upon the helpful Context class method called openFileOutput(). Use this method to create files in the default location under the application data directory:

```
/data/data/<package name>/files/
```

For example, the following code snippet creates and opens a file called Filename.txt. We write a single line of text to the file and then close the file:

```
import java.io.FileOutputStream;

...

FileOutputStream fos;
```

Table 12.1 Important **android.content.Context** File Management Methods

Method	Purpose
Context.deleteFile()	Deletes a private application file by name. Note: You can also use the File class methods.
Context.fileList()	Gets a list of all files in the /files subdirectory.
Context.getCacheDir()	Retrieves the application /cache subdirectory.
Context.getDir()	Creates or retrieves an application subdirectory by name.
Context.getExternalCacheDir()	Retrieves the /cache subdirectory on the external file system (API Level 8).
Context.getExternalFilesDir()	Retrieves the /files subdirectory on the external file system (API Level 8).
Context.getFilesDir()	Retrieves the application /files subdirectory.
Context.getFileStreamPath()	Returns the absolute file path to the application /files subdirectory.
Context.openFileInput()	Opens a private application file for reading.
Context.openFileOutput()	Opens a private application file for writing.

```
String strFileContents = "Some text to write to the file.";
fos = openFileOutput("Filename.txt", MODE_PRIVATE);
fos.write(strFileContents.getBytes());
fos.close();
```

We can append data to the file by opening it with the mode set to MODE_APPEND:

```
import java.io.FileOutputStream;
...
FileOutputStream fos;
String strFileContents = "More text to write to the file.";
fos = openFileOutput("Filename.txt", MODE_APPEND);
fos.write(strFileContents.getBytes());
fos.close();
```

The file we created has the following path on the Android file system:

```
/data/data/<package name>/files/Filename.txt
```

Figure 12.1 shows a screen capture of an Activity that is configured to collect text input from a user, and then writes the information to a text file when Send is clicked.

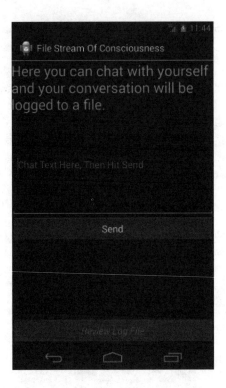

Figure 12.1   A screen capture of an `Activity`
that is capable of writing to a text file.

Reading from Files in the Default Application Directory

Again we have a shortcut for reading files stored in the default `/files` subdirectory. The following code snippet opens a file called `Filename.txt` for read operations:

```
import java.io.FileInputStream;

...

String strFileName = "Filename.txt";

FileInputStream fis = openFileInput(strFileName);
```

Figure 12.2 shows a screen capture of an `Activity` that is configured to read the information from a text file upon launching of the `Activity`.

Reading Raw Files Byte by Byte

You handle file-reading and file-writing operations using standard Java methods. The `java.io.InputStreamReader` and `java.io.BufferedReader` are used for reading bytes

Figure 12.2   A screen capture of an `Activity` reading from
a text file and displaying the contents.

and characters from different types of primitive file types. Here's a simple example of how
to read a text file, line by line, and store it in a `StringBuffer`:

```
FileInputStream fis = openFileInput(filename);

StringBuffer sBuffer = new StringBuffer();

BufferedReader dataIO = new BufferedReader (new InputStreamReader(fis));

String strLine = null;

while ((strLine = dataIO.readLine()) != null) {
    sBuffer.append(strLine + "\n");
}

dataIO.close();
fis.close();
```

Table 12.2 **Important XML Utilities**

Package or Class	Purpose
`android.sax.*`	Framework to write standard SAX handlers
`android.util.Xml`	XML utilities, including the `XMLPullParser` creator
`org.xml.sax.*`	Core SAX functionality (project: *http://www.saxproject.org*)
`javax.xml.*`	SAX and limited DOM, Level 2 Core support
`org.w3c.dom`	Interfaces for DOM, Level 2 Core
`org.xmlpull.*`	`XmlPullParser` and `XMLSerializer` interfaces as well as a SAX2 Driver class (project: *http://xmlpull.org*)

Reading XML Files

The Android SDK includes several utilities for working with XML files, including SAX, an XML Pull Parser, and limited DOM, Level 2 Core support. Table 12.2 lists the packages helpful for XML parsing on the Android platform.

Your XML parsing implementation will depend on which parser you choose to use. Back in Chapter 6, "Managing Application Resources," we discussed including raw XML resource files in your application package. Here is a simple example of how to load an XML resource file and parse it using an `XmlPullParser`.

The XML resource file contents, as defined in the `/res/xml/my_pets.xml` file, are as follows:

```
<?xml version="1.0" encoding="UTF-8"?>

<!-- Our pet list -->

<pets>

    <pet type="Bunny" name="Bit"/>

    <pet type="Bunny" name="Nibble"/>

    <pet type="Bunny" name="Stack"/>

    <pet type="Bunny" name="Queue"/>

    <pet type="Bunny" name="Heap"/>

    <pet type="Bunny" name="Null"/>

    <pet type="Fish" name="Nigiri"/>

    <pet type="Fish" name="Sashimi II"/>

    <pet type="Lovebird" name="Kiwi"/>

</pets>
```

The following code illustrates how to parse the preceding XML using a special pull parser designed for XML resource files:

```
XmlResourceParser myPets = getResources().getXml(R.xml.my_pets);

int eventType = -1;

while (eventType != XmlResourceParser.END_DOCUMENT) {
    if(eventType == XmlResourceParser.START_DOCUMENT) {
        Log.d(DEBUG_TAG, "Document Start");
    } else if(eventType == XmlResourceParser.START_TAG) {
        String strName = myPets.getName();
        if(strName.equals("pet")) {
            Log.d(DEBUG_TAG, "Found a PET");
            Log.d(DEBUG_TAG,
                "Name: "+myPets.getAttributeValue(null, "name"));
            Log.d(DEBUG_TAG,
                "Species: "+myPets.
                getAttributeValue(null, "type"));
        }
    }
    eventType = myPets.next();
}
Log.d(DEBUG_TAG, "Document End");
```

Tip

You can review the complete implementation of this parser in the `ResourceRoundup` project found in the Chapter 6 code directory.

Working with Other Directories and Files on the Android File System

Using `Context.openFileOutput()` and `Context.openFileInput()` method calls is great if you have a few files and you want them stored in the application's private `/files` sub-directory, but if you have more sophisticated file management needs, you need to set up your own directory structure. To do this, you must interact with the Android file system using the standard `java.io.File` class methods.

The following code retrieves the `File` object for the `/files` application subdirectory and retrieves a list of all filenames in that directory:

```
import java.io.File;

...

File pathForAppFiles = getFilesDir();

String[] fileList = pathForAppFiles.list();
```

Here is a more generic method to create a file on the file system. This method works anywhere on the Android file system you have permission to access, not just the `/files` subdirectory:

```
import java.io.File;

import java.io.FileOutputStream;

...

File fileDir = getFilesDir();

String strNewFileName = "myFile.dat";

String strFileContents = "Some data for our file";

File newFile = new File(fileDir, strNewFileName);

newFile.createNewFile();

FileOutputStream fo =

    new FileOutputStream(newFile.getAbsolutePath());

fo.write(strFileContents.getBytes());

fo.close();
```

You can use `File` objects to manage files within a desired directory and create subdirectories. For example, you might want to store "track" files within "album" directories. Or perhaps you want to create a file in a directory other than the default. Let's say you want to cache some data to speed up your application's performance and how often it accesses the network. In this instance, you might want to create a cache file. There is also a special application directory for storing cache files. Cache files are stored in the following location on the Android file system, retrievable with a call to the `getCacheDir()` method:

```
/data/data/<package name>/cache/
```

The external cache directory, found via a call to the `getExternalCacheDir()` method, is not treated the same in that files are not automatically removed from it.

Warning

Applications are responsible for managing their own cache directory and keeping it to a reasonable size (1MB is commonly recommended). The system places no limit on the number of files in a cache directory. The Android file system deletes cache files from the internal cache directory (`getCacheDir()`) as needed when internal storage space is low, or when the user uninstalls the application.

The following code gets a `File` object for the `/cache` application subdirectory, creates a new file in that specific directory, writes some data to the file, closes the file, and then deletes it:

```
File pathCacheDir = getCacheDir();
String strCacheFileName = "myCacheFile.cache";
String strFileContents = "Some data for our file";

File newCacheFile = new File(pathCacheDir, strCacheFileName);
newCacheFile.createNewFile();

FileOutputStream foCache =
    new FileOutputStream(newCacheFile.getAbsolutePath());
foCache.write(strFileContents.getBytes());
foCache.close();

newCacheFile.delete();
```

Creating and Writing Files to External Storage

Applications should store large amounts of data on external storage (using the SD card) rather than on limited internal storage. You can access external file storage, such as the SD card, from within your application as well. This is a little trickier than working within the confines of the application directory, as SD cards are removable, and so you need to check to see if the storage is mounted before use.

Tip

You can monitor file and directory activity on the Android file system using the `FileObserver` class (`android.os.FileObserver`). You can monitor storage capacity using the `StatFs` class (`android.os.StatFs`).

You can access external storage on the device using the `Environment` class (`android.os.Environment`). Begin by using the `getExternalStorageState()` method to check the mount status of external storage. You can store private application files on external storage, or you can store public shared files such as media. If you want to store private application files, use the getExternalFilesDir() method of the Context class because these files will be cleaned up if the application is uninstalled later. The external cache is accessed using the similar getExternalCacheDir() method. However, if you want to store shared files such as pictures, movies, music, ringtones, or podcasts on external storage, you can use the getExternalStoragePublicDirectory() method of the Environment class to get the top-level directory used to store a specific file type.

Tip

Applications that use external storage are best tested on real hardware, as opposed to the emulator. You'll want to make sure you thoroughly test your application with various external storage states, including mounted, unmounted, and read-only modes. Each device may have different physical paths, so directory names should not be hard-coded.

Summary

There are a variety of ways to store and manage application data on the Android platform. The method you use depends on what kind of data you need to store. Applications have access to the underlying Android file system, where they can store their own private files, as well as limited access to the file system at large. It is important to follow best practices, such as performing disk operations asynchronously, when working on the Android file system, because mobile devices have limited storage and computing power.

Quiz Questions

1. What are the constant values of the Android file permission modes of MODE_PRIVATE and MODE_APPEND?

2. True or false: Storing files using the MODE_WORLD_READABLE and MODE_WORLD_WRITEABLE permissions is the new recommended way for exposing your application's data to others.

3. What is the top-level directory for storing Android application data on the Android file system?

4. What is the name of the Context class method call for creating files under the application data directory?

5. What is the name of the Context class method call for retrieving the external cache directory?

6. True or false: The android.os.Environment.getExternalStorageMountStatus() method is used for determining the mount state of a device's external storage.

Exercises

1. Using the Android documentation, describe how to hide media files saved to a public external file directory to prevent Android's media scanner from including the media files in other applications.

2. Create an application that is able to display the result of whether the SD card is available or not prior to accessing the external storage system.

3. Create an application for storing image files to the Pictures/ directory of external storage.

References and More Information

Android SDK Reference regarding the java.io package:
   http://d.android.com/reference/java/io/package-summary.html
Android SDK Reference regarding the Context interface:
   http://d.android.com/reference/android/content/Context.html
Android SDK Reference regarding the File class:
   http://d.android.com/reference/java/io/File.html
Android SDK Reference regarding the Environment class:
   http://d.android.com/reference/android/os/Environment.html
Android API Guides: "Using the Internal Storage":
   http://d.android.com/guide/topics/data/data-storage.html#filesInternal
Android API Guides: "Using the External Storage":
   http://d.android.com/guide/topics/data/data-storage.html#filesExternal

13
Leveraging Content Providers

Applications can access data within other applications on the Android system through content provider interfaces and expose internal application data to other applications by becoming a content provider. Content providers are the way applications can access user information, including contact data, images, audio and video on the device, and much more. In this chapter, we take a look at some of the content providers available on the Android platform and what you can do with them.

Warning

Always run content provider code on test devices, not your personal devices. It is very easy to accidentally wipe out all of the Contacts database, your browser bookmarks, or other types of data on your devices. Consider this fair warning, because we discuss operations such as how to query (generally safe) and modify (not so safe) various types of device data in this chapter.

Exploring Android's Content Providers

Android devices ship with a number of built-in applications, many of which expose their data as content providers. Your application can access content provider data from a variety of sources. You can find the content providers included with Android in the package `android.provider`. Table 13.1 lists some useful content providers in this package.

Now let's look at some of the most popular and official content providers in more detail.

Tip

The code examples provided in this chapter use the `CursorLoader` class for performing cursor queries on a background thread using the `loadInBackground()` method. This prevents your application from blocking on the UI thread when performing cursor queries. This approach has replaced the `Activity` class method `managedQuery()` for performing cursor queries that block the UI thread and is officially deprecated. If you are targeting devices earlier than Honeycomb, you'll want to import the `CursorLoader` class from the Android Support Package using `android.support.v4.content.CursorLoader` rather than importing the class from `android.content.CursorLoader`.

Table 13.1 **Useful Built-in Content Providers**

Provider	Purpose
AlarmClock	Set alarms within the Alarm Clock application (API Level 9)
Browser	Browser history and bookmarks
CalendarContract	Calendar and event information (API Level 14)
CallLog	Sent and received calls
ContactsContract	Phone contact database or phonebook (API Level 5)
MediaStore	Audio/visual data on the phone and external storage
SearchRecentSuggestions	Search suggestions appropriate to the application
Settings	System-wide device settings and preferences
UserDictionary	A dictionary of user-defined words for use with predictive text input (API Level 3)
VoicemailContract	A single unified place for the user to manage voicemail content from different sources (API Level 14)

Using the **MediaStore** Content Provider

You can use the MediaStore content provider to access media on the phone and on external storage devices. The primary types of media you can access are audio, images, and video. You can access these different types of media through their respective content provider classes under android.provider.MediaStore.

Most of the MediaStore classes allow full interaction with the data. You can retrieve, add, and delete media files from the device. There are also a handful of helper classes that define the most common data columns that can be requested.

Table 13.2 lists some commonly used classes you can find under android.provider .MediaStore.

> **Tip**
>
> Many of the code examples provided in this section are taken from the SimpleContent Provider application. The source code for the SimpleContentProvider application is provided for download on the book's website.

The following code demonstrates how to request data from a content provider. A query is made to the MediaStore to retrieve the titles of all the audio files on the SD card of the handset and their respective durations. This code requires that you load some audio files onto the virtual SD card in the emulator.

```
String[] requestedColumns = {
    MediaStore.Audio.Media.TITLE,
    MediaStore.Audio.Media.DURATION
};
```

Table 13.2 **Common MediaStore Classes**

Class	Purpose
Audio.Albums	Manages audio files organized by album
Audio.Artists	Manages audio files organized by artist
Audio.Genres	Manages audio files belonging to a particular genre
Audio.Media	Manages audio files on the device
Audio.Playlists	Manages audio files that are part of a particular playlist
Files	Lists all media files (API Level 11)
Images.Media	Manages image files on the device
Images.Thumbnails	Retrieves thumbnails for the image files
Video.Media	Manages video files on the device
Video.Thumbnails	Retrieves thumbnails for the video files

```
CursorLoader loader = new CursorLoader(this,

                    MediaStore.Audio.Media.EXTERNAL_CONTENT_URI,

                    requestedColumns, null, null, null);

Cursor cur = loader.loadInBackground();

Log.d(DEBUG_TAG, "Audio files: " + cur.getCount());

Log.d(DEBUG_TAG, "Columns: " + cur.getColumnCount());

int name = cur.getColumnIndex(MediaStore.Audio.Media.TITLE);

int length = cur.getColumnIndex(MediaStore.Audio.Media.DURATION);

cur.moveToFirst();

while (!cur.isAfterLast()) {

    Log.d(DEBUG_TAG, "Title" + cur.getString(name));

    Log.d(DEBUG_TAG, "Length: " +

        cur.getInt(length) / 1000 + " seconds");

    cur.moveToNext();

}
```

The MediaStore.Audio.Media class has predefined strings for every data field (or column) exposed by the content provider. You can limit the audio file data fields requested as part of the query by defining a String array with the column names required. In this case, we limit the results to only the track title and the duration of each audio file.

We then use a CursorLoader and access the cursor using a loadInBackground() method call. The first parameter of the CursorLoader is the application context. The second parameter is the predefined URI of the content provider you want to query. The third parameter is the list of columns to return (audio file titles and durations). The fourth and fifth parameters control any selection-filtering arguments, and the sixth parameter provides a sort method for the results. We leave these `null` because we want all audio files at this location. By using the `loadInBackground()` method, we get a `Cursor` as a result. We then examine our `Cursor` for the results.

Using the `CallLog` Content Provider

Android provides a content provider to access the call log on the handset via the class `android.provider.CallLog`. At first glance, the `CallLog` might not seem to be a useful provider for developers, but it has some nifty features. You can use the `CallLog` to filter recently dialed calls, received calls, and missed calls. The date and duration of each call are logged and tied back to the Contacts application for caller identification purposes.

The `CallLog` is a useful content provider for customer relationship management (CRM) applications. The user can also tag specific phone numbers with custom labels within the Contacts application.

To demonstrate how the `CallLog` content provider works, let's look at a hypothetical situation where we want to generate a report of all calls to a number with the custom label `HourlyClient123`. Android allows for custom labels on these numbers, which we leverage for this example:

```
String[] requestedColumns = {

    CallLog.Calls.CACHED_NUMBER_LABEL,

    CallLog.Calls.DURATION

};

CursorLoader loader = new CursorLoader(this,

        CallLog.Calls.CONTENT_URI,

        requestedColumns,

        CallLog.Calls.CACHED_NUMBER_LABEL + " = ?",

        new String[] { "HourlyClient123" },

        null);

Cursor calls = loader.loadInBackground();

Log.d(DEBUG_TAG, "Call count: " + calls.getCount());

int durIdx = calls.getColumnIndex(CallLog.Calls.DURATION);

int totalDuration = 0;

calls.moveToFirst();

while (!calls.isAfterLast()) {
```

```
    Log.d(DEBUG_TAG, "Duration: " + calls.getInt(durIdx));

    totalDuration += calls.getInt(durIdx);

    calls.moveToNext();

}

Log.d(DEBUG_TAG, "HourlyClient123 Total Call Duration: " + totalDuration);
```

This code is similar to the code shown for the `MediaStore` audio files. Again, we start with listing our requested columns: the call label and the duration of the call. This time, however, we don't want to get every call in the log, only those with a label of `HourlyClient123`. To filter the results of the query to this specific label, it is necessary to specify the fourth and fifth parameters of the `CursorLoader`. Together, these two parameters are equivalent to a database `WHERE` clause. The fourth parameter specifies the format of the `WHERE` clause with the column name, with selection parameters (shown as ?) for each selection argument value. The fifth parameter, the `String` array, provides the values to substitute for each of the selection arguments (?) in order as you would do for a simple SQLite database query.

We use the same method to iterate the records of the `Cursor` and add up all the call durations.

Accessing Content Providers That Require Permissions

Your application needs a special permission to access the information provided by the `CallLog` content provider. You can declare the `<uses-permission>` tag using the Android IDE Wizard, or you can add the following to your `AndroidManifest.xml` file:

```
<uses-permission

    android:name="android.permission.READ_CONTACTS">

</uses-permission>
```

Although it's a tad confusing, there is no `CallLog` provider permission. Instead, applications that access the `CallLog` use the `READ_CONTACTS` permission. Although the values are cached within this content provider, the data is similar to what you might find in the contacts provider.

Tip

You can find all available permissions in the class `android.Manifest.permission`.

Using the `Browser` Content Provider

Another useful built-in content provider is the `Browser`. The `Browser` content provider exposes the user's browser site history and bookmarked websites. You access this content provider via the `android.provider.Browser` class. As with the `CallLog` class, you can use the information provided by the `Browser` content provider to generate statistics and to provide cross-application functionality. You might use the `Browser` content provider to add a bookmark for your application support website.

In this example, we query the `Browser` content provider to find the top five most frequently visited bookmarked sites.

```
String[] requestedColumns = {
    Browser.BookmarkColumns.TITLE,
    Browser.BookmarkColumns.VISITS,
    Browser.BookmarkColumns.BOOKMARK
};

CursorLoader loader = new CursorLoader(this,
            Browser.BOOKMARKS_URI,
            requestedColumns,
            Browser.BookmarkColumns.BOOKMARK + "=1",
            null,
            Browser.BookmarkColumns.VISITS + " DESC limit 5");
Cursor faves = loader.loadInBackground();

Log.d(DEBUG_TAG, "Bookmarks count: " + faves.getCount());

int titleIdx = faves.getColumnIndex(Browser.BookmarkColumns.TITLE);
int visitsIdx = faves.getColumnIndex(Browser.BookmarkColumns.VISITS);
int bmIdx = faves.getColumnIndex(Browser.BookmarkColumns.BOOKMARK);

faves.moveToFirst();

while (!faves.isAfterLast()) {
    Log.d("SimpleBookmarks", faves.getString(titleIdx) + " visited "
        + faves.getInt(visitsIdx) + " times : "
        + (faves.getInt(bmIdx) != 0 ? "true" : "false"));
    faves.moveToNext();
}
```

Again, the requested columns are defined, the query is made, and the cursor iterates through the results.

Note that the `CursorLoader` has become substantially more complex. Let's take a look at the parameters to this method in more detail. The second parameter, `Browser` `.BOOKMARKS_URI`, is a URI for all browser history, not only the bookmarked items. The third parameter defines the requested columns for the query results. The fourth parameter specifies that the bookmark property must be `true`. This parameter is needed in order to filter within the query. Now the results are only browser history entries that have been bookmarked. The fifth parameter, selection arguments, is used only when replacement values are used. It is not used in this case, so the value is set to null. Last, the sixth parameter specifies an order for the results (most visited in descending order). Retrieving browser history information requires setting the READ_HISTORY_BOOKMARKS permission.

Tip

Notice that we also tacked a LIMIT statement onto the sixth parameter of CursorLoader. Although this is not specifically documented, we've found limiting the query results in this way works well and might even improve application performance in some situations where the query results are lengthy. Keep in mind that if the internal implementation of a content provider verified that the last parameter was only a valid ORDER BY clause, this may not always work. We are also taking advantage of the fact that most content providers are backed by SQLite. This need not be the case.

Using the `CalendarContract` Content Provider

Introduced officially in Android 4.0 (API Level 14), the CalendarContract provider allows you to manage and interact with the user's calendar data on the device. You can use this content provider to create one-time and recurring events in a user's calendar, set reminders, and more, provided the device user has appropriately configured calendar accounts (for example, Microsoft Exchange). In addition to the fully featured content provider, you can also quickly trigger a new event to be added to the user's calendar using an Intent, like this:

```
Intent calIntent = new Intent(Intent.ACTION_INSERT);

calIntent.setData(CalendarContract.Events.CONTENT_URI);

calIntent.putExtra(CalendarContract.Events.TITLE,
                "My Winter Holiday Party");

calIntent.putExtra(CalendarContract.Events.EVENT_LOCATION,
                "My Ski Cabin at Tahoe");

calIntent.putExtra(CalendarContract.Events.DESCRIPTION,
                "Hot chocolate, eggnog and sledding.");

startActivity(calIntent);
```

Here, we seed the calendar event title, location, and description using the appropriate intent Extras. These fields will be set in a form that displays for the user, who will then need to confirm the event in the Calendar app. To learn more about the Calendar Contract provider, see *http://d.android.com/guide/topics/providers/calendar-provider.html* and *http://d.android.com/reference/android/provider/CalendarContract.html*.

Using the `UserDictionary` Content Provider

Another useful content provider is the UserDictionary provider. You can use this content provider for predictive text input on text fields and other user input mechanisms.

Individual words stored in the dictionary are weighted by frequency and organized by locale. You can use the `addWord()` method within the `UserDictionary.Words` class to add words to the custom user dictionary.

Using the `VoicemailContract` Content Provider

The `VoicemailContract` content provider was introduced in API Level 14. You can use this content provider to add new voicemail content to the shared provider so that all voicemail content is accessible in one place. Application permissions, such as the `ADD_VOICEMAIL` permission, are necessary for accessing this provider. For more information, see the Android SDK documentation for the `VoicemailContract` class at *http:// d.android.com/reference/android/provider/VoicemailContract.html*.

Using the `Settings` Content Provider

Another useful content provider is the `Settings` provider. You can use this content provider to access the device settings and user preferences. Settings are organized much as they are in the Settings application—by category. You can find information about the `Settings` content provider in the `android.provider.Settings` class. If your application needs to modify system settings, you'll need to register the `WRITE_SETTINGS` or `WRITE_SECURE_SETTINGS` permissions in your application's Android manifest file.

Introducing the `ContactsContract` Content Providers

The Contacts database is one of the most commonly used applications on Android devices. People always want contact information handy for contacting friends, family, co-workers, and clients. Additionally, most devices show the identity of a contact based on the Contacts application, including nicknames, photos, or icons.

Android provides a built-in Contacts application, and the contact data is exposed to other Android applications using the content provider interface. As an application developer, this means you can leverage the user's contact data within your application for a more robust user experience.

The content provider for accessing user contacts was originally called `Contacts`. Android 2.0 (API Level 5) introduced an enhanced contacts management content provider class to manage the data available from the user's contacts. This provider, called `ContactsContract`, includes a subclass called `ContactsContract.Contacts`. This is the preferred contacts content provider moving forward.

Your application needs special permission to access the private user information provided by the `ContactsContract` content provider. You must declare a `<uses-permission>` tag using the permission `READ_CONTACTS` to read this information. If your application modifies the Contacts database, you'll need the `WRITE_CONTACTS` permission as well.

Tip

Some of the code examples provided in this section are taken from the `SimpleContacts` application. The source code for the `SimpleContacts` application is provided for download on the book's website.

Working with the **ContactsContract** Content Provider

The more recent contacts content provider, `ContactsContract.Contacts`, introduced in API Level 5 (Android 2.0), provides a robust contact content provider that suits the more robust Contacts application that has evolved along with the Android platform.

Tip

The `ContactsContract` content provider was further enhanced in Android 4.0 (Ice Cream Sandwich, API Level 14) to incorporate substantive social networking features. Some of the new features include managing the device user's identity, favorite methods of communication with specific contacts, as well as a new `INVITE_CONTACT` Intent type for applications to use to make contact connections. The device user's personal profile is accessible through the `ContactsContract.Profile` class (which requires the `READ_PROFILE` application permission). The device user's preferred methods of communicating with specific contacts can be accessed through the new `ContactsContract.DataUsageFeedback` class. For more information, see the Android SDK documentation for the `android.provider.ContactsContract` class.

The following code utilizes the `ContactsContract` provider:

```
String[] requestedColumns = {
    ContactsContract.Contacts.DISPLAY_NAME,
    ContactsContract.CommonDataKinds.Phone.NUMBER,
};

CursorLoader loader = new CursorLoader(this,
            ContactsContract.Data.CONTENT_URI,
            requestedColumns, null, null, "display_name desc limit 1");
Cursor contacts = loader.loadInBackground();

int recordCount = contacts.getCount();
Log.d(DEBUG_TAG, "Contacts count: " + recordCount);

if (recordCount > 0) {
    int nameIdx = contacts
        .getColumnIndex(ContactsContract.Contacts.DISPLAY_NAME);
    int phoneIdx = contacts
        .getColumnIndex(ContactsContract.CommonDataKinds.Phone.NUMBER);

    contacts.moveToFirst();
    Log.d(DEBUG_TAG, "Name: " + contacts.getString(nameIdx));
    Log.d(DEBUG_TAG, "Phone: " + contacts.getString(phoneIdx));
}
```

Here, we can see that the code is using a query URI provided from the `Contacts Contract` provider called `ContactsContract.Data.CONTENT_URI`. Second, you're

Table 13.3 **Commonly Used `ContactsContract` Data Column Classes**

Class	Purpose
`ContactsContract.CommonDataKinds`	Defines a number of frequently used contact columns such as email, nickname, phone, and photo.
`ContactsContract.Contacts`	Defines the consolidated data associated with a contact. Some aggregation may be performed.
`ContactsContract.Data`	Defines the raw data associated with a single contact.
`ContactsContract.PhoneLookup`	Defines the phone columns and can be used to quickly look up a phone number for caller identification purposes.
`ContactsContract.StatusUpdates`	Defines the social networking columns and can be used to check the instant messaging status of a contact.

requesting different column names. The column names of the `ContactsContract` provider are organized more thoroughly to allow for far more dynamic contact configurations. This can make your queries slightly more complex. Luckily, the `ContactsContract.CommonDataKinds` class has a number of frequently used columns defined together. Table 13.3 shows some of the commonly used classes that can help you work with the `ContactsContract` content provider.

Tip

New additions have been made to the `ContactsContract` content provider in Android 4.3, providing the ability to query the contacts data for any changes. You now have the ability to determine the recently deleted contacts with `ContactsContract.DeletedContacts`. This is an extremely useful feature because prior to this addition, there was no standard way for an application to determine which contacts had been changed or deleted.

For more information on the `ContactsContract` provider, see the Android SDK documentation: *http://d.android.com/reference/android/provider/ContactsContract.html*.

Modifying Content Provider Data

Content providers are not only static sources of data. They can also be used to add, update, and delete data, if the content provider application has implemented this functionality. Your application must have the appropriate permissions (that is, `WRITE_CONTACTS` as opposed to `READ_CONTACTS`) to perform some of these actions. Let's use the `ContactsContract` content provider and give some examples of how to modify the Contacts database.

Adding Records

Using the ContactsContract content provider, we can, for example, add a new record to the Contacts database programmatically. The code that follows adds a new contact named Ian Droid with a phone number of 6505551212, as shown here:

```
ArrayList<ContentProviderOperation> ops = new
ArrayList<ContentProviderOperation>();

int contactIdx = ops.size();

ContentProviderOperation.Builder op =

ContentProviderOperation.newInsert(ContactsContract.RawContacts.CONTENT_URI);

op.withValue(ContactsContract.RawContacts.ACCOUNT_NAME, null);

op.withValue(ContactsContract.RawContacts.ACCOUNT_TYPE, null);

ops.add(op.build());

op = ContentProviderOperation.newInsert(ContactsContract.Data.CONTENT_URI);

op.withValue(ContactsContract.Data.MIMETYPE,
        ContactsContract.CommonDataKinds.StructuredName.CONTENT_ITEM_TYPE);

op.withValue(ContactsContract.CommonDataKinds.StructuredName.DISPLAY_NAME,
        "Ian Droid");

op.withValueBackReference(ContactsContract.Data.RAW_CONTACT_ID,
        contactIdx);

ops.add(op.build());

op = ContentProviderOperation.newInsert(ContactsContract.Data.CONTENT_URI);

op.withValue(ContactsContract.CommonDataKinds.Phone.NUMBER,
        "6505551212");

op.withValue(ContactsContract.CommonDataKinds.Phone.TYPE,
        ContactsContract.CommonDataKinds.Phone.TYPE_WORK);

op.withValue(ContactsContract.CommonDataKinds.Phone.MIMETYPE,
        ContactsContract.CommonDataKinds.Phone.CONTENT_ITEM_TYPE);

op.withValueBackReference(ContactsContract.Data.RAW_CONTACT_ID,
        contactIdx);

ops.add(op.build());

getContentResolver().applyBatch(ContactsContract.AUTHORITY, ops);
```

Here, we use the ContentProviderOperation class to create an ArrayList of operations to insert records into the Contacts database on the device. The first record we add with newInsert() is the ACCOUNT_NAME and ACCOUNT_TYPE of the contact. The second record we add with newInsert() is a name for the ContactsContract .CommonDataKinds.StructuredName.DISPLAY_NAME column. We need to create the contact with a name before we can assign information, such as phone numbers. Think of this as creating a row in a table that provides a one-to-many relationship to a phone number table. The third record we add with newInsert() is a phone number for the contact that we are adding to the Contacts database.

We insert the data in the database found at the ContactsContract.Data.CONTENT_URI path. We use a call to getContentResolver().applyBatch() to apply all three Content Provider operations at once using the ContentResolver associated with our Activity.

Tip

At this point, you might be wondering how the structure of the data can be determined. The best way is to thoroughly examine the documentation for the specific content provider with which you want to integrate your application.

Updating Records

Inserting data isn't the only change you can make. You can update one or more rows as well. The following block of code shows how to update data within a content provider. In this case, we update a phone number field for a specific contact.

```
String selection = ContactsContract.Data.DISPLAY_NAME + " = ? AND " +
        ContactsContract.Data.MIMETYPE + " = ? AND " +
        String.valueOf(ContactsContract.CommonDataKinds.Phone.TYPE) + " = ? ";

String[] selectionArgs = new String[] {
        "Ian Droid",
        ContactsContract.CommonDataKinds.Phone.CONTENT_ITEM_TYPE,
        String.valueOf(ContactsContract.CommonDataKinds.Phone.TYPE_WORK)
};

ArrayList<ContentProviderOperation> ops =
        new ArrayList<ContentProviderOperation>();

ContentProviderOperation.Builder op =
        ContentProviderOperation.newUpdate(ContactsContract.Data.CONTENT_URI);
op.withSelection(selection, selectionArgs);
op.withValue(ContactsContract.CommonDataKinds.Phone.NUMBER, "6501234567");
ops.add(op.build());

getContentResolver().applyBatch(ContactsContract.AUTHORITY, ops);
```

Again, we use the `ContentProviderOperation` class to create an `ArrayList` of operations to update a record in the Contacts database on the device—in this case, the phone number field previously given a `TYPE_WORK` attribute. This replaces any current phone number stored in the `NUMBER` field with a `TYPE_WORK` attribute currently stored with the contact. We add the `ContentProviderOperation` with the `newUpdate()` method and once again use `applyBatch()` on the `ContentResolver` class to complete our change. We can then confirm that only one row was updated.

Deleting Records

Now that you have cluttered up your Contacts application with sample user data, you might want to delete some of it. Deleting data is fairly straightforward. Another reminder: you should use these examples only on a test device, so you don't accidentally delete all of your contact data from your device.

Deleting All Records

The following code deletes all rows at the given URI. Keep in mind that you should execute operations like this with extreme care.

```
ArrayList<ContentProviderOperation> ops =
        new ArrayList<ContentProviderOperation>();

ContentProviderOperation.Builder op =
ContentProviderOperation.newDelete(ContactsContract.RawContacts.CONTENT_URI);
ops.add(op.build());

getContentResolver().applyBatch(ContactsContract.AUTHORITY, ops);
```

The `newDelete()` method deletes all rows at a given URI, which in this case includes all rows at the `RawContacts.CONTENT_URI` location (in other words, all contact entries).

Deleting Specific Records

Often you want to select specific rows to delete by adding selection filters to remove rows matching a particular pattern.

For example, the following `newDelete()` operation matches all contact records with the name `Ian Droid`, which we used when we created the contact previously in the chapter.

```
String selection = ContactsContract.Data.DISPLAY_NAME + " = ? ";
String[] selectionArgs = new String[] { "Ian Droid" };

ArrayList<ContentProviderOperation> ops =
        new ArrayList<ContentProviderOperation>();

ContentProviderOperation.Builder op =
```

```
ContentProviderOperation.newDelete(ContactsContract.RawContacts.CONTENT_URI);
op.withSelection(selection, selectionArgs);
ops.add(op.build());

getContentResolver().applyBatch(ContactsContract.AUTHORITY, ops);
```

Using Third-Party Content Providers

Any application can implement a content provider to share its information safely and securely with other applications on a device. Some applications use content providers only to share information internally—within their own brand, for example. Others publish the specifications for their providers so that other applications can integrate with them.

If you poke around in the Android source code, or run across a content provider you want to use, consider this: a number of other content providers are available on the Android platform, especially those used by some of the typically installed Google applications (Calendar, Messaging, and so on). Be aware, though, that using undocumented content providers, simply because you happen to know how they work or have reverse-engineered them, is generally not a good idea. Use of undocumented and non-public content providers can make your application unstable. This post on the Android Developers Blog makes a good case for why this sort of hacking should be discouraged in commercial applications: *http://android-developers.blogspot.com/2010/05/be-careful-with-content-providers.html*.

Summary

Your application can leverage the data available within other Android applications, if they expose that data as content providers. Content providers such as `MediaStore`, `Browser`, `CallLog`, and `ContactsContract` can be leveraged by other Android applications, resulting in a robust, immersive experience for users. Applications can also share data among themselves by becoming content providers. Becoming a content provider involves implementing a set of methods that manage how and what data you expose for use in other applications.

Quiz Questions

1. What is the name of the content provider for accessing media on the phone and on external storage devices?

2. True or false: The `MediaStore.Images.Thumbnails` class is for retrieving thumbnails for image files.

3. What permission is required for accessing information provided by the `CallLog` content provider?

4. True or false: The `READ_HISTORY` permission is required for accessing the browser history information of the `Browser` content provider.

5. What is the method call for adding words to the custom user dictionary of the UserDictionary provider?

6. True or false: The Contacts content provider was added in API Level 5.

Exercises

1. Using the Android documentation, determine all the tables associated with the ContactsContract content provider.

2. Create an application that is able to add words that a user enters into an EditText field to the UserDictionary content provider.

3. Create an application that is able to add an email address for a contact using the ContactsContract content provider. As we have said before, always run content provider code on test devices, not your personal devices.

References and More Information

Android SDK Reference regarding the android.provider package:
   http://d.android.com/reference/android/provider/package-summary.html
Android SDK Reference regarding the AlarmClock content provider:
   http://d.android.com/reference/android/provider/AlarmClock.html
Android SDK Reference regarding the Browser content provider:
   http://d.android.com/reference/android/provider/Browser.html
Android SDK Reference regarding the CallLog content provider:
   http://d.android.com/reference/android/provider/CallLog.html
Android SDK Reference regarding the Contacts content provider:
   http://d.android.com/reference/android/provider/Contacts.html
Android SDK Reference regarding the ContactsContract content provider:
   http://d.android.com/reference/android/provider/ContactsContract.html
Android SDK Reference regarding the MediaStore content provider:
   http://d.android.com/reference/android/provider/MediaStore.html
Android SDK Reference regarding the Settings content provider:
   http://d.android.com/reference/android/provider/Settings.html
Android SDK Reference regarding the SearchRecentSuggestions content provider:
   http://d.android.com/reference/android/provider/SearchRecentSuggestions.html
Android SDK Reference regarding the UserDictionary content provider:
   http://d.android.com/reference/android/provider/UserDictionary.html
Android API Guides: "Content Providers":
   http://d.android.com/guide/topics/providers/content-providers.html

14
Designing Compatible Applications

There are now hundreds of different Android devices on the market worldwide—from smartphones to tablets and televisions. In this chapter, you learn how to design and develop Android applications that are compatible with a variety of devices despite differences in screen size, hardware, or platform version. We offer numerous tips for designing and developing your application to be compatible with many different devices. Finally, you learn how to internationalize your applications for foreign markets.

Maximizing Application Compatibility

With dozens of manufacturers developing Android devices, we've seen an explosion of different device models—each with its own market differentiators and unique characteristics. Users now have choices, but these choices come at a cost. This proliferation of devices has led to what some developers call *fragmentation* and others call *compatibility issues*. Terminology aside, it has become a challenging task to develop Android applications that support a broad range of devices. Developers must contend with devices that support different platform versions (see Figure 14.1), hardware configurations (including optional hardware features) such as OpenGL versions (see Figure 14.2), and variations in screen sizes and densities (see Figure 14.3). The list of device differentiators is lengthy, and it grows with each new device.

Although fragmentation makes the Android app developer's life more complicated, it's still possible to develop for and support a variety of devices—even all devices—within a single application. When it comes to maximizing compatibility, you'll always want to use the following strategies:

- Whenever possible, choose the development option that is supported by the widest variety of devices. In many cases, you can detect device differences at runtime and provide different code paths to support different configurations. Just make sure you inform your quality assurance team of this sort of application logic so it can be understood and thoroughly tested.

- Whenever a development decision limits the compatibility of your application (for example, using an API that was introduced in a later API level or introducing a

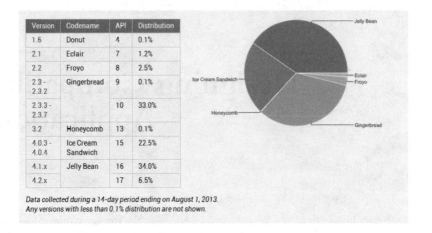

Version	Codename	API	Distribution
1.6	Donut	4	0.1%
2.1	Eclair	7	1.2%
2.2	Froyo	8	2.5%
2.3 - 2.3.2	Gingerbread	9	0.1%
2.3.3 - 2.3.7		10	33.0%
3.2	Honeycomb	13	0.1%
4.0.3 - 4.0.4	Ice Cream Sandwich	15	22.5%
4.1.x	Jelly Bean	16	34.0%
4.2.x		17	6.5%

Data collected during a 14-day period ending on August 1, 2013.
Any versions with less than 0.1% distribution are not shown.

Figure 14.1   Android device statistics regarding platform version (source: *http://d.android.com/about/dashboards/index.html#Platform*).

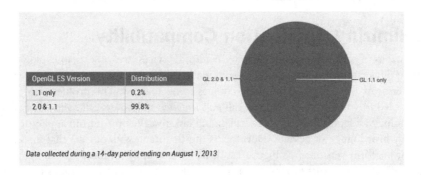

OpenGL ES Version	Distribution
1.1 only	0.2%
2.0 & 1.1	99.8%

Data collected during a 14-day period ending on August 1, 2013

Figure 14.2   Android device statistics regarding OpenGL versions (source: *http://d.android.com/about/dashboards/index.html#OpenGL*).

hardware requirement such as camera support), assess the risk and document this limitation. Determine whether you are going to provide an alternative solution for devices that do not support this requirement.

- Consider screen size and density differences when designing application user interfaces. It is often possible to design very flexible layouts that look reasonable in both portrait and landscape modes, as well as different screen resolutions and sizes. However, if you don't consider these factors early, you will likely have to make changes (sometimes painful ones) later on to accommodate the differences.

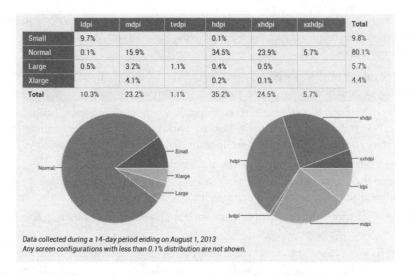

	ldpi	mdpi	tvdpi	hdpi	xhdpi	xxhdpi	Total
Small	9.7%			0.1%			9.8%
Normal	0.1%	15.9%		34.5%	23.9%	5.7%	80.1%
Large	0.5%	3.2%	1.1%	0.4%	0.5%		5.7%
Xlarge		4.1%		0.2%	0.1%		4.4%
Total	10.3%	23.2%	1.1%	35.2%	24.5%	5.7%	

Data collected during a 14-day period ending on August 1, 2013
Any screen configurations with less than 0.1% distribution are not shown.

Figure 14.3   Android device statistics regarding screen sizes and densities (source: *http://d.android.com/about/dashboards/index.html#Screens*).

- Test on a wide range of devices early in the development process to avoid unpleasant surprises late in the game. Make sure the devices have different hardware and software, including different versions of the Android platform, different screen sizes, and different hardware capabilities.

- Whenever necessary, provide alternative resources to help smooth over differences between device characteristics (we talk extensively about alternative resources later in this chapter).

- If you do introduce software and hardware requirements to your application, make sure you register this information in the Android manifest file using the appropriate tags. These tags, used by the Android platform as well as third parties such as Google Play, help ensure that your application is installed only on devices that are capable of meeting its requirements.

Now let's look at some of the strategies you can use to target different device configurations and languages.

Designing User Interfaces for Compatibility

Before we show you the many ways you can provide custom application resources and code to support specific device configurations, it's important to remember that you can often avoid needing them in the first place. The trick is to design your initial default solution to be flexible enough to cover any variations. When it comes to user interfaces, keep them simple and don't overcrowd them. Also, take advantage of the many powerful tools at your disposal:

- As a rule of thumb, design for normal-size screens and medium resolution. Over time, devices trend toward larger screens with higher resolution.

- Use fragments to keep your screen designs independent from your application `Activity` classes and provide for flexible workflows. Leverage the Android Support Library to provide newer support libraries to older platform versions.

- For `View` and `Layout` control width and height attributes, use `match_parent` (also called the deprecated `fill_parent`) and `wrap_content` so that controls scale for different screen sizes and orientation changes, instead of using fixed pixel sizes.

- For dimensions, use the flexible units, such as `dp` and `sp`, as opposed to fixed-unit types, such as `px`, `mm`, and `in`.

- Avoid using `AbsoluteLayout` and other pixel-perfect settings and attributes.

- Use flexible layout controls such as `RelativeLayout`, `LinearLayout`, `TableLayout`, and `FrameLayout` to design a screen that looks great in both portrait and landscape modes and on a variety of different screen sizes and resolutions. Try the "working square" principle for organizing screen content—we will talk more about this in a moment.

- Encapsulate screen content in scalable container controls such as `ScrollView` and `ListView`. Generally, you should scale and grow screens in only one direction (vertically or horizontally), not both.

- Don't provide exact position values for screen elements, sizes, and dimensions. Instead, use relative positions, weights, and gravity. Spending time up front to get these right saves time later.

- Provide application graphics of reasonable quality, and always keep the original (larger) sizes around in case you need different versions for different resolutions at a later time. There is always a trade-off in terms of graphics quality versus file size. Find the sweet spot where the graphic scales reasonably well for changes in screen characteristics, without bulking up your application or taking too long to display. Whenever possible, use stretchable graphics, such as Nine-Patch, which allow a graphic to change size based on the area in which it is displayed.

Tip

Looking for information about the device screen? Check out the `DisplayMetrics` utility class, which, when used in conjunction with the window manager, can determine all sorts of information about the display characteristics of the device at runtime:

```
DisplayMetrics currentMetrics = new DisplayMetrics();
WindowManager wm = getWindowManager();
wm.getDefaultDisplay().getMetrics(currentMetrics);
```

Working with Fragments

Fragments were discussed in detail in Chapter 9, "Partitioning the User Interface with Fragments," but they deserve another mention here, in relation to designing compatible applications. All applications can benefit from the screen workflow flexibility provided by `Fragment`-based designs. By decoupling screen functionality from specific `Activity` classes, you have the option of pairing up that functionality in different ways, depending on the screen size, orientation, and other hardware configuration options. As new types of Android devices hit the market, you'll be well placed for supporting them if you do this work up front—in short, future-proofing your user interfaces.

Tip

There's little excuse not to use fragments, even if you are supporting legacy Android versions as far back as Android 1.6 (99% of the market). Simply use the Android Support Library to include these features in your legacy code. It's just a right-click away in the Android IDE. With most non-`Fragment`-based APIs deprecated, it's clearly the path along which the platform designers are leading developers.

Leveraging the Android Support Library

Fragments and several other new features of the Android SDK (such as loaders) are so important for future device compatibility that there are Android support libraries to bring these APIs to older device platform versions, as far back as Android 1.6. To use the Android Support Library with your application, take the following steps:

1. Use the Android SDK Manager to download the Android Support Library.
2. Find your project in the `Package Explorer` or `Project Explorer`.
3. Right-click the project and choose `Android Tools`, `Add Support Library....` The most updated library will be downloaded, and your project settings will be modified to use the newest library.
4. Begin using the APIs available as part of the Android Support Library. For example, to create a class extending `FragmentActivity`, you need to import `android.support.v4.app.FragmentActivity`.

Supporting Specific Screen Types

Although you generally want to try to develop your applications to be screen independent (support all types of screens, small and large, high density and low), you can specify the types of screens your application can support explicitly when necessary in the Android manifest file. Here are some of the basics for supporting different screen types within your application:

- Explicitly state which screen sizes your application supports using the `<supports-screens>` Android manifest file tag. For more information on this Android manifest tag, see *http://d.android.com/guide/topics/manifest/supports-screens-element.html.*

- Design flexible layouts that work with different-size screens.

- Provide the most flexible default resources you can, and add appropriate alternative layout and drawable resources for different screen sizes, densities, aspect ratios, and orientations as needed.

- Test, test, test! Make sure you review how your application behaves on devices with different screen sizes, densities, aspect ratios, and orientations regularly as part of your quality assurance testing cycle.

Tip

For a very detailed discussion of how to support different types of screens, from the smallest smartphones to the largest tablets and televisions, see the Android Developer website: *http://d.android.com/guide/practices/screens_support.html.*

It's also helpful to understand how legacy applications are automatically scaled for larger and newer devices using what is called *screen compatibility mode*. Depending on the version of the Android SDK that your application originally targeted, the behavior on newer platform versions may be subtly different. This mode is on by default but can be disabled by your application. Learn more about screen compatibility mode at the Android Developer website: *http://d.android.com/guide/practices/screen-compat-mode.html.*

Working with Nine-Patch Stretchable Graphics

Phone screens come in various dimensions. It can save you a lot of time to use stretchable graphics to enable a single graphic to scale appropriately for different screen sizes and orientations or different lengths of text. Android supports Nine-Patch Stretchable Graphics for this purpose. Nine-Patch Stretchable Graphics are simply PNG graphics that have patches, or areas of the image, defined to scale appropriately, instead of the entire image scaling as one unit. We discuss how to create stretchable graphics in Appendix A, "Mastering the Android Development Tools."

Using the "Working Square" Principle

Another way to design for different screen orientations is to try to keep a "working square" area where most of your application's user activity (meaning where users look and click on the screen) takes place. This area remains unchanged (or changes little beyond just rotating) when the screen orientation changes. Only functionality displayed outside the "working square" changes substantially when screen orientation changes (see Figure 14.4).

One example of a "working square" is the Camera application on the Nexus 4. In portrait mode, the camera controls are on the bottom of the viewfinder (see Figure 14.5, left); when the device is rotated clockwise into landscape mode, the camera controls stay in the same place but now they are on the right side of the viewfinder (see Figure 14.5, right).

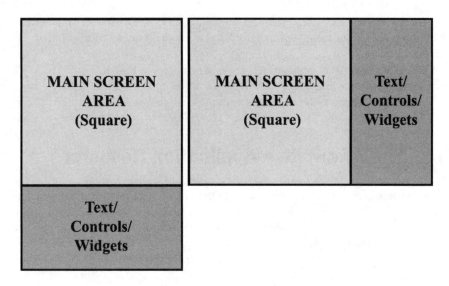

Figure 14.4   The "working square" principle.

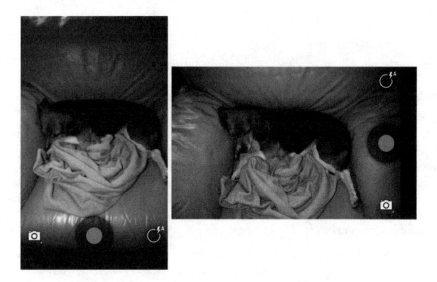

Figure 14.5   Nexus 4 Camera application using a form
of the "working square" principle.

The viewfinder area would be considered the "working square"—the area that remains uncluttered. The controls are kept outside that area, so the user can compose his or her photos and videos.

When you're using the application, the rotation appears to have had little effect. The controls moved from being below the viewfinder to being to the right of the viewfinder. It just so happens, though, that they remain in the same location on the screen. This is part of the elegance of the "working square" principle.

Providing Alternative Application Resources

Few application user interfaces look perfect on every device. Most require some tweaking and some special case handling. The Android platform allows you to organize your project resources so that you can tailor your applications to specific device criteria. It can be useful to think of the resources stored at the top of the resource hierarchy naming scheme as *default resources* and the specialized versions of those resources as *alternative resources*.

Here are some reasons you might want to include alternative resources within your application:

- To support different user languages and locales
- To support different device screen sizes, densities, dimensions, orientations, and aspect ratios
- To support different device docking modes
- To support different device input methods
- To provide different resources depending on the device's Android platform version

Understanding How Resources Are Resolved

Here's how it works. Each time a resource is requested within an Android application, the Android operating system attempts to find the resource that is the best possible match for the job. In many cases, applications provide only one set of resources. Developers can include alternative versions of those same resources as part of their application packages. The Android operating system always attempts to load the most specific resources available—the developer does not have to worry about determining which resources to load because the operating system handles this task.

There are four important rules to remember when creating alternative resources:

1. The Android platform always loads the most specific, most appropriate resource available. If an alternative resource does not exist, the default resource is used. Therefore, it's important to know your target devices, design for the defaults, and add alternative resources judiciously in order to keep your projects manageable.

2. Alternative resources must always be named exactly the same as the default resources and stored in the appropriately named directory, as dictated by a special

alternative resource qualifier. If a string is called `strHelpText` in the `/res/values/strings.xml` file, it must be named the same in the `/res/values-fr/strings.xml` (French) and `/res/values-zh/strings.xml` (Chinese) string files. The same goes for all other types of resources, such as graphics or layout files.

3. Good application design dictates that alternative resources should almost always have a default counterpart so that regardless of the device configuration, some version of the resource will always load. The only time you can get away without a default resource is when you provide every kind of alternative resource. One of the first steps the system takes when finding a best matching resource is to eliminate resources that are contradictory to the current configuration. For example, in portrait mode, the system would not even attempt to use a landscape resource, even if that is the only resource available. Keep in mind that new alternative resource qualifiers are added over time, so although you might think your application provides complete coverage of all alternatives now, it might not in the future.

4. Don't go overboard creating alternative resources because they add to the size of your application package and can have performance implications. Instead, try to design your default resources to be flexible and scalable. For example, a good layout design can often support both landscape and portrait modes seamlessly—if you use appropriate layouts, user interface controls, and scalable graphics resources.

Organizing Alternative Resources with Qualifiers

Alternative resources can be created for many different criteria, including, but not limited to, screen characteristics, device input methods, and language or regional differences. These alternative resources are organized hierarchically within the `/res` resource project directory. You use directory qualifiers (in the form of directory name suffixes) to specify a resource as an alternative resource to load in specific situations.

A simple example might help to drive this concept home. The most common example of when alternative resources are used has to do with the default application icon resources created as part of a new Android project in the Android IDE. An application could simply provide a single application icon graphics resource, stored in the `/res/drawable` directory. However, different Android devices have different screen densities. Therefore, alternative resources are used instead: `/res/drawable-hdpi/ic_launcher.png` is an application icon suitable for high-density screens, `/res/drawable-ldpi/ic_launcher.png` is the application icon suitable for low-density screens, and so on. Note that in each case, the alternative resource is named the same. This is important. Alternative resources must use the same names as the default resources. This is how the Android system can match the appropriate resource to load—by its name.

Here are some additional important facts about alternative resources:

- Alternative resource directory qualifiers are always applied to the default resource directory name, for example, `/res/drawable-qualifier`, `/res/values-qualifier`, `/res/layout-qualifier`.

- Alternative resource directory qualifiers (and resource filenames) must always be lowercase, with one exception: region qualifiers.

- Only one directory qualifier of a given type may be included in a resource directory name. Sometimes this has unfortunate consequences—you might be forced to include the same resource in multiple directories. For example, you cannot create an alternative resource directory called `/res/drawable-ldpi-mdpi` to share the same icon graphic. Instead, you must create two directories: `/res/drawable-ldpi` and `/res/drawable-mdpi`. Frankly, when you want different qualifiers to share resources instead of providing two copies of the same resource, you're often better off making those your default resources and then providing alternative resources for those that do not match `ldpi` and `mdpi`—that is, `hdpi`. As we said, it's up to you how you go about organizing your resources; these are just our suggestions for keeping things under control.

- Alternative resource directory qualifiers can be combined or chained, with each qualifier separated from the next by a dash. This enables developers to create very specific directory names and therefore very specialized alternative resources. These qualifiers must be applied in a specific order, and the Android operating system always attempts to load the most specific resource (that is, the resource with the longest matching path). For example, you can create an alternative resource directory for French language (qualifier `fr`), Canadian region (qualifier `rCA`—CA is a region qualifier and is therefore capitalized) string resources (stored in the values directory) as follows: `/res/values-fr-rCA/strings.xml`.

- You need to create alternative resources only for the specific resources you require—not every resource in a given file. If you need to translate only half the strings in the default `strings.xml` file, provide alternative strings only for those specific string resources. In other words, the default `strings.xml` resource file might contain a superset of string resources and the alternative string resource files a subset—only the strings requiring translation. Common examples of strings that do not get localized are company and brand names.

- No custom directory names or qualifiers are allowed. You may use only the qualifiers defined as part of the Android SDK. These qualifiers are listed in Table 14.1.

- Always try to include default resources—that is, those resources saved in directories without any qualifiers. These are the resources that the Android operating system will fall back on when no specific alternative resource matches the criteria. If you don't, the system falls back on the closest matching resource based upon the directory qualifiers—one that might not make sense.

Table 14.1 **Important Alternative Resource Qualifiers**

Directory Qualifier	Example Values	Description
Mobile country code and mobile network code	`mcc310` (United States) `mcc310-mnc004` (United States, Verizon)	The mobile country code (MCC), optionally followed by a dash, and a mobile network code (MNC) from the SIM card in the device.
Language and region code	`en` (English) `ja` (Japanese) `de` (German) `en-rUS` (American English) `en-rGB` (British English)	The language code (ISO 639-1 two-letter language code), optionally followed by a dash, and the region code (a lowercase `r` followed by the region code as defined by ISO 3166-1-alpha-2).
Layout direction	`ldltr` `ldrtl`	The application's layout direction, either left to right or right to left. Resources such as layouts, values, or drawables can use this rule. Requires setting the application attribute `supportsRtl` as `true` in your manifest file. Added in API Level 17.
Screen pixel dimensions. Several qualifiers for specific screen dimensions, including smallest width, available width, and available height.	`sw<N>dp` (smallest width) `w<N>dp` (available width) `h<N>dp` (available height) Examples: `sw320dp` `sw480dp` `sw600dp` `sw720dp` `h320dp` `h540dp` `h800dp` `w480dp` `w720dp` `w1080dp`	DP-specific screen requirements. `swXXXdp`: Indicates the smallest width that this resource qualifier supports. `wYYYdp`: Indicates the minimum width. `hZZZdp`: Indicates the minimum height. The numeric value can be any width the developer desires, in `dp` units. Added in API Level 13.
Screen size	`small` `normal` `large` `xlarge` (added in API Level 9)	Generalized screen size. A `small` screen is generally a low-density QVGA or higher-density VGA screen. A `normal` screen is generally a medium-density HVGA screen or similar. A `large` screen has at least a medium-density VGA screen or other screen with more pixels than an HVGA display. An `xlarge` screen has at least a medium-density HVGA screen and is generally tablet size or larger. Added in API Level 4.

(continues)

Table 14.1 **Continued**

Directory Qualifier	Example Values	Description
Screen aspect ratio	long notlong	Whether or not the device is a wide-screen device. WQVGA, WVGA, FWVGA screens are long screens. QVGA, HVGA, and VGA screens are notlong screens. Added in API Level 4.
Screen orientation	port land	When a device is in portrait mode, the port resources will be loaded. When the device is in landscape mode, the land resources will be loaded.
UI mode	car desk appliance television	Load specific resources when the device is in a car or desk dock. Load specific resources when the device is a television display. Load specific resources when the device is an appliance and has no display. Added in API Level 8.
Night mode	night notnight	Load specific resources when the device is in night mode or not. Added in API Level 8.
Screen pixel density	ldpi mdpi hdpi xhdpi (added in API Level 8) xxhdpi (added in API Level 16) tvdpi (added in API Level 13) nodpi	Low-density screen resources (approx. 120dpi) should use the ldpi option. Medium-density screen resources (approx. 160dpi) should use the mdpi option. High-density screen resources (approx. 240dpi) should use the hdpi option. Extra-high-density screen resources (approx. 320dpi) should use the xhdpi option. Extra-extra-high-density screen resources (approx. 480dpi) should use the xxhdpi option. Television screen resources (approx. 213dpi, between mdpi and hdpi) should use the tvdpi option. Use the nodpi option to specify resources that you do not want to be scaled to match the screen density of the device. Added in API Level 4.

Directory Qualifier	Example Values	Description
Touchscreen type	`notouch` `finger`	Resources for devices without touchscreens should use the `notouch` option. Resources for devices with finger-style (capacitive) touchscreens should use the `finger` option.

Keyboard type and availability	`keysexposed`
	`keyshidden`
	`keyssoft`
		Use the `keysexposed` option for resources when a keyboard is available (hardware or soft keyboard).
		Use the `keyshidden` option for resources when no hardware or software keyboard is available.
		Use the `keyssoft` option for resources when the soft keyboard is available.

Text input method	`nokeys`
	`qwerty`
	`12key`
		Use the `nokeys` option for resources when the device has no hardware keys for text input.
		Use the `qwerty` option for resources when the device has a QWERTY hardware keyboard for text input.
		Use the `12key` option for resources when the device has a 12-key numeric keypad for text input.

Navigation key availability	`navexposed` `navhidden`	Use `navexposed` for resources when the navigational hardware buttons are available to the user. Use `navhidden` for resources when the navigational hardware buttons are not available to the user (such as when the phone case is slid shut).

Navigation method	`nonav`
	`dpad`
	`trackball`
	`wheel`
		Use `nonav` if the device has no navigation buttons other than a touchscreen.
		Use `dpad` for resources where the primary navigation method is a directional pad.
		Use `trackball` for resources where the primary navigation method is a trackball.
		Use `wheel` for resources where the primary navigation method is a directional wheel.

(continues)

Table 14.1 **Continued**

Directory Qualifier	Example Values	Description
Android platform	v3 (Android 1.5) v4 (Android 1.6) v7 (Android 2.1.X) v8 (Android 2.2.X) v9 (Android 2.3–2.3.2) v10 (Android 2.3.3–2.3.4) v12 (Android 3.1.X) v13 (Android 3.2.X) v14 (Android 4.0.X) v15 (Android 4.0.3) v16 (Android 4.1.2) v17 (Android 4.2.2) v18 (Android 4.3)	Load resources based on the Android platform version, as specified by the API level. This qualifier will load resources for the specified API level or higher. Note: There are some known issues with this qualifier. See the Android documentation for details.

Now that you understand how alternative resources work, let's look at some of the directory qualifiers you can use to store alternative resources for different purposes. Qualifiers are tacked onto the existing resource directory name in a strict order, shown in descending order in Table 14.1.

Good examples of alternative resource directories with qualifiers are

- `/res/values-en-rUS-port-finger`
- `/res/drawables-en-rUS-land-mdpi`
- `/res/values-en-qwerty`

Bad examples of alternative resource directories with qualifiers are

- `/res/values-en-rUS-rGB`
- `/res/values-en-rUS-port-FINGER-wheel`
- `/res/values-en-rUS-port-finger-custom`
- `/res/drawables-rUS-en`

The first bad example does not work because you can have only one qualifier of a given type, and this one violates that rule by including both `rUS` and `rGB`. The second bad example violates the rule that qualifiers (with the exception of the region) are always lowercase. The third bad example includes a custom attribute defined by the developer, but these are not currently supported. The last bad example violates the order in which the qualifiers must be placed: language first, then region, and so on.

Providing Resources for Different Orientations

Let's look at a very simple application that uses alternative resources to customize screen content for different orientations. The `SimpleAltResources` application (see the book's sample code for a complete implementation) has no real code to speak of—check the `Activity` class if you don't believe us. Instead, all interesting functionality depends on the resource folder qualifiers. These resources are as follows:

- The default resources for this application include the application icon and a picture graphic stored in the `/res/drawable` directory, the layout file stored in the `/res/layout` directory, and the color and string resources stored in the `/res/values` directory. These resources are loaded whenever a more specific resource is not available to load. They are the fallbacks.

- There is a portrait-mode alternative picture graphic stored in the `/res/drawable-port` directory. There are also portrait-mode-specific string and color resources stored in the `/res/values-port` directory. If the device is in portrait orientation, these resources—the portrait picture graphic, the strings, and the colors—are loaded and used by the default layout.

- There is a landscape-mode alternative picture graphic stored in the `/res/drawable-land` directory. There are landscape-mode-specific string and color (basically reversed background and foreground colors) resources stored in the `/res/values-land` directory as well. If the device is in landscape orientation, these resources—the landscape picture graphic, the strings, and the colors—are loaded and used by the default layout.

Figure 14.6 illustrates how the application loads different resources based on the orientation of the device at runtime. This figure shows the project layout, in terms of resources, as well as what the screen looks like in different device orientations.

Using Alternative Resources Programmatically

There is currently no easy way to request resources of a specific configuration programmatically. For example, the developer cannot programmatically request the French or English version of the string resource. Instead, the Android system determines the resource at runtime, and developers refer only to the general resource variable name.

Organizing Application Resources Efficiently

It's easy to go too far with alternative resources. You could provide custom graphics for every different permutation of device screen, language, or input method. However, each time you include an application resource in your project, the size of your application package grows.

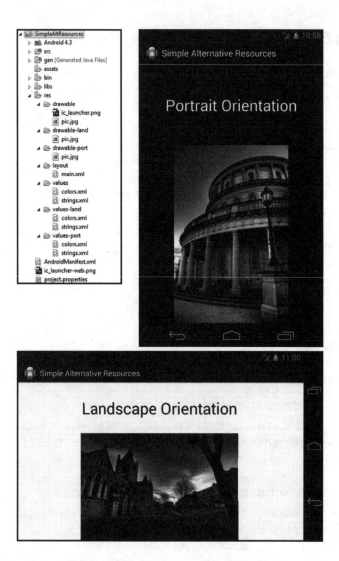

Figure 14.6   Using alternative resources
for portrait and landscape orientations.

There are also performance issues with swapping out resources too frequently—
generally when runtime configuration transitions occur. Each time a runtime event such
as an orientation or keyboard state change occurs, the Android operating system restarts
the underlying Activity and reloads the resources. If your application is loading a lot
of resources and content, these changes come at a cost to application performance and
responsiveness.

Choose your resource organization scheme carefully. Generally, you should make the most commonly used resources your defaults and then carefully overlay alternative resources only when necessary. For example, if you are writing an application that routinely shows videos or displays a game screen, you might want to make landscape mode resources your defaults and provide alternative portrait mode resources because they are not as likely to be used.

Retaining Data across Configuration Changes

An `Activity` can keep data around through these transitions by using the `onRetain NonConfigurationInstance()` method to save data and the `getLastNon ConfigurationInstance()` method to restore this data after the transition. This functionality can be especially helpful when your `Activity` has a lot of setup or preloading to do. When using fragments, all you need to do is set a flag to retain a `Fragment` instance across these changes.

Handling Configuration Changes

In cases where your `Activity` does not need to reload alternative resources on a specific transition, you might want to consider having the `Activity` class handle the transition to avoid having your `Activity` restart. The Camera application mentioned earlier could use this technique to handle orientation changes without having to reinitialize the camera hardware internals, redisplay the viewfinder window, or redisplay the camera controls (the `Button` controls simply rotate in place to the new orientation—very slick).

For an `Activity` class to handle its own configuration changes, your application must

- Update the `<activity>` tag in the Android manifest file for that specific `Activity` class to include the `android:configChanges` attribute. This attribute must specify the types of changes the `Activity` class handles itself.

- Implement the `onConfigurationChanged()` method of the `Activity` class to handle the specific changes (by type).

Targeting Tablets, TVs, and Other New Devices

There has been tremendous growth in the types of devices supported by the Android platform. Whether we're talking tablets, TVs, or toasters, there's something for everyone. These new devices make for an exciting time for application developers. New devices mean new groups and demographics of users using the platform. These new types of Android devices, however, pose some unique challenges for Android developers.

Targeting Tablet Devices

Tablets come in a variety of sizes and default orientations, from many different manufacturers and carriers. Luckily, from a developer's perspective, tablets can be considered just another Android device, provided that you haven't made any unfortunate development assumptions.

Android tablets run the same platform versions that traditional smartphones do—there is nothing special. Most tablets these days run Android 4.0 and higher. Here are some tips for designing, developing, and publishing Android applications for tablet devices:

- **Design flexible user interfaces:** Regardless of what devices your applications are targeting, use flexible layout designs. Use `RelativeLayout` to organize your user interfaces. Use relative dimension values such as `dp` instead of specific ones such as `px`. Use stretchable graphics such as Nine-Patch.

- **Take advantage of fragments:** Fragments make for much more flexible user interface navigation by decoupling screen functionality from specific activities.

- **Leverage alternative resources:** Provide alternative resources for various device screen sizes and densities.

- **Screen orientation:** Tablets often default to landscape mode, but this is not always the case. Some tablets, especially smaller ones, use portrait defaults.

- **Input mode differentiators:** Tablets often rely solely on touchscreen input. Some configurations also have a few other physical buttons, but this is unusual because Honeycomb, the first platform revision to truly support tablets, moved the typical hardware buttons to the touchscreen.

- **UI navigational differences:** Users hold and tap on tablets in a different fashion from the way they do on smartphones. In portrait and landscape modes, tablet screens are substantially wider than their smartphone equivalents. Applications such as games that rely on the user cradling the device in his or her hands like a traditional game controller may struggle with all the extra room on a tablet. The user's thumbs might easily reach or access the two halves of a smartphone screen but not be able to do the same on a tablet.

- **Feature support:** Certain hardware and software features are not usually available on tablets. For example, telephony is not always available. This has implications for unique device identifiers; many used to rely on the telephony identifier that may not be present. The point is, hardware differences can also lead to other, less obvious impacts.

Targeting Google TV Devices

Google TV is another type of device that Android developers can target. Users can browse Google Play for compatible applications and download them much as they would to other Android devices.

In order to develop Google TV applications, developers use the Android SDK as well as a Google TV add-on, which can be downloaded using the Android SDK Manager.

There are some subtle differences between development for Google TV devices and targeting smartphones and tablets. Let's look at some development tips for targeting Google TV devices:

- **Screen density and resolution:** Google TV devices currently run at two resolutions. The first is 720p (aka "HD" and `tvdpi`), or 1280 × 720 pixels. The second is 1080p (aka "Full HD" and `xhdpi`), or 1920 × 1080 pixels. These correspond to `large` screen size.

- **Screen orientation:** Google TV devices need only landscape-oriented layouts.

- **Not pixel perfect:** One caveat regarding Google TV development is not to rely on the exact number of pixels on the screen. Televisions don't always expose every single pixel. Therefore, your screen designs should be flexible enough to accommodate small adjustments when you've had a chance to test your applications on real Google TV devices. Use of `RelativeLayout` is highly recommended. See *https:// developers.google.com/tv/android/docs/gtv_displayguide#DisplayResolution* for more information on this issue.

- **Input mode limitations:** Unlike tablets or smartphones, Google TV devices are not within arm's reach and do not have touchscreens. This means no gestures, no multitouch, and so on. The Google TV interface uses a directional pad (or D-pad)— that is, arrow keys for up, down, left, and right along with a `Select` button and media keys ("Play," "Pause," and so on). Some configurations also have a mouse or keyboard.

- **UI navigational differences:** The input type limitations with Google TV devices may mean you need to make some changes to your application's screen navigation. Users can't easily skip over focusable items on the screen. For instance, if your UI has a row of items, with the two most common on the far left and far right for convenient access with thumb clicks, these items may be inconveniently separated for the average Google TV user.

- **Android manifest file settings:** A number of Android manifest file settings should be configured appropriately for the Google TV. Review the Google TV documentation for details: *https://developers.google.com/tv/android/docs/ gtv_androidmanifest*.

- **Google Play filters:** Google Play uses Android manifest file settings to filter applications and provide them to the appropriate devices. Certain features, such as those defined using the `<uses-feature>` tag, may exclude your application from Google TV devices. One example of this is when applications require features such as touchscreen, camera, and telephony. For a complete list of features supported and unsupported by the Google TV, see the following page: *https://developers.google.com/ tv/android/docs/gtv_android_features*.

- **Feature support:** Certain hardware and software features (sensors, cameras, telephony, and so on) are not available on Google TV devices.

- **Native Development Kit:** For Google TV devices based on Android 4.2.2, NDK support has been added. There is currently no NDK support for Google TV devices prior to Android 4.2.2.

- **Supported media formats:** There are subtle differences between the media formats supported by the Android platform (*http://d.android.com/guide/appendix/ media-formats.html*) and those supported on the Google TV platform (*https:// developers.google.com/tv/android/docs/gtv_media_formats*).

Tip

For more information on developing for Google TV devices, see the Google TV Android Developers Guide at *https://developers.google.com/tv/android/*.

Targeting Google Chromecast Devices

Google Cast is a new screen-sharing feature introduced recently. Chromecast is an HDMI dongle that users connect to their TV and control with one of their devices, such as a smartphone, tablet, or computer.

Android 4.3 (API Level 18) received the MediaRouter APIs (android.media.MediaRouter) so developers can integrate screen-sharing capabilities into their applications. To learn more about the MediaRouter APIs, see *http://developer.android.com/reference/android/media/MediaRouter.html*. To learn more about Google Cast, see *https://developers.google.com/cast/*.

Summary

Compatibility is a vast topic, and we've given you a lot to think about. During design and implementation, always consider if your choices are going to introduce roadblocks to device compatibility. Quality assurance personnel should always vary the devices used for testing as much as possible—certainly don't rely solely on emulator configurations for testing coverage. Use best practices that encourage compatibility, and do your best to keep compatibility-related resources and code streamlined and manageable.

If you take only two concepts away from this chapter, one should be that alternative resources and fragments can be used to great effect. They enable a flexibility that can go a long way toward achieving compatibility, whether it's for screen differences or internationalization. The other is that certain Android manifest file tags can help ensure that your applications are installed only on devices that meet certain prerequisites, or requirements, such as a certain version of OpenGL ES or the availability of camera hardware.

Quiz Questions

1. True or false: To design user interfaces for compatibility, as a rule of thumb, design for normal-size screens and medium resolution.

2. What percentage of Android devices currently on the market support the use of fragments?

3. What manifest file tag is used to explicitly state which screen sizes your application supports?

4. True or false: The directory /res/drawables-rGB-MDPI is a good example of an alternative resource directory with a qualifier.

5. What are the possible values for the layout direction alternative resource directory qualifier?

6. True or false: You can request resources of a specific configuration programmatically.

7. What is the method call you should implement in your `Activity` class for handling configuration changes?

Exercises

1. Read through the "Best Practices" topic of the Android API Guides (*http://d .android.com/guide/practices/index.html*) to learn more about how to build apps that work for a wide range of devices.

2. Using the "Best Practices" Android API Guides, determine what the typical sizes in dp units are for `small`, `normal`, `large`, and `xlarge` screens.

3. Using the "Best Practices" Android API Guides, determine what scaling ratio you should follow between the four densities of low, medium, high, and extra-high.

References and More Information

Android SDK Reference regarding the application `Dialog` class:
   http://d.android.com/reference/android/app/Dialog.html
Android SDK Reference regarding the Android Support Library:
   http://d.android.com/tools/extras/support-library.html
Android API Guides: "Screen Compatibility Mode":
   http://d.android.com/guide/practices/screen-compat-mode.html
Android API Guides: "Providing Alternative Resources":
   http://d.android.com/guide/topics/resources/providing-resources.html#AlternativeResources
Android API Guides: "How Android Finds the Best-Matching Resource":
   http://d.android.com/guide/topics/resources/providing-resources.html#BestMatch
Android API Guides: "Handling Runtime Changes":
   http://d.android.com/guide/topics/resources/runtime-changes.html
Android API Guides: "Android Compatibility":
   http://d.android.com/guide/practices/compatibility.html
Android API Guides: "Supporting Multiple Screens":
   http://d.android.com/guide/practices/screens_support.html
ISO 639-2 languages:
   http://www.loc.gov/standards/iso639-2/php/code_list.php
ISO 3166 country codes:
   http://www.iso.org/iso/home/standards/country_codes.htm

V

Publishing and Distributing Android Applications

15

Learning the Android Software Development Process

The mobile development process is similar to the traditional desktop software process, with a couple of distinct differences. Understanding how these differences affect your mobile development team is critical to running a successful project. This insight into the mobile development process is invaluable to those new to mobile development and veteran developers alike, to those in management and planning, as well as to the developers and testers in the trenches. In this chapter, you learn about the peculiarities of mobile development as they pertain to each stage of the software development process.

An Overview of the Mobile Development Process

Mobile development teams are often small in size and project schedules are short in length. The entire project lifecycle is often condensed, and whether you're a team of one or one hundred, understanding the mobile development considerations for each part of the development process can save you a lot of wasted time and effort. Some hurdles a mobile development team must overcome include

- Choosing an appropriate software methodology
- Understanding how target devices dictate the functionality of your application
- Performing thorough, accurate, and ongoing feasibility analyses
- Mitigating the risks associated with preproduction devices
- Keeping track of device functionality through configuration management
- Designing a responsive, stable application on a memory-restrictive system
- Designing user interfaces for a variety of devices with different user experiences
- Testing the application thoroughly on the target devices
- Incorporating third-party requirements that affect where you can sell your application
- Deploying and maintaining a mobile application
- Reviewing user feedback, crash reports, and ratings, and deploying timely application updates

Choosing a Software Methodology

Developers can easily adapt most modern software methodologies to mobile development. Whether your team opts for traditional rapid application development (RAD) principles or more modern variants of agile software development, such as Scrum, mobile applications have some unique requirements.

Understanding the Dangers of Waterfall Approaches

The short development cycle might tempt some to use a waterfall approach, but developers should beware of the inflexibility that comes with this choice. It is generally a bad idea to design and develop an entire mobile application without taking into account the many changes that tend to occur during the development cycle (see Figure 15.1). Changes to target devices (especially preproduction models, though sometimes shipping devices can have substantial software changes), ongoing feasibility, and performance concerns and the need for quality assurance (QA) to test early and often on the target devices themselves, (not just the emulator) make it difficult for strict waterfall approaches to succeed with mobile projects.

Figure 15.1   The dangers of waterfall development
(graphic courtesy of Amy Tam Badger).

Understanding the Value of Iteration

Because of the speed at which mobile projects tend to progress, iterative methods have been the most successful strategies adapted to mobile development. Rapid prototyping gives developers and QA personnel ample opportunity to evaluate the feasibility and performance of the mobile application on the target devices and adapt as needed to the changes that inevitably occur over the course of the project.

Gathering Application Requirements

Despite the relative simplicity of a mobile application's feature set compared to a traditional desktop application, requirements analyses for a mobile application can be more complex. The mobile user interface must be elegant and the application must be fault tolerant, not to mention responsive in a resource-constrained environment. You must often tailor requirements to work across a number of devices—devices that might have vastly different user interfaces and input methods. Having great variation in target platforms can make development assumptions tricky. It's not unlike the differences Web developers might need to accommodate when developing for different Web browsers (and versions of Web browsers).

Determining Project Requirements

When multiple devices are involved (which is almost always the case with Android), we have found several approaches to be helpful for determining project requirements. Each approach has its benefits and its drawbacks. These approaches are

- The lowest common denominator method
- The customization method

Using the Lowest Common Denominator Method

With the lowest common denominator method, you design the application to run *sufficiently* well across a number of devices. In this case, the primary target for which you develop is the device configuration with the fewest features—basically, the most inferior device. Only requirements that can be met by all devices are included in the specification in order to reach the broadest range of devices—requirements such as input methods, screen resolution, and the platform version. With this method, you'll often put a stake in the ground for a specific Android API level and then tailor your application further using Android manifest file settings and Google Play filters.

> **Note**
>
> The lowest common denominator method is roughly equivalent to developing a desktop application with these minimum system requirements—Windows 2000 and 128MB of RAM—on the assumption that the application will be forward compatible with the latest version of Windows (and every other version in between). It's not ideal, but in some cases the trade-offs are acceptable.

Some light customization, such as resources and the final compiled binary (and the version information), is usually feasible with the lowest common denominator method. The main benefit of this method is that there is only one major source code tree to work with; bugs are fixed in one place and apply for all devices. You can also easily add other devices without changing much code, provided they, too, meet the minimum hardware requirements. The drawbacks include the fact that the resulting generalized application does not maximize any device-specific features, nor can it take advantage of new platform features. Also, if a device-specific problem arises or you misjudge the lowest common denominator and later find that an individual device lacks the minimum requirements, the team might be forced to implement a workaround (hack) or branch the code at a later date, losing the early benefits of this method but keeping all the drawbacks.

Tip

The Android SDK makes it easy for developers to target multiple platform versions within a single application package. Developers should take care to identify target platforms early in the design phase. That said, over-the-air firmware updates to users do occur, so the platform version on a given device is likely to change over time. Always design your applications with forward compatibility in mind, and make contingency plans for distributing application upgrades to existing applications as necessary.

When using more modern SDK features, such as fragments or loaders, one of the easiest ways to get your application to support more devices is by using the Android Support Package and the support libraries. Using the support libraries will allow you to write your application following best practices such as supporting single-pane and multipane layouts, while allowing your application to also work on older devices that do not have built-in support for those modern SDK features. Increasing the market size for your application could be as simple as importing the support libraries into your application's code, rather than importing the standard SDK libraries.

Using the Customization Method

Google Play provides management capabilities to implement a customized application for particular devices by leveraging multiple APK support. Multiple APK support allows you to create multiple APKs of your application, each of which targets a specific set of device configurations, or even a specific device. The different configurations that you are able to target are as follows:

- Different API levels
- Different GL textures
- Different screen sizes
- Any combination of different API levels, different GL textures, and/or different screen sizes

This customization method gives you complete control over how your application functions on a specific set of target devices, or even one particular device, if you desire to have that level of fine-grained control over the capabilities your application provides.

Google Play allows developers to tie multiple APK files together under a single product name. This allows developers to create optimal packages that don't contain a lot of resources not needed by every device. For example, a "small-screen package" wouldn't need resources for tablets and televisions.

Tip

To learn more about how to implement and manage multiple APK support for your application, see the following URLs: *http://d.android.com/training/multiple-apks/index.html* and *http://d.android.com/google/play/publishing/multiple-apks.html*.

This method works well for specialized applications with a small number of target devices but does not scale easily from a build or product management perspective.

Generally, developers will come up with a core application framework (classes or packages) shared across all versions of the application. All versions of a client/server application would likely share the same server and interact with it in the same way, but the client implementation is tailored to take advantage of specific device features, when they are available. The primary benefit of this technique is that users receive an application that leverages all the features their device (or API level) has to offer. Some drawbacks include source code fragmentation (many branches of the same code), increased testing requirements, and the fact that it can be more difficult to add new devices in the future.

For customization, you should also think about which screen sizes you will support. You may have an application that should work only on small screens, such as smartphones, or you may want to support only tablets or TVs. Regardless, you should provide screen-specific layouts, adding to your application manifest the types of screens your application supports for Google Play filtering, and packaging different drawable resource files.

Taking Advantage of the Best of Both Methods

In truth, mobile development teams usually use a hybrid approach, incorporating some aspects from both methods. It's pretty common to see developers define classes of devices based on functionality. For example, a game application might group devices based on graphics performance, screen resolution, or input methods. A location-based service (LBS) application might group devices based on the available internal sensors. Other applications might develop one version for devices with built-in front-facing cameras and one version for those without. These groupings are arbitrary and set by the developer to keep the code and testing manageable. They will, in large part, be driven by the details of a particular application and any support requirements. In many cases, these features can be detected at runtime as well, but add enough of them together and the code paths can become overly complex when having two or more applications would actually be easier.

Tip

A single, unified version of an application is usually cheaper to support than multiple versions. However, a game might sell better with custom versions that leverage the distinct advantages and features of a specific class of devices. A vertical business application would likely benefit more from a unified approach that works the same, is easier to train users across multiple devices, and would thus have lower support costs for the business.

Developing Use Cases for Mobile Applications

You should first write use cases in general terms for the application before adapting them to specific device classes, which impose their own limitations. For example, a high-level use case for an application might be "Enter Form Data," but the individual devices might use different input methods, such as hardware versus software keyboards, and so on. Following this approach allows you to chart application user flows independent of specific user interface components or user experience best practices most appropriate for a given device, form factor, or even platform. Considering that the most successful mobile applications these days need to have both Android and iOS versions, starting your use case development independent from the platform can help keep your app's identity in parity, while still recognizing and embracing platform differences upon implementation.

Tip

Developing an application for multiple devices is much like developing an application for different operating systems and input devices (such as handling Mac keyboard shortcuts versus those on Windows)—you must account for subtle and not-so-subtle differences. These differences might be obvious, such as not having a keyboard for input, or not so obvious, such as device-specific bugs or different conventions for soft keys. See Chapter 14, "Designing Compatible Applications," for a discussion of device compatibility.

Incorporating Third-Party Requirements and Recommendations

In addition to the requirements imposed by your internal requirements analyses, your team needs to incorporate any requirements imposed by others. Third-party requirements can come from any number of sources, including

- Android SDK License Agreement requirements
- Google Play requirements (if applicable)
- Google Cloud Messaging API License Agreement requirements (if applicable)
- Other Google license requirements (if applicable)
- Other third-party API requirements (if applicable)
- Other application store requirements (if applicable)
- Mobile carrier/operator requirements (if applicable)
- Application certification requirements (if applicable)
- Android design guidelines and recommendations (if applicable)
- Other third-party design guidelines and recommendations (if applicable)

Incorporating these requirements into your project plan early is essential not only for keeping your project on schedule but also so that these requirements are built into the application from the ground up, as opposed to applied as an afterthought, which can be risky.

Managing a Device Database

As your mobile development team builds applications for a growing number of devices, it becomes more and more important to keep track of your application's target devices and related information for revenue estimation and maintenance purposes. Creating a device database is a great way to keep track of both marketing and device specification details for target devices. When we say *database,* we mean anything from a Microsoft Excel spreadsheet to a little SQL database. The point is that the information is shared across the team or company and kept up-to-date. It can also be helpful to break devices into classes, such as those that support OpenGL ES 2.0 or those without camera hardware.

Tip

Depending on the resources available to you, you may not be able to keep track of every single device you plan to target. In that case, you should instead keep track of the class of devices that you plan to target and gather and maintain statistics of common device characteristics rather than specific device characteristics.

The device database is best implemented early, when project requirements are just determined and target devices are determined. Figure 15.2 illustrates how you can track device information and how different members of the application development team can use it.

Tip

Readers have asked us for our take on using personal devices for testing purposes. Is it safe? Is it smart? The short answer is that you can use your personal device for testing safely in most cases. It's highly unlikely that you will "break" or "brick" your device to the point where a factory reset won't fix it. However, protecting your data is another problem entirely. For example, if your application acts on the Contacts database, your real contacts may be messed with, by bugs or other coding mistakes. Sometimes using personal devices is convenient, especially for small development teams without a big hardware budget. Make sure you understand the ramifications of doing so.

Determining Which Devices to Track

Some companies track only the devices they actively develop for, whereas others also track devices they might want to include in the future, or lower-priority devices. You can include devices in the database during the requirements phase of a project but also later as a change in project scope. You can also add devices as subsequent porting projects long after the initial application has been released.

Storing Device Data

You should design the device database to contain any information about a given device that would be helpful for developing and selling applications. This might require that someone be tasked with keeping track of a continual stream of information from

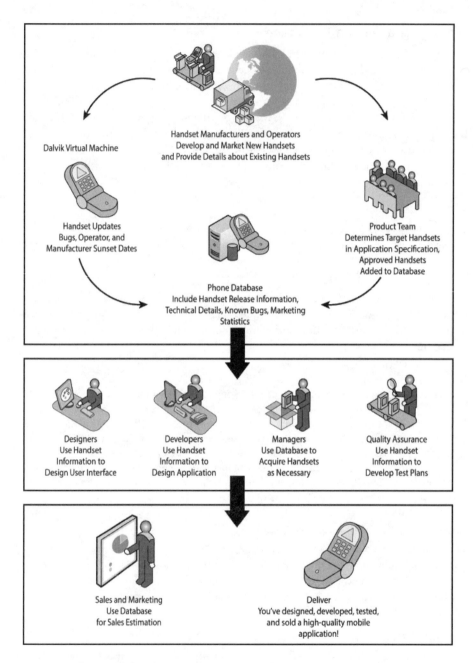

Figure 15.2   How a development team uses the device database.

carriers and manufacturers. Still, this information can be useful for all mobile projects at a company. This data should include the following:

- Important device technical specification details (screen resolution, hardware details, supported media formats, input methods, and localization).

- Any known issues with devices (bugs and important limitations).

- Device carrier information (any firmware customizations, release and sunset dates, and expected user statistics, such as if a device is highly anticipated and expected to sell a lot, or is well received for vertical market applications, and so on).

- API level data and firmware upgrade information. (As information becomes available, changes might have no impact on the application or warrant an entirely separate device entry; keep in mind that different carriers roll out upgrades on different schedules, so keeping track of this information at a too-fine-grained level may not be feasible.)

- Actual testing device information (which devices have been purchased or loaned through manufacturer or carrier loaner programs, how many are available, and so on).

You can also cross-reference the device carrier information with sales figures from the carrier, application stores, and internal metrics. Your application's ratings and reviews, as well as any crash reports by device, should also be documented.

The actual testing device information is often best implemented as a library checkout system. Team members can reserve devices for testing and development purposes. When a loaner device needs to be returned to the manufacturer, it's easy to track. This also facilitates sharing devices across teams.

Using Device Data

Remember that the database can be used for multiple mobile development projects. Device resources can be shared, and sales statistics can be compared to see on which devices your applications perform best. Different team members (or roles) can use the device database in different ways:

- Product designers use the database to develop the most appropriate application user interface for the target devices.

- Media artists use the database to generate application assets such as graphics, videos, and audio in supported media file formats and resolutions appropriate for the target devices.

- Project managers use the database to determine the devices that must be acquired for development and testing purposes on the project and development priorities.

- Software developers use the database to design and develop applications compatible with target device specifications.

- QA personnel use the database to design and develop the target device specifications for test plans and to test the application thoroughly.

- Marketing and sales professionals use the database to estimate sales figures for released applications. For example, it is important to be aware that application sales will drop as device availability drops.

The information in the database can also help determine the most promising target devices for future development and porting. Android devices have built-in ways for users to report when your application crashes. When users report a crash, the information is sent to Google, and Google then presents it to you from within the Google Play Developer Console. Tracking this information will help you improve the quality of your applications over the long term.

Using Third-Party Device Databases

There are third-party databases for device information, including screen size and internal device details and carrier support details, but subscribing to such information can be costly for a small company. Many mobile developers instead choose to create a custom device database with only the devices they are interested in and the specific data they need for each device, which is often absent from open and free databases. WURFL (*http://wurfl.sourceforge.net*), for instance, is better for mobile Web development than for application development.

Assessing Project Risks

In addition to the normal risks any software project must identify, mobile projects need to be aware of the outside influences that can affect their project schedule and whether the project requirements can be met. Some of the risk factors include identifying and acquiring target devices and continually reassessing application feasibility.

Identifying Target Devices

Just as most sane software developers wouldn't write a desktop application without first deciding what operating systems (and their versions) the application would run on, mobile developers must consider the target devices their application will run on. Each device has different capabilities, a different user interface, and unique limitations.

Target devices are generally determined in one of two ways:

- There's a popular "killer" device you want to develop for.
- You want to develop an application for maximum coverage.

In the first instance, you have your initial target device (or class of devices) figured out. In the second instance, you want to look at the available (and soon-to-be-available) devices on the market and adjust your application specifications to cover as many as is reasonably feasible.

Tip

On the Android platform, you normally do not target individual devices specifically, but device features or classes (for example, those running a specific platform version or having specific hardware configurations). You can limit the devices upon which your application will be installed using Android manifest tags, which act as market filters.

There may be instances when your application is targeting only a specific niche, such as Google TV or Google Glass. In this case, your application would probably not be useful for a smartphone or tablet; on the other hand, if your application is more general, such as a game, you should make every effort to determine the different targets and types of devices your application will work on, such as smartphones, phablets, tablets, and TVs.

Understanding How Manufacturers and Operators Fit In

It is also important to note that we've seen popular product lines, such as the Droid, Galaxy, One, Desire, EVO, or Optimus line of Android devices, customized by a number of manufacturers. A carrier often ships its custom version of a device, including a different user experience or skin, as well as big bundles of custom applications (taking up a bunch of space on the device). The carrier might also disable specific device features, which could effectively make it impossible for your application to run. You must take all these factors into account when considering your application requirements and capabilities. Your application's running requirements must match the features shared across all target devices and handle optional feature use appropriately in all cases.

Understanding How Devices Come and Go over Time

New devices are developed all the time. Carriers and manufacturers retire (sunset) devices all the time. Different carriers might carry the same (or similar) device but might sunset (retire) the device at different times. A carrier may also release a particular device much sooner than other carriers, for various reasons.

Tip

Developers should set a policy, made clear to users, of how long an application will be supported after the carrier or manufacturer stops supporting a specific device. This policy might need to be different for various carriers because carriers impose their own support requirements.

Developers need to understand how different kinds of device models can move through the worldwide marketplace. Some devices are available (or become popular) only in certain geographic regions. Sometimes devices are released worldwide, but often they are released regionally.

Historically, it has been common for a device (or new generation of devices) to become available initially in market-driving regions of eastern Asia, including South Korea and Japan, and then show up in Europe, North America, and Australia, where device users often upgrade every year or two and pay premium rates for applications. Finally, these same devices become available in Central and South America, China, and India, where subscribers often don't have landlines or the same levels of income. Regions such as China and India must often be treated as entirely separate mobile marketplaces—with more affordable devices requiring vastly different revenue models. Here, applications sell for less, but revenue is instead derived from the huge and growing subscriber base.

Acquiring Target Devices

The earlier you can get your hands on the target devices, the better off you are. Sometimes this is as easy as going to the store and buying a new device.

It is quite common for an application developer to target upcoming devices—devices not yet shipping or available to consumers. There is a great competitive advantage to having your application ready to run the moment consumers have the device in their hands for the first time. For preproduction devices, you can join manufacturer and operator developer programs. These programs help you keep abreast of changes to the device lines (upcoming models, discontinued models). Many of these programs also include preproduction device loan programs, enabling developers to get their hands on the device before consumers do.

Tip

If you are just getting started acquiring Android devices, consider a Google Experience device, such as one of the Nexus handsets like the Nexus 4, 7, or 10. See *http://www.google .com/nexus/* for more information.

There are risks for developers writing applications for specific preproduction devices because device shipment dates often slide and the platform might have unstable or bug-prone firmware. Devices are delayed or canceled. Device features (especially new and interesting ones) are not set in stone until the device ships and the developer verifies that those features work as expected. Exciting new devices are announced all the time—devices you might want your application to support. Your project plan must be flexible enough to change and adapt with the market as necessary.

Tip

Sometimes you don't need to acquire specific devices to test with them. Various online services allow you to remotely install and test on real devices that are accessible and controllable through remote services. Most of these services have some sort of charge that must be weighed against the cost of actually owning the device outright.

Determining the Feasibility of Application Requirements

Mobile developers are at the mercy of the device limitations, which vary in terms of memory and processing power, screen type, and platform version. Mobile developers do not really have the luxury traditional desktop application developers have of saying an application requires "more memory" or "more space." Device limitations are pretty much fixed, and if a mobile application is to run, it runs within the device's limitations, or not at all. Technically speaking, most Android devices have some hardware flexibility, such as the ability to use external storage devices such as SD cards, but we're still talking about limited resources.

You can do true feasibility assessment only on the physical device, not the software emulator. Your application might work beautifully in the emulator but falter on the actual device. Mobile developers must constantly revisit feasibility, application responsiveness, and performance throughout the development process.

Understanding Quality Assurance Risks

The QA team has its work cut out for it because the testing environment is generally less than ideal.

Testing Early, Testing Often

Get those target devices in hand as early as possible. For preproduction devices, it can take months to get the hardware in hand from the manufacturer. Cooperating with carrier device loaner programs and buying devices from retail locations is frustrating but sometimes necessary. Don't wait until the last minute to gather the test hardware. We have seen many developers wonder why their applications run slow on certain older devices only to realize that testing on a fast development computer or brand-new device with a dedicated network connection is not the same as testing on the actual device.

Testing on the Device

It cannot be said enough: *Testing on the emulator is helpful, but testing on the device is essential.* In reality, it doesn't matter if the application works on the emulator—no one uses an emulator in the real world.

Although you can perform factory resets on devices and wipe user data, there is often no easy way to completely "wipe" a device and return it to a clean starting state, so the QA team needs to determine and stick to a testing policy of what is considered a clean state on the device. Testers might need to learn to flash devices with different firmware versions and understand subtle differences between platform versions, as well as how underlying application data is stored on the device (for example, SQLite databases, private application files, and cache usage).

Mitigating the Risk of Limited Real-World Testing Opportunities

In some ways, every QA tester works within a controlled environment. This is doubly true for mobile testers. They often work with devices that are not on real networks and preproduction devices that might not match those in the field. Add to this that because testing generally takes place in a lab, the location (including primary cell tower, satellite fixes and related device signal strength, availability of data services, LBS information, and locale information) is fixed. The QA team needs to get creative to mitigate the risks of testing too narrow a range of these factors. For example, it is essential to test all applications when the device has no signal (and in airplane mode and such) to make sure they don't crash and burn under such conditions that we all experience at some point. A variety of testing tools, some better suited to developers and white-box testers, are available to assist in application development. Some of the most suitable tools include Exerciser Monkey, monkeyrunner, and JUnit.

Testing Client/Server and Cloud-Friendly Applications

Make sure the QA team understands its responsibilities. Mobile applications often have network components and server-side functionality. Make sure thorough server and service testing is part of the test plan—not just the client portion of the solution that is implemented on the device. This might require the development of desktop or Web applications to exercise network portions of the overall solution.

Writing Essential Project Documentation

You might think that with its shorter schedules, smaller teams, and simpler functionality, mobile software project documentation would be less onerous. Unfortunately, this is not the case—quite the opposite. In addition to the traditional benefits any software project enjoys from good documentation, it serves a variety of purposes in mobile development. Consider documenting the following for your project:

- Requirements analysis and prioritization
- Risk assessment and management
- Application architecture and design
- Feasibility studies, including performance benchmarking
- Technical specifications (overall, server, device-specific client)
- Detailed user interface specifications (general, service specific)
- Test plans, test scripts, test cases (general, device specific)
- Scope change documentation

Much of this documentation is common in the average software development project. But perhaps your team finds that skimping on certain aspects of the documentation process has been doable in the past. Before you think of cutting corners in a mobile development project, consider some of these documentation requirements for a successful project. Some project documentation might be simpler than that of larger-scale software projects, but other portions might need to be fleshed out in finer detail—especially user interface and feasibility studies.

Developing Test Plans for Quality Assurance Purposes

Quality assurance relies heavily on the functional specification documentation and the user interface documentation. Screen real estate is valuable on the small screens of mobile devices, and user experience is vital to the successful mobile project. Test plans need to provide complete coverage of the application user interface, yet be flexible enough to address higher-level user experience issues that may meet the requirements of the test plan but just aren't positive experiences.

Understanding the Importance of User Interface Documentation

There's no such thing as a killer application with a poorly designed user interface. Thoughtful user interface design is one of the most important details to nail down during the design phase of any mobile software project. You must thoroughly document application workflow (application state) at the screen-by-screen level and can include detailed specifications for key usage patterns and how to gracefully fall back when certain keys or features are missing. You should clearly define usage cases in advance.

Leveraging Third-Party Testing Facilities

Some companies opt to have QA done offsite by a third party; most QA teams require detailed documentation, including use case workflow diagrams, to determine correct application behavior. If you do not provide adequate, detailed, and accurate documentation to the testing facility, you will not get deep, detailed, and accurate test results. By providing detailed documentation, you raise the bar from "it works" to "it works correctly." What might seem straightforward to some people might not be to others.

Providing Documentation Required by Third Parties

If you are required to submit your application for review to a software certification program, or in some cases to a mobile application store, part of your submission is likely to be some documentation about your application. Some stores require, for example, that your application include a Help feature or technical support contact information. Certification programs might require you to provide detailed documentation on application functionality, user interface workflow, and application state diagrams.

Providing Documentation for Maintenance and Porting

Mobile applications are often ported to additional devices and other mobile platforms. This porting work is frequently done by a third party, making the existence of thorough functional and technical specifications even more crucial.

Leveraging Configuration Management Systems

Many wonderful source control systems are out there for developers, and most that work well for traditional development work fine for a mobile project. Versioning your application, on the other hand, is not necessarily as straightforward as you might think.

Choosing a Source Control System

Mobile development considerations impose no surprise requirements for source control systems. Some considerations for developers evaluating how to handle configuration management for a mobile project are

- Ability to keep track of source code (Java) and binaries (Android packages and so on)
- Ability to keep track of application resources by device configuration (graphics and so on)
- Integration with the developer's chosen development environment (the Android IDE, Android Studio, or Eclipse)

One point to consider is integration between the development environment (such as the Android IDE) and your source control system. Common source control systems, such as Subversion, CVS, Git, and Mercurial, work well with Eclipse and Android Studio. Git source control is integrated with the Android IDE as the default source control software. Check to see if your favorite source control system works with your chosen Android development environment.

Implementing an Application Version System That Works

Developers should also make an early decision on a versioning scheme that takes into account the device particulars and the software build. It is often not sufficient to version the software by build alone (that is, Version 1.0.1).

Mobile developers often combine the traditional versioning scheme with the target device configuration or device class supported (Version 1.0.1.*Important Characteristic/ Device Class Name*). This helps QA, technical support personnel, and end users who might not know the model names or features of their devices or know them only by marketing names developers are often unaware of. For example, an application developed with camera support might be versioned 1.0.1.Cam, where Cam stands for "Camera Support," whereas the same application for a device without camera support might have a version such as 1.0.1.NoCam, where NoCam stands for the "No Camera Support" source branch. If you had two different maintenance engineers supporting the different source code trees, you would know just by the version name whom to assign bug fixes.

Just to make things a tad more confusing, you need to plan your upgrade versions as well. If an upgrade spawns a rebuild of your application, you might want to version it appropriately: Version 1.0.1.NoCam.Upg1, and such. Yes, this can get out of control, so don't go overboard, but if you design your versioning system intelligently up front, it can be useful later when you have different device builds floating around internally and with users. Finally, you also have to keep track of the `versionCode` attribute associated with your application.

Also, be aware of what distribution methods support multiple application packages or binaries as the same application and which require each binary to be managed independently. There are several good reasons not to have all of your code and resources in a single binary. Application package size, for example, can get large and unmanageable when the application attempts to support multiple device resolutions using alternative resources.

Designing Mobile Applications

When designing an application for mobile, the developer must consider the constraints the device imposes and decide what type of application framework is best for a given project.

Understanding Mobile Device Limitations

Applications are expected to be fast, responsive, and stable, but developers must work with limited resources. You must keep in mind the memory and processing power constraints of all target devices when designing and developing mobile applications.

Exploring Common Mobile Application Architectures

Mobile applications have traditionally come in two basic models: standalone applications and network-driven applications.

Standalone applications are packaged with everything they require and rely on the device to do all the heavy lifting. All processing is done locally, in memory, and is subject to the limitations of the device. Standalone applications might use network functions, but they do not rely on them for core application functionality. An example of a reasonable standalone application is a basic Solitaire game. A user can play the game when the device is in airplane mode without issue.

Network-driven applications provide a lightweight client on the device but rely on the network (or the cloud) to provide a good portion of their content and functionality. Network-driven applications are often used to offload intensive processing to a server. They also benefit from the ability to deliver additional content or functionality on the fly, long after the application has been installed. Developers also like network-driven applications because this architecture enables them to build one smart application server or cloud service with device clients for many different operating systems to support a larger audience of users. Good examples of network-driven applications include

- Applications that leverage cloud-based services, application servers, or Web services
- Customizable content such as ringtone and wallpaper applications
- Applications with noncritical process- and memory-intensive operations that can be offloaded to a powerful server and the results delivered back to the client
- Any application that provides additional features at a later date without a full update to the binary

How much you rely on the network to assist in your application's functionality is up to you. You can use the network to provide only content updates (popular new ringtones), or you can use it to dictate how your application looks and behaves (for instance, adding new menu options or features on the fly). If your application is truly network based, such as a Web app, and does not need access to any device-specific features, you may not even need to build a native application with an installable APK. In that case, you may prefer to have users access your application through a browser.

Designing for Extensibility and Maintenance

Applications can be written with a fixed user interface and a fixed feature set, but they need not be. Network-driven applications can be more complex to design but offer flexibility for the long term. Here's an example: Let's say you want to write a wallpaper application. Your application can be a standalone version, partially network driven, or completely network driven. Regardless, your application has two required functions:

- Display a set of images and allow the user to choose one.
- Take the chosen image and set it as the wallpaper on the device.

A super-simple standalone wallpaper application might come with a fixed set of wall-papers. If they're a generic size for all target devices, you might need to reformat them for the specific device. You could write this application, but it would waste space and processing. You can't update the wallpapers available, and it is generally just a bad design.

The partially network-driven wallpaper application might enable the user to browse a fixed menu of wallpaper categories, which show images from a generic image server. The application downloads a specific graphic and then formats the image for the device. As the developer, you can add new wallpaper images to the server anytime, but you need to build a new application every time you want to add a new device configuration or screen size. If you want to change the menu to add live wallpapers at a later date, you need to write a new version of your application. This application design is feasible, but it isn't using its resources wisely either and isn't particularly extensible. However, you could use the single application server and write applications for Android, iPhone, Windows RT, BREW, J2ME, and BlackBerry 10 clients, so you are still in a better position than you were with the standalone wallpaper application.

The fully network-driven version of the wallpaper application does the bare minimum on the device. The client enables the server to dictate what the client user interface looks like, what menus to display, and where to display them. The user browses the images from the application server just as with the partially network-driven version, but when the user chooses a wallpaper, the mobile application just sends a request to the server: "I want this wallpaper and I am this kind or type of device, with such-and-such screen resolution." The server formats and resizes the image (any process-intensive operations) and sends the perfectly tailored wallpaper down to the application, which the application then sets as the wallpaper. Adding support for more devices is straightforward—simply deploy the lightweight client with any necessary changes and add support for that device configuration to the server. Adding a new menu item is just a server change, resulting in all devices (or whichever devices the server dictates) getting that new category. You need to update the client only when a new function requires the client to change, such as to add support for live wallpapers. The response time of this application depends on network performance, but the application is the most extensible and dynamic. However, this application is basically useless when the device is in airplane mode.

Standalone applications are straightforward. This approach is great for one-shot applications and those that are meant to be network independent. Network-driven applications require a bit more forethought and are sometimes more complicated to develop but might save a lot of time and provide users with fresh content and features for the long run.

Designing for Application Interoperability

Mobile application designers should consider how they will interface with other applications on the device, including other applications written by the same developer. Here are some issues to address:

- Will your application rely on other content providers?
- Are these content providers guaranteed to be installed on the device?

- Will your application act as a content provider? What data will it provide?
- Will your application have background features? Act as a service?
- Will your application rely on third-party services or optional components?
- Will your application use publicly documented Intent mechanisms to access third-party functionality? Will your application provide the same?
- How will your application user experience suffer when optional components are not available?
- Will your application require substantial device resources such as battery life? Will it play nice?
- Will your application expose its functionality through a remote interface such as Android Interface Definition Language (AIDL)?

Developing Mobile Applications

Mobile application implementation follows the same principles as other platforms. The steps mobile developers take during implementation are fairly straightforward:

- Write and compile the code.
- Run the application in the software emulator.
- Test and debug the application in the software emulator or test device.
- Package and deploy the application to the target devices.
- Test and debug the application on the target devices.
- Incorporate changes from the team and repeat until the application is complete.

Note

We talk more about development strategies for building solid Android applications in Chapter 16, "Designing and Developing Bulletproof Android Applications."

Testing Mobile Applications

Testers face many challenges, including device fragmentation (many devices, each with different features—some call this "compatibility"), defining device states (what is a clean state?), and handling real-world events (device calls, loss of coverage). Gathering the devices needed for testing can be costly and difficult.

The good news for mobile QA teams is that the Android SDK includes a number of useful tools for testing applications on both the emulator and the device. There are many opportunities for leveraging white-box testing.

You must modify defect-tracking systems to handle testing across device configurations and carriers. For thorough testing, QA team members generally cannot be given the device and told to "try to break it." There are many shades of gray for testers between black-box and white-box testing. Testers should know their way around the Android emulator and the other utilities provided with the Android SDK. Mobile QA involves a lot of edge case testing. Again, a preproduction model of a device might not be exactly the same as what eventually ships to consumers.

> **Note**
>
> We discuss testing Android applications in detail in Chapter 18, "Testing Android Applications."

Controlling the Test Release

In some situations, you may wish to take complete control of to whom your application will be released for testing. Rather than making your application available to the entire world all at once, releasing your application on a smaller scale may be the ideal test plan. Here are the common ways for controlling the test release of an application:

- **Private controlled testing:** In this situation, developers invite users to a controlled setting, such as an office. They observe users interacting with the application, and then make changes based on feedback from those test users. The developers then implement any updates, invite more testers to interact with the application, and so on, until the design receives positive feedback. Only then would they release the application to more users. Private testing usually involves not allowing the application to leave the facilities on a test user's device; sometimes you may even want to provide your own testing device to ensure that the application never leaves your facilities.

- **Private group testing:** In this situation, developers prove their APK file to a very small set of test users, and then collect feedback in a manner suitable for the situation. They then use the feedback to make the necessary changes, rerelease the APK to the same test users, or new test users, and continue receiving feedback and updating accordingly, until they begin receiving positive responses from users. The application is usually not on a strict lockdown policy, such as never leaving the building, but rather has a more limited but semi-open test distribution. One new feature of Google Play that may help you facilitate this type of test release is a Private Channel Release. If you have a Google Apps domain, you can launch your application in a controlled and private way to users of your particular domain.

- **Google Play Staged Rollouts:** Google Play provides many new features for controlling to whom your application is released. Using these facilities may ease how you test your application with real users. Staged Rollouts is a new feature of Google Play that allows you to offer your application to alpha and beta test groups for collecting early feedback, prior to releasing your application to all Google Play users.

Deploying Mobile Applications

Developers need to determine what methods they use to distribute applications. With Android, you have a number of options. You can market applications yourself and leverage marketplaces such as Google Play. Consolidated mobile marketplaces, such as Handango, also have Android distribution channels of which you can take advantage.

Note

We discuss publication of Android applications in detail in Chapter 19, "Publishing Your Android Application."

Determining Target Markets

Developers must take into account any requirements imposed by third parties offering application distribution mechanisms. Specific distributors might impose rules for what types of applications they distribute on your behalf. They might impose quality requirements such as testing certifications (although none specific to Android applications existed at the time this book went to print) and accompanying technical support, documentation and adherence to common user interface workflow standards, and performance metrics for responsive applications. Distributors might also impose content restrictions such as barring objectionable content.

Tip

The most popular distribution channels for Android applications have been changing over time. Google Play remains the first stop in Android app publication, but both the Amazon Appstore and Facebook App Center have become effective hubs for Android app distribution. Other app stores are also available; some cater to special user groups and niche application genres, whereas others distribute for many different platforms.

Supporting and Maintaining Mobile Applications

Developers cannot just develop an application, publish it, and forget about it—even the simplest of applications likely requires some maintenance and the occasional upgrade. Generally speaking, mobile application support requirements are minimal if you come from a traditional software background, but they do exist.

Carriers and operators generally serve as the front line of technical support to end users. As a developer, you aren't usually required to have 24/7 responsive technical support staff or toll-free device numbers and such. In fact, the bulk of application maintenance can fall on the server side and be limited to content maintenance—for example, posting new media such as ringtones, wallpapers, videos, or other content. This may not seem obvious at first. After all, you've provided your email address and website when the user downloaded your application, right? Although that may be the case, your average user still calls the company on the bill first (in other words, the carrier) for support if the device is not functioning properly.

That said, the device firmware changes quickly, and mobile development teams need to stay on top of the market. Here are some of the maintenance and support considerations unique to mobile application development.

Track and Address Crashes Reported by Users

Google Play—the most popular way to distribute Android applications—has built-in features enabling users to submit crash and bug reports regarding an application. Monitor your developer account and address these issues in a timely fashion in order to maintain your credibility and keep your users happy.

Testing Firmware Upgrades

Android handsets receive frequent (some say *too* frequent) firmware upgrades. This means that the Android platform versions you initially tested and supported become obsolete and the handsets on which your application is installed can suddenly run new versions of the Android firmware. Although upgrades are supposed to be backward compatible, this hasn't always proven true. In fact, many developers have fallen victim to poor upgrade scenarios, in which their applications suddenly cease to function properly. Always retest your applications after a major or minor firmware upgrade occurs in the field.

Maintaining Adequate Application Documentation

Maintenance is often not performed by the same engineers who developed the application in the first place. Here, keeping adequate development and testing documentation, including specifications and test scripts, is even more vital.

Managing Live Server Changes

Always treat any live server and Web or cloud service with the care it deserves. This means you need to appropriately time your backups and upgrades. You need to safeguard data and maintain user privacy at all times. You should manage rollouts carefully because live mobile application users might rely on the app's availability. Do not underestimate the server-side development or testing needs. Always test server rollouts and service upgrades in a safe testing environment before "going live."

Identifying Low-Risk Porting Opportunities

If you've implemented the device database we talked about previously in the chapter, now is the ideal time to analyze device similarities to identify easy porting projects. For example, you might discover that an application was originally developed for a specific class of device, but now several popular devices are on the market with similar specifications. Porting an existing application to these new devices is sometimes as straightforward as generating a new build (with appropriate versioning) and testing the application on the new devices. If you defined your device classes well, you might even get lucky and not have to make any changes at all when new devices come out.

Application Feature Selection

When determining what features your application will support, make sure to think about the costs versus the benefits of supporting a particular feature. Adding new features is always the easy part, but removing them from your application is not. Once users become accustomed to a feature, if that feature goes missing, your users may never use your application again. They may even go as far as writing a negative review and giving your app an extremely low rating. Always make sure that a particular feature is of use to the users of your application, rather than just cluttering a user interface with things for users to do, only to realize that you should not have added a given feature in the first place.

Summary

Mobile software development has evolved over time and differs in some important ways from traditional desktop software development. In this chapter, you gained some practical advice for adapting traditional software processes to mobile—from identifying target devices to testing and deploying your application to the world. There's always room for improvement when it comes to software processes. Ideally, some of these insights can help you to avoid the pitfalls new mobile companies sometimes fall into or simply to improve the processes of veteran teams.

Quiz Questions

1. True or false: The waterfall software methodology is preferable to the iteration and rapid prototyping approach for Android development.

2. What are the approaches the authors have found helpful for determining project requirements?

3. When is the best time to implement a device database?

4. True or false: Since the Android emulator has been made available, testing on real devices is not essential.

5. What are the steps mobile developers take during implementation?

Exercises

1. Come up with an idea for an application, then determine and explain the best approach to take for determining project requirements.

2. Create a list of requirements for the application idea you came up with in the previous exercise.

3. Identify the target devices for the application idea that you came up with in the first exercise, and create a simple device database outlining the important features that are relevant to your application idea.

References and More Information

Wikipedia on the software development process:
>   *http://en.wikipedia.org/wiki/Software_development_process*

Wikipedia on the waterfall development process:
>   *http://en.wikipedia.org/wiki/Waterfall_model*

Wikipedia on rapid application development (RAD):
>   *http://en.wikipedia.org/wiki/Rapid_application_development*

Wikipedia on iterative and incremental development:
>   *http://en.wikipedia.org/wiki/Iterative_and_incremental_development*

Extreme Programming:
>   *http://www.extremeprogramming.org*

Android Training: "Designing for Multiple Screens":
>   *http://d.android.com/training/multiscreen/index.html*

Android Training: "Creating Backward-Compatible UIs":
>   *http://d.android.com/training/backward-compatible-ui/index.html*

Android API Guides: "Supporting Multiple Screens":
>   *http://d.android.com/guide/practices/screens_support.html*

Android API Guides: "Supporting Tablets and Handsets":
>   *http://d.android.com/guide/practices/tablets-and-handsets.html*

Android Google Services: "Filters on Google Play":
>   *http://d.android.com/google/play/filters.html*

16

Designing and Developing Bulletproof Android Applications

In this chapter, we cover tips and techniques from our years in the trenches of mobile software design and development. We also warn you—the designers, developers, and managers of mobile applications—of the various and sundry pitfalls you should do your best to avoid. Reading this chapter all at one time when you're new to mobile development might be a bit overwhelming. Instead, consider reading specific sections when planning the parts of the overall process. Some of our advice might not be appropriate for your particular project, and processes can always be improved. Ideally, this information about how mobile development projects succeed (or fail) will give you some insight into how you might improve the chances of success for your own projects.

Best Practices in Designing Bulletproof Mobile Applications

The "rules" of mobile application design are straightforward and apply across all platforms. These rules were crafted to remind us that our applications often play a secondary role on the device. Many Android devices are, at the end of the day, smartphones first. These rules also make it clear that we do operate, to some extent, because of the infrastructure managed by the carriers and device manufacturers. These rules are echoed throughout the Android SDK License Agreement and third-party application marketplace terms and conditions.

The "rules" are as follows:

- Don't abuse the user's trust.
- Don't interfere with device telephony and messaging services (if applicable).
- Don't break or otherwise tamper with or exploit the device hardware, firmware, software, or OEM components.
- Don't abuse or cause problems on operator networks.

Now perhaps these rules sound like no-brainers, but even the most well-intentioned developers can accidentally break them if they aren't careful and don't test their applications thoroughly before distribution. This is especially true for applications that leverage networking support and low-level hardware APIs on the device, and those that store private user data such as names, locations, and contact information.

Meeting Mobile Users' Demands

Mobile users also have their own set of demands for applications they install on their devices. Applications are expected to

- "Enchant me," "Simplify my life," and "Make me amazing" (from the Android design documentation found here: *http://d.android.com/design/get-started/creative-vision.html*)
- Have straightforward, intuitive user interfaces that are easy to get up and running
- Get the job done with minimal frustration to the user (provide visual feedback and follow common Android design patterns) and minimal impact on device performance (battery usage, network and data usage, and so on)
- Be available 24 hours a day, seven days a week (remote servers or services always on, always available, not running in someone's closet)
- Include a Help and/or About screen for feedback and support contact information
- Honor private user information and treat it with care

Designing User Interfaces for Mobile Devices

Designing effective user interfaces for mobile devices, especially for applications that run on a number of different devices, is something of a black art. We've all seen bad mobile application user interfaces. A frustrating user experience can turn a user off your brand; a good experience can win a user's loyalty. Great experiences give your application an edge over the competition, even if your functionality is similar. An elegant, well-designed user interface can win over users even when the application functionality is behind that of the competition. Said another way, doing something really well is more important than cramming too many features into an app and doing them badly.

Here are some tips for designing great mobile user interfaces:

- Fill screens sparingly; too much information on one screen overwhelms the user.
- Be consistent with user interface workflows, menu types, and buttons. Also, consider making the user interface consistent with Android design patterns.
- Design your applications using fragments, even if you aren't targeting tablet devices. (The Android Support Package makes this possible for nearly all target versions.)
- Make touch mode "hit areas" large enough (48dp) and space them appropriately (8dp).
- Streamline common use cases with clear, consistent, and straightforward interfaces.
- Use big, readable fonts and large icons.

- Integrate tightly with other applications on the system using standardized controls, such as the `QuickContactBadge`, content providers, and search adapters.

- Keep localization in mind when designing text-heavy user interfaces. Some languages are lengthier than others.

- Reduce the number of keys or clicks needed as much as possible.

- Do not assume that specific input mechanisms (such as specific buttons or a keyboard) are available on all devices.

- Try to design the default use case of each screen to require only the user's thumb. Special cases might require other buttons or input methods, but encourage "thumbing" by default.

- Size resources such as graphics appropriately for target devices. Do not include oversize resources and assets, because they bulk up your application package, load more slowly, and are generally less efficient.

- In terms of "friendly" user interfaces, assume that users do not read the application permissions when they approve them to install your application. If your application does anything that could cause users to incur significant fees or shares private information, consider informing them again (as appropriate) when your application performs such actions. Basically, take a "no surprises" approach, even if the permissions and your privacy policy also state the same thing.

> **Note**
>
> We discussed how to design Android applications that are compatible with a wide range of devices, including how to develop for different screen sizes and resolutions, in Chapter 14, "Designing Compatible Applications." We also discuss designing for the user experience in Chapter 17, "Planning the Android Application Experience."

Designing Stable and Responsive Mobile Applications

Mobile device hardware has come a long way in the past few years, but developers must still work with limited resources. Users do not usually have the luxury of upgrading the RAM and other hardware in Android devices. Android users may, however, take advantage of removable storage devices such as SD cards to provide some extra space for application and media storage. Spending some time up front to design a stable and responsive application is important for the success of the project. The following are some tips for designing robust and responsive mobile applications:

- Don't perform resource-intensive or lengthy operations on the main UI thread. Always use asynchronous tasks, threads, or background services to offload blocking operations.

- Use efficient data structures and algorithms; these choices manifest themselves in app responsiveness and happy users.

- Use recursion with care; these functional areas should be code reviewed and performance tested.

- Keep application state at all times. The Android `Activity` stack makes this work well, but you should take extra care to go above and beyond.

- Save your state using appropriate lifecycle callbacks, and assume that your application will be suspended or stopped at any moment. If your application is suspended or closed, you cannot expect a user to verify anything (click a button and so on). If your application resumes gracefully, your users will be grateful.

- Start up fast and resume fast. You cannot afford to have the user twiddling thumbs waiting for your application to start. Instead, you need to strike a delicate balance between preloading and on-demand data because your application might be suspended (or closed) with no notice.

- Inform users during long operations by using progress bars. Consider offloading heavy processing to a server instead of performing these operations on the device because they might drain battery life beyond the limits users are willing to accept.

- Ensure that long operations are likely to succeed before embarking on them. For example, if your application downloads large files, check for network connectivity, file size, and available space before attempting the download.

- Minimize the use of local storage, because most devices have very limited amounts. Use external storage, when appropriate. Be aware that SD cards (the most common external storage option) can be ejected and swapped; your application should handle this gracefully.

- Understand that data calls to content providers and across the AIDL barrier come at a cost to performance, so make these calls judiciously.

- Verify that your application resource consumption model matches your target audience. Gamers might anticipate shorter battery life on graphics-intensive games, but productivity applications should not drain the battery unnecessarily and should be lightweight for people "on the go" who do not always have their device charging.

Tip

Written by the Google Android team, the Android Developers Blog (*http://android-developers .blogspot.com*) is a fantastic resource. This blog provides detailed insight into the Android platform, often covering topics not discussed in the Android platform documentation. Here, you can find tips, tricks, best practices, and shortcuts on relevant Android development topics such as memory management (`Context` management), `View` optimization (avoiding deep `View` hierarchies), and layout tricks to improve UI speed. Savvy Android developers visit this blog regularly and incorporate these practices and tips into their projects. Keep in mind that Google's Android Developer guys and gals are often focused on educating the rest of us about the latest API-level features; their techniques and advice may not always be suitable for implementation with older target platforms.

Designing Secure Mobile Applications

Many mobile applications integrate with core applications such as the Phone, Camera, and Contacts. Make sure you take all the precautions necessary to secure and protect private user data such as names, locations, and contact information used by your application. This includes safeguarding personal user data on application servers and during network transmission.

> **Tip**
>
> If your application accesses, uses, or transmits private data, especially usernames, passwords, or contact information, it's a good idea to include an End User License Agreement (EULA) and a privacy policy with your application. Also keep in mind that privacy laws vary by country.

Handling Private Data

To begin with, limit the private or sensitive data your application stores as much as possible. Don't store this information in plain text, and don't transmit it over the network without safeguards. Do not try to work around any security mechanisms imposed by the Android framework. Store private user data in private application files, which are private to the application, and not in shared parts of the operating system. Do not expose application data in content providers without enforcing appropriate permissions on other applications. Use the encryption classes available in the Android framework when necessary.

Transmitting Private Data

The same cautions should apply to any remote network data storage (such as application servers or cloud storage) and network transmission. Make sure any servers or services that your application relies on are properly secured against identity or data theft and invasion of privacy. Treat any servers your application uses like any other part of the application—test these areas thoroughly. Any private data transmitted should be secured using typical security mechanisms such as SSL. The same rules apply when enabling your application for backups using services such as Android Backup Service.

Designing Mobile Applications for Maximum Profit

For billing and revenue generation, mobile applications generally fall into one or more of the following categories:

- Free applications (including those with advertising revenue)
- Single payment (pay once)
- In-app products (pay for specific content, such as a ringtone, a Sword of Smiting, or a new level pack)

- Subscription billing (payments recurring on a schedule, often seen with productivity and service applications)

- Outside billing and membership supplementation (mobile access to content such as premium TV for current paying subscribers)

Applications can use multiple types of billing, depending on which marketplaces and billing APIs they use (Google Play, for example, will be limiting billing methods to Google Wallet). No specific billing APIs are built into the Android framework. With Android in general, third parties can provide billing methods or APIs, so technically the sky's the limit. There is an optional Google Play In-app Billing API add-on for use with Google Play (and only Google Play). Google Play provides support for accepting various payment methods for Google Play, including credit cards, direct carrier billing, gift cards, and Google Play balance values.

When designing your mobile applications, consider the functional areas where billing can come into play and factor this into your design. Consider the transactional integrity of specific workflow areas of the application that can be charged for. For example, if your application has the capability to deliver data to the device, make sure this process is transactional in nature so that if you decide to charge for this feature, you can drop in the billing code, and when the user pays, the delivery occurs, or the entire transaction is rolled back.

Note

You will learn more about the different methods currently available to market your application in Chapter 19, "Publishing Your Android Application."

Following the Android Application Quality Guidelines

Users' expectations of application quality rise with every new iteration of Android. Luckily, Google has put in a great deal of effort researching what a quality application is like, its employees have designed quite a few quality applications themselves, and the best part is that they have designed a set of standards that you can use to measure your application's quality.

There are three quality guidelines recommended in the Android documentation that you should seriously consider:

- **Core app quality:** Core app quality criteria are the most basic standards that all of your applications should follow, and they should also be validated on each and every device that you plan on targeting. The core app quality guidelines include criteria for how to assess your application's visual design and user interaction, functional behavior criteria, stability and performance criteria, and Google Play promotional criteria. The guidelines also provide a sort of step-by-step procedural approach to testing your application to determine if it meets these recommended criteria. You can learn more about how to meet the core app quality guidelines here: *http:// d.android.com/distribute/googleplay/quality/core.html.*

- **Tablet app quality:** If you are building an application for tablets, you still need to make sure that you meet the core app quality criteria. In addition, Google provides an additional set of quality criteria for developers writing applications for tablets. The guidelines for tablets are presented as a checklist of recommendations. You can learn more about the checklist for tablet app quality here: *http://d.android.com/ distribute/googleplay/quality/tablet.html.*

- **Improving app quality:** Even if your application meets the criteria and recommendations for creating a quality application, your efforts should not end there. User demand and application competition are setting the bar for quality higher and higher. To keep up with demand and to outshine your competition, the Android documentation provides a set of strategies that you can begin thinking about and implementing in your application quality analysis. To learn more about the strategies for continuously improving your application's quality, visit *http://d.android.com/ distribute/googleplay/strategies/app-quality.html.*

Currently, there are no requirements that your application actually adhere to these quality guidelines, but if you would like your application to achieve success, these guidelines are where to begin focusing your efforts.

Leveraging Third-Party Quality Standards

There are no certification programs specifically designed for Android applications. However, as more applications are developed, third-party standards might be designed to differentiate quality applications from the masses. For example, mobile marketplaces may impose quality requirements, and certainly programs have been created with some recognized body's endorsement or stamp of approval. The Amazon Appstore for Android puts apps through some testing before they are made available for sale. Google Play has an Editors' Choice category of applications. Developers with an eye on financial applications would do well to consider conformance requirements.

Warning

With Android, the market is expected to manage itself to a greater extent than in some other mobile platform markets. Do not make the mistake of interpreting that as "no rules" when it really means "few rules imposed by the system." Strong licensing terms are in place to keep malware and other malicious code out of users' hands, and applications do indeed get removed for misbehavior, just as they do when they sneak through onto other platform markets.

Designing Mobile Applications for Ease of Maintenance and Upgrades

Generally speaking, it's best to make as few assumptions about the device configurations as possible when developing a mobile application. You'll be rewarded later when you want to port your application or provide an easy upgrade. You should carefully consider what assumptions you make.

Leveraging Application Diagnostics

In addition to adequate documentation and easy-to-decipher code, you can leverage some tricks to help maintain and monitor mobile applications in the field. Building lightweight auditing, logging, and reporting into your application can be highly useful for generating your own statistics and analytics. Relying on third-party information, such as that generated with market reports, could cause you to miss some key pieces of data that are useful to you. For example, you can easily keep track of

- How many users install the application
- How many users launch the application for the first time
- How many users regularly use the application
- What the most popular usage patterns and trends are
- What the least popular usage patterns and features are
- What devices (determined by application versioning or other relevant metrics) are the most popular

Often you can translate these figures into rough estimates of expected sales, which you can later compare with actual sales figures from third-party marketplaces. You can streamline and, for example, make the most popular usage patterns the most visible and efficient in terms of user experience design. Sometimes you can even identify potential bugs, such as features that are not working at all, just by noting that a feature has never been used in the field. Finally, you can determine which device targets are most appropriate for your specific application and user base.

You can gather interesting information about your application from numerous sources, including the following:

- Google Play sales statistics, ratings, and bug/crash reports, as well as those available on other distribution channels.
- Application integration with statistics-gathering APIs such as Google Analytics or other third-party application monitoring services.
- For applications relying on network servers, quite a lot of information can be determined by looking at server-side statistics.
- Feedback sent directly to you, the developer, through email, user reviews, or other mechanisms made available to your users.

Tip

Never collect personal data without the user's knowledge and consent. Gathering anonymous diagnostics is fairly commonplace, but avoid keeping any data that can be considered private. Make sure your sample sizes are large enough to obfuscate any personal user details, and make sure to factor out any live QA testing data from your results (especially when considering sales figures).

Designing for Easy Updates and Upgrades

Android applications can easily be upgraded in the field. The application update and upgrade processes do pose some challenges to developers, though. When we say *updating,* we mean modifying the Android manifest version information and redeploying the updated application on users' devices. When we say *upgrading,* we mean creating an entirely new application package with new features and deploying it as a separate application that the user needs to choose to install and that does not replace the old application.

From an update perspective, you need to consider what conditions necessitate an update in the field. For example, do you draw the line at crashes or feature requests? You also want to consider the frequency with which you deploy updates—you need to schedule updates so that they come up frequently enough to be truly useful, but not so often that users are constantly updating their application.

Tip

You should build application content updates into the application functionality as a feature (often network driven) as opposed to necessitating an over-the-air actual application update. By enabling your applications to retrieve fresh content on the fly, you keep your users happy longer, and applications stay relevant.

When considering upgrades, decide the manner in which you will migrate users from one version of your application to the next. Will you leverage the Android Backup Service features so that your users can transition seamlessly from one device to the next, or will you provide your own backup solution? Consider how you will inform users of existing applications that a major new version is available.

Tip

Google provides a service known as the Android Backup Service, which allows developers to persist user application data to the cloud for easy restoration. This service is used for storing application data and settings and is not meant to be a database back end for your application. To learn more about the Android Backup Service, refer to the following URL: *http://d .android.com/google/backup/index.html.*

Leveraging Android Tools for Application Design

The Android SDK and developer community provide a number of useful tools and resources for application design. You might want to leverage the following tools during this phase of your development project:

- The Graphical Layout Editor is a good place to start for rapid proof of concept. You can find more about the Graphical Layout Editor here: *http://d.android.com/tools/ help/adt.html#graphical-editor.*
- Use the Android emulator before you have specific devices. You can use different AVD configurations to simulate different device configurations and platform versions.

- The DDMS tool is very useful for memory profiling.
- The Hierarchy Viewer in Pixel Perfect mode enables accurate user interface design. Along with lint, it can also be used to optimize your layout designs.
- The Draw Nine-Patch tool can create stretchable graphics for mobile use.
- Real devices may be your most important tool. Use real devices for feasibility research and application proof-of-concept work whenever possible. Do not design solely using the emulator. The Developer Options within the Settings application are useful tools for developing and debugging on actual hardware.
- The technical specifications for specific devices, often available from manufacturers and carriers, can be invaluable for determining the configuration details of target devices.

Avoiding Silly Mistakes in Android Application Design

Last but not least, here is a list of some of the silly mistakes Android designers should do their best to avoid:

- Designing or developing for months without performing feasibility testing on the device (basically "waterfall testing")
- Designing for a single device, platform, language, or hardware configuration
- Designing as if your device has a large amount of storage and processing power and is always plugged into a power source
- Developing for the wrong version of the Android SDK (verify the device SDK version)
- Trying to adapt applications to smaller screens after the fact by having the device "scale"
- Deploying oversize graphics and media assets with an application instead of sizing them appropriately

Best Practices in Developing Bulletproof Mobile Applications

Developing applications for mobile is not that different from traditional desktop development. However, developers might find developing mobile applications more restrictive, especially resource constrained. Again, let's start with some best practices or "rules" for mobile application development:

- Test assumptions regarding feasibility early and often on the target devices.
- Keep application size as small and efficient as possible.

- Choose efficient data structures and algorithms appropriate to mobile.
- Exercise prudent memory management.
- Assume that devices are running primarily on battery power.

Designing a Development Process That Works for Mobile Development

A successful project's backbone is a good software process. It ensures standards and good communication and reduces risks. We talked about the overall mobile development process in Chapter 15, "Learning the Android Software Development Process." Again, here are a few general tips for successful mobile development processes:

- Use an iterative development process.
- Use a regular, reproducible build process with adequate versioning.
- Communicate scope changes to all parties—changes often affect testing most of all.

Testing the Feasibility of Your Application Early and Often

It cannot be said enough: You must test developer assumptions on real devices. There is nothing worse than designing and developing an application for a few months only to find that it needs serious redesign to work on an actual device. Just because your application works on the emulator does not, *in any way,* guarantee that it will run properly on the device. Some functional areas to examine carefully for feasibility include

- Functionality that interacts with peripherals and device hardware
- Network speed and latency
- Memory footprint and usage
- Algorithm efficiency
- User interface suitability for different screen sizes and resolutions
- Device input method assumptions
- File size and storage usage

We know, we sound like a broken record—but, truly, we've seen this mistake made over and over again. Projects are especially vulnerable to this when target devices aren't yet available. What happens is that engineers are forced closer to the waterfall method of software development with a big, bad surprise after weeks or months of development on some vanilla-style emulator.

We don't need to explain again why waterfall approaches are dangerous, do we? You can never be too cautious about this stuff. Think of this as the preflight safety speech of mobile software development.

Using Coding Standards, Reviews, and Unit Tests to Improve Code Quality

Developers who spend the time and effort necessary to develop efficient mobile applications are rewarded by their users. The following is a representative list of some of the efforts you can make:

- Centralizing core features in shared Java packages. (If you have shared C or C++ libraries, consider using the Android NDK.)
- Developing for compatible versions of the Android SDK (know your target devices).
- Using the right level of optimization, including coding with RenderScript or using the NDK, where appropriate.
- Using built-in controls and widgets appropriate to the application, customizing only where needed.

You can use system services to determine important device characteristics (screen type, language, date, time, input methods, available hardware, and so on). If you make any changes to system settings from within your application, be sure to change the settings back when your application exits or pauses, if appropriate.

Defining Coding Standards

Developing a set of well-communicated coding standards for the development team can help drive home some of the important requirements of mobile applications. Some standards might include

- Implementing robust error handling as well as handling exceptions gracefully.
- Moving lengthy, process-intensive, or blocking operations off the main UI thread.
- Avoiding creating unnecessary objects during critical sections of code or user interface behavior, such as animations and response to user input.
- Releasing objects and resources you aren't actively using.
- Practicing prudent memory management. Memory leaks can render your application useless.
- Using resources appropriately for future localization. Don't hard-code strings and other assets in code or layout files.
- Avoiding obfuscation in the code itself unless you're doing so for a specific reason (such as using Google's License Verification Library, or LVL). Comments are worthwhile. However, you should consider obfuscation later in the development process to protect against software piracy using built-in ProGuard support.
- Considering using standard document generation tools such as `Javadoc`.
- Instituting and enforcing naming conventions—in code and in database schema design.

Performing Code Reviews

Performing code inspections can improve the quality of project code, help enforce coding standards, and identify problems before QA gets their hands on a build and spends time and resources testing it.

It can also be helpful to pair developers with the QA tester who tests their specific functional areas to build a closer relationship between the teams. If testers understand how the application and Android operating system function, they can test the application more thoroughly and successfully. This might or might not be done as part of a formal code review process. For example, a tester can identify defects related to type safety just by noting the type of input expected (but not validated) on a form field of a layout or by reviewing the Submit or Save button-handling function with the developer. This would help circumvent the time spent to file, review, fix, and retest validation defects. Reviewing the code in advance doesn't reduce the testing burden but rather helps reduce the number of easily caught defects.

Developing Code Diagnostics

The Android SDK provides a number of packages related to code diagnostics. Building a framework for logging, unit testing, and exercising your application to gather important diagnostic information, such as the frequency of method calls and performance of algorithms, can help you develop a solid, efficient, and effective mobile application. It should be noted that diagnostic hooks are almost always removed prior to application publication because they impose significant performance reductions and greatly reduce responsiveness.

Using Application Logging

In Chapter 3, "Writing Your First Android Application," we discussed how to leverage the built-in logging class `android.util.Log` to implement diagnostic logging, which can be monitored via a number of Android tools, such as the `LogCat` utility (available within DDMS, Android Debug Bridge, or ADB, the Android IDE, Android Studio, and the Android Development Plugin for Eclipse).

Developing Unit Tests

Unit testing can help developers move one step closer to the elusive 100% of code coverage testing. The Android SDK includes extensions to the `JUnit` framework for testing Android applications. Automated testing is accomplished by creating test cases, in Java code, that verify that the application works the way you designed it. You can do this automated testing for both unit testing and functional testing, including user interface testing.

Basic `JUnit` support is provided through the `junit.framework` and `junit.runner` packages. Here, you find the familiar framework for running basic unit tests with helper classes for individual test cases. You can combine these test cases into test suites. There are utility classes for your standard assertions and test result logic.

The Android-specific unit-testing classes are part of the `android.test` package, which includes an extensive array of testing tools designed specifically for Android applications. This package builds upon the `JUnit` framework and adds many interesting features, such as the following:

- Simplified hooking of test instrumentation (`android.app.Instrumentation`) with `android.test.InstrumentationTestRunner`, which you can run via `adb` shell commands
- Performance testing (`android.test.PerformanceTestCase`)
- Single `Activity` (or `Context`) testing (`android.test.ActivityUnitTestCase`)
- Full application testing (`android.test.ApplicationTestCase`)
- Services testing (`android.test.ServiceTestCase`)
- Utilities for generating events such as touch events (`android.test.TouchUtils`)
- Many more specialized assertions (`android.test.MoreAsserts`)
- User interface testing with `uiautomator`, the API for which is included by adding the `uiautomator.jar` to your project (`com.android.uiautomator.*`)
- `View` validation (`android.test.ViewAsserts`)

Handling Defects Occurring on a Single Device

Occasionally, you have a situation when you need to provide code for a specific device. Google and the Android team tell you that when this happens, it's a bug, so you should tell them about it. By all means, do so. However, this won't help you in the short term. Nor will it help you if they fix it in a subsequent revision of the platform but carriers don't roll out the update and fix for months, if ever, to specific devices.

Handling bugs that occur only on a single device can be tricky. You don't want to branch code unnecessarily, so here are some of your choices:

- If possible, keep the client generic and use the server to serve up device-specific items.
- If the conditions can be determined programmatically on the client, try to craft a generic solution that enables developers to continue to develop under one source code tree, without branching.
- If the device is not a high-priority target, consider dropping it from your requirements if the cost-benefit ratio suggests that a workaround is not cost-effective. Not all markets support excluding individual devices, but Google Play does.
- If required, branch the code to implement the fix. Make sure to set your Android manifest file settings such that the branched application version is installed only on the appropriate devices.
- If all else fails, document the problem only and wait for the underlying "bug" to be addressed. Keep your users in the loop.

Leveraging Android Tools for Development

The Android SDK comes with a number of useful tools and resources for application development. The development community adds even more useful utilities to the mix. You might want to leverage the following tools during this phase of your development project:

- The Android IDE, Eclipse with the ADT plugin, or Android Studio
- The Android emulator and physical devices for testing
- The Android DDMS tool for debugging and interaction with the emulator or device
- The ADB tool for logging, debugging, and shell access tools
- The `sqlite3` command-line tool for application database access (available via the `adb` shell)
- The Android Support Package for including the support libraries to avoid writing custom case code
- The Hierarchy Viewer for user interface debugging of views

Numerous other tools also are available as part of the Android SDK. See the Android documentation for more details.

Avoiding Silly Mistakes in Android Application Development

Here are some of the frustrating and silly mistakes Android developers should try to avoid:

- Forgetting to register new activities, services, and necessary permissions to the `AndroidManifest.xml` file
- Forgetting to display `Toast` messages using the `show()` method
- Hard-coding information such as network information, test user information, and other data into the application
- Forgetting to disable diagnostic logging before release
- Forgetting to remove test-configured email addresses or websites in code before release
- Distributing live applications with debug mode enabled

Summary

Be responsive, stable, and secure—these are the tenets of Android development. In this chapter, we armed you—the software designers, developers, and project managers—with tips, tricks, and best practices for mobile application design and development based on real-world knowledge and experience from veteran mobile developers. Feel free to pick and choose which information works well for your specific project, and keep in mind that the software process, especially the mobile software process, is always open to improvement.

Quiz Questions

1. What are some application diagnostics that you should consider keeping track of?

2. What is the difference between designing for updates and designing for upgrades?

3. What are some of the Android tools recommended to leverage during application design?

4. True or false: One best practice is to assume that devices are running primarily while plugged in.

5. What are some of the Android tools recommended to leverage during development?

6. True or false: It is a good practice to enable diagnostic logging before release.

Exercises

1. Read the Android documentation Training titled "Best Practices for Security & Privacy" (*http://d.android.com/training/best-security.html*).

2. Read the Android documentation Training titled "Best Practices for User Experience & UI" (*http://d.android.com/training/best-ux.html*).

3. Read the Android documentation Training titled "Improving App Quality after Launch" (*http://d.android.com/distribute/googleplay/strategies/app-quality.html*).

References and More Information

Android Training: "Performance Tips":
  http://d.android.com/training/articles/perf-tips.html
Android Training: "Keeping Your App Responsive":
  http://d.android.com/training/articles/perf-anr.html
Android Training: "Designing for Seamlessness":
  http://d.android.com/guide/practices/seamlessness.html
Android API Guides: "User Interface":
  http://d.android.com/guide/topics/ui/index.html
Android Design: "Design Principles":
  http://d.android.com/design/get-started/principles.html
Android Distribute: "App Quality":
  http://d.android.com/distribute/googleplay/quality/index.html
Google Analytics: "Google Analytics SDK for Android v2 (Beta)—Overview":
  https://developers.google.com/analytics/devguides/collection/android/v2/

17

Planning the Android Application Experience

Knowing how to use the newest Android APIs is a great start, but there is more to building Android applications than just programming a bunch of code and adding more features to your application. Implementing a slick-looking user interface is also wonderful, but if it is difficult to figure out how to use your application and it does not provide any real benefit to the user, it will most likely never become that "killer app." In order to truly set your application apart from the myriad of other applications available to users, you really must think differently about what user problem your application solves. Solving that problem in a graceful way, rather than developing an application that is just a collection of Android features, is one of the best pieces of advice the authors have to share.

The purpose of this chapter is to present many different concepts and techniques that should enable you to make better decisions about how to design your application with your users in mind. The information presented in this chapter is not exhaustive, nor is it meant to be the default methodology that you have to use when planning your applications. Rather, the information should be adapted to fit your particular development situation. The authors have seen that the most successful projects are not always performed by developers who follow one particular rigorous development methodology that has been handed to them. Usually, the most successful projects are completed by developers who work together to create their own system and develop a methodology that works best for them, within their own resource constraints.

Thinking about Objectives

When starting a new Android development project, it is always a good idea to set some expectations early on, before writing code. The most helpful expectations to think about are in the form of objectives. Usually, there are at least two parties who have objectives in relation to a given Android development project, if not more. People who use your application obviously have reasons for doing so; therefore, they have objectives they are working to achieve with your application. On the other hand, you, the developer or team of developers, have reasons for building the application. In addition, besides users and team, there may be additional stakeholders who have objectives in relation to your project.

User Objectives

Users install an application usually because of a need they are trying to fulfill. User objectives may vary widely; for example, users who are forgetful may be looking for an application that can keep track of important information for them, such as a note-taking application or a calendar application. On the other hand, certain users may want to be entertained by a game but have only short bursts of time they can devote to playing.

Focusing your development efforts around a clear set of user objectives should help you determine who your target users will be. As an application developer, if you try to fulfill the objectives of too many different types of users, you may end up not pleasing any users at all. If you set out without thinking about who your target users are, you may end up building a note-taking game for a forgetful busy user looking for help remembering important information while being entertained in short bursts.

Not only will knowing your users' objectives help you focus your development efforts to create a superior experience for a particular type of user, but it will also help you discover if there are applications that may already be fulfilling the same or similar needs. Building an application that is just like other applications already available is not a good use of your efforts. But narrowing in on the pain points that your target users have, and knowing what the current competition is, should help you make better decisions with your development efforts.

Take the time early on to think about what a realistic set of user objectives is for a particular need you want your application to fill, and think about how to differentiate yourself from the competition. Then design your application to fulfill those objectives. You may be pleasantly surprised when your users thank you for fulfilling their needs.

Team Objectives

Whether you are a team of one working alone on your Android project, or one person on a team of many at a large corporation, your team is probably building the application with specific objectives in mind. Those team objectives could be achieving 5,000 downloads in the first month or generating $50,000 in revenue in the first quarter. Other examples of team objectives could be releasing the first version of an application in one month, or something different altogether, such as generating a measurable quantity of brand recognition.

Whatever those team objectives are, it is a good idea to start thinking about them as early as possible. Fulfilling your users' objectives is only part of the equation. Failure to have a clear set of team objectives may result in developing software that is late or over budget, or it may even result in the project never being completed.

Objectives of Other Stakeholders

Not all Android application projects have other stakeholders involved, but some projects do. Other stakeholders could include advertisers that provide ads for placing within your application. Their objectives may be to maximize their revenues, maintaining their brand recognition without harming the user experience of your application. Think about other stakeholders in addition to users and team early in the planning process.

Not thinking about the needs of other stakeholders up front may result in harming any types of business partnerships that you may have developed with those stakeholders. Failure to consider their needs could damage your relationship.

Techniques for Focusing Your Product Efforts

Knowing that you should target your project efforts around a clear set of objectives is the first step. Now we will discuss practical techniques that you can begin using right now to help you think about what your users' objectives are and how you can fulfill them.

Personas

One way to keep your target user or users in mind during your Android project is to create a fictional persona. The purpose of using a persona during development is to think about your users' problems from their perspective. Defining that persona and the problems the persona has is just one way to fine-tune not just who the target users will be, but also how to differentiate your product from other available applications.

Personas are fairly easy to create. Some of the information that you should consider defining for your fictional personas includes

- Name
- Gender
- Age range
- Occupation
- Android sophistication level
- Favorite applications
- Most-used Android features
- Attitude toward or awareness of your application's objective
- Education
- Income
- Marital status
- Hobbies

This list is not comprehensive, but it is a good start to help you narrow in on exactly who your target users are. You should create only one or two different personas. As we mentioned earlier in this chapter, if you try to please every single type of user, your application may never actually solve any particular need for any users at all.

You can create these personas on paper and keep them nearby and visible while you work. Sometimes it even helps to attach a picture of a person to this fictional character;

that way your character has a face to go with the name. Then when you are making decisions for your Android application, you can refer back to your target user to see if you are fulfilling that user's needs.

Entity Discovery and Organization

Early in your project's life, you should start thinking about the entities, classes, and objects that describe the information within your application. Drawing simple diagrams on paper can help you determine how to organize your code. Here are a few techniques that you can use:

- **Domain modeling:** A domain model provides names for all of the entities used within a project. The domain model usually evolves over the life of a project. It usually includes the entity names, which should be nouns, and their relationships to other entities.

- **Class modeling:** A class model is very similar to a domain model, just more specific. A class model is usually derived from a domain model but includes much more detail. This diagram usually includes class names, attributes, operations, and relationships to other classes.

- **Entity relationship modeling:** An entity relationship model is used specifically for describing an application's data model. The data model describes the tables of a database. This diagram usually includes the entity names, their attributes, relationships to other entities, and cardinalities.

With the information you gather from these diagrams, combined with the Android classes that your project requires, it becomes increasingly important to think about where and how to implement classes in relation to one another as your project progresses. The larger your project gets without proper organization and planning, the more your code base becomes like spaghetti code: that is, unstructured, tangled, overly complex, and very difficult to follow.

Use Cases and Use Case Diagrams

Another way to think about your target users is to develop a set of use cases and use case diagrams for how they will use your application. A use case generally describes the scenarios and interactions that an actor (or user) has with your application, and a use case diagram visually represents the actor and the application and the interactions that occur between them. You should think about use cases as actions that your target user is trying to do when using your application. Use cases are good for helping you determine how your application behaves when a user interacts with it.

Here is a simple use case for a task management application:

On first launch, the application displays an empty task management screen asking the user to enter the first task. An Add Task button is available on the task

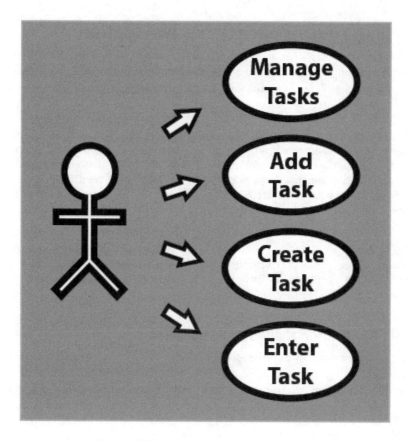

Figure 17.1   A simplistic use case diagram
for a task management application.

management screen, and when the user selects it, the application responds by presenting an `Enter Task` form for entering a new task. The entry form includes a
`Create Task` button. After the user enters a new task into the form, the user presses
the `Create Task` button, and the application then creates and stores the task. Then
the task management screen displays the task just created for the user to review.

Figure 17.1 is a diagram of this use case.

The quickest way to create a use case diagram is to draw it on paper or on a whiteboard, although you may also use a graphics editing program or something more sophisticated such as a use case management and diagramming application if you so choose.
Usually, the simplest and quickest tools for drawing use cases are the most effective, and
drawing them by hand is highly recommended.

Charting Your Application's Navigation

Now that you are on track for understanding who your target users are and how they intend to use your application, take some time to figure out how to implement navigation so users can accomplish the tasks that you will be providing.

Tip

Before we talk about how to design navigation within your own application, you should take a moment to read about how users navigate within the Android System UI, if you have not already done so. You can learn more at the following URL: *http://d.android.com/design/ get-started/ui-overview.html*. This article will help you learn about the different screens within Android—the `Home`, `All Apps`, and `Recents` screens—in addition to different system bars, such as the `status bar`, `navigation bar`, and `combined bar`.

Tip

Many of the code examples provided in this section are taken from the `SimpleNavigation` application. The source code for this application is provided for download on the book's website.

Android Application Navigation Scenarios

In order to understand how to program navigation within your application, you first must understand the different types of navigation that Android provides. There is more than one way that Android allows users to navigate to and within an application as well as to and from one application and another. The following sections describe the navigation scenarios that Android allows.

Entry Navigation

Entry navigation is how a user navigates into an application. There are many different ways this can occur, such as from a `Home` screen widget, from the `All Apps` screen, from a notification listed within the `status bar`, or even from another application altogether.

Lateral Navigation

Lateral navigation is mainly for applications that have screens residing on the same hierarchy level within an application. If your application has more than one screen residing on the same level, you may want to provide users the ability to navigate laterally across that particular hierarchy level by implementing swipe navigation, tabs, or both. Figure 17.2 is a depiction of lateral navigation.

To implement lateral navigation for activities, all you need to do is make a call to `startActivity()` using an `Intent` with the lateral `Activity` and ensure that each of the activities is on the same hierarchy level. If your activities are on the same hierarchy level but not the top level, you can define the `parentActivityName` attribute in your manifest and set the parent `Activity` to be the same for each of the activities that should reside on the same hierarchy level.

Figure 17.2   A depiction of navigating an Android application laterally.

Descendant Navigation

Descendant navigation is used when your application has more than one hierarchy level. This means that users can navigate deeper into your application's hierarchy levels. Usually, this is done by creating a new `Activity` with `startActivity()`. Figure 17.3 shows a depiction of navigating from a top-level `Activity` to a lower-level `Activity`.

To implement descendant navigation, make sure that the descendant `Activity` declares `parentActivityName` in your application manifest and set the `Activity` to be the ancestor. Then, from the ancestor `Activity`, create an `Intent` with the descendant `Activity`, and simply call `startActivity()`.

Back Navigation

Back navigation is used when a user clicks the `Back` button located on the Android navigation bar or presses a hardware `Back` button. The default behavior navigates the user to the last `Activity` or `Fragment` that was placed on the back stack. To override this behavior, call `onBackPressed()` from within your `Activity`. Figure 17.4 shows a depiction of navigating back within an application after having performed the lateral navigation seen in Figure 17.2.

You do not have to do anything special to implement back navigation in your application, unless you are working with fragments. With fragments, if you want to navigate back, you need to make sure that you add your `Fragment` to the back stack with a call to `addToBackStack()`.

Ancestral Navigation

Ancestral navigation, or up navigation, is used when your application has more than one hierarchy level and you must provide a means for navigating to a higher level. Figure 17.5

Figure 17.3 A depiction of performing descendant
navigation within an Android application.

Figure 17.4 A depiction of navigating back after having navigated laterally
as in Figure 17.2.

Figure 17.5   Showing up navigation as enabled.

Figure 17.6   A depiction of performing ancestral navigation
within an Android application.

shows up navigation enabled within an application, and Figure 17.6 shows a depiction
of performing ancestral navigation after having performed descendant navigation as in
Figure 17.3.

To implement ancestral navigation within your application, you must do two
things. The first is to make sure that your descendant Activity defines the correct parentActivityName attribute within your application manifest. Then, in the
onCreate() method of your Activity, simply call the following:

```
getActionBar().setDisplayHomeAsUpEnabled(true);
```

External Navigation

External navigation is when the user navigates from one application to another. Sometimes this is done in order to retrieve a result from another application using `startActivityForResult()`, or it could be done to leave the current application altogether.

Launching Tasks and Navigating the Back Stack

A task is one or more activities that are used for accomplishing a specific goal. The back stack is where Android manages these activities with a last-in-first-out ordering. As the activities of a task are created, they are added to the back stack in order. If the default behavior applies to an `Activity`, and the user presses the `Back` button, Android removes the last `Activity` added to the stack. In addition, if the user instead were to press the `Home` button, the task would then move itself and the activities to the background. The task may be resumed by the user at a later time, as moving it to the background does not destroy the `Activity` or task.

Tip

You may customize the default behavior of activities in the back stack. To learn how this can be done, you should read the following Android documentation: *http://d.android.com/guide/ components/tasks-and-back-stack.html#ManagingTasks*.

Navigating with Fragments

We have covered extensively how the various navigation scenarios work when using activities. With fragments, let's just say that how navigation should be handled depends. If you have implemented a descendant `ViewPager` with fragments, and there are dozens or potentially hundreds of fragments that a user could page through, it is probably not a good idea to add each of the fragments to the back stack just to give the user the ability to navigate back up to its ancestor `Activity`. If so, and the user has a habit of using the `Back` button rather than the `Up` button, he or she may become extremely frustrated at having to navigate through dozens of fragments just to get to the ancestral `Activity`. It is clear that ancestral navigation should be used to handle this scenario, but not every user knows to use the `Up` button.

When the `Fragment` count is small, supporting back navigation should be OK. When designing your application, think about what a user would experience if you do support adding each and every `Fragment` to the back stack. After all, your application may require supporting that for various reasons, but be sure to be conscious of how users may experience your application.

Planning Application Navigation

Now that you know about the different ways that Android handles both system and application navigation, you should be ready to plan how users navigate through your application. You can begin planning your navigation by thinking about user flows and creating screen maps.

User Flows

A user flow is the path the user takes through an application to accomplish a particular goal. This goal may be closely related to one or more use cases, as many times a user must take multiple actions in order to accomplish a particular goal. When designing user flows, remember to keep the steps to the minimum required in order to accomplish the goal while maintaining an optimal experience for the user. Too many steps may lead to unnecessary confusion or frustration.

You should also limit the number of user flows your application provides. As we mentioned earlier, you should not try to create a solution for every type of user. Instead, specialize by fulfilling a need that helps users make their lives easier. A few user flows per application are common, but you probably will design at least one or two key flows that a user performs frequently.

Screen Maps

One way to determine the user flows or key flows for your application is by designing a screen map. A screen map is a way to visualize the relationships among the screens of your application. The organization of a screen map will vary from application to application. Some maps may involve just one or two screens, whereas others could have dozens.

You can assemble a screen map by first creating a list of all the screens that your application will need, then connecting them to show their navigational relationships. Figure 17.7 shows an extremely simple screen map of the hierarchical relationship between the screens for the `SimpleNavigation` sample application accompanying this chapter.

When designing your screen maps, there are a few things you should be aware of:

- A screen does not necessarily mean you need an `Activity`. Instead, use reusable fragments for displaying like content.

- Group content fragments together when in a multipane layout and separately when in a single-pane layout.

- When possible, use one or more of the navigation design patterns that are commonly recommended for use in Android applications.

Tip

To learn more about creating screen maps and planning your application's navigation, please read the Android documentation found here: *http://d.android.com/training/design-navigation/index.html*.

Android Navigation Design Patterns

There are many design patterns commonly found within Android applications. Many of these patterns are highlighted within the Android documentation due to their effectiveness. We describe a few of these common navigation design patterns here.

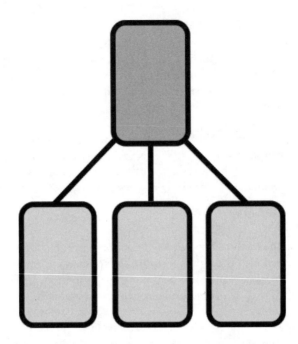

Figure 17.7   An extremely simple screen map showing the hierarchical
relationship of the activities of the `SimpleNavigation` code sample.

Tabs

Use fixed (Figure 17.8, left) or scrollable (Figure 17.8, right) tabs when you have three or
fewer related content sections within the same hierarchy level. Implementing fixed tabs
with swipe functionality using `ViewPager` is recommended.

Drop-down

Use drop-down navigation (shown in Figure 17.9) when your application has more than
three content sections within the same hierarchy level and when the other patterns are
not appropriate.

Navigation Drawer

Use the navigation drawer when you have more than three top-level sections within your
application and if you need to provide quick access to lower-level sections in addition to
the top-level sections. Figure 17.10 shows an application using a navigation drawer. More
information on using the navigation drawer can be found at the Android documentation
website: *http://d.android.com/training/implementing-navigation/nav-drawer.html.*

Master Detail Flow

Use the master detail flow with fragments when using views such as lists or grids, one
`Fragment` for the list or grid and the other `Fragment` for the associated detail view. When

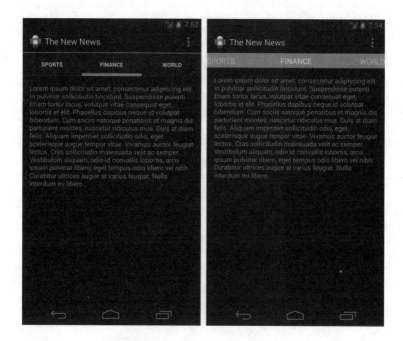

Figure 17.8   Two different types of tab design patterns for Android applications: fixed (left) and scrollable (right).

Figure 17.9   An Android application using drop-down navigation.

Figure 17.10   A screenshot of an application using the navigation drawer.

selecting an item in the Fragment list or grid on a single-pane layout, launch a new Activity to display the Fragment detail view. Figure 17.11 shows a master detail flow application running in a single-pane layout, the left side showing the master list Activity and the right side showing the detail Activity. In multipane layout, touching an item within the list or grid should display the accompanying detail Fragment alongside the list or grid. Figure 17.12 shows the same master detail flow application from Figure 17.11, only this time within a multipane layout with the master list Fragment on the left and the detail Fragment on the right.

Targets

Use targets such as buttons when your application needs to replace the current screen entirely and none of the other patterns apply. Figure 17.13 shows the SimpleNavigation application launcher Activity with three target navigational buttons.

Encouraging Action

Determining how to navigate your application is only half the battle when designing your product. The other challenge is figuring out how to get your users to perform the actions made available within your application.

Actions differ from navigation as they are usually designed to permanently alter the user's data. With that said, there are a few common design patterns that have evolved on the Android platform for presenting actions to users.

Figure 17.11 Two screenshots of a master detail flow application
shown in a single-pane layout.

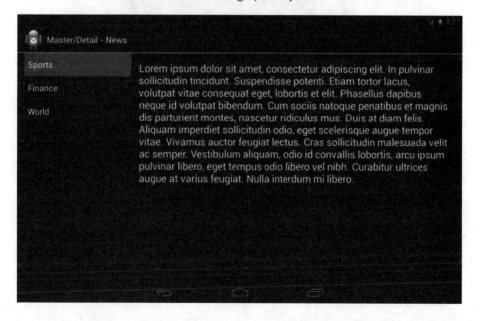

Figure 17.12 A screenshot of a master detail flow application
shown in a multipane layout.

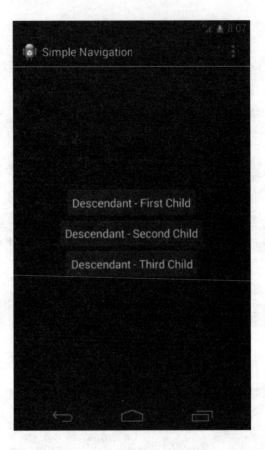

Figure 17.13   A screenshot of the `SimpleNavigation` sample
application displaying three descendant `Activity` navigation buttons.

Menus

The concept of presenting menus to users to provoke action from them has been around
since Android API Level 1. With Android API Level 11, menus have been replaced with
a newer design pattern known as the `ActionBar` for presenting actions to users. For applications prior to API Level 11, you may want to consider implementing menus for presenting actions to your users. There are three different types of menus available for use:

- **Options menu:** An options menu is where you should present actions available
  to a particular `Activity`. The maximum number of actions that you can present
  within an options menu is six. If you need to include more than six menu items,
  an overflow menu will be created and your actions will be accessible from there. It

is a good idea to order your most common actions to be presented in the options menu first.

- **Context menu:** You can use a context menu to present actions when a selection event is initiated by a user from a long press. If your `Activity` supports a context menu upon a selection event, once an item has been selected, a dialog will be displayed presenting the various actions that you support.

- **Pop-up menu:** A pop-up menu looks like an overflow-style menu item and is used for displaying actions relevant to the content displayed within an `Activity`.

Action Bars

As mentioned in the preceding section, the `ActionBar` has become the preferred way to present actions to users. The `ActionBar` is where to place actions that you want to make available to a particular `Activity`. You can add actions to or remove them from the `ActionBar` from within an `Activity` or `Fragment`.

Tip

Many of the code examples provided in this section are taken from the `SimpleActionBar` application. The source code for this application is provided for download on the book's website.

You can use an `ActionBar` to display various elements, which are detailed in the following sections.

Application Icon

You may place your application's icon within the `ActionBar`. If your application supports up navigation, the application icon would be where a user would press to navigate up a level.

View Control

A `View` control may be placed on your `ActionBar` for enabling actions such as search or navigation using tabs or a drop-down menu.

Action Buttons

Action buttons are usually icons, text, or both icons and text for displaying the actions you would like to make available to users from within your `Activity`. Figure 17.14 shows two action buttons, the `Add` and `Close` buttons, each with an associated icon.

To add action buttons to the `ActionBar` you must add a menu layout to your `Activity`. Here is the menu layout used in the `SimpleActionBar` application:

```
<menu xmlns:android="http://schemas.android.com/apk/res/android" >

    <item

        android:id="@+id/menu_add"

        android:icon="@android:drawable/ic_menu_add"
```

```
        android:orderInCategory="2"

        android:showAsAction="ifRoom|withText"

        android:title="@string/action_add"/>

    <item

        android:id="@+id/menu_close"

        android:icon="@android:drawable/ic_menu_close_clear_cancel"

        android:orderInCategory="4"

        android:showAsAction="ifRoom|withText"

        android:title="@string/action_close"/>

    <item

        android:id="@+id/menu_help"

        android:icon="@android:drawable/ic_menu_help"

        android:orderInCategory="5"

        android:showAsAction="never"

        android:title="@string/action_help"/>

</menu>
```

Then, in your `Activity`, you need to inflate the menu using the `onCreateOptionsMenu()` method like so:

```
@Override

public boolean onCreateOptionsMenu(Menu menu) {

    getMenuInflater().inflate(R.menu.simple_action_bar, menu);

    return true;

}
```

This will add the action items to the `ActionBar`. Notice the item icon attributes in our menu layout. Android provides default icons for many common action types such as add, close, clear, cancel, or help. Using these default icons will save you a great amount of time, in addition to providing a consistent user experience across all applications that use those icons. Using your own icons may seem desirable, but doing so may confuse users who are not used to seeing the icon you provide for a common action.

Action Overflow

Action items that you are not able to fit on the main `ActionBar` will be placed within the overflow section. Make sure to order your action items in the order of their importance and frequency of use. Figure 17.14 also shows an action overflow menu item named `Help`. This action item is accessible only after the overflow icon in the upper-right corner of the screen is touched.

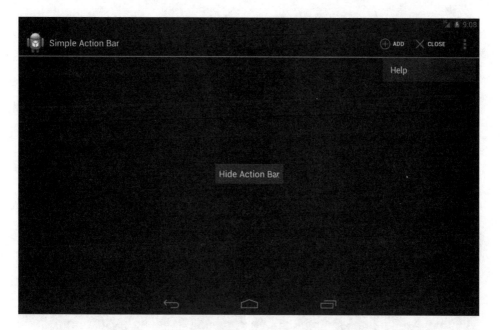

Figure 17.14   A screenshot of the `SimpleActionBar` sample application showing both action buttons and their icons along with an action overflow menu item.

If your application supports both small screens and large tablets, you may want your `ActionBar` to display differently based on the type of device. Since there is more room on the `ActionBar` on large tablets, you are able to fit more actions. With smaller screens, rather than having all of the actions displayed in the overflow, you are able to tell your application that you would like to split the `ActionBar` (see Figure 17.15, left). This means that your `ActionBar` will also appear at the bottom of the screen if there are more actions than will fit in the top `ActionBar`. To support a split `ActionBar`, set the `uiOptions` attribute within either the `<application>` or `<activity>` tag of your application's manifest file like so:

```
android:uiOptions="splitActionBarWhenNarrow"
```

In certain scenarios, you may want to hide the `ActionBar`. This can be useful if your application requires going into full-screen mode, or if you have designed a game and don't always want the `ActionBar` to be present. In order to hide the `ActionBar`, just add the following to your `Activity`:

```
getActionBar().hide();
```

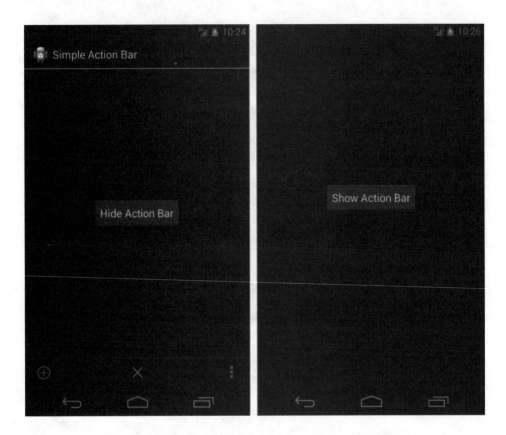

Figure 17.15   Two screenshots of the `SimpleActionBar`
sample application showing (left) a visible split `ActionBar`
with two action buttons and (right) no visible `ActionBar`
after the `Hide Action Bar` button is pressed.

If you need to show the `ActionBar` again at a later point, you can do so with the
following:

```
getActionBar().show();
```

In Figure 17.15, in the left screenshot, the `ActionBar` is displayed; in the right screenshot, it is hidden.

In order to make your action item respond to touch events, you need to override
the `onOptionsItemSelected()` method in your `Activity`. Here is how we defined the
method in the `SimpleActionBar` sample application:

```
@Override
public boolean onOptionsItemSelected(MenuItem item) {
    switch (item.getItemId()) {
```

```
case R.id.menu_add:

    Toast.makeText(this, "Add Clicked", Toast.LENGTH_SHORT).show();

    return true;

case R.id.menu_close:

    finish();

    return true;

case R.id.menu_help:

    Toast.makeText(this, "Help Clicked", Toast.LENGTH_SHORT).show();

    return true;

default:

    return super.onOptionsItemSelected(item);

    }

}
```

The `onOptionsItemSelected()` allows us to detect which item in the menu was interacted with, and we use a simple `switch()` statement to determine which item was selected using the IDs we defined within the menu layout file. Our example is very simple. For the `Add` and `Help` action items, we simply make a `Toast` display to the screen, and the `Close` action item actually ends the `Activity` by calling the `finish()` method.

ActionBar Compatibility

To add an `ActionBar` to legacy applications running on devices with Android versions all the way back to 2.1 (API Level 7), you can use the Android Support Library (Revision 18) in your project. Rather than using the regular `Activity` or `FragmentActivity` classes, you must use the `ActionBarActivity` class, which extends the `FragmentActivity` class of the v4 Support Library. In addition, you must set the theme of your application or `Activity` to `Theme.AppCompat`. Finally, in order to access the `ActionBar` in your code, you must call the `getSupportActionBar()` method.

Contextual Action Mode

Contextual action mode is useful for displaying actions you would like to make available to users when they have selected something from within an `Activity`.

Dialogs

Dialogs are yet another way to present actions to your users. The best time to use a `Dialog` is when your application needs to confirm or acknowledge an action a user has taken that will permanently alter the user's data.

If you allow users to edit their application data directly from within a `Dialog`, you should present actions within the `Dialog` for the user to either confirm or deny the changes before actually committing them.

Actions Originating from Your Application's Content

You may need to make certain actions available from within your application's content areas. If so, there are various UI elements that you can use for enabling actions. These UI elements include

- Buttons
- Check boxes
- Radio buttons
- Toggle buttons and switches
- Spinners
- Text fields
- Seek bars
- Pickers

For a detailed look at these various user interface controls, see Chapter 7, "Exploring User Interface Building Blocks."

Communicating Your Application's Identity

To set your application apart from other applications, you should think about the identity that you would like users to associate with your product. Some of the most common ways to communicate identity are as follows:

- Develop consistent style guidelines and follow those guidelines throughout your application.
- Choose a specific color palette and theme for your application. Use colors to establish uniformity or contrast among the different visual elements of your user interface.
- Create a unique application launcher icon that your users will remember. Try to associate the purpose of your application with the design of your icon. In addition, any other icons that you create should instantly communicate to users what the icon means.
- Emphasize content with various font styles.
- Use white space or empty space effectively.
- Do not cram user interface components together. Instead, use padding and margins to provide spacing between user interface components.
- If you plan on having your application run on different-size displays, make sure your application remains flexible with its layouts to accommodate differences across devices displays.

Tip

For a comprehensive overview of style recommendations, see the Android documentation that can be found here: *http://d.android.com/design/style/index.html.*

Designing Screen Layouts

Before investing a great deal of time or money in developing your application, you should spend some time deciding how you would like your user interface layout to appear. There are a few different methods you can use for determining your screen layouts.

Sketches

You should start making decisions about your layouts very early on by quickly creating rough sketches, on paper or on a whiteboard, to determine how your screens and their visual components should be organized in their layout. This is a very quick way to determine any screens that may be required and should help uncover any usability issues prior to investing a lot of time in writing code. Don't be concerned with accuracy or detail at this stage.

Wireframes

Wireframes are slightly more sophisticated and structured than sketches but serve a similar purpose. Once you determine that your sketches are appropriate, a more structured wireframe may be created to further solidify how the application layout should appear. Wireframes typically do not involve details such as color, images, or typography. Like sketches, you may create wireframes on paper or on a whiteboard, with a little more attention to accuracy and detail. You may even want to consider using a software program for designing your wireframes.

Design Comps

A design comp is a high-fidelity mock-up of an application's layouts. Usually, it would be created in a graphic design program. In a design comp, your application's identity should be taken seriously, as this is usually the stage where major decisions on the branding of an application are made. You may even want more than one design comp created, to allow you to choose the one that communicates your application's identity best. A design comp is created prior to finalizing the design and identity, and prior to spending a great amount of time coding the design.

Tip

Google provides a great set of high-fidelity stencils, icons, colors, and fonts that can be used for making design comps. The stencils include real-looking mock-ups of common Android user interface controls. When you are ready to create your design comps, you may opt to roll your own, although using these downloads will make your job a whole lot easier and save you a great amount of time. Many different formats are available for download, so you can choose your graphics editor of choice. You can download these files here: *http://d.android.com/design/downloads/index.html.*

Reacting Properly with Visual Feedback

Provide visual feedback following your style guidelines, to let users know that something is about to happen or has happened when they interact with the user interface, especially when the interaction involves initiating application operations or behaviors.

Some ways to provide visual feedback include

- Using color states, animations, and transitions.
- Displaying alert messages or dialogs to confirm or acknowledge before making a final decision. An alternative to confirming or acknowledging is the Undo pattern, similar to what is found in the Gmail application. When a user deletes an email, rather than asking for confirmation or acknowledgment, a `Toast` message with an Undo option is made available in case the message was unintentionally deleted.
- Using `Toast` messages to provide feedback that does not require important decisions to be confirmed or acknowledged.
- Displaying validation when users interact with forms or provide input, letting them know whether they have provided the correct type or format.

Observing Target Users for Usability

The quicker you present your design to actual target users, the quicker you will be able to discover any problems in your application's design. In addition, observing the users' interactions with your application and receiving their feedback could prove to be invaluable and help you get your design right.

You may want to start presenting your design to friends or family. This is definitely a cheap way to begin testing usability. The only problem is that your friends or family may not fit the profile of your target user. Therefore, you may need to use other means to find your target users. Once you have found them, have them test your design and see what you can learn from their interactions with it.

Mocking Up the Application

The fastest way to receive feedback on your design is to present your work to your target users even before you have written any code. You may be wondering how this is done, but the answer is simple. As we recommended earlier in this chapter, you may have already created rough sketches on paper. If so, presenting these mock-ups to users, without a real working application, is definitely the most cost-effective approach to testing your design up front, with very little effort.

UI Storyboards

A UI storyboard is usually a collection of screen mock-ups derived from designs. You may want to create a storyboard of all the screens required for your application, or you may decide that you just want to test the most important user flows. Usually, you would present the UI storyboard in paper format and ask a target user to begin using the storyboard as if it were an actual application.

There are drawbacks to presenting just a UI storyboard to a target user, especially because the design is not working on an actual device. But the immediate benefits that you receive may far outweigh the drawbacks. As we mentioned earlier, presenting a storyboard to a user, even if it is a series of paper mock-ups, may actually help you uncover major design issues early on.

Prototypes

You may consider building a prototype. A prototype is similar to a UI storyboard, only more sophisticated in that the prototype actually works on a real device. The prototype's functionality is usually extremely limited and is definitely not meant to be a real application. Depending on the effort you want to invest, the prototype may be merely capable of navigating through your screens and used just to validate the user flows, or you may decide that you would like to spend more time providing some of the most important functions of your application.

A prototype usually does not have much styling, if any, but it should reflect how you presume the layout will actually appear. The main point of the prototype is not to impress users with the beauty of the application, but to help uncover any usability issues that may not be readily apparent. Presenting your target users a minimally functioning prototype is another great way to discover any usability issues early in the development process.

Testing the Release Build

You should present your release build to your target users prior to an official launch to validate your design. Even if you have tested and verified your application's usability with UI storyboards or with a prototype, you still want to be sure that the real application does not have any major usability issues.

The release build is usually much more sophisticated than a prototype and more than likely has received styling and an application identity. Problems not apparent in the storyboard or prototype phases may be evident when your target users begin testing the release build. One reason may be due to any styling that may have been applied. Major styling decisions typically are not applied to storyboards or prototypes, so usability issues caused from styling are not uncovered until real users test the release build.

Testing and validating your design prior to release is just as important and valuable to the overall success of your application as it is early on in the process.

Summary

In this chapter, you have learned many different methods for planning the Android application experience. You have learned how to think about your application from your users' perspective and have picked up valuable tips for how to structure your application. You have also learned that focusing on one or two key flows can help set your application apart from your competitors. You have also learned different methods and patterns used for implementing user navigation and actions. You have also learned that getting your application in front of users as quickly as possible may be the best way to validate your design. Go forth with the knowledge learned in this chapter and begin creating incredible Android application experiences for your users.

Quiz Questions

1. What is required to perform lateral navigation between activities?

2. What must you define in your application manifest for supporting lateral, descendant, or ancestral navigation?

3. What method should you override to change the default behavior of a Back press within your application?

4. What method do you call in your Activity to support up navigation?

5. What attribute and value do you add to your <application> or <activity> XML to support a split ActionBar?

6. What method do you use in an Activity to hide the ActionBar?

Exercises

1. Come up with a simple application idea. Create your first persona and define one or two main use cases for your idea.

2. Make a list of screens that will be required for implementing your idea, and create a screen map.

3. Create a simple mock-up of the application on paper and ask someone to use the paper mock-up. Determine if there is anything wrong with your application or if there is anything you could do to improve the design after presenting it.

References and More Information

Wikipedia: persona (user experience):
  http://en.wikipedia.org/wiki/Persona_(user_experience)
Wikipedia: use case:
  http://en.wikipedia.org/wiki/Use_case
Android Training: "Best Practices for User Experience & UI":
  http://d.android.com/training/best-ux.html
Android API Guides: "Tasks and Back Stack":
  http://d.android.com/guide/components/tasks-and-back-stack.html
Android Design: "Patterns":
  http://d.android.com/design/patterns/index.html

Android API Guides: "Supporting Tablets and Handsets":
  http://d.android.com/guide/practices/tablets-and-handsets.html
Android Distribute: "App Quality":
  http://d.android.com/distribute/googleplay/quality/index.html
Android Training: "Advertise without Compromising User Experience":
  http://d.android.com/training/monetization/ads-and-ux.html
Android Design: "Downloads":
  http://d.android.com/design/downloads/index.html
Android Design: "Videos":
  http://d.android.com/design/videos/index.html
YouTube: Android Developers Channel: "Android Design in Action":
  https://www.youtube.com/playlist?list=PLWz5rJ2EKKc8j2B95zGMb8muZvrIy-wcF

Testing Android Applications

Test early, test often, test on the device. That is the quality assurance mantra we consider most important when it comes to testing Android applications. Testing your applications need not be an onerous process. Instead, you can adapt traditional QA techniques, such as automation and unit testing, to the Android platform with relative ease. In this chapter, we discuss our tips and tricks for testing Android applications. We also warn you—the project managers, software developers, and testers of mobile applications—of the various and sundry pitfalls you should do your best to avoid. We also provide a practical unit example, in addition to introducing many tools available for automating Android application testing.

Best Practices in Testing Mobile Applications

Like all QA processes, mobile development projects benefit from a well-designed defect-tracking system, regularly scheduled builds, and planned, systematic testing. There are also plentiful opportunities for white-box and black-box testing as well as opportunities for automation.

Designing a Mobile Application Defect-Tracking System

You can customize most defect-tracking systems to work for the testing of mobile applications. The defect-tracking system must encompass tracking of issues for specific device defects and problems related to any centralized application servers (if applicable).

Logging Important Defect Information

A good mobile defect-tracking system includes the following information about a typical device defect:

- Application build version information, language, and so on
- Device configuration and state information, including device type, Android platform version, and important specs
- Screen orientation, network state, sensor information
- Steps to reproduce the problem using specific details about exactly which input methods were used (touch versus click)
- Device screenshots that can be taken using DDMS or the Hierarchy Viewer tool provided with the Android SDK

Tip

It can be helpful to develop a simple glossary of standardized terms for certain actions on the devices, such as touch mode gestures, click versus tap, long click versus press and hold, clear versus back, and so on. This helps make the steps to reproduce a defect more precise for all parties involved.

Redefining the Term *Defect* for Mobile Applications

It's also important to consider the larger definition of the term *defect*. Defects might occur on all devices or on only some devices. Defects might also occur in other parts of the application environment, such as on a remote application server. Some types of defects typical of mobile applications include the following:

- Crashing, unexpected terminations, forced closures, app not responding (ANR) events, and various other terms used for unexpected behavior that result in the application no longer running or responding

- Features not functioning correctly (improper implementation)

- Using too much disk space on the device

- Inadequate input validation (typically, "button mashing")

- State management problems (startup, shutdown, suspend, resume, power off)

- Responsiveness problems (slow startup, shutdown, suspend, resume)

- Inadequate state change testing (failures during interstate changes, such as an unexpected interruption during resume)

- Usability issues related to input methods, font sizes, and cluttered screen real estate; cosmetic problems that cause the screen to display incorrectly

- Pausing or "freezing" on the main UI thread (failure to implement asynchronous tasks, threading)

- Feedback indicators missing (failure to indicate progress)

- Integration with other applications on the device causing problems

- Application "not playing nicely" on the device (draining battery, disabling power-saving mode, overusing network resources, incurring extensive user charges, obnoxious notifications)

- Using too much memory, not freeing memory or releasing resources appropriately, and not stopping worker threads when tasks are finished

- Not conforming to third-party agreements, such as the Android SDK License Agreement, Google Maps API terms, marketplace terms, or any other terms that apply to the application

- Application client or server not handling protected/private data securely, including ensuring that remote servers or services have adequate uptime and security measures taken

Managing the Testing Environment

Testing mobile applications poses a unique challenge to the QA team, especially in terms of configuration management. The difficulty of such testing is often underestimated. Don't make the mistake of thinking that mobile applications are easier to test because they have fewer features than desktop applications and are, therefore, simpler to validate. The vast variety of Android devices available on the market today makes testing different installation environments tricky.

Warning

Ensure that all changes in project scope are reviewed by the QA team. Adding new devices sometimes has little impact on the development schedule but can have significant consequences in terms of testing schedules.

Managing Device Configurations

Device fragmentation is one of the biggest challenges the mobile tester faces. Android devices come in various form factors with different screens, platform versions, and underlying hardware. They come with a variety of input methods such as hardware buttons, keyboards, and touchscreens. They come with optional features, such as cameras, enhanced graphics support, fingerprint readers, and even 3D displays. Many Android devices are smartphones, but non-phone devices such as Android tablets, TVs, and other devices are becoming more and more popular with each Android SDK release. Keeping track of all the devices, their abilities, and so on is a big job, and much of the work falls on the testing team.

QA personnel must have a detailed understanding of the functionality of each target device, including familiarity with what features are available and any device-specific idiosyncrasies that exist. Whenever possible, testers should test each device as it is used in the field, which might not be the device's default configuration or language. This means changing input modes, screen orientations, and locale settings. It also means testing with battery power, not just plugging the device into a power source while sitting at a desk.

Tip

Be aware of how third-party firmware modifications can affect how your application works on the device. For example, let's assume you've gotten your hands on an unbranded version of a target device and testing has gone well. However, if certain carriers take that same device but remove some default applications and load it up with others, this is valuable information to the tester. Many devices ditch the stock Android user experience for more custom user interfaces, like HTC's Sense and Samsung's TouchWiz user interfaces. Just because your application runs flawlessly on the "vanilla" device doesn't mean that this is how most users' devices are configured by default. Do your best to get test devices that closely resemble the devices users will have in the field. The various default styles may not display as you expect with your user interface.

One hundred percent testing coverage is impossible, so QA must develop priorities thoughtfully. As we discussed in Chapter 15, "Learning the Android Software

Development Process," developing a device database can greatly reduce the confusion of mobile configuration management, help determine testing priorities, and keep track of physical hardware available for testing. Using AVD configurations, the emulator is also an effective tool for extending coverage to simulate devices and situations that would not be covered otherwise.

Tip

If you have trouble configuring devices for real-life situations, you might want to look into the device "labs" available through some carriers. Instead of participating in loaner programs, developers visit the carrier's onsite lab where they can rent time on specific devices. Here, a developer can install an application and test it—not ideal for recurring testing but much better than no testing—and some labs are staffed with experts to help out with device-specific issues.

Determining Clean Starting State on a Device

There is currently no good way to "image" a device so that you can return to the same starting state again and again. The QA testing team needs to define what a "clean" device is for the purposes of test cases. This can involve a specific uninstall process, some manual cleanup, or sometimes a factory reset.

Tip

Using the Android SDK tools, such as DDMS and ADB, developers and testers can have access to the Android file system, including application SQLite databases. These tools can be used to monitor and manipulate data on the emulator. For example, testers might use the sqlite3 command-line interface to "wipe" an application database or fill it with test data for specific test scenarios. For use on devices, you may need to "root" the devices first. Rooting a device is beyond the scope of this book, and we do not recommend doing so on test devices.

While we're on the topic of "clean" states, here is another issue to consider. You may have heard that you can "root" most Android devices, allowing access to underlying device features not openly accessible through the public Android SDK. Certainly there are apps (and developers writing apps) that require this kind of access (some are even published on Google Play). Generally speaking, though, we feel that rooted devices do not make good testing and development devices for most teams. You want to develop and test on devices that resemble those in the hands of users; most users do not root their devices.

Mimicking Real-World Activities

It is nearly impossible (and certainly not cost-effective for most companies) to set up a complete isolated environment for mobile application testing. It's fairly common for networked applications to be tested against test (mock) application servers and then go "live" on production servers with similar configurations. However, in terms of device configuration, mobile software testers must use real devices with real service to test mobile applications properly. If the device is a phone, it needs to be able to make and receive phone calls, send and receive text messages, determine location using LBS services, and basically do anything a phone would normally do.

Testing a mobile application involves more than just making sure the application works properly. In the real world, your application does not exist in a vacuum but is one of many installed on the device. Testing a mobile application involves ensuring that the software integrates well with other device functions and applications. For example, let's say you were developing a game. Testers must verify that calls received while the game is being played cause the game to automatically pause (keep state) and that calls can be answered or ignored without issue.

This also means testers must install other applications on the device. A good place to start is with the most popular applications for the device. Testing your application with these other applications installed, combined with real use, can reveal integration issues or usage patterns that don't mesh well with the rest of the device.

Sometimes testers need to be creative when it comes to reproducing certain types of events. For example, testers must ensure that an application behaves appropriately when mobile handsets lose network connectivity or coverage.

Tip

Unlike with some other mobile platforms, testers actually have to take special steps to make most Android devices lose coverage above and beyond holding them wrong. To test loss of signal, you could go out and test your application in a highway tunnel or elevator, or you could just place the device in the refrigerator. Don't leave it in the cold too long, though, because this will drain the battery. Tin cans work great, too, especially those that have cookies in them. First, eat the cookies; then place the device in the can to seal off the signal. This advice also holds true for testing applications that leverage location-based services.

Maximizing Testing Coverage

All test teams strive for 100% testing coverage, but most also realize such a goal is not reasonable or cost-effective (especially with dozens of Android devices available around the world). Testers must do their best to cover a wide range of scenarios, the depth and breadth of which can be daunting—especially for those new to mobile. Let's look at several specific types of testing and how QA teams have found ways—some tried-and-true and others innovative—to maximize coverage.

Validating Builds and Designing Smoke Tests

In addition to a regular build process, it can be helpful to institute a build acceptance test policy (also sometimes called build validation, smoke testing, or sanity testing). Build acceptance tests are short and targeted at key functionality to determine whether the build is good enough for more thorough testing to be completed. This is also an opportunity to quickly verify bug fixes expected to be in the build before a complete retesting cycle occurs. Consider developing build acceptance tests for multiple Android platform versions to run simultaneously.

Automating Testing

Mobile build acceptance testing is frequently done manually on the highest-priority target device; however, this is also an ideal situation for an automated "sanity" test. By creating an automated test script that runs using the Android SDK's test tool, called `monkeyrunner`, the team can increase its level of confidence that a build is worth further testing, and the number of bad builds delivered to QA can be minimized. Based on a set of Python APIs, you can write scripts that install and run applications on emulators and devices, send specific keystrokes, and take screenshots. When combined with the `JUnit` unit-testing framework, you can develop powerful automated test suites.

Testing on the Emulator versus the Device

When you can get your hands on the actual device your users have, focus your testing there. However, devices and the service contracts that generally come with them can be expensive. Your test team cannot be expected to set up test environments on every carrier or in every country where your application is used. There are times when the Android emulator can reduce costs and improve testing coverage. Some of the benefits of using the emulator include

- Ability to simulate devices when they are not available or in short supply
- Ability to test difficult test scenarios not feasible on live devices
- Ability to be automated like any other desktop software

Testing Before Devices Are Available Using the Emulator

Developers often target up-and-coming devices or platform versions not yet available to the general public. These devices are often highly anticipated, and developers who are ready with applications for these devices on Day 1 of release often experience a sales bump because fewer applications are available to these users—less competition, more sales.

The latest version of the Android SDK is usually released to developers several months prior to when the general public receives over-the-air updates. Also, developers can sometimes gain access to preproduction devices through carrier and manufacturer developer programs. However, developers and testers should be aware of the dangers of testing on preproduction devices. The hardware is generally beta quality. The final technical specifications and firmware can change without notice. Release dates can slip, and the device might never reach production.

When preproduction devices cannot be acquired, testers can do some functional testing using emulator AVD configurations that attempt to closely match the target platform, thus lessening the risks for a compact testing cycle when these devices go live and allowing developers to release applications faster.

Understanding the Dangers of Relying on the Emulator

Unfortunately, the emulator is more of a generic Android device that only simulates many of the device internals—despite all the options available within the AVD configuration.

Tip

Consider developing a document describing the specific AVD configurations used for testing different device configurations as part of the test plan.

The emulator does not represent the specific implementation of the Android platform that is unique to a given device. It does not use the same hardware to determine signal, networking, or location information. The emulator can "pretend" to make and receive calls and messages, or take pictures or video. At the end of the day, it doesn't matter if the application works on the emulator if it doesn't work on the actual device.

Testing Strategies: Black- and White-Box Testing

The Android tools provide ample tools for black-box and white-box testing:

- Black-box testers might require only testing devices and test documentation. For black-box testing, it is even more important that testers have a working knowledge of the specific devices, so providing device manuals and technical specifications also aids in more thorough testing. In addition to such details, knowing device nuances as well as device standards can greatly help with usability testing. For example, if a dock is available for the device, knowing that it's either landscape or portrait mode is useful.

- White-box testing has never been easier on mobile. White-box testers can leverage the many affordable tools, including the Android IDE, Android Studio, and the Eclipse development environment (which all are available for free) and the many debugging tools available as part of the Android SDK. White-box testers use the Android emulator, DDMS, and ADB especially. They can also take advantage of the powerful unit-testing framework uiautomator and the Hierarchy Viewer for user interface debugging. For these tasks, the tester requires a computer with a development environment similar to the developer's as well as knowledge of Java, Python, and the various typical tools available for developers.

Testing Mobile Application Servers and Services

Testers often focus on the client portion of the application and sometimes neglect to thoroughly test the server portion. Many mobile applications rely on networking or the cloud. If your application depends on a server or remote service to operate, testing the server side of your application is vital. Even if the service is not your own, you need to test thoroughly against it so you know it behaves as the application expects it to behave.

Warning

Users expect applications to be available anytime, day or night, 24/7. Minimize server or service downtimes and make sure the application notifies users appropriately (and doesn't crash and burn) if a service is unavailable. If the service is outside your control, it might be worthwhile to look at what service-level agreements are offered.

Here are some guidelines for testing remote servers or services:

- Version your server builds. You should manage server rollouts like any other part of the build process. The server should be versioned and rolled out in a reproducible way.

- Use test servers. Often, QA tests against a mock server in a controlled environment. This is especially true if the live server is already operational with real users.

- Verify scalability. Test the server or service under load, including stress testing (many users, simulated clients).

- Test the server security (hacking, SQL injection, and such).

- Ensure data transmissions to and from the server are secure and not easily sniffed (SSL, HTTPS, valid certificates).

- Ensure that your application handles remote server maintenance or service interruptions gracefully—scheduled or otherwise.

- Test your old clients against new servers to ensure expected, graceful application behavior. Consider versioning your server communications and protocols in addition to your client builds.

- Test server upgrades and rollbacks and develop a plan for how you are going to inform users if and when services are down.

These types of testing offer yet more opportunities for automated testing to be employed.

Testing Application Visual Appeal and Usability

Testing a mobile application is not only about finding dysfunctional features, but also about evaluating the usability of the application. Report areas of the application that lack visual appeal or are difficult to navigate or use. We like to use the walking-and-chewing-gum analogy when it comes to mobile user interfaces. Mobile users frequently do not give the application their full attention. Instead, they walk or do something else while they use it. Applications should be as easy for the user as chewing gum.

Tip

Consider conducting usability studies to collect feedback from people who are not familiar with the application. Relying solely on the product team members, who see the application regularly, can blind the team to application flaws.

Leveraging Third-Party Standards for Android Testing

Make a habit of trying to adapt traditional software-testing principles to mobile. Encourage QA personnel to develop and share these practices within your company.

Again, no certification programs are specifically designed for Android applications at this time; however, nothing is stopping the mobile marketplaces from developing them.

Consider looking over the certification programs available in other mobile platforms, such as the extensive testing scripts and acceptance guidelines used by Windows, Apple, and BREW platforms, and adjusting them for your Android applications. Regardless of whether you plan to apply for a specific certification, conforming to well-recognized quality guidelines can improve your application's quality.

Handling Specialized Test Scenarios

In addition to functional testing, there are a few other specialized testing scenarios that any QA team should consider.

Testing Application Integration Points

It's necessary to test how the application behaves with other parts of the Android operating system. For example:

- Ensuring that interruptions from the operating system are handled properly (incoming messages, calls, and powering off)
- Validating content provider data exposed by your application, including such uses as through a Live Folder
- Validating functionality triggered in other applications via an `Intent`
- Validating any known functionality triggered in your application via an `Intent`
- Validating any secondary entry points to your application as defined in `AndroidManifest.xml`, such as application shortcuts
- Validating alternative forms of your application, such as App Widgets
- Validating service-related features, if applicable

Testing Application Upgrades

When possible, perform upgrade tests of both the client and the server or service side of things. If upgrade support is planned, have development create a mock upgraded Android application so that QA can validate that data migration occurs properly, even if the upgraded application does nothing with the data.

Tip

Users receive Android platform updates over the air on a regular basis. The platform version on which your application is installed might change over time. Some developers have found that firmware upgrades have broken their applications, necessitating upgrades. Always retest your applications when a new version of the SDK is released, so that you can upgrade users before your applications have a chance to break in the field.

If your application is backed by an underlying database, you'll want to test versioning your database. Does a database upgrade migrate existing data or delete it? Does the migration work from all versions of the application to the current version, or just the last version?

Testing Device Upgrades

Applications are increasingly using the cloud and backup services available on the Android platform. This means that users who upgrade their devices can seamlessly move their data from one device to another. So if they drop their smartphone in a hot tub or crack their tablet screen, their application data can often be salvaged. If your application leverages these services, make sure you test whether these transitions work.

Testing Product Internationalization

It's a good idea to test internationalization support early in the development process—on both the client and the server or services. You're likely to run into some problems in this area related to screen real estate and issues with strings, dates, times, and formatting.

Tip

If your application will be localized for multiple languages, test in a foreign language—especially a verbose one. The application might look flawless in English but be unusable in German, where words are generally longer.

Testing for Conformance

Make sure to review any policies, agreements, and terms to which your application must conform and make sure your application complies. For example, Android applications must by default conform to the Google Play Developer Distribution Agreement and, when applicable, other Google Play services terms of service. Other distribution means and add-on packages may add further terms that your application must abide by.

Installation Testing

Generally speaking, installation of Android applications is straightforward; however, you need to test installations on devices with low resources and low memory as well as test installation from the specific marketplaces when your application "goes live." If the manifest install location allows external media, be sure to test various low or missing resource scenarios.

Backup Testing

Don't forget to test features that are not readily apparent to the user, such as the backup and restore services and the sync features.

Performance Testing

Application performance matters in the mobile world. The Android SDK has support for calculating performance benchmarks within an application and monitoring memory and resource usage. Testers should familiarize themselves with these utilities and use them often to help identify performance bottlenecks and dangerous memory leaks and misused resources.

One common performance issue we see frequently with new Android developers is trying to do everything on the main UI thread. Time- and resource-intensive work, such as network downloads, XML parsing, graphics rendering, and other such tasks, should be moved off the main UI thread so that the user interface remains responsive. This helps avoid so-called force close (or FC) issues and negative reviews saying as much.

The Debug class (android.os.Debug) has been around since Android was first released. This class provides a number of methods for generating trace logs that can then be analyzed using the traceview test tool. Android 2.3 introduced a new class called StrictMode (android.os.StrictMode) that can be used to monitor applications, track down latency issues, and banish ANRs. There's also a great write-up about StrictMode on the Android Developers Blog, available at *http://android-developers .blogspot.com/2010/12/new-gingerbread-api-strictmode.html*.

Here's another good example of a common performance issue we see from new Android application developers. Many do not realize that, by default, Android screens (backed by activities) are restarted every time the screen orientation changes. Unless the developer takes the appropriate actions, nothing is cached by default. Even basic applications really need to take care of how their lifecycle management works. Tools are available to do this efficiently. Yet, we frequently run into very inefficient ways of doing this—usually due to not handling lifecycle events at all.

Testing In-App Billing

Billing is too important to leave to guesswork. Test it. The Google Play Developer Console allows developers to test application billing. Testing in-app billing requires an actual device with the most recent version of Google Play installed. Making sure billing works correctly could help prevent loss of revenue.

Testing for the Unexpected

Regardless of the workflow you design, understand that users do random, unexpected things—on purpose and by accident. Some users are "button mashers," whereas others forget to set the keypad lock before putting the device in their pocket, resulting in a weird set of key presses. Rotating the screen frequently, sliding a physical keyboard in and out, or fiddling with other settings often triggers unexpected configuration changes. A phone call or text message inevitably comes in during the most remote edge cases. Your application must be robust enough to handle this. The Exerciser Monkey command-line tool can help you test for this type of event.

Testing to Increase Your Chances of Being a "Killer App"

Every mobile developer wants to develop a "killer app"—those applications that go viral, rocket to the top of the charts, and make millions a month. Most people think that if they just find the right idea, they'll have a killer app on their hands. Developers are always scouring the top-ten lists and Google Play's Editors' Choice category, trying to figure out how to develop the next great app. But let us tell you a little secret: if there's one thing that all "killer apps" share, it's a higher-than-average quality standard. No clunky, slow, obnoxious, or difficult-to-use application ever makes it to the big leagues. Testing and enforcing quality standards can mean the difference between a mediocre application and a killer app.

If you spend any time examining the mobile marketplace, you'll notice that a number of larger mobile development companies publish a variety of high-quality applications with a shared look and feel. These companies leverage user interface consistency as well as shared and above-average quality standards to build brand loyalty and increase market share, while hedging their bets that perhaps just one of their many applications will have that magical combination of great idea and quality design. Other, smaller companies often have the great ideas but struggle with the quality aspects of mobile software development. The inevitable result is that the mobile marketplace is full of fantastic application ideas badly executed with poor user interfaces and crippling defects.

Leveraging Android SDK Tools for Android Application Testing

The Android SDK and developer community provide a number of useful tools and re-sources for application testing and quality assurance. You might want to leverage the following tools during this phase of your development project:

- The physical devices for testing and bug reproduction
- The Android emulator for automated testing and testing of builds when devices are not available
- The Android DDMS tool for debugging and interaction with the emulator or device, as well as for taking screenshots
- The ADB tool for logging, debugging, and shell access tools
- The Exerciser Monkey command-line tool for stress testing of input (available via the adb shell command)
- The monkeyrunner API for automating running unit test suites and for writing functional and framework unit tests
- The uiautomator testing framework, a command-line tool and a set of APIs for automating user interface tests to run on one or more devices by writing UI func-tional test cases (requires API Level 16 and SDK Tools, Revision 21 or higher)
- The UiAutomation class is used for automating and simulating user interactions that span multiple applications and allows you to inspect the user interface to determine if your tests have passed or failed (added in API Level 18)
- The logcat command-line tool, which can be used to view log data generated by the application (best used with debug versions of your application)
- The traceview application, which can be used to view and interpret the tracing log files you can generate from your app
- The sqlite3 command-line tool for application database access (available via the adb shell command)
- The Hierarchy Viewer for user interface debugging, performance tweaking, and pixel-perfect screenshots of the device
- The lint tool, which can be used to optimize the layout resources of an application

- The `systrace` tool for analyzing display and performance execution times of your application's processes
- The `bmgr` command-line tool, which can help test backup management features of your application, if applicable

It should be noted that although we have used the Android tools, such as the Android emulator and DDMS debugging tools, with the Android IDE, these are standalone tools that can be used by QA personnel without the need for source code or a development environment.

Tip

The tools discussed in Appendix A, "Mastering the Android Development Tools," and throughout this book are valuable not just to developers; these tools provide testers with much more control over device configuration.

Avoiding Silly Mistakes in Android Application Testing

Here are some of the frustrating and silly mistakes and pitfalls that Android testers should try to avoid:

- Not testing the server or service components used by an application as thoroughly as the client side.
- Not testing with the appropriate version of the Android SDK (device versus development build versions).
- Not testing on the device and assuming the emulator is enough.
- Not testing the live application using the same system that users use (billing, installation, and such). Buy your own app.
- Neglecting to test all entry points to the application.
- Neglecting to test in different coverage areas and network speeds.
- Neglecting to test using battery power. Don't always have the device plugged in.

Android Application Testing Essentials

The Android SDK offers many different methods for testing your application. Some test methods available are runnable from within an IDE, others from the command line, but many times you are able to run them using either an IDE or the command line. Many of these test methods require writing a test program to run against your application.

Writing a test program to run against your application may sound intimidating at first. After all, you are writing a lot of code already just to build an application. If you are new to the concept of writing test code, you may be wondering why you should spend the time learning how to write more code to test your application.

The answer is simple. Writing tests helps automate a great amount of the testing process, rather than having to manually verify that your code is working correctly. An example should help. Let's say you build an application that allows users to create, read, update, and delete data. Many times these actions are performed on a data model. Writing tests against the data model allows you to verify that the data model code is functioning as it should, providing the correct results when queried, storing the correct results when saved, and deleting the correct information when deleted.

On the other hand, when a user takes an action within your application, you usually would like to provide some sort of visual feedback. Writing tests against your views allows you to verify that when a user does take a particular action, the views are displaying the correct information every step of the way.

Tip

Tests should be designed to determine what the results of your application code should be. As long as your application's requirements remain the same, your tests should always expect the same results, even if you change your application's underlying code. In the case that one of your tests fails, as long as the expectation is the same and you have written your tests correctly, you probably have made a mistake somewhere in your application's logic.

You may be thinking that your app is too simple for testing or that there is no way that an error could possibly be in your code because you are sure that you have covered every possible scenario. If you believe this to be true, and even though you programmed the application to do only what the app is supposed to do, just remember that your users are not programmers, nor do they limit their expectations to what you believe your application provides. Your users may think your application provides a scenario that you have not actually created for them, and when they try to use this imagined scenario, your application will more than likely explode in their hands. That is when the negative reviews start rolling in. Even if the feature never existed in the first place, your users most likely don't care and will blame the problem on you even if it wasn't your fault they tried to do something they weren't supposed to.

Since you are the application programmer, you are bound to come across one or two errors while coding. As your application grows, and you release new features, how do you know for sure that the results you expected last week are still the same as the results your application is providing this week?

Unit Testing with JUnit

One way to ensure that your application is working properly, and continues to work properly over long periods of time, is to write unit tests. A unit test is designed to test small units of your application's logic. For example, you may always expect a particular value to be created when a user does something. A unit test ensures that every time your code changes, the actual result of that unit of code is as expected. The alternative way to test that your application is creating that particular value properly would be to install your application and try out each and every feature in every possible order while taking into account every possible scenario to see if the result is as expected every time you update your code. This method quickly becomes cumbersome and time-consuming as your application grows and becomes very difficult to track.

Android provides unit testing based on the JUnit testing framework. Many of Android's testing classes directly inherit their functionality from JUnit. This means that you can write unit tests to test Java code, or you could write more Android-specific tests. Both JUnit and the Android SDK tools test classes are available from within the Android IDE, Eclipse with the ADT plugin, and Android Studio. Unit testing is a very big topic. The following content is not meant to be comprehensive, but rather to serve as an introduction to how you can start unit testing your Android applications to create software that is less error prone.

There are two approaches to writing unit tests. One approach is to write the application first and to write the tests last. The other approach is to write the tests first and the application code last. We will be working with an application that has already been written to ease ourselves into understanding unit tests. There are many reasons you would want to write your tests before your application logic; this approach is known as Test Driven Development (TDD).

We will not cover TDD in this book, but once you have a feel for how we create our first working test project, you should be more comfortable moving on to the test-first approach. We will point out that using TDD helps with deciding up front what your application results should be, and therefore you write your unit tests with those results in mind. Knowing what the expected results should be without having written the application logic means that your tests will fail. Then you move on to writing your application, knowing what results to produce, until all your tests pass.

Just to clarify, this does not mean that you write every single one of your tests up front before writing any code. Instead, you write a single unit test and then move on to writing the application code to make that individual unit test pass. Once we are through, you should be able to see how TDD could have been applied to the following example. TDD is a vast topic, and there are many great resources out there for learning it.

Introducing the `PasswordMatcher` Application

In order to learn how to perform unit testing, we first need an application that we can unit test. We have provided a simple application that shows two `EditText` fields that have an `inputType` of `textPassword`. This means that any text typed into the fields will be anonymous. We also have a `Button` with an `onClick` listener that determines if the two passwords entered into each of the `EditText` boxes are equal. Figure 18.1 shows what the user interface for the application looks like.

Tip

Many of the code samples provided in this chapter are taken from the `PasswordMatcher` application and the `PasswordMatcherTest` application. The source code for these applications is provided for download on the book's website.

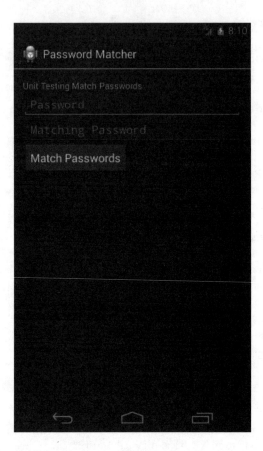

Figure 18.1 The `PasswordMatcher` application showing
two `EditText` boxes and a `Button`.

Let's take a look at the contents of the `layout` file for the `PasswordMatcher` application. The name of the file is `activity_password_matcher.xml`.

```
<LinearLayout xmlns:android="http://schemas.android.com/apk/res/android"
  xmlns:tools="http://schemas.android.com/tools"
    android:layout_width="match_parent"
    android:layout_height="match_parent"
    android:orientation="vertical"
    android:paddingBottom="@dimen/activity_vertical_margin"
    android:paddingLeft="@dimen/activity_horizontal_margin"
    android:paddingRight="@dimen/activity_horizontal_margin"
    android:paddingTop="@dimen/activity_vertical_margin"
    tools:context=".PasswordMatcherActivity" >
```

```xml
<TextView
    android:id="@+id/title"
    android:layout_width="match_parent"
    android:layout_height="wrap_content"
    android:contentDescription="@string/display_title"
    android:text="@string/match_passwords_title" />
<EditText
    android:id="@+id/password"
    android:layout_width="match_parent"
    android:layout_height="wrap_content"
    android:hint="@string/password"
    android:inputType="textPassword"
    android:text="" />
<EditText
    android:id="@+id/matchingPassword"
    android:layout_width="match_parent"
    android:layout_height="wrap_content"
    android:hint="@string/matching_password"
    android:inputType="textPassword"
    android:text="" />
<Button
    android:id="@+id/matchButton"
    android:layout_width="wrap_content"
    android:layout_height="wrap_content"
    android:contentDescription="@string/submit_match_password_button"
    android:text="@string/match_password_button" />
<TextView
    android:id="@+id/passwordResult"
    android:layout_width="match_parent"
    android:layout_height="wrap_content"
    android:contentDescription="@string/match_password_notice"
    android:visibility="gone" />
</LinearLayout>
```

The layout is a LinearLayout that contains a TextView for displaying our application title, two EditText views with the text initially set to be an empty string, a Button, and a final TextView for displaying the results of our Button onClick response that has a visibility of GONE. This visibility setting means that the TextView will not appear when the application is first launched, nor will it take up any visual space.

The code for our PasswordMatcherActivity is as follows:

```java
public class PasswordMatcherActivity extends Activity {
    EditText password;
    EditText matchingPassword;
    TextView passwordResult;

    @Override
    protected void onCreate(Bundle savedInstanceState) {
        super.onCreate(savedInstanceState);
        setContentView(R.layout.activity_password_matcher);
        password = (EditText) findViewById(R.id.password);
        matchingPassword = (EditText) findViewById(R.id.matchingPassword);
        passwordResult = (TextView) findViewById(R.id.passwordResult);
        Button button = (Button) findViewById(R.id.matchButton);
        button.setOnClickListener(new View.OnClickListener() {
            @Override
            public void onClick(View v) {
                String p = password.getText().toString();
                String mp = matchingPassword.getText().toString();
                if (p.equals(mp) && !p.isEmpty() && !mp.isEmpty()) {
                    passwordResult.setVisibility(View.VISIBLE);
                    passwordResult.setText(R.string.passwords_match_notice);
                    passwordResult.setTextColor(getResources().getColor(
                            R.color.green));
                } else {
                    passwordResult.setVisibility(View.VISIBLE);
                    passwordResult.setText(R.string.passwords_do_not_match_notice);
                    passwordResult.setTextColor(getResources().getColor(
                            R.color.red));
                }
            }
        });
    }
}
```

As you see, the `onClick` method checks to see that our two passwords are equal and that they are not empty. If either of the passwords is empty or they are not equal, we change the visibility setting of the `TextView` to `View.VISIBLE`, set the text to display an error message, and set the text color to red. If the passwords are equal and not empty, we change the visibility setting of the `TextView` to `View.VISIBLE`, set the text to display a success message, and set the text color to green.

Determining What Our Tests Should Prove

Let's think about what results our application should produce. Our application requests the user to input data into two text fields, and then responds with a result when the user clicks the button. Here are the results that we would like our tests to make sure our application produces:

- When a user leaves either one of the password fields empty or both password fields empty, assert that our application has displayed a red error message.

- When a user enters two passwords that do not match, assert that our application has displayed a red error message.

- When a user enters two matching passwords, assert that our application has displayed a green success message.

Now that we know what results our application should produce, we are set up pretty well for knowing how to write our tests. In order to make sure our application produces those results, we will write tests that assert these assumptions, and that the actual results are as expected.

Creating an Android Test Project

In order to write our tests, we must first create an Android test project. The test code is not part of our `PasswordMatcher` application. Instead, we create a `PasswordMatcherTest` package to house our test classes.

The steps for creating a test project are as follows:

1. In the Android IDE, go to `File`, `New`, `Other`, and under the `Android` folder, select `Android Test Project`, and press `Next` (see Figure 18.2).

2. On the `Create Android Project` page, type the Project Name of `Password MatcherTest` and click `Next` (see Figure 18.3).

3. On the `Select Test Target` page, make sure `An existing Android Project` is selected, choose the `PasswordMatcher` project, and click `Next` (see Figure 18.4).

4. On the `Select Build Target` page, choose `Android 4.3` and click `Finish` (see Figure 18.5).

Figure 18.2   Creating an Android test project in the Android IDE.

Figure 18.3   Naming the test project in the Android IDE.

Figure 18.4   Linking the test project to the `PasswordMatcher` application in the Android IDE.

Figure 18.5   Selecting the `Build Target` of the test project within the Android IDE.

Now that our test project has been created, upon first glance the project looks very much like a regular Android application. As we can see in Figure 18.6, the folder structure is very similar and has many of the same files that we are used to seeing, such as the `AndroidManifest.xml`.

Upon looking at the contents of the manifest file, we can clearly see the differences (see Figure 18.7).

The manifest includes the following:

```
<instrumentation
    android:name="android.test.InstrumentationTestRunner"
    android:targetPackage="com.introtoandroid.passwordmatcher" />
<application
    android:icon="@drawable/ic_launcher"
    android:label="@string/app_name" >
    <uses-library android:name="android.test.runner" />
</application>
```

Figure 18.6   Viewing the test project directory
structure within the Android IDE.

```
PasswordMatcherTest Manifest ⊠
   <?xml version="1.0" encoding="utf-8"?>
   <manifest xmlns:android="http://schemas.android.com/apk/res/android"
       package="com.introtoandroid.passwordmatcher.test"
       android:versionCode="1"
       android:versionName="1.0" >

       <uses-sdk android:minSdkVersion="9" />

       <instrumentation
           android:name="android.test.InstrumentationTestRunner"
           android:targetPackage="com.introtoandroid.passwordmatcher" />

       <application
           android:icon="@drawable/ic_launcher"
           android:label="@string/app_name" >
           <uses-library android:name="android.test.runner" />
       </application>

   </manifest>
```

⊞ Manifest Ⓐ Application Ⓟ Permissions Ⓘ Instrumentation ⊟ AndroidManifest.xml

Figure 18.7   Viewing the manifest file of the test
project within the Android IDE.

The <instrumentation> element is required for our test projects. This declaration allows our test application to "hook" into the Android system. We specify the name of the InstrumentationTestRunner class and include our PasswordMatcher package as the targetPackage against which our tests will run. We can also see that this application has a <uses-library> element that references android.test.runner. Another important aspect is that the test package name is com.introtoandroid.passwordmatcher.test. This is almost the same as the target application package, except that .test has been added to the end of the package. All test projects created using the Android tools have .test appended to the name of the package under test.

We do not yet have a source file or any classes defined in our source package for this project. Let's go ahead and create one within the Android IDE so we can begin writing code by following these steps:

1. From inside the Android IDE Package Explorer, right-click on the package com.introtoandroid.passwordmatcher.test found within the src folder of the project PasswordMatcherTest, choose New, and then choose Class. Type the name PasswordMatcherTest as the Class name (Figure 18.8). The Superclass default entry must be changed, so choose Browse, type

Figure 18.8   Creating the `PasswordMatcherTest.java` file.

`android.test.ActivityInstrumentationTestCase2` into the "Choose a type" text field entry, and click OK (Figure 18.9). Finally, click Finish to create the Java class file.

2. Now that we have our class file created, there are a few errors that we need to fix. We must first import the `PasswordMatcherActivity` file and the resource files associated from our `PasswordMatcher` project. The import statements should be as follows:

```
import com.introtoandroid.passwordmatcher.PasswordMatcherActivity;

import com.introtoandroid.passwordmatcher.R;
```

3. We must also modify the extend class associated with the `ActivityInstrumentationTestCase2<T>` from T to `PasswordMatcherActivity`. Our new declaration should be `ActivityInstrumentationTestCase2<PasswordMatcherActivity>`.

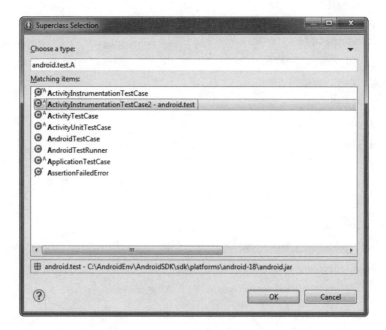

Figure 18.9   Choosing a superclass type for the test class.

4. We have one more error that needs to be fixed before we can write any code, and that is to add a class constructor. Go ahead and add the following code to your class:

```
public PasswordMatcherTest() {
    super(PasswordMatcherActivity.class);
}
```

We are now ready to begin writing our tests for this project.

Writing the Tests

There are a few standard steps to take when writing tests. First, we need to create a setup method that will set up our test project with any information that we will need to access from within the tests. This is the place where we want to access our PasswordMatcherActivity, which will allow us to gain access to any of the views that we may need throughout the tests. We must create a few variables for accessing

our views in addition to importing any classes that may be required. Here are
the import statements:

```
import android.widget.Button;

import android.widget.EditText;

import android.widget.TextView;
```

Here are the variables we need to access in our test project:

```
TextView title;

EditText password;

EditText matchingPassword;

Button button;

TextView passwordResult;

PasswordMatcherActivity passwordMatcherActivity;
```

And here is our setUp() method:

```
protected void setUp() throws Exception {

    super.setUp();

    passwordMatcherActivity = getActivity();

    title = (TextView) passwordMatcherActivity.findViewById(R.id.title);

    password = (EditText) passwordMatcherActivity.findViewById(R.id.password);

    matchingPassword = (EditText)

            passwordMatcherActivity.findViewById(R.id.matchingPassword);

    button = (Button) passwordMatcherActivity.findViewById(R.id.matchButton);

    passwordResult = (TextView)

passwordMatcherActivity.findViewById(R.id.passwordResult);

}
```

This method gets the PasswordMatcherActivity using the getActivity() method,
so that we can start accessing our views using the findViewById method.

Now we can begin writing test cases to ensure that our application is behaving
correctly. We should start by testing the initial state of the application to make sure
the starting state is correct. Even though the initial state will always be the same, it is a
good idea to know that the application starts as expected, because if something is not
working correctly when our application begins changing state, we have already verified that our starting state is as expected, and that rules out the starting state from being the culprit.

Tip

When using JUnit 3 for Android testing, all test case methods must begin with the word `test`, such as `testPreConditions()` or `testMatchingPasswords()`. Prepending the word `test` to method names lets JUnit know that the method is in fact a test method and not just a standard method. Only the methods that start with the word `test` will be run as test cases.

The elements of our application that change their state during execution are the two `EditText` elements and the `TextView` result notice. Ensuring that our test starts with the correct inputs gives us confidence that our actual test methods will start with the correct values. Let's begin by writing our very first test case for making sure the starting state of our application is as expected.

```java
public void testPreConditions() {
    String t = title.getText().toString();
    assertEquals(passwordMatcherActivity.getResources()
            .getString(R.string.match_passwords_title), t);
    String p = password.getText().toString();
    String pHint = password.getHint().toString();
    int pInput = password.getInputType();
    assertEquals(EMPTY_STRING, p);
    assertEquals(passwordMatcherActivity.getResources()
            .getString(R.string.password), pHint);
    assertEquals(129, pInput);
    String mp = matchingPassword.getText().toString();
    String mpHint = matchingPassword.getHint().toString();
    int mpInput = matchingPassword.getInputType();
    assertEquals(EMPTY_STRING, mp);
    assertEquals(passwordMatcherActivity.getResources()
            .getString(R.string.matching_password), mpHint);
    assertEquals(129, mpInput);
    String b = button.getText().toString();
    assertEquals(passwordMatcherActivity.getResources()
            .getString(R.string.match_password_button), b);
    int visibility = passwordResult.getVisibility();
    assertEquals(View.GONE, visibility);
}
```

Android Unit-Testing APIs and Assertions

Before we run our first test, let's take a moment to introduce assertions. If you are new to unit testing, you probably have not yet been exposed to the assert methods. An assertion compares the expected value the application should be creating (the expected value provided by you) with the actual value that the test receives upon running the application.

There are many standard `JUnit` assertion methods that you have at your disposal, but there are also many Android-specific assertion methods.

The `testPreConditions()` method begins by getting the text value of the `TextView` with the id of `title`. We then use the `assertEquals()` method and pass in the value that our test expects the `text` attribute to be, with the value that the `getText()` method actually provides. When you run the test, if the values are equal, this means that one particular assertion of the test passes. We continue getting the `text` value, `hint` value, and `inputType` of both `EditText` fields and use the `assertEquals()` method to make sure the expected value matches the actual value. We also get the `text` value of the `Button` and check to see if it matches the expected value. We finish the method by making sure that the visibility of the `passwordResult` notice is not showing and is equal to the `View.GONE` value.

If all of the assertions pass, this means that the entire test should pass and that the starting values of our application are the values they are supposed to be.

Running Your First Test Using the Android IDE

To run your first test using the Android IDE or Eclipse with the ADT plugin installed, select your test project in the Android IDE, right-click the project, go to `Debug As`, then choose `Android JUnit Test`. We want to ensure that the `testPreConditions()` test method is starting with the correct values.

> **Note**
>
> Make sure that you have an emulator running on your computer, or that you have a real device connected to your computer in debug mode for your test to run. If you have more than one device or emulator attached to your computer, you may be presented with a selection UI to choose a device on which to run the test.

Your test should begin running, and you must wait until the test completes to determine if it passes.

Analyzing the Test Results

Once the test completes, you should see a new window open within the IDE titled `JUnit`. If your test has been written correctly, you should see the results as shown in Figure 18.10 that indicate the test has passed.

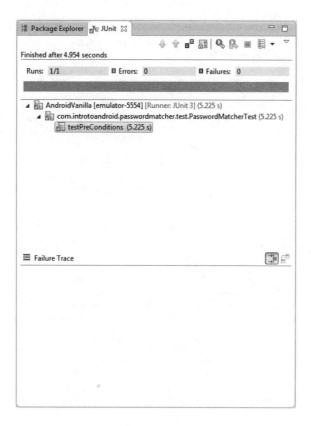

Figure 18.10   The Android IDE showing that the
testPreConditions() method has passed.

The JUnit window provides a few useful details about the test once it has finished. You should see that the test was run on a particular device and port; in this particular case, the device was an emulator named AndroidVanilla on port 5554. You should also see that the test class that was run was com.introtoandroid.passwordmatcher.test .PasswordMatcherTest. Also notice that the testPreConditions() method was run. An icon (📇) provides a visual indication that the test run completed successfully. Also note the time it took to complete the overall test in addition to the time it took to complete the testPreConditions() method.

Notice the 🔍 icon. This icon allows you to rerun your test without needing to use the Debug As option. The 🔍 icon allows you to rerun your failed tests. This is useful when you have quite a few tests and you just want to work on the failing tests and narrow in on tests that you need to correct.

Figure 18.11 The Android IDE showing that the
`testPreConditions()` method has failed the test.

A failed test means that the expected results do not match the actual results. The  icon lets you know that a test has failed. In the case that the test failed, you would see a window like the one depicted in Figure 18.11.

You should also notice that the `Failure Trace` section of the `JUnit` window shown in Figure 18.11 lists a stack trace that could be useful to help you track down where the failure is originating.

An error in the test means that there is an error in the test code, and you must fix the error before you can determine if the test will pass or fail (see Figure 18.12). The  icon lets you know if a particular test has an error present.

Again, the `Failure Trace` section of the `JUnit` window lets you know where the error is originating; in this case, the error is a `NullPointerException`.

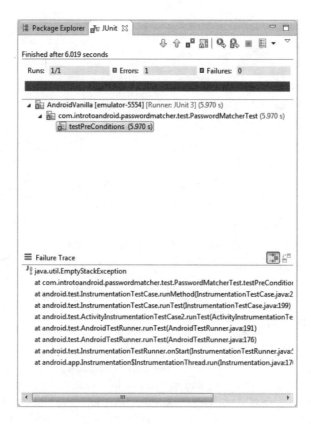

Figure 18.12   The Android IDE showing that the `testPreConditions()` method has an error that must be fixed before the test can pass or fail.

Adding Additional Tests

The test project includes a few additional tests, but we will cover only one of those tests here, as they are very similar. Please see the `PasswordMatcherTest` project for the full code listing providing all the test methods. The test that we will discuss is the `test MatchingPasswords()` method. As the name of the method suggests, this test will determine if the passwords we provide the application match and, if so, will let us know if the expected visual outcome of the test matches what the application actually outputs when provided the matching password inputs.

Here is our `testMatchingPasswords()` method:

```
public void testMatchingPasswords() {

    TouchUtils.tapView(this, password);

    sendKeys(GOOD_PASSWORD);
```

```
TouchUtils.tapView(this, matchingPassword);

sendKeys(GOOD_PASSWORD);

TouchUtils.clickView(this, button);

String p = password.getText().toString();

assertEquals("abc123", p);

String mp = matchingPassword.getText().toString();

assertEquals("abc123", mp);

assertEquals(p, mp);

int visibility = passwordResult.getVisibility();

assertEquals(View.VISIBLE, visibility);

String notice = passwordResult.getText().toString();

assertEquals(passwordMatcherActivity.getResources()

        .getString(R.string.passwords_match_notice), notice);

int noticeColor = passwordResult.getCurrentTextColor();

assertEquals(passwordMatcherActivity.getResources()

        .getColor(R.color.green), noticeColor);

}
```

This test does a few things. Since we have initialized our views in the setUp() method, we can begin testing our application. We start the method by calling the TouchUtils.tapView() method. The TouchUtils class provides methods for simulating touch events within our application. Calling the tapView() method on the password EditText field grabs the focus of the field and allows the test to use the sendKeys() method to enter a GOOD_PASSWORD value into the EditText field. We continue the test by grabbing the focus of the matching Password EditText field and use the sendKeys() method for the test to enter the same GOOD_PASSWORD value into the second EditText field. We then use the getText() method to get the text value of each of the EditText values to ensure that the values are equals to the GOOD_PASSWORD value the test entered, and then check to make sure that both EditText values are equal to each other. The test then checks the passwordResult TextView to see if the visibility has been set to View.VISIBLE and further checks to see if the value of the text is actually what we expect the value to be. Finally, we get the text color value of the passwordResult TextView and check to make sure that the value is equal to green.

When you run the test, you should see the PasswordMatcher application start up, and you should also notice that both EditText values automatically begin receiving password input into their respective fields, followed by the Button named Match Passwords receiving a click. After the Button receives the click from the test, you should finally see the TextView display as visible, and the PasswordMatcherActivity should now display a green success notice that reads Passwords match! (see Figure 18.13).

Figure 18.13   The `PasswordMatcher` application displaying a `TextView`
with a green color indicating that the passwords entered match.

After we run our test, we should see that the test passes, and this means that the application responded as expected (see Figure 18.14).

Here are just a few classes, located in the `android.test` package, that you may want to be aware of. For a full listing with descriptions, see the Android documentation.

- **`ActivityInstrumentationTestCase2<T>`**: used for functional testing of a single `Activity`
- **`MoreAsserts`**: additional assertion methods specific to Android
- **`TouchUtils`**: used to perform touch events
- **`ViewAsserts`**: assertion methods used for making assertions about views

More Android Automated Testing Programs and APIs

Automated testing is a very powerful tool that you should use when developing your Android applications. `JUnit` for Android is just one of the automated testing tools that the

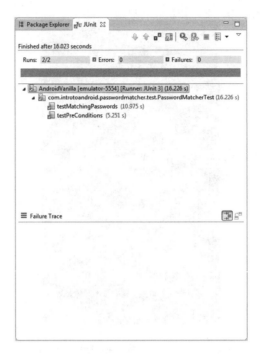

Figure 18.14   The Android IDE displaying a successful test run.

Android SDK provides. Other tools that the Android SDK provides for testing applications that deserve a mention are as follows:

- **UI/Application Exerciser Monkey**: This program, named `monkey`, can be run from the command line using an `adb` shell command. Use this tool for stress testing your application, which generates and sends your test device random events while your application is running. This is useful for uncovering bugs that may be present when random events are thrown at your application.

- **monkeyrunner**: This is a testing API for writing Python programs for taking control of the automated testing process. A `monkeyrunner` program runs outside the Android emulator or device and can be used for running unit tests, installing and uninstalling your `.apk` file, testing across multiple devices, taking screenshots of your application during a running test cycle, and many more useful features.

- **uiautomator**: This is a testing framework and command-line tool that was added in API Level 16. The `uiautomator` tool is used for running tests from the command line using an `adb` shell command. You can use this tool for automating user interface tests across one or more devices and for automating the functional testing of your user interface.

- **UiAutomation**: This is a testing class for simulating user events and for leveraging the `AccessibilityService` APIs for inspecting user interfaces during automated tests. You can use this class for simulating user events that span multiple applications. This class was added in API Level 18.

Summary

In this chapter, we armed you—the keepers of application quality—with real-world knowledge for testing Android applications, in addition to introducing a real example of how to test your Android applications with unit tests.

Whether you're a team of one or one hundred, testing your applications is critical for project success. Luckily, the Android SDK provides a number of tools for testing applications, as well as a powerful unit-testing framework and other sophisticated testing APIs. By following standard QA techniques and leveraging these tools, you can ensure that the application you deliver to your users is the best it can be.

Quiz Questions

1. True or false: One typical defect common to mobile applications is an application using too much disk space on the device.
2. Name three specialized test scenarios that any QA team should consider.
3. What is the name of the unit-testing library available for testing Android applications?
4. When creating an Android test project, what word is automatically appended to the end of the package name under test by the Android tools?
5. When using `JUnit 3` for testing Android applications, what prefix must your test methods begin with?
6. True or false: Testing the default starting values of your application is overkill.
7. What Android test class is used for performing touch events from within unit tests?

Exercises

1. Read through the Testing topic within the Android documentation, at the following URL: *http://d.android.com/tools/testing/index.html*.
2. Using the `PasswordMatcherTest` project, determine how to run the test project from the command line and provide the command for doing so.
3. Add an additional test method to the `PasswordMatcherTest` project that uses a method from the `ViewAsserts` class to determine if each of the views of the `PasswordMatcher` application is on the screen. Write the method and make sure the test passes.

References and More Information

Android Tools: "Testing":

http://d.android.com/tools/testing/index.html

Android Tools: "Testing Fundamentals":

http://d.android.com/tools/testing/testing_android.html

Android Tools: "monkeyrunner":

http://d.android.com/tools/help/monkeyrunner_concepts.html

Android Tools: "UI/Application Exerciser Monkey":

http://d.android.com/tools/help/monkey.html

Android Tools: "UI Testing":

http://d.android.com/tools/testing/testing_ui.html

Android Tools: "uiautomator":

http://d.android.com/tools/help/uiautomator/index.html

Android Reference: "UiAutomation":

http://d.android.com/reference/android/app/UiAutomation.html

Wikipedia on software testing:

http://en.wikipedia.org/wiki/Software_testing

Software Testing Help:

http://www.softwaretestinghelp.com

19

Publishing Your Android Application

After you've developed and tested your application, the next logical step is to publish it so that other people can enjoy it. You might even want to make some money. A variety of distribution opportunities are available to Android application developers. Many developers choose to sell their applications through mobile marketplaces such as Google Play. Others develop their own distribution mechanisms—for example, they might sell their applications from a website. You may even want to have fine-grained control over who can install your application using new features with the Google Play Developer Console. Regardless, developers should consider which distribution options they plan to use during the application design and development process, because some distribution choices might require code changes or impose restrictions on content.

Choosing the Right Distribution Model

The application distribution methods you choose to employ depend on your goals and target users. Here are some questions you should ask yourself:

- Is your application ready for prime time, or are you considering a beta period to iron out the kinks?

- Are you trying to reach the broadest audience, or have you developed a vertical market application? Determine who your users are, which devices they are using, and their preferred methods for seeking out and downloading applications.

- How will you price your application? Is it freeware or shareware? Are the payment models (single payment versus subscription model versus ad-driven revenue) you require available on the distribution mechanisms you want to leverage?

- Where do you plan to distribute? Verify that any application markets you plan to use are capable of distributing within those countries or regions.

- Are you willing to share a portion of your profits? Distribution mechanisms such as Google Play take a percentage of each sale in exchange for hosting your application and distributing and collecting application revenue on your behalf.

- Do you require complete control over the distribution process, or are you will-ing to work within the boundaries and requirements imposed by third-party marketplaces? This might require compliance with further license agreements and terms.

- If you plan to distribute yourself, how will you do so? You might need to develop more services to manage users, deploy applications, and collect payments. If so, how will you protect user data? What trade laws must you comply with?

- Have you considered creating a free trial version of your application? If the distri-bution system under consideration has a return policy, consider the ramifications. You need to ensure that your application has safeguards to minimize the number of users who buy your app, use it, and return it for a full refund. For example, a game might include safeguards such as a free trial version and a full-scale version with more game levels than could possibly be completed within the refundable time period.

Protecting Your Intellectual Property

You've spent time, money, and effort to build a valuable Android application. Now you want to distribute it but perhaps you are concerned about reverse engineering of trade secrets and software piracy. As technology rapidly advances, it's impossible to perfectly protect against either.

If you're accustomed to developing Java applications, you might be familiar with code obfuscation tools. These are designed to strip easy-to-read information from compiled Java byte codes, making the decompiled application more difficult to understand and reverse engineer. Some tools, such as ProGuard (*http://proguard.sourceforge.net*), support Android applications because they can run after the `.jar` file is created and before it's converted to the final package file used with Android. ProGuard support is built into Android projects created with the Android tools.

Google Play also supports a licensing service called the License Verification Library (LVL). This is available as a Google Play add-on but works on Android API Level 3 and higher. It applies only to paid applications distributed through Google Play. It requires application support—code additions—to be fully utilized, and you should seriously con-sider obfuscating your code if you use it. The service's primary purpose is to verify that a paid application installed on a device was properly purchased by the user. You can find out more at the Android Developer website: *http://d.android.com/google/play/licensing/index.html*.

You may also be concerned about rogue applications impersonating your brand or performing trademark and/or copyright infringement. Google has many mechanisms set up for reporting infringements, so if this does occur, you should report those infringe-ments to protect your brand. In addition to using the mechanisms Google provides for reporting infringements, you may also need to consult with legal counsel.

Following the Policies of Google Play

When you publish your application to Google Play, you must agree to certain policies that Google enforces. One of those policies is the Developer Distribution Agreement, which can be found here: *http://play.google.com/about/developer-distribution-agreement.html*. By accepting the agreement, you are agreeing to not perform certain prohibited actions that are outlined within the agreement.

Another term of service that you agree to is the Developer Program Policies as defined here: *http://play.google.com/about/developer-content-policy.html*. This includes rules that prohibit spam, restrict content, and govern ad implementations, and it even outlines subscription and cancellation policies. Staying up-to-date on the current policies of Google Play is very important to avoid any negative repercussions for failure to comply with them.

Billing the User

Unlike some other mobile platforms you might have used, the Android SDK does not currently provide built-in billing APIs that work directly from within applications. Instead, billing APIs are normally add-on APIs that are provided by the distribution channels.

For selling your applications on Google Play, you must register for a Google Wallet Merchant account. Once registered, you need to connect your Google Wallet Merchant account to your Developer Console account. Google Wallet is the billing provider for processing application payments from within Google Play.

Google Play allows you to sell your application in 130 different countries, enabling you to accept the currencies that your users are used to spending. Users will be able to make purchases from their Android devices or from the Web, and Google Play provides an easy way to track and manage the entire process. Google Play accepts many different forms of payment, including direct carrier billing, credit card, gift card, or a stored Google Play balance. Any revenue that you generate is paid out to you in monthly installments to your Google Wallet Merchant account.

If an application needs to charge ad hoc fees for goods sold within the application (that is, subscriptions or in-app products), the application developer must implement an in-app billing mechanism. Google Play provides an In-app Billing API for billing support within any application published to Google Play (*http://d.android.com/google/play/billing/index.html*).

Rolling your own in-app billing system? Most Android devices can leverage the Internet, so using online billing services and APIs—PayPal, Amazon, or others, for example—is a common choice. Check with your preferred billing service to make sure it specifically allows mobile use and that the billing methods your application requires are available, feasible, and legal for your target users. Similarly, make sure any distribution channels you plan to use allow these billing mechanisms (as opposed to their own).

Leveraging Ad Revenue

Another method to make money from users is to have an ad-supported mobile business model. Android itself has no specific rules against using advertisements within applications. However, different markets may impose their own rules for what's allowed. For instance, Google's AdMob Ads service allows developers to place ads within their applications. (Read more at *https://developers.google.com/mobile-ads-sdk/docs/*.) Several other companies provide similar services.

Collecting Statistics Regarding Your Application

Before you publish, you may want to consider adding some statistics collection to your application to determine how your users use it. You can write your own statistics-collection mechanisms, or you can use third-party add-ons such as the Google Analytics App Tracking SDK for Android. Ensure that you always inform your users if you are collecting information about them, and incorporate your plans into your clearly defined EULA and privacy policy. Statistics can help you not just see how many people are using your application, but also how they are actually using it.

Now let's look at the steps you need to take to package and publish your application.

Packaging Your Application for Publication

Developers must take several steps when preparing an Android application for publication and distribution. Your application must also meet several important requirements imposed by the marketplaces. The following steps are required for publishing an application:

1. Prepare and perform a release candidate build of the application.
2. Verify that all requirements for the marketplace are met, such as configuring the Android manifest file properly. For example, make sure the application name and version information are correct and the `debuggable` attribute is set to `false`.
3. Package and digitally sign the application.
4. Test the packaged application release thoroughly.
5. Update and include all the required resources for the release.
6. Make sure that your servers or services used by your application are stable and production ready.
7. Publish the application.

The preceding steps are required but not sufficient to guarantee a successful deployment. Developers should also take these steps:

1. Thoroughly test the application on all target handsets.
2. Turn off debugging, including `Log` statements and any other logging.

3. Verify permissions, making sure to add ones for services used and to remove any that aren't used, regardless of whether they are enforced by the handsets.

4. Test the final, signed version with all debugging and logging turned off.

Now, let's explore each of these steps in more detail, in the order they might be performed.

Preparing Your Code for Packaging

An application that has undergone a thorough testing cycle might need changes made to it before it is ready for a production release. These changes convert it from a debuggable, preproduction application into a release-ready application.

Setting the Application Name and Icon

An Android application has default settings for the icon and label. The icon appears in the application launcher and can appear in various other locations, including marketplaces. As such, an application is required to have an icon. You should supply alternative icon drawable resources for various screen resolutions. The label, or application name, is also displayed in similar locations and defaults to the package name. You should choose a short, user-friendly name that displays under the application icon in launcher screens.

Versioning the Application

Next, proper versioning is required, especially if updates could occur in the future. The version name is up to the developer. The version code, though, is used internally by the Android system to determine if an application is an update. You should increment the version code for each new update of an application. The exact value doesn't matter, but it must be greater than the previous version code. Versioning within the Android manifest file is discussed in Chapter 5, "Defining Your Application Using the Android Manifest File."

Verifying the Target Platforms

Make sure your application sets the `<uses-sdk>` tag in the Android manifest file correctly. This tag is used to specify the minimum and target platform versions that the application can run on. This is perhaps the most important setting after the application name and version information.

Configuring the Android Manifest for Filtering

If you plan to publish through the Google Play store, you should read up on how this distribution system uses certain tags within the Android manifest file to filter applications available to users. Many of these tags, such as `<supports-screens>`, `<uses-configuration>`, `<uses-feature>`, `<uses-library>`, `<uses-permission>`, and `<uses-sdk>`, were discussed in Chapter 5. Set each of these items carefully, because you don't want to accidentally put too many restrictions on your application. Make sure you test your application thoroughly after configuring these Android manifest file settings. For more information on how Google Play filters work, see *http://d.android.com/google/play/filters.html*.

Preparing Your Application Package for Google Play

Google Play has strict requirements for application packages. When you upload your application to the Android Developer Console, the package is verified and any problems are communicated to you. Most often, problems occur when you have not properly configured your Android manifest file.

Google Play uses the `android:versionName` attribute of the `<manifest>` tag within the Android manifest file to display version information to users. It also uses the `android:versionCode` attribute internally to handle application upgrades. The `android:icon` and `android:label` attributes must also be present because both are used by Google Play to display the application name to the user with a visual icon.

Warning

The Android SDK allows the `android:versionName` attribute to reference a string resource. Google Play, however, does not. An error is generated if a string resource is used.

Disabling Debugging and Logging

Next, you should turn off debugging and logging. Disabling debugging involves removing the `android:debuggable` attribute from the `<application>` tag of the `AndroidManifest.xml` file or setting it to `false`. You can turn off the logging code within Java in a variety of different ways, from just commenting it out to using a build system that can do this automatically.

Tip

A common method for conditionally compiling debug code is to use a class interface with a single, `public static final boolean` that's set to `true` or `false`. When this is used with an `if` statement and set to `false`, because it's immutable, the compiler should not include the unreachable code, and it certainly won't be executed. We recommend using some method other than just commenting out the `Log` lines and other debug code.

Tip

If you don't specify the `android:debuggable` attribute, incremental builds will automatically turn it on and export/release builds will leave it off. Specifying the value as `true` will also cause export/release builds to actually do a debug build.

Verifying Application Permissions

Finally, the permissions used by the application should be reviewed. Include all permissions that the application requires, and remove any that are not used. Users appreciate this.

Packing and Signing Your Application

Now that the application is ready for publication, the file package—the .apk file—needs to be prepared for release. The package manager of an Android device will not install a package that has not been digitally signed. Throughout the development process, the Android tools have accomplished this through signing with a debug key. The debug key cannot be used for publishing an application to the wider world. Instead, you need to use a true key to digitally sign the application. You can use the private key to digitally sign the release package files of your Android application, as well as any upgrades. This ensures that the application (as a complete entity) is coming from you, the developer, and not some other source (imposters!).

> **Warning**
>
> A private key identifies the developer and is critical to building trust relationships between developers and users. It is very important to secure private key information.

Google Play requires that your application's digital signature validity period end after October 22, 2033. This date might seem like a long way off and, for mobile, it certainly is. However, because an application must use the same key for upgrading and because applications that are designed to work closely together with special privileges and trust relationships must also be signed with the same key, the key could be chained forward through many applications. Thus, Google is mandating that the key be valid for the foreseeable future so application updates and upgrades are performed smoothly for users.

> **Note**
>
> Finding a third-party certificate authority that will issue a key is optional, but self-signing is the most straightforward solution. Within Google Play, there is no benefit to using a third-party certificate authority.

Although self-signing is typical of Android applications, and a certificate authority is not required, creating a suitable key and securing it properly are critical. The digital signature for Android applications can impact certain functionality. The expiry of the signature is verified at installation time, but after it's installed, an application continues to function even if the signature has expired.

You can export and sign your Android package file from within the Android IDE as follows (or you can use the command-line tools):

1. In the Android IDE, right-click the appropriate application project and choose the Android Tools, Export Signed Application Package... option. (Alternatively, after right-clicking the appropriate package, you can choose Export, expand the Android section, and choose Export Android Application, which defaults to a signed application.)

2. Click the Next button.

3. Select the project to export (the one you right-clicked before is the default, or you can select `Browse...` to choose another project) and click `Next`.

4. On the `Keystore selection` screen, choose the `Create new keystore` option and enter a file location (where you want to store the key) as well as a password for managing the keystore. (If you already have a keystore, choose `Browse` to pick your keystore file and then enter the correct password.)

Warning

Make sure you choose a strong password for the keystore. Remember where the keystore is located, too. The same one is required to publish an upgrade to your application. If it's checked into a revision-control system, the password helps protect it. However, you should consider adding an extra layer of privilege required to get to it.

5. Click the `Next` button.

6. On the `Key Creation` screen, enter the details of the key, as shown in Figure 19.1.

7. Click the `Next` button.

Figure 19.1   Creating a new key for exporting
a signed Android application in the Android IDE.

8. On the `Destination and key/certificate checks` screen, enter a destination for the application package file.

9. Click the `Finish` button.

You have now created a fully signed and certified application package file. The application package is ready for publication. For more information about signing, see the Android Developer website: *http://d.android.com/tools/publishing/app-signing.html.*

Note

If you are not using the Android IDE, you can use the `keytool` and `jarsigner` command-line tools available within the JDK, in addition to the `zipalign` utility provided with the Android SDK, to create a suitable key and sign an application package file (`.apk`). Although `zipalign` is not directly related to signing, it optimizes the application package for more efficient use on Android. The Android IDE runs `zipalign` automatically after the signing step.

Testing the Release Version of Your Application Package

Now that you have configured your application for production, you should perform a full final testing cycle, paying special attention to subtle changes to the installation process. An important part of this process is to verify that you have disabled all debugging features so that logging has no negative impact on the functionality and performance of the application.

Including All Required Resources

Before releasing your application, you need to make sure that all the required resources are available for access from your application. Testing that these resources are working properly and accessible is extremely important. Also, be sure that the most recent versions of these resources are included.

Readying Your Servers or Services

Make sure that your servers or any third-party services that your application accesses are stable and work well in a production setting. The last thing you want is to have a strong application with a weak back end. If your application is accessible via the Web, and not just a standalone application, ensuring proper and stable access to your servers and services should be a priority.

Distributing Your Application

Now that you've prepared your application for publication, it's time to get it out to users—for fun and profit. Before you publish, you may want to consider setting up an application website, tech support email address, help and feedback forum, Twitter/Facebook/Google+/social network *du jour* account, and any other infrastructure you may want or need to support your published application.

Publishing to Google Play

Google Play is the most popular mechanism for distributing Android applications at the time of this writing. This is where a typical user purchases and downloads applications. As of this writing, it's available to most, but not all, Android devices. As such, we show you how to check your package for preparedness, sign up for an Android Developer Console account, and submit your application for download to Google Play.

Note

Google Play is updated frequently. We have made every attempt to provide the latest steps for uploading and managing applications. However, these steps and the user interfaces described in this section may change at any time. Please review the Google Play Developer Console website (*https://play.google.com/apps/publish*) for the latest information.

Signing Up for Publishing to Google Play

To publish applications through Google Play, you must register for a publisher account and set up a Google Wallet Merchant account.

Note

As of this writing, only developers ("merchants") residing in certain approved countries may sell priced applications on Google Play due to international laws, as described here: *https://support.google.com/googleplay/android-developer/answer/150324?hl=en*. Developers from many other countries can register for publisher accounts, but they may publish only free applications at this time. For a complete list of supported publisher countries, see *https://support.google.com/googleplay/android-developer/answer/136758?hl=en*.

To sign up for a Google Play publisher account, you need to follow these steps:

1. Go to the Google Play Developer Console sign-up website at *https://play.google.com/apps/publish*, as shown in Figure 19.2.

2. Sign in with the Google account you want to use. If you do not yet have a Google account, click the Sign Up button and create one first.

3. You must first agree to the Google Play Developer Distribution Agreement by ticking the check box, as shown in Figure 19.3, then press Continue to payment. As of this writing, a $25 (USD) one-time registration fee is required to publish applications.

4. Note that Google Wallet is used for registration payment processing, so you must also set up a Google Wallet account, if you don't already have one, as shown in Figure 19.4.

5. Once the Google Wallet account has been set up, you must then accept the $25 registration fee (shown in Figure 19.5).

6. You then proceed to Complete your Account details (see Figure 19.6). Enter the required information and click Complete registration.

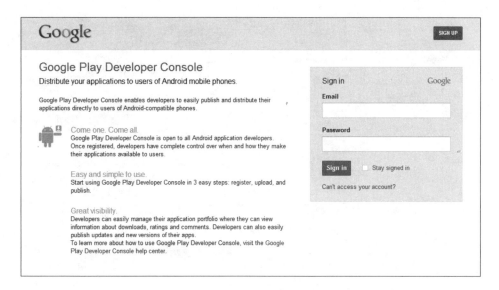

Figure 19.2   The Google Play publisher sign-in page.

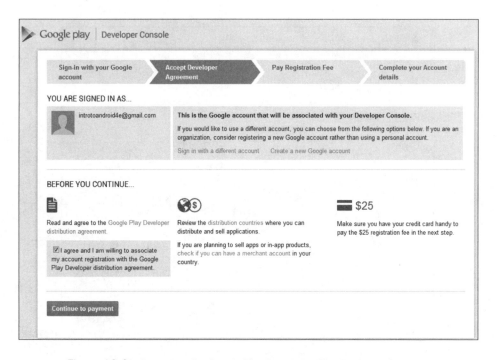

Figure 19.3   Accepting the Google Play Developer Distribution Agreement.

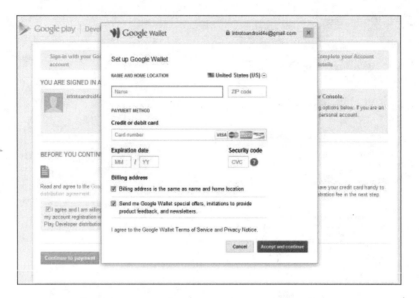

Figure 19.4   Setting up a Google Wallet account.

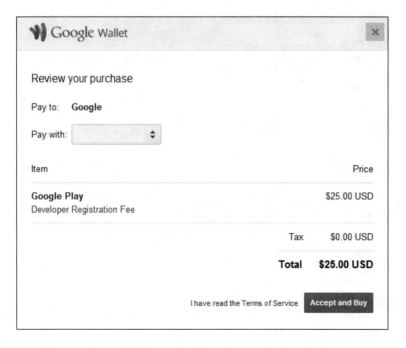

Figure 19.5   Accepting the $25 registration fee.

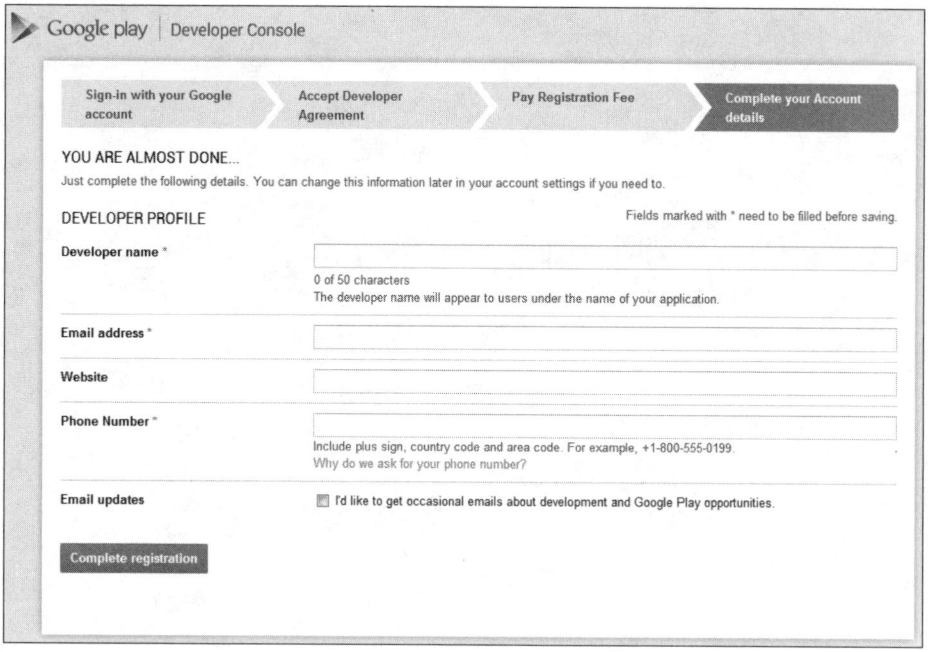

Figure 19.6   Complete your account details page.

Tip

Always print out the actual agreement you sign as part of the registration process, in case it changes in the future.

When you successfully complete these steps, you are presented with the home screen of the Google Play Developer Console, as seen in Figure 19.7. Signing up and paying to be an Android Developer does not create a Google Wallet Merchant account. A merchant account is used for payment processing purposes. From the Developer Console, you should be able to set up a merchant account by following the link in the lower-right section of the screen. If you are creating a paid app, feel free to set this up at any time.

Uploading Your Application to Google Play

Now that you have an account registered for publishing applications to Google Play and have a signed application package, you are ready to upload it for publication.

From the main page of the Google Play Developer Console website, sign in and click the Publish an Android App on Google Play button. You should now see an Add New Application dialog, as seen in Figure 19.8.

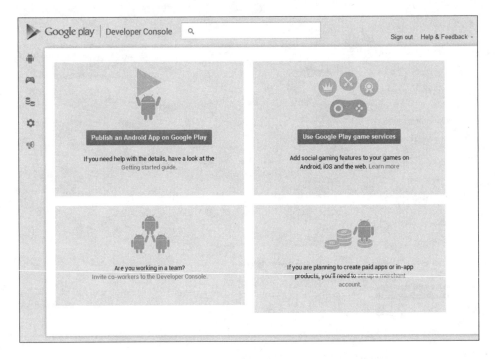

Figure 19.7   The Developer Console start page.

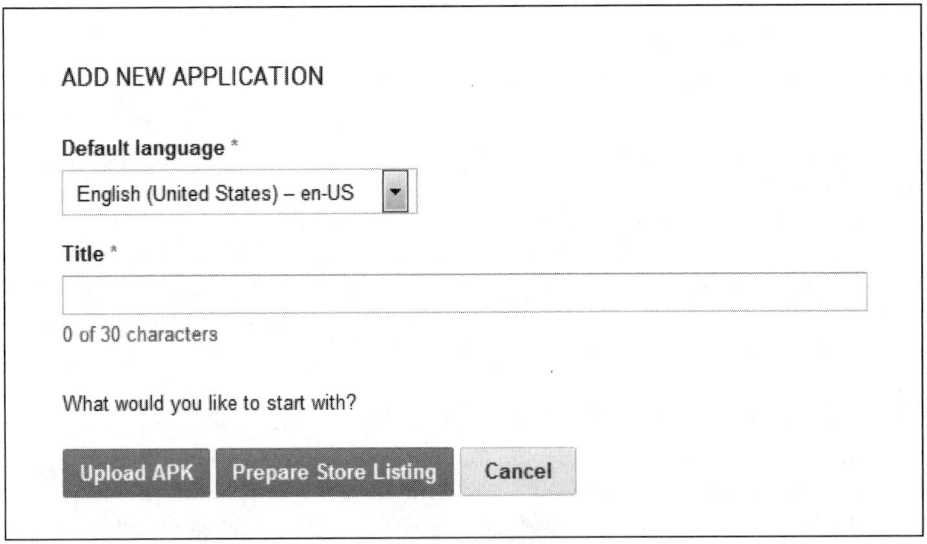

ADD NEW APPLICATION

Default language *

English (United States) – en-US

Title *

0 of 30 characters

What would you like to start with?

Upload APK   Prepare Store Listing   Cancel

Figure 19.8   The Add New Application dialog.

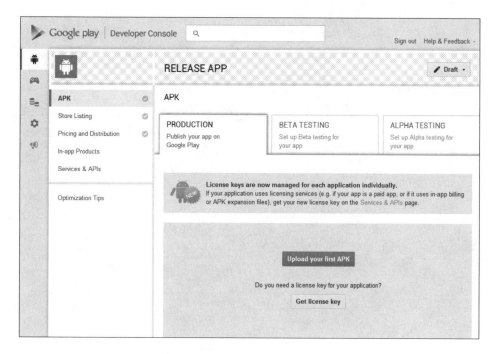

Figure 19.9   Google Play application upload form.

From this page, you can create a new listing in the Developer Console for your application. In order to publish a new application, enter a Title and click the `Upload APK` button on this dialog. You will now see a new application listing requesting that you `Upload your first APK` (see Figure 19.9). There are three options for uploading presented: Production, Beta Testing, and Alpha Testing. The Beta and Alpha Testing options are for performing a Staged Rollout, which will be discussed later in this chapter.

When you click the `Upload your first APK` button, you are presented with a dialog that allows you to upload an `.apk` file from your file system by dragging and dropping the file onto the upload space or by browsing and selecting the file.

Uploading Application Marketing Assets

The `Store Listing` tab associated with your application begins with the `Product Details` section (see Figure 19.10). Here, you can perform the following tasks:

- Provide additional translations of your application.
- Enter an application title, description, promo text, and recent changes information.
- Upload screenshots demonstrating your application on different-size devices, in particular a phone, a 7-inch tablet, and a 10-inch tablet.

Figure 19.10   Google Play `Store Listing` and `Product Details` form.

- Provide a high-resolution version of your application icon, a feature graphic, a promo graphic, and a promo video.
- Enter categorization data for your application.
- Provide contact details for your application.
- Link to a privacy policy that your application provides.

Configuring Pricing and Distribution Details

The `Pricing and Distribution` tab associated with your application allows you to enter pricing information for your application (see Figure 19.11). Here, you can do the following:

- Specify whether the application is free or paid.
- Specify the countries where you would like to distribute your application.
- Opt in to Google Play for Education.
- Provide consent for acknowledging that your application abides by the Android content guidelines and export laws of your country.

Figure 19.11   Developer Console `Pricing and Distribution` tab.

Note

Currently, a 30% transaction fee is imposed for hosting applications within the Android Market. Prices can range from $0.99 to $200 (USD), and similar ranges are available in other supported currencies. For more details, see *https://support.google.com/googleplay/android-developer/answer/138412*.

Configuring Additional Application Options

There are a few other tabs associated with your application that allow you to configure additional setup tasks:

- Specify in-app products for your application. This requires adding the `BILLING` permission to your APK and setting up a merchant account.
- Manage services and APIs such as Google Cloud Messaging (GCM), Licensing and In-app Billing, and Google Play Game Services.
- Implement additional optimization tips for improving your app listing on Google Play.

Managing Other Developer Console Options

In addition to managing your applications, you can also set up Google Play Game Services and review detailed financial reports for your paid applications. To review financial reports, you must have a merchant account set up to enable paid apps. Financial information is downloadable in CSV format.

Google Play Game Services

A new addition to Google Play is the Google Play Game Services APIs. These APIs allow you to add leaderboards, achievements, and real-time and multiplayer services and to save game data using the Cloud Save APIs. From the Developer Console, you must accept the Google APIs terms of service before you can begin integrating Game Services into your application.

> **Note**
>
> Google Play Game Services APIs provide many useful tools for game developers, but there are no rules prohibiting non-game applications from using these APIs.

Publishing Your Application to Google Play

Once you have entered all the required information, you should be ready to transition your application from a draft to publishing on Google Play. Once you publish, your application appears in Google Play almost immediately. After publication, you can see statistics, including ratings, active installs, and crashes in the All Applications section of the Developer Console (see Figure 19.12).

> **Tip**
>
> Receiving crash reports from a specific device? Check your application's market filters in the Android manifest file. Are you including and excluding the appropriate devices? You can also exclude specific devices by adjusting the Supported Devices settings of the application listing.

Managing Your Application on Google Play

Once you've published your application to Google Play, you will need to manage it. Some considerations include understanding how the Google Play return policy works, managing application upgrades, and, if necessary, removing your application from publication.

Understanding the Google Play Application Return Policy

Google Play currently has a 15-minute refund policy on applications. That is to say, a user can use an application for 15 minutes and then return it for a full refund. However, this applies only to the first download and first return. If a particular user has already returned your application and wants to "try it again," he or she must make a final

Figure 19.12   Viewing application statistics
within the Google Play Developer Console.

purchase—and can't return it a second time. Although this limits abuse, you should still be aware that if your application has limited reuse appeal, you might find that you have a return rate that's too high and need to pursue other methods of monetization.

Upgrading Your Application on Google Play

You can upgrade existing applications from the Android Developer Console. Simply upload a new version of the same application using the Android manifest file tag `android:versionCode`. When you publish it, users receive an Update Available notification, prompting them to download the upgrade.

Warning

Application updates must be signed with the same private key as the original application. For security reasons, the Android package manager does not install the update over the existing application if the key is different. This means you need to keep the key corresponding with the application in a secure, easy-to-find location for future use.

Removing Your Application from Google Play

You can also use the Unpublish action in the Android Developer Console to remove the application from Google Play. The Unpublish action is immediate, but your application entry in the Google Play store application might be cached on handsets that have viewed or downloaded your application. Keep in mind that unpublishing the application makes it unavailable to new users but does not remove it from existing users' devices.

Google Play Staged Rollouts

In the case that you are not yet ready to offer your application for download to the entire world, you are able to distribute it as a prerelease version using Staged Rollouts. This allows you to define alpha and beta test groups, so you are able to generate feedback prior to offering your application to all of Google Play. Any reviews provided will not be visible in the Google Play store, which provides you an opportunity to fix any defects that may generate negative reviews before they affect the perception of your application.

Publishing to the Google Play Private Channel

If you have a Google Apps domain, Google allows you to launch and distribute your application in a private way to the users of your Google Apps domain. The distribution occurs through the Google Play store and can be useful if your application should be restricted to only those within your organization. Rather than having to set up your own distribution mechanisms for internal distribution, you are able to leverage all of the powerful features that Google Play provides, without needing to make your application available to users other than the group that should have access.

Translating Your Application

Since Google Play is available to users in 130 different countries, and growing, you should think about translating your application into different languages early in the development process. There are simple measures that you can take to prepare your application for localization, including the following:

- Design your application with localization in mind from Day 1.
- Know which languages you may want to target first.
- Do not hard-code strings into your application. Instead, use string resources for any text, so when the time comes, all you need to do is have the string resources translated.
- The Google Play Developer Console is now offering a pilot program for translation; once accepted, you will be able to hire professional translators to translate the string resources you provide. This helps to streamline the translation process and provides a simple way to find translators.
- Make sure once your application has been translated that you also test the application in each language. Some translations may require more textual content, thereby pushing your user interface out of whack. Testing for this scenario is important because users won't want to use an application that does not display properly.

Publishing Using Other Alternatives

Google Play is not the only place available to distribute your Android applications. Many alternative distribution mechanisms are available to developers. Application requirements, royalty rates, and licensing agreements vary by store. Third-party application stores are free to enforce whatever rules they want on the applications they accept, so read the fine print carefully. They might enforce content guidelines, require additional technical support, and enforce digital signing requirements. Only you and your team can determine which are suitable for your specific needs.

Tip

Android is an open platform, which means there is nothing to prevent a handset manufacturer or an operator (or even you) from developing an Android application store.

Here are a few alternative marketplaces where you might consider distributing your Android applications:

- **Amazon Appstore** is an example of an Android-specific distribution website for free and paid applications (*http://amazon.com/appstore*).

- **Samsung Apps** is an app store managed by one of the most successful Android device manufacturers on the market (*http://apps.samsung.com*).

- **GetJar** boasts about having over 100 million users, so this is definitely an Android market to consider adding your application to (*http://www.getjar.com/*).

- **Soc.io Mall** (formerly AndAppStore) is an Android-specific distribution site for free applications, e-books, and music using an on-device store (*http://mall.soc.io*).

- **Handango** distributes mobile applications across a wide range of devices with various billing models (*http://www.handango.com*).

- **AT&T Apps** is an example of a store run by the carrier AT&T for its mobile subscribers (*http://www.att.com/shop/apps.html*).

Self-Publishing Your Application

You can distribute Android applications directly from a website, server, or email. The self-publishing method is most appropriate for vertical market applications, content companies developing mobile marketplaces, and big-brand websites wanting to drive users to their branded Android applications. It can also be a good way to get beta feedback from end users.

Although self-distribution is perhaps the easiest method of application distribution, it might also be the hardest to market, protect, and make money in. The only requirement for self-distribution is to have a place to host the application package file.

There are downsides to self-distribution. The Google Play licensing service will not be available to help you protect your application from piracy. In addition, Google Play's In-app Billing service is not available to apps outside Google Play; therefore, you will have

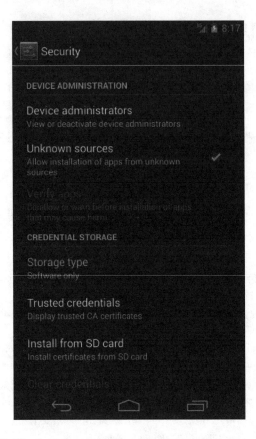

Figure 19.13 Settings application showing the required check box for downloading from unknown sources.

to manage the billing aspects yourself. Furthermore, end users must configure their devices to allow packages from unknown sources. This setting is found under the `Security` section of the device's Settings application, as shown in Figure 19.13. This option is not available on all consumer devices in the market.

After that, the final step the user must take is to enter the URL of the application package into the Web browser on the handset and download the file (or click a link to it). When the file is downloaded, the standard Android install process occurs, asking the user to confirm the permissions and, optionally, confirm an update or replacement of an existing application if a version is already installed.

Summary

You've now learned how to design, develop, test, and deploy professional-grade Android applications. In this final chapter, you learned how to prepare your application package for publication using a variety of revenue models. You also learned about different distribution strategies. Whether you publish through Google Play, alternative markets, your own website, email, or some combination of these options, you can now build a robust application from the ground up and distribute it for profit (or fame!).

So, now it's time to go out there, fire up your favorite IDE, and build some amazing applications. We want to encourage you to think outside the box. The Android platform leaves the developer with a lot more freedom and flexibility than most other mobile platforms. Take advantage of this. Use what works and reinvent what doesn't. You might just find yourself with a killer app.

Finally, if you're so inclined, we'd love to know about all the exciting applications you're building. You'll find our contact information in the Introduction to this book. Best of luck!

Quiz Questions

1. What is the name of the obfuscation tool provided with the Android SDK?
2. True or false: The In-app Billing APIs have been added to the Android SDK.
3. What is the name of the Google third-party add-on for collecting statistics regarding your application?
4. What is the difference between the manifest settings `versionName` and `versionCode`?
5. True or false: You should disable logging before uploading your application to Google Play.
6. True or false: You are not allowed to self-sign applications that you want to upload to Google Play.
7. What type of merchant account is required for Google Play in order to create paid applications?

Exercises

1. Read through the "Publishing Overview" section and accompanying subsections from the Android documentation found at the following URL: *http://d.android .com/tools/publishing/publishing_overview.html*.
2. Read through all of the sections and subsections from the Distribute tab from the Android Developers website found at the following URL: *http://d.android.com/ distribute/index.html*.
3. Publish your first real application on Google Play.

References and More Information

The Google Play website:
   https://play.google.com/store
Android Tools: "Publishing Overview":
   http://d.android.com/tools/publishing/publishing_overview.html

Android Developers Distribute: Publishing:
  http://d.android.com/distribute/googleplay/publish/index.html
Android Tools: "ProGuard"
  http://d.android.com/tools/help/proguard.html
Android Google Services: "Filters on Google Play":
  http://d.android.com/google/play/filters.html
Android Google Services: Google Play Distribution: "Application Licensing":
  http://d.android.com/google/play/licensing/index.html
Android Google Services: Games:
  http://d.android.com/google/play-services/games.html
Android Developers Distribute: Policies: "Google Play Policies and Guidelines":
  http://d.android.com/distribute/googleplay/policies/index.html

VI

Appendixes

A

Mastering the Android
Development Tools

Android developers are fortunate to have many tools at their disposal to help facilitate the design and development of quality applications. Some of the Android development tools are integrated by default into the Android IDE, which is included in the ADT Bundle, or integrated with Eclipse after installing the ADT plugin, whereas other Android development tools must be used from the command line. In this appendix, we walk through a number of the most important tools available for use with Android. Knowledge of ADT will help you develop Android applications faster and with fewer roadblocks.

Note

This appendix covers the existing tools available at the time of this writing, and not the new Android Studio, as that product is still very new and not feature complete. To see exactly which tools were used during the writing of this book, check out the book's Introduction and read the section "Development Environment Used in This Book."

When this appendix discusses an IDE, the focus is on the Android IDE. Whenever we refer to the Android IDE, the same instructions apply to Eclipse with the ADT plugin. Because the Android IDE and Eclipse with the ADT plugin installed are equivalent, from here on, we will mention only the Android IDE.

Note

The Android development tools are updated frequently. We have made every attempt to provide the latest steps for the latest tools. However, these steps and the user interfaces described in this appendix may change at any time. Please review the Android Development website (*http://d.android.com/tools/help/index.html*) and our book website (*http://introductiontoandroid.blogspot.com*) for the latest information.

Using the Android Documentation

Although it is not a tool per se, the Android documentation is a key resource for Android developers. An HTML version of the Android documentation is provided in the /docs subfolder of the Android SDK, and the documentation should always be your first stop when you encounter a problem. You can also access the latest help documentation online at the Android Developer website, *http://developer.android.com/index.html* (or *http://d .android.com* for short). The Android documentation is organized and searchable and is divided into three main categories with several sections per category, as shown in Figure A.1:

- **Design:** This tab provides information about designing Android applications.
  - **Get Started:** When designing your application, you must start somewhere. This section is a great resource for learning how to get started designing your Android application.
  - **Style:** This links to quite a few sections that are useful for understanding how to visually style your applications. Topics such as themes, color, iconography, and typography are explained here.
  - **Patterns:** This link provides many sections describing common design patterns found throughout Android applications. Providing a pleasant and consistent experience to our users is important, and many of the problems associated with design issues are described here.
  - **Building Blocks:** This link comprises many sections explaining the many common types of user interface elements. Each section further describes how to use a specific element.
  - **Downloads:** This link provides many downloadable resources that are useful for designing Android applications. Provided for download are controls and icons following the typography and color guidelines of Android. You are able to download all files as one .zip, or you may choose to download only the files that are relevant to your design goals.
  - **Videos:** This section provides many videos from design sessions presented during the Google I/O conference. These videos are useful for learning tips and tricks directly from the Android team.
- **Develop:** This tab provides information for developing Android applications.
  - **Training:** The training section includes tutorials for using specific classes and provides code samples that you are free to use within your applications. The tutorials are listed in order of how one should proceed through learning about Android development, and many important topics are discussed in depth. These trainings are an invaluable resource to Android developers.
  - **API Guides:** This tab provides in-depth explanations of many Android topics, classes, or packages. Although related to the Training section, the API Guides provide a much deeper explanation of particular features of the Android API.
  - **Reference:** This tab includes a searchable package and class index of all Android APIs provided as part of the Android SDK in a Javadoc-style format. You will spend most of your time on this tab, looking up Java class documentation, checking method parameters, and performing other similar tasks.

- **Tools:** The Tools tab is the definitive resource for learning about the Android Developer Tools plugin that comes bundled with the Android IDE. Many of these tools are covered throughout this book and are usable from either your IDE or the command line. One particular section of the Tools tab, the Tools Help section, is particularly useful for learning how to use both the SDK Tools and the Platform Tools.
- **Get the SDK:** This section provides downloads for the Android SDK. Included for download are the Android SDK Bundle and the SDK Tools, and each is available for Windows, Mac, and Linux.
- **Google Services:** This tab provides tutorials, code samples, and API guides for integrating Google services into your Android application.
- **Distribute:** This tab provides information about distributing Android applications.
  - **Google Play:** This tab provides an introduction to Google Play. Having a good understanding of Google Play is important before launching your application. This section covers how to gain visibility, monetize your application, and control distribution.
  - **Publishing:** The Publishing section teaches developers what they need to know to publish their applications with Google Play. Explanations of the Developer Console are provided in addition to a Publishing Checklist that developers should follow to ensure they have a successful launch.
  - **Promoting:** This section covers promoting your applications outside Google Play. Google provides many tools for making this an easy process, such as the Device Art Generator, which can be used for adding screenshots of your application to real device art for use within your advertising copy. This section also provides instructions for branding guidelines for incorporating the Android and Google Play brands into the advertising copy of your applications.
  - **App Quality:** This section provides resources for maximizing the quality of your applications. There is a list of criteria for evaluating application quality, and tips are provided for how to improve quality.
  - **Policies:** This section consists of guidelines developers must follow. Failure to follow these guidelines may result in removal of your application from Google Play. Understanding these policies will help you comply with them.
  - **Spotlight:** This section highlights some applications that have been successfully distributed within Google Play. Learning how others have achieved success is always helpful for understanding how those principles may be applied to your application.
  - **Open Distribution:** This section discusses alternative distribution methods to Google Play. Although Google Play is a great source for achieving success, there are other options developers should know about, and these are briefly discussed here.

Figure A.1 shows a screenshot of the Android SDK Reference tab of the website.

Now is a good time to learn your way around the Android SDK documentation. First, check out the online documentation, and then try the local documentation.

Tip

Different features of the Android SDK are applicable to different versions of the platform. New APIs, classes, interfaces, and methods have been introduced over time. Therefore, each item in the documentation is tagged with the API level when it was first introduced. To see whether an item is available in a specific platform version, check its API level, usually listed along the right side of the documentation. You can also filter the documentation to a specific API level, so that it displays only the SDK features available for that platform version (see Figure A.1, left center).

Keep in mind that this book is designed to be a companion guide in your journey to mastering Android development. It covers Android fundamentals and tries to distill a lot of information into an easily digestible format to get you up and running quickly. It then provides you with a thorough understanding of what is available and feasible on the Android platform. It is not an exhaustive SDK reference, but a guide to best practices. You'll

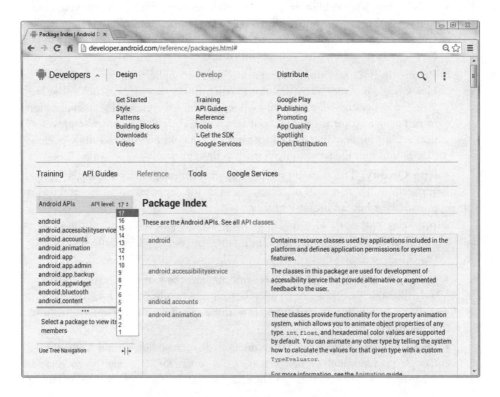

Figure A.1   The Android Developer website.

need to become intimately familiar with the Android SDK Java class documentation in order to be successful at designing and developing Android applications in the long run.

Leveraging the Android Emulator

Although we introduced the Android emulator as a core tool in Chapter 2, "Setting Up Your Android Development Environment," it's worth mentioning again. The Android emulator is probably the most powerful tool at a developer's disposal, along with the Android SDK and Android Virtual Device Managers (which we also talked about fairly extensively in other chapters of this book). It is important for developers to learn to use the emulator and understand its limitations. The Android emulator is integrated with the Android IDE. For more information about the emulator, please check out Appendix B, "Quick-Start Guide: The Android Emulator." We suggest that you review this detailed appendix after you have looked over the other materials covered in this appendix.

Figure A.2 shows a sample application included with the Android SDK called `App Navigation` and what it looks like when running in the Android emulator.

You can also find exhaustive information about the emulator on the Android Developer website: *http://d.android.com/tools/help/emulator.html.*

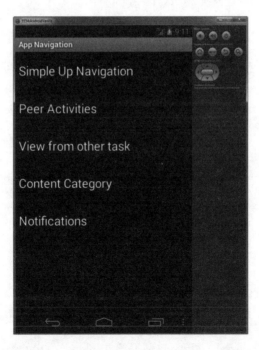

Figure A.2   The Android emulator in action running the `App Navigation` sample application.

Viewing Application Log Data with LogCat

You learned how to log application information in Chapter 3, "Writing Your First Android Application," using the `android.util.Log` class. The log output appears in the `LogCat` pane of the Android IDE (available in the `Debug` and `DDMS` perspectives of the Android IDE). You can also interact with `logcat` directly.

Even when you have a great debugger, incorporating logging support into your applications is very useful. You can then monitor your application's log output, generated on either the emulator or an attached device. Log information can be invaluable for tracking down difficult bugs and reporting application state during the development phase of a project.

Log data is categorized by severity. When you create a new class in your project, we recommend defining a unique debug tag string for that class so that you can easily track down where a log message originated. You can use this tag to filter the logging data and find only the messages you are interested in. You can use the `LogCat` utility from within the Android IDE to filter your log messages to the debug tag string you supplied for your application. To learn how to do this, check out the "Creating Custom Log Filters" section in Appendix D, "Android IDE and Eclipse Tips and Tricks."

Finally, there are some performance trade-offs to consider when it comes to logging. Excessive logging impacts device and application performance. At a minimum, debug and verbose logging should be used only for development purposes and removed prior to application publication.

Debugging Applications with DDMS

When it comes to debugging on the emulator or device, you need to turn your attention to the `Dalvik Debug Monitor Service` (DDMS) tool. DDMS is a debugging utility that is integrated into the Android IDE through a special perspective. It is also available as a standalone executable in the `/tools` directory of the Android SDK installation.

The DDMS perspective in the Android IDE (see Figure A.3) provides a number of useful features for interacting with emulators and handsets and debugging applications. You use DDMS to view and manage processes and threads running on the device, view heap data, attach to processes to debug, and a variety of other tasks.

You can find out all about DDMS and how to use its features in Appendix C, "Quick-Start Guide: Android DDMS." We suggest that you review this detailed appendix after you have looked over the other material covered in this appendix.

Using Android Debug Bridge (ADB)

The Android Debug Bridge (ADB) is a client/server command-line tool that enables developers to debug Android code on the emulator and the device using the Android IDE. Both the DDMS and the Android Developer Tools use ADB to facilitate interaction between the development environment and the device (or emulator). You can find the `adb.exe` command-line tool in the `/platform-tools` directory of the Android SDK.

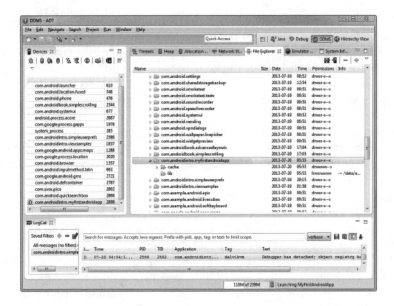

Figure A.3 Using DDMS integrated into the Android IDE perspective.

Developers can also use ADB to interact with the device file system, install and uninstall Android applications manually, and issue shell commands. For example, the logcat and sqlite3 shell commands enable you to access logging data and application databases.

For an exhaustive ADB reference, see the Android SDK documentation at *http://d.android.com/tools/help/adb.html.*

Using the Resource Editors and UI Designer

The Android IDE is a solid, well-designed development environment for Java applications. When using the Android IDE, you have access to a bunch of simple Android-specific tools to help you design, develop, debug, and publish applications. Like all applications, Android apps are made up of functionality (Java code) and data (resources such as strings and graphics). The functionality is handled with the Android IDE Java editor and compiler. The ADT plugin integrated into the IDE adds numerous special editors for creating Android-specific resource files to encapsulate application data such as strings and user interface resource templates called layouts.

Note

The Android tools team has been hard at work integrating Android support into another IDE for developers. This IDE is known as Android Studio, which is based on the Community Edition of IntelliJ IDEA. We should continue to see more energy put into Android Studio, as well as feature parity with Android IDE and Eclipse with the ADT plugin.

Most Android resources are stored in specially formatted XML files. The resource editors and UI designer that come as part of the ADT plugin allow you to work with application resources in a structured, graphical way, or by editing the raw XML. Two examples of resource editors include the string resource editor and the Android manifest file editor. The generic resource editor will load when you are working with XML files in the /res project directory hierarchy, such as string, style, or dimension resources.

The Android manifest file resource editor will load when you open the Android manifest file associated with your project. Figure A.4 shows that the resource editor for editing Android manifest files consists of numerous tabs, which organize the contents of that resource type. Note that the last tab is always the XML tab, where you can edit the XML resource file manually, if necessary.

Android layout (user interface templates) resources are also technically XML files. However, some people prefer to be able to drag and drop controls, move them around, and preview what the user interface would look like to an actual user. Recent updates to the ADT plugin have greatly improved UI designer features for developers.

The UI designer loads whenever you open an XML file within the /res/layout project directory hierarchy. You can use the UI designer in Graphical Layout mode, which allows you to drag and drop controls and see what your application will look like with a variety of AVD-style configuration options (Android API level, screen resolution, orientation, theme, and more), as shown in Figure A.5. You can also switch to XML editing mode to edit controls directly or set specific properties.

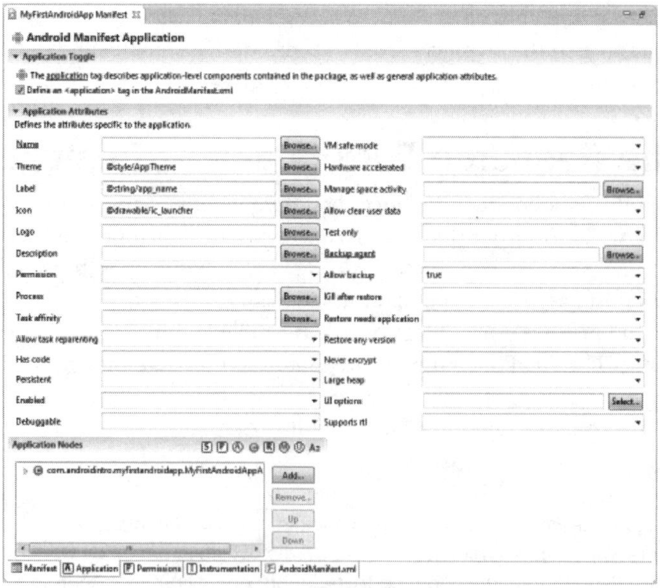

Figure A.4   Editing the Android manifest file in the Android IDE.

Figure A.5   Using the UI designer in the Android IDE.

 Tip

We recommend anchoring the `Properties` pane of the Android IDE to the right of the UI designer to edit properties of a selected control in a more structured manner, as seen in the lower right of Figure A.5.

We discussed the details of designing and developing user interfaces, as well as working with layouts and user interface controls, in Chapter 7, "Exploring User Interface Building Blocks," and Chapter 8, "Designing with Layouts." For now, we just want you to be aware that your application user interface components are generally stored as resources, and that ADT provides some helpful tools for designing and managing these resources.

Using the Android Hierarchy Viewer

The Android Hierarchy Viewer is a tool that identifies layout component relationships (the hierarchy) and helps developers design, debug, and profile their user interfaces. Developers can use this tool to inspect the user interface control properties and develop pixel-perfect layouts. The Hierarchy Viewer is available as a standalone executable in the `/tools` sub-directory of your Android SDK installation, as well as an Android IDE perspective. Figure A.6 shows what the Hierarchy Viewer looks like when first launched and connected to an emulator instance, before any of the graphical views are shown. The application to be inspected has a package name called `com.example.android.appnavigation`.

The Hierarchy Viewer is a visual tool that can be used to inspect your application user interfaces in ways that allow you to identify and improve your layout designs. You can

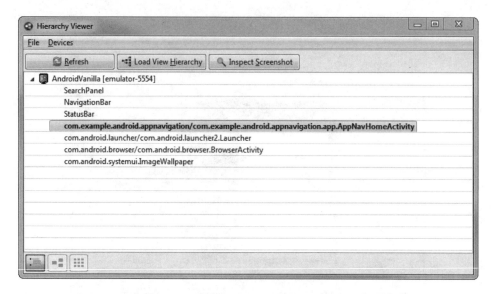

Figure A.6   Screenshot of the Android Hierarchy Viewer standalone
app when first launched.

drill down on specific user interface controls and inspect their properties at runtime. You
can save screenshots of the current application state on the emulator or the device.

The Hierarchy Viewer application is divided into two main modes:

- **Layout View mode:** This mode shows the hierarchy of user interface controls
  loaded by your application in tree form. You can zoom in and select specific controls
  to find out lots of information about their current state; there is also profiling information to help you optimize your controls.

- **Pixel Perfect mode:** This mode shows the user interface pixels in a zoomed-in
  grid fashion. This is useful for designers who need to look at very specific layout
  arrangements or line up views on top of images.

You can switch between the modes by using the buttons in the bottom-left corner of
the tool.

Launching the Hierarchy Viewer

To launch the Hierarchy Viewer with your application in the emulator, perform the following steps:

1. Launch your Android application in the emulator.

2. Navigate to the Android SDK tools subdirectory and launch the Hierarchy
   Viewer application (`hierarchyviewer.bat` on Windows), or use the `Hierarchy
   View` Android IDE perspective. We find using the standalone executable more

convenient because we often want to tweak the user interface using the Android IDE while we work.

3. Choose your emulator instance from the `Device` listing.

4. Select the application you want to view from the options available. The application must be running on that emulator to show up on the list.

Working in Layout View Mode

The Layout View mode is invaluable for debugging drawing issues related to your application user interface controls. If you wonder why something isn't drawing correctly, try launching the Hierarchy Viewer and checking the properties for that control at runtime.

Note

When you load an application in the Hierarchy Viewer, you will want to be aware of the fact that your application user interface does not begin at the root of the hierarchy in the tree view. In fact, there are several layers of layout controls above your application content that will appear as parent controls of your content. For example, the system `status bar` and `title bar` are higher-level controls. Your application contents are actually child controls within a `FrameLayout` control called `@id/content`. When you load layout contents using the `setContentView()` method within your `Activity` class, you are specifying what to load within this high-level `FrameLayout`.

Figure A.7 shows the Hierarchy Viewer loaded in Layout View mode.

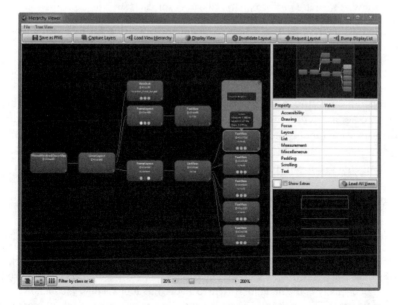

Figure A.7   The Hierarchy Viewer tool (Layout View mode).

When you first load your application in Layout View mode, you will see several panes of information. The main pane shows the parent/child control relationships as a tree view. Each tree node represents a user interface control on the screen and shows the control's unique identifier, type, and profiling information for optimization purposes (more on this in a moment). There are also a number of smaller panes on the right side of the screen. The loupe/zoom pane allows you to quickly navigate a large tree view. The property pane shows the various properties for each tree node, when highlighted. Finally, the wireframe model of the currently loaded user interface is displayed, with a red box highlighting the currently selected control.

Tip

You'll have better luck navigating your application `View` objects with the Hierarchy Viewer tool if you set your `View` object ID properties to friendly names you can remember instead of the autogenerated sequential ID tags provided by default. For example, a `Button` control called `SubmitButton` is more descriptive than `Button01`.

You can use the Hierarchy Viewer tool to interact and debug your application user interface. Specifically, you can use the Invalidate and Request Layout features that correspond to the `View.invalidate()` and `View.requestLayout()` functions of the UI thread. These functions initiate `View` objects and draw or redraw them as necessary.

Optimizing Your User Interface

You can also use the Hierarchy Viewer to optimize your user interface contents. If you have used this tool before, you may have noticed all the little red, yellow, and green dots in the tree view. These are performance indicators for each specific control:

- The left dot represents how long the measuring operation for this view takes.
- The middle dot represents how long the layout-rendering operation for this view takes.
- The right dot represents how long the drawing operation for this view takes.

Indicators represent how each control renders in relation to other controls in the tree. They are not a strict representation of a bad or good control, per se. A red dot means that this view renders the slowest, compared to all views in the hierarchy. A yellow dot means that this view renders in the bottom 50% of all views in the hierarchy. A green dot means that this view renders in the top 50% of all views in the hierarchy. When you click a specific view within the tree, you will also see the actual performance times on which these indicators are based.

Tip

The Hierarchy Viewer provides control-level precision profiling. But it won't tell you if your user interface layouts are organized in the most efficient way. For that, you'll want to check out the `lint` command-line tool (formerly the `layoutopt` command-line tool) available in the `/tools` subdirectory of the Android SDK installation. This tool will help you identify unnecessary layout controls in your user interface, among other inefficiencies. Find out more at the Android Developer website: *http://d.android.com/tools/debugging/debugging-ui.html#lint*.

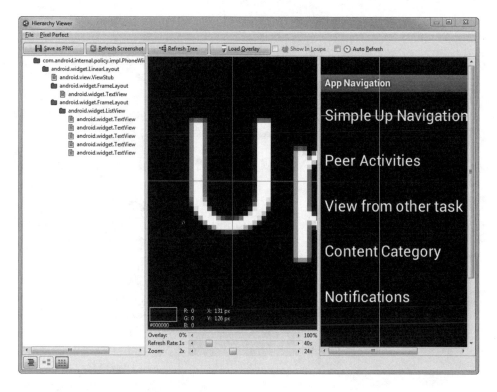

Figure A.8   The Hierarchy Viewer tool (Pixel Perfect mode).

Working in Pixel Perfect Mode

You can use the Pixel Perfect mode to closely inspect your application user interface. You can also load PNG mock-up files to overlay your user interface and adjust your application's look. You can access the Pixel Perfect mode by clicking the button with the nine pixels on it at the bottom left of the Hierarchy Viewer.

Figure A.8 illustrates how you can inspect the currently running application screen at the pixel level by using the loupe feature of this mode.

Working with Nine-Patch Stretchable Graphics

Android supports Nine-Patch Stretchable Graphics, which provide flexibility for supporting different user interface characteristics, orientations, and device screens. Nine-Patch Stretchable Graphics can be created from PNG files using the draw9patch tool included with the /tools directory of the Android SDK.

Nine-Patch Stretchable Graphics are simply PNG graphics that have patches, or areas of the image, defined to scale appropriately, instead of the entire image being scaled as

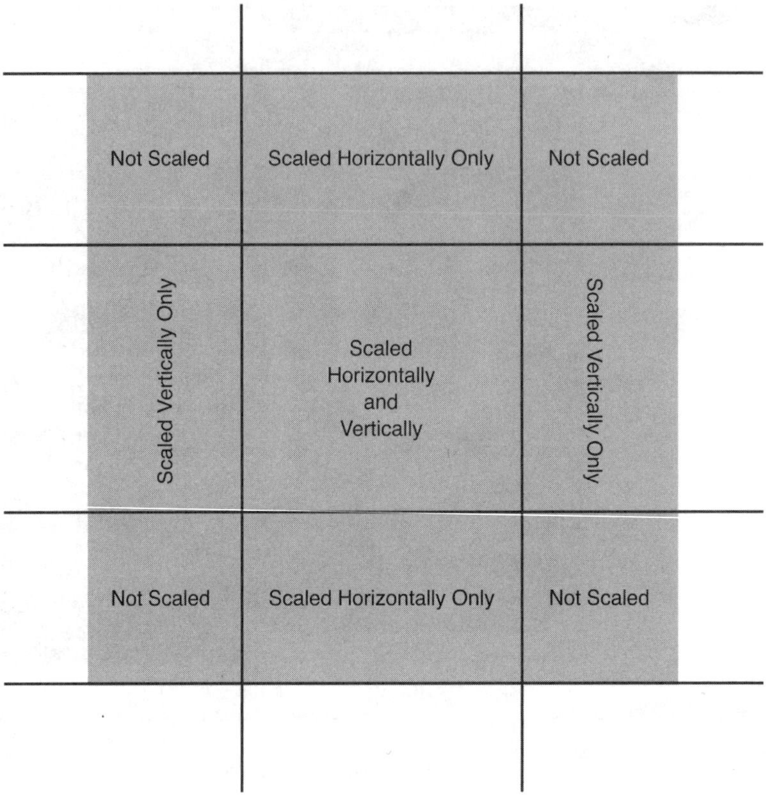

Figure A.9   How a Nine-Patch graphic of a square is scaled.

one unit. Figure A.9 illustrates how the image (shown as the square) is divided into nine patches. Often the center segment is transparent.

The interface for the draw9patch tool is straightforward. In the left pane, you can define the guides to your graphic to specify how it scales when stretched. In the right pane, you can preview how your graphic behaves when scaled with the patches you defined. Figure A.10 shows a simple PNG file loaded in the tool, prior to its guides being set.

To create a Nine-Patch Stretchable Graphic file from a PNG file using the draw9patch tool, perform the following steps:

1. Launch draw9patch.bat in your Android SDK tools subdirectory.

2. Drag a PNG file onto the pane (or use File, Open Nine-Patch).

3. Click the Show patches check box at the bottom of the left pane.

4. Set your Patch scale appropriately (set it higher to see more marked results).

5. Click along the left edge of your graphic to set a horizontal patch guide.

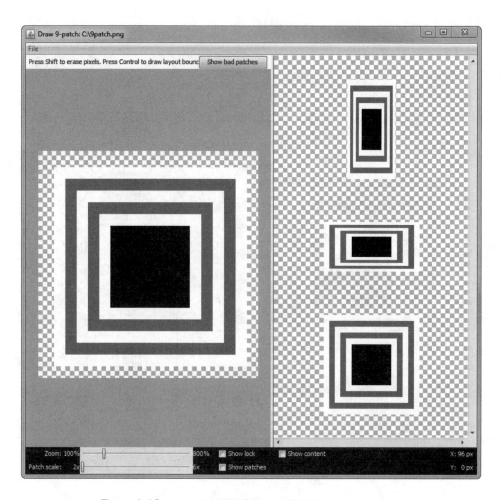

Figure A.10   A simple PNG file before Nine-Patch processing.

6. Click along the top edge of your graphic to set a vertical patch guide.

7. View the results in the right pane; move the patch guides until the graphic stretches as desired. Figures A.11 and A.12 illustrate two possible guide configurations.

8. To delete a patch guide, press Shift and click the guide pixel (black) or left–click the guide pixel.

9. Save your graphics file. Nine-Patch graphics should end with the extension .9.png (for example, little_black_box.9.png).

10. Include your graphics file as a resource in your Android project and use it just as you would a normal PNG file.

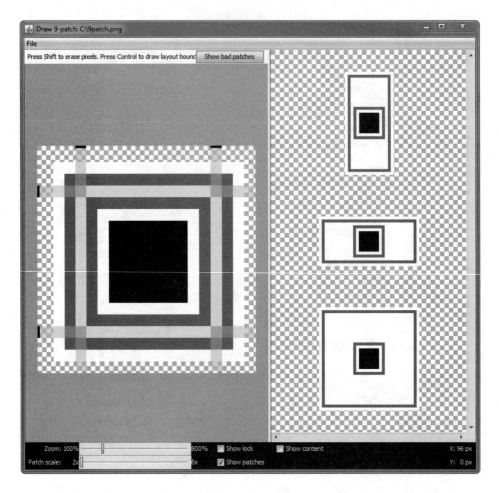

Figure A.11   A Nine-Patch PNG file after Nine-Patch processing with some patch guides defined.

Working with Other Android Tools

Although we've already covered the most important tools, a number of other special-purpose utilities are included with the Android SDK. Many of these tools provide the underlying functionality that has been integrated into the Android IDE. However, if you are not using the Android IDE, these tools may be used on the command line.

A complete list of the development tools that come as part of the Android SDK is available on the Android Developer website at *http://d.android.com/tools/help/index.html*.

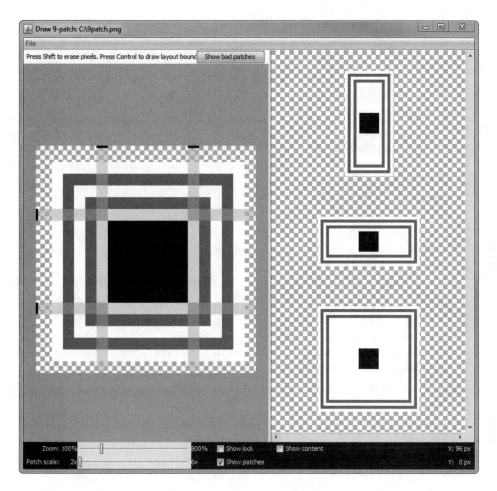

Figure A.12   A Nine-Patch PNG file after Nine-Patch processing with some different patch guides defined.

There, you'll find a description of each tool as well as a link to its official documentation. Here is a list of some useful tools we haven't yet discussed:

- **android**: This command-line tool provides much the same functionality as the Android SDK and Android Virtual Device Managers; it also helps you create and manage projects if you are not using the Android IDE.
- **bmgr**: This shell tool is accessed through the adb command line to interact with the Android Backup Manager.

- **`dmtracedump, hprof-conv, traceview`:** These tools are used for diagnostics, debug logging, and profiling of applications.

- **`etc1tool`:** This command-line tool lets you convert between PNG files and compressed Ericsson Texture Compression (ETC1) files. The specification for ETC1 is available at *http://www.khronos.org/registry/gles/extensions/OES/OES_compressed_ETC1_RGB8_texture.txt.*

- **`logcat`:** This shell tool is accessed through the adb command line to interact with the platform logging tool, LogCat. Although you'll normally access log output through the Android IDE, you can also use this shell tool to capture, clear, and redirect log output (a useful feature if you're doing any automation, or not using the Android IDE). Although the command-line logcat tool is used to provide better filters, the Android IDE logcat view has brought this filtering power to the graphical version.

- **`mksdcard`:** This command-line tool lets you create SD card disk images independent of a specific AVD.

- **`monkey, monkeyrunner`:** These are tools you can use to test your application and implement automated testing suites. We discussed unit testing and test opportunities for applications in Chapter 18, "Testing Android Applications."

- **ProGuard:** This is a tool for obfuscating and optimizing application code. We talked more about ProGuard, and specifically how to protect the intellectual property of an application, in Chapter 19, "Publishing Your Android Application."

- **`sqlite3`:** This shell tool is accessed through the adb command line to interact with SQLite databases.

- **`systrace`:** This is a performance analysis tool for learning about the execution of applications.

- Tracer for OpenGL ES: This tool allows you to analyze the execution of OpenGL ES code to understand how an application is processing and executing graphics.

- **`uiautomator`:** This is an automated functional UI testing framework for creating and running user interface tests for an application.

- **`zipalign`:** This command-line tool is used to align an APK file after it has been signed for publication. This tool is necessary only if you do not use the Android IDE Export Wizard to compile, package, sign, and align your application. We discussed these steps in Chapter 19, "Publishing Your Android Application."

Summary

The Android SDK ships with a number of powerful tools to help with common Android development tasks. The Android documentation is an essential reference for developers. The Android emulator can be used for running and debugging Android applications virtually, without the need for an actual device. The DDMS debugging tool, which is integrated into the Android IDE as a perspective, is useful for monitoring emulators and devices. ADB is the powerful command-line tool behind many of the features of DDMS and the ADT plugin. The Hierarchy Viewer and lint tools can be used to design and optimize your user interface controls, and the Nine-Patch tool allows you to create stretchable graphics for use within your apps. There are also a number of other tools to aid developers with different development tasks, from design to development, testing, and publication.

Quiz Questions

1. True or false: DDMS is available as a standalone executable.
2. Which SDK subdirectory folder holds the adb command-line tool?
3. True or false: Android string resource files are stored in the json format.
4. What are the two modes for working with Android layout files using the Android IDE?
5. Which tool is used for inspecting and optimizing the user interface?

Exercises

1. Using the Android documentation, create a list of the logcat command-line options.
2. Using the Android documentation, determine which adb command is used for printing a list of all attached emulator instances.
3. Using the Android documentation, describe how to use DDMS for tracking the memory allocation of objects.

References and More Information

Google's Android Developers Online SDK Reference:
   http://d.android.com/reference/packages.html
Android Tools: "Android Emulator":
   http://d.android.com/tools/help/emulator.html
Android Tools: "Using DDMS":
   http://d.android.com/tools/debugging/ddms.html
Android Tools: "Android Debug Bridge":
   http://d.android.com/tools/help/adb.html
Android Tools: "Draw 9-Patch":
   http://d.android.com/tools/help/draw9patch.html
Android Tools: "Optimizing your UI":
   http://d.android.com/tools/debugging/debugging-ui.html

B

Quick-Start Guide: The Android Emulator

The most useful tool provided with the Android SDK is the emulator. Developers use the emulator to quickly develop Android applications for a variety of hardware. This Quick-Start Guide is not a complete documentation of the emulator commands. Instead, it is designed to get you up and running with common tasks. Please see the emulator documentation provided with the Android SDK for a complete list of features and commands.

The Android emulator is integrated with the Android IDE, which is included in the ADT Bundle, or integrated with Eclipse after installing the ADT plugin. The emulator is also available within the /tools directory of the Android SDK, and you can launch it as a separate process. The best way to launch the emulator is by using the Android Virtual Device Manager.

When this appendix discusses an IDE, the focus is on the Android IDE. Whenever we refer to the Android IDE, the same instructions apply to Eclipse with the ADT plugin. Because the Android IDE and Eclipse with the ADT plugin are equivalent, from here on, we will mention only the Android IDE.

Simulating Reality: The Emulator's Purpose

The Android emulator (shown in Figure B.1) simulates a real device environment where your applications run. As a developer, you can configure the emulator to closely resemble the devices on which you plan to deploy your applications.

Here are some tips for using the emulator effectively:

- You can use keyboard commands to easily interact with the emulator.
- Mouse clicking within the emulator window works, as do scrolling and dragging. So do the keyboard arrow buttons. Don't forget the side buttons, such as the volume control. These work, too.
- If your computer has an Internet connection, so does your emulator. The browser works. You can toggle networking using the F8 key.

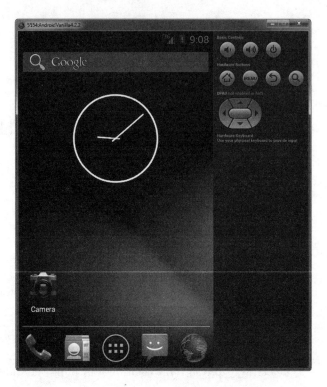

Figure B.1   A typical Android emulator.

- Different Android platform versions show slightly different underlying user experiences (the basics of the Android operating system) on the emulator. For example, older platform targets have a basic Home screen and use an application drawer to store installed applications, whereas the newer smartphone-centric platform versions such as Android 4.2+ use sleeker controls and an improved Home screen, and the Honeycomb (Android 3.0+) platform targets include the holographic theme and ActionBar navigation. The emulator uses the basic user interface, which is frequently overridden, or skinned, by manufacturers and carriers. In other words, the operating system features of the emulator might not match what real users see.

- The Settings application can be useful for managing system settings. You can use the Settings application to configure the user settings available within the emulator, including networking, screen options, and locale options.

- The Dev Tools application can be useful for setting development options. These include many useful tools, from a terminal emulator to a list of installed packages. Additionally, tools for accounts and sync testing are available. JUnit tests can be launched directly from here.

- To switch between portrait and landscape modes of the emulator, use the 7 and 9 keys on the numeric keypad (or the Ctrl+F11 and Ctrl+F12 keys).

- You can use the F6 key to emulate a trackball with your mouse. This takes over exclusive control of your mouse, so you must use F6 to get control back again.

- The Menu button is a context menu for the given screen. Keep in mind that newer devices do not always have the physical keys such as Home, Menu, Back, and Search.

- Invoke the application lifecycle: To easily stop an application, just press Home (on the emulator) and you'll get onPause() and onStop() Activity lifecycle events. To resume, launch the application again. To pause the application, press the Power button (on emulator). Only the onPause() method will be called. You'll need to press the Power button a second time to activate the display to be able to unlock the emulator to see the onResume() method call.

- Notifications such as incoming SMS messages appear in the status bar, along with indicators for simulated battery life, signal strength and speed, and so on.

Warning

One of the most important things to remember when working with the emulator is that it is a powerful tool, but it is no substitute for testing on the true target device. The emulator often provides a much more consistent user experience than a physical device, which moves around in the physical world, through tunnels and cell signal dead zones, with many other applications running and sucking down battery and resources. Always budget time and resources to thoroughly exercise your applications on target physical devices and in common situations as part of your testing process.

Working with Android Virtual Devices

The Android emulator is a not a real device, but a generic Android system simulator for testing purposes. Developers can simulate different types of Android devices by creating AVD configurations.

Tip

It can be helpful to think of an AVD as providing the emulator's personality. Without an AVD, an emulator is an empty shell, not unlike a CPU with no attached peripherals.

Using AVD configurations, Android emulators can simulate

- Different target platform versions
- Different screen sizes and resolutions
- Different input methods
- Different network types, speeds, and strengths
- Different underlying hardware configurations
- Different external storage configurations

Figure B.2   AVD configurations described in different emulator settings.

Each emulator configuration is unique, as described within its AVD profile, and stores its data persistently, including installed applications, modified settings, and the contents of its emulated SD card. A number of emulator instances with different AVD configurations are shown in Figure B.2.

Using the Android Virtual Device Manager

To run an application in the Android emulator, you must configure an Android Virtual Device (AVD). To create and manage AVDs, you can use the Android Virtual Device Manager from within the Android IDE or use the `android` command-line tool provided with the Android SDK in the `/tools` subdirectory. Each AVD configuration contains important information describing a specific type of Android device, including the following:

- The friendly, descriptive name for the configuration
- The target Android platform version
- The screen size, aspect ratio, and resolution
- Hardware configuration details and features, including how much RAM is available, which input methods exist, and optional hardware details such as camera support
- Simulated external storage (virtual SD cards)

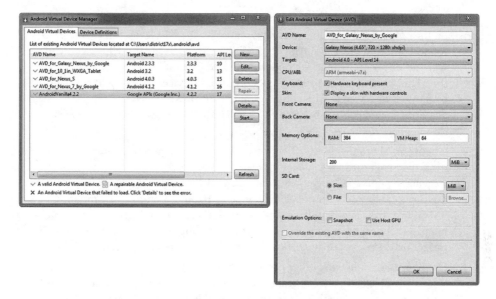

Figure B.3   The Android Virtual Device Manager (left) can be used to
create AVD configurations (right).

Figure B.3 illustrates how you can use the Android Virtual Device Manager to create
and manage AVD configurations.

Creating an AVD

Follow these steps to create an AVD configuration within the Android IDE:

1. Launch the Android Virtual Device Manager from within the Android IDE by
    clicking the little green Android device icon (📱) on the toolbar. You can also
    launch it by selecting `Window, Android Virtual Device Manager` from the
    Android IDE menu.

2. Click the `Android Virtual Devices` menu item (Figure B.3, left). The configured
    AVDs are displayed as a list.

3. Click the `OK` button to create a new AVD (Figure B.3, right).

4. Choose a name for the AVD. If you are trying to simulate a specific device, you
    might want to name it as such. For example, a name such as `Nexus7` might refer to
    an AVD that simulates the Nexus 7 tablet running the Android 4.1.2 platform.

5. Choose a Device for the AVD. In this case, since we are naming our device
    `Nexus7`, we can choose the `Nexus 7 (7.27", 800 × 1280: tvdpi)` device from
    the device selection drop-down.

6. Choose a build Target. This represents the version of the Android platform running on the emulator. The platform is represented by the API level. For example, to support Android 4.2.2, use API Level 17. However, this is also where you choose whether or not to include the optional Google APIs. If your application relies on the Maps application and other Google Android services, you should choose the target with the Google APIs. For a complete list of API levels and which Android platforms they represent, see *http://d.android.com/guide/topics/manifest/uses-sdk-element.html#ApiLevels*.

7. Choose an SD card capacity. This capacity can be configured in kibibytes or mibibytes. Each SD card image takes up space on your hard drive and takes a long time to generate; don't make your card capacities too large, or they will hog your hard drive space. Choose a reasonable size, such as 1024MiB or less. The minimum is 9MiB. Just make sure you have adequate disk space on your development computer and choose an appropriate size for your testing needs. If you're dealing with images or videos, you may need to allocate much more capacity.

8. Configure or modify any other hardware characteristics that you would like enabled or disabled. If your application will be using a front or back camera, you may choose to emulate these cameras, or, provided your host computer has camera hardware, you may attach them to your AVD. If you want to disallow using your host computer's hardware keyboard, or remove the skin and hardware controls when running the emulator, you may deselect the default options. We have found it easier to keep these options enabled. There are also Emulation Options you should consider enabling such as the Snapshot or Use Host GPU. Snapshot eliminates the wait time for launching an AVD by persisting the AVD's state between executions, and Use Host GPU leverages the host's graphics processor for rendering OpenGL ES within the AVD.

9. Click the OK button and wait for the operation to complete. Because the Android Virtual Device Manager formats the memory allocated for SD card images, creating an AVD configuration sometimes takes a few moments.

Creating AVDs with Custom Hardware Settings

As mentioned earlier, you can choose specific hardware configuration settings within your AVD configurations. You need to know what the default settings are to determine whether you need to override them. Some of the hardware options available are shown in Table B.1.

Tip

You can save time, money, and a lot of grief by spending a bit of time up front configuring AVDs that closely match the hardware upon which your application will run. Share the specific settings with your fellow developers and testers. We often create device-specific AVDs and name them after the device.

Table B.1 **Important Hardware Profile Options**

Hardware Property Option	Description	Default Value
Device RAM size `hw.ramSize`	Physical RAM on the device, in megabytes	96
Touchscreen support `hw.touchScreen`	Touchscreen exists on the device	Yes
Trackball support `hw.trackBall`	Trackball exists on the device	Yes
Keyboard support `hw.keyboard`	QWERTY keyboard exists on the device	Yes
GPU emulation `hw.gpu.enabled`	Emulate OpenGL ES GPU	No
D-pad support `hw.dPad`	Directional pad exists on the device	Yes
GSM modem support `hw.gsmModem`	GSM modem exists on the device	Yes
Camera support `hw.camera`	Camera exists on the device	No
Camera pixels (horizontal) `hw.camera.maxHorizontalPixels`	Maximum horizontal camera pixels	640
Camera pixels (vertical) `hw.camera.maxVerticalPixels`	Maximum vertical camera pixels	480
GPS support `hw.gps`	GPS exists on the device	Yes
Battery support `hw.battery`	Device can run on a battery	Yes
Accelerometer support `hw.accelerometer`	Accelerometer exists on the device	Yes
Audio recording support `hw.audioInput`	Device can record audio	Yes
Audio playback support `hw.audioOutput`	Device can play audio	Yes
SD card support `hw.sdCard`	Device supports removable SD card	Yes
Cache partition support `disk.cachePartition`	Device supports cache partition	Yes
Cache partition size `disk.cachePartition.size`	Device cache partition size in megabytes	66
Abstracted LCD density `hw.lcd.density`	Generalized screen density	160
Max VM app heap size `vm.heapSize`	Maximum heap size an application can allocate before being killed by the operating system	Depends on target and options: 16, 24, 32, 48, 64

Launching the Emulator with a Specific AVD

After you have configured the AVD you want to use, you are ready to launch the emulator. Although there are a number of ways to do this, there are four methods you will likely use on a regular basis:

- From within the Android IDE, you can configure the application's Debug or Run configuration to use a specific AVD.
- From within the Android IDE, you can configure the application's Debug or Run configuration to enable the developer to choose an AVD manually upon launch.
- From within the Android IDE, you can launch an emulator directly from within the Android Virtual Device Manager.
- The emulator is available within the /tools directory of the Android SDK and can be launched as a separate process from the command line (generally necessary only if you are not using the Android IDE).

Maintaining Emulator Performance

The Android emulator is slow if you do not choose any special configuration options when setting up your virtual devices or if you do not follow well-known tricks. That said, here are a few tips that will help ensure the best and speediest emulator experience possible:

- Enable the Snapshot feature in your AVD. Then, before you start using your AVD, launch it once, let it boot up, and shut it down to set a baseline snapshot. This is especially important with the newest platform versions such as Jelly Bean. Subsequent launches will be faster and more stable. You can even turn off saving a new snapshot to speed up exiting and it will continue to use the old snapshot.
- Launch your emulator instances before you need them, such as when you first launch the Android IDE, so that when you're ready to debug, they're already running.
- Keep the emulator running in the background between debugging sessions in order to quickly install, reinstall, and debug your applications. This saves valuable minutes of waiting for the emulator to boot up. Instead, simply launch the Debug configuration from the Android IDE and the debugger reattaches.
- Keep in mind that application performance is much slower when the debugger is attached. This applies to both running in the emulator and on a device.
- If you've been using an emulator for testing many apps, or just need a very clean environment, consider re-creating the AVD from scratch. This will give you a new environment clean of any past changes or modifications. This can help speed up the emulator, too, if you have lots of apps installed.

Tip

If your development machine has an Intel processor that supports hardware vir-tualization, you can take advantage of a special Android emulator system image that Intel provides to further speed up your development environment. To learn more about how to install and set up an Intel Android 4.2 Jelly Bean x86 emula-tor system image, see the following URL: *http://software.intel.com/en-us/articles/android-4-2-jelly-bean-x86-emulator-system-image.*

Configuring Emulator Startup Options

The Android emulator has a number of configuration options above and beyond those set in the AVD profile. These options are configured in the Android IDE Debug and Run configurations for your specific applications, or when the emulator is launched from the command line. Some emulator startup settings include numerous disk image, debug, media, network, system, UI, and help settings. For a complete list of emulator startup options, consult the Android emulator documentation: *http://d.android.com/tools/help/emulator.html#startup-options.*

Launching an Emulator to Run an Application

The most common way to launch the emulator involves launching a specific emulator instance with a specific AVD configuration, either through the Android Virtual Device Manager or by choosing a Run or Debug configuration for your project in the Android IDE and installing or reinstalling the latest incarnation of your application.

Tip

Remember that you can create Run configurations and Debug configurations separately, with different options, using different startup options and even different AVDs.

To create a Debug configuration for a specific project within the Android IDE, take the following steps:

1. Choose Run, Debug Configurations (or right-click the project and choose Debug As...).
2. Double-click on Android Application.
3. Name your Debug configuration (we often use the project name).
4. Choose the project by clicking on the Browse button.
5. Switch to the Target tab and choose the appropriate Deployment Target Selection Mode. Either choose a specific AVD to use with the emulator (only those matching your application's target SDK are shown) or select the Always prompt to pick device option to be prompted upon launch to choose an AVD on the fly.

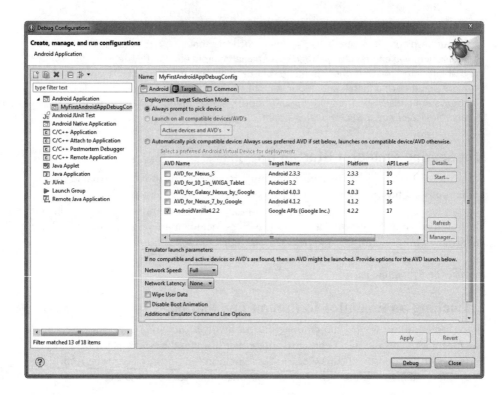

Figure B.4   Creating a `Debug` configuration in the Android IDE.

Tip

If you have Android devices connected via USB when you attempt to run or debug your application from the Android IDE, you will be prompted to choose your target at runtime despite having selected a specific AVD. This enables you to redirect the install or reinstall operation to a device other than an emulator. You can always force this behavior by choosing the `Always prompt to pick device` option for your `Deployment Target Selection Mode` on the `Target` tab of your `Debug` configuration. We find setting the mode to `Always prompt to pick device` helps if you switch between debugging on emulators and devices frequently, and setting a specific target is more useful when debugging with only a specific AVD emulator instance.

6. Configure any emulator startup options on the `Target` tab. You can enter any options not specifically shown on the tab as normal command-line options in the `Additional Emulator Command Line Options` field.

The resulting `Debug` configuration might look something like Figure B.4.

You can create `Run` configurations in a very similar fashion. If you set a specific AVD for use in the `Deployment Target Selection Mode` settings, that AVD is used with the

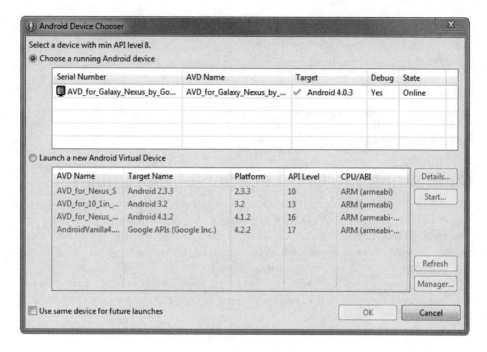

Figure B.5   The Android Device Chooser.

emulator whenever you debug your application in the Android IDE. However, if you choose the `Always prompt to pick device` option, you are prompted to select an AVD from the Android Device Chooser when you first try to debug the application, as shown in Figure B.5. After you have launched that emulator, the Android IDE pairs the emulator with your project for the duration of your debugging session.

Launching an Emulator from the Android Virtual Device Manager

Sometimes you just want to launch an emulator on the fly—for example, to have a second emulator running to interact with your first emulator to simulate calls, text messages, and such. In this case, you can simply launch it from the Android Virtual Device Manager. To do this, take the following steps:

1. Launch the Android Virtual Device Manager from within the Android IDE (▤) on the toolbar. You can also launch it by selecting `Window`, `Android Virtual Device Manager` from the Android IDE menu.

2. Click the `Android Virtual Devices` menu item on the left menu. The configured AVDs are displayed as a list.

3. Select an existing AVD configuration from the list or create a new AVD that matches your requirements.

4. Hit the Start button.

5. Configure any launch options necessary.

6. Hit the Launch button. The emulator now launches with the AVD you requested.

Warning

You cannot run multiple instances of the same AVD configuration simultaneously. If you think about it, this makes sense because the AVD configuration keeps the state and persistent data.

Configuring the GPS Location of the Emulator

To develop and test applications that use Google Maps support with location-based services, you need to create an AVD with a target that includes the Google APIs. After you have created the appropriate AVD and launched the emulator, you need to configure its location. The emulator does not have location sensors, so the first thing you need to do is seed your emulator with GPS coordinates.

To configure your emulator with pretend coordinates, launch your emulator (if it is not already running) with an AVD supporting the Google APIs and follow these steps:
In the emulator:

1. Press the Home key to return to the Home screen.

2. Find and launch the Maps application.

3. Click through the various startup dialogs, if this is the first time you've launched the Maps application.

4. Choose the My Location menu item (⊙) and enable location on the device if it is not already enabled.

In the Android IDE:

5. Click the DDMS perspective in the top-right corner of the Android IDE.

6. You see an Emulator Control pane on the upper-right side of the IDE. Scroll down to the Location Controls.

7. Manually enter the longitude and latitude of your location. Note that they are in reverse order. For example, Yosemite Valley has the coordinates Longitude: –19.588542 and Latitude: 37.746761.

8. Click Send.

Back in the emulator, notice that the map now shows the location you seeded. Your screen should display your location as Yosemite, as shown in Figure B.6. This location persists across emulator launches.

You can also use GPX 1.1 coordinate files to send a series of GPS locations through DDMS to the emulator, if you prefer. GPX 1.0 files are not supported by DDMS.

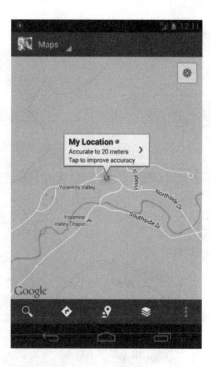

Figure B.6   Setting the location of the emulator to Yosemite Valley.

Tip

Wondering where we got the coordinates for Yosemite? To find a specific set of coordinates for use, you can go to *http://maps.google.com*. Navigate to the location you want the coordinates for. Next, right-click the location and choose "What's here?" The latitude and longitude will be placed in the search field.

Calling between Two Emulator Instances

You can have two emulator instances call each other using the Dialer application provided on the emulator. The emulator's "phone number" is its port number, which can be found in the title bar of the emulator window. To simulate a phone call between two emulators, you must perform the following steps:

1. Launch two different AVDs so two emulators are running simultaneously. (Using the Android AVD and SDK Manager is easiest.)
2. Note the port number of the emulator you want to receive the call.
3. In the emulator that makes the call, launch the Dialer application.
4. Type the port number you noted as the number to call. Press Enter (or Send).

Figure B.7   Simulating a phone call between two emulators.

5. You see (and hear) an incoming call on the receiving emulator instance. Figure B.7 shows an emulator with port 5556 (left) using the `Dialer` application to call the emulator on port 5554 (right).

6. Answer the call by pressing `Send` or swiping across the `Dialer` app.

7. Pretend to chat for a bit. Figure B.8 shows a call in progress.

8. You can end either emulator call at any time by pressing the `End` key.

Messaging between Two Emulator Instances

You can send SMS messages between two emulators, exactly as previously described for simulating calls, by using the emulator port numbers as SMS addresses. To simulate a text message between two emulators, you must perform the following steps:

1. Launch two instances of the emulator.

2. Note the port number of the emulator you want to receive the text message.

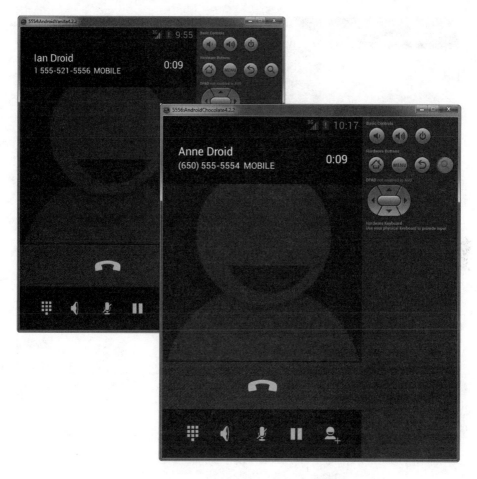

Figure B.8   Two emulators with a phone call in progress.

3. In the emulator that sends the text, launch the `Messaging` application.

4. Type the port number you noted as the "To" field for the text message. Enter a text message, as shown in Figure B.9 (left). Press the `Send` button.

5. You see (and hear) an incoming text message on the receiving emulator instance. Figure B.9 (center, top) shows an emulator with port 5554 receiving a text message from the emulator on port 5556 (left).

6. View the text message by pulling down the `status bar` or launching the `Messaging` app.

7. Pretend to chat for a bit. Figure B.9 (right, bottom) shows a text message conversation in progress.

Figure B.9   Emulator at port 5556 (left) crafting a text message to send to
another emulator at port 5554 (center, right).

Interacting with the Emulator through the Console

In addition to using the DDMS tool to interact with the emulator, you can also connect directly to the Emulator console using a Telnet connection and then issue commands. For example, to connect to the Emulator console of the emulator using port 5554, you would do the following:

```
telnet localhost 5554
```

You can use the Emulator console to issue commands to the emulator. To end the session, just type quit or exit. You can shut down this instance of the emulator using the kill command.

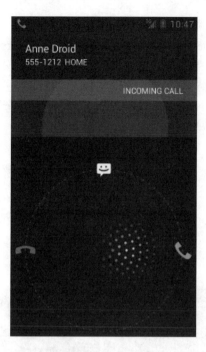

Figure B.10   Incoming call from 555-1212 (configured as a contact named
Anne Droid), prompted via the Emulator console.

 Warning

You may need to enable Telnet on your system in order to proceed through the following sections if this has not already been done.

Using the Console to Simulate Incoming Calls

You can simulate incoming calls to the emulator from specified numbers. The console command for issuing an incoming call is

```
gsm call <number>
```

For example, to simulate an incoming call from the number 555-1212, you would issue the following console command:

```
gsm call 5551212
```

The result of this command in the emulator is shown in Figure B.10. The name "Anne Droid" shows up because we have an entry in the Contacts database that ties the phone number 555-1212 to a contact named Anne Droid.

Using the Console to Simulate SMS Messages

You can simulate SMS messages to the emulator from specified numbers as well, just as you can from DDMS. The command for issuing an incoming SMS is

```
sms send <number> <message>
```

For example, to simulate an incoming SMS from the number 555-1212, you would issue the following command:

```
sms send 5551212 What's up!
```

In the emulator, you get a notification on the status bar informing you of a new message. It even displays the contents on the bar for a moment and then rolls away, showing the Message icon. You can pull down the status bar to see the new message or launch the Messaging application. The result of the preceding command in the emulator is shown in Figure B.11.

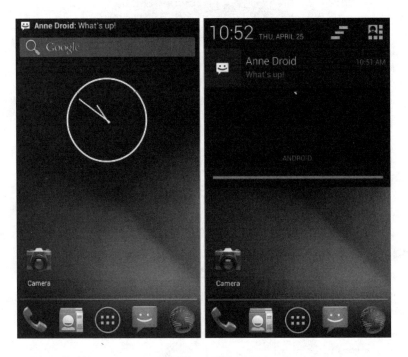

Figure B.11   An incoming SMS from 555-1212 (configured as a contact named Anne Droid), prompted via the Emulator console.

Using the Console to Send GPS Coordinates

You can use the Emulator console to issue GPS commands to the emulator. The command for a simple GPS fix is

```
geo fix <longitude> <latitude> [<altitude>]
```

For instance, to set the fix for the emulator to the top of Mount Everest, launch the Maps application in the emulator by selecting Menu, My Location. Then, within the Emulator console, issue the following command to set the device's coordinates appropriately:

```
geo fix 86.929837 27.99003 8850
```

Using the Console to Monitor Network Status

You can monitor the network status of the emulator and change the network speed and latency on the fly. The command for displaying network status is

```
network status
```

Typical results from this request look something like this:

```
Current network status:
 download speed:        0 bits/s (0.0 KB/s)
 upload speed:          0 bits/s (0.0 KB/s)
 minimum latency: 0 ms
 maximum latency: 0 ms
OK
```

Using the Console to Manipulate Power Settings

You can manage "fake" power settings on the emulator using the power commands. You can turn the battery capacity to 99% charged as follows:

```
power capacity 99
```

You can turn the AC charging state to off (or on) as follows:

```
power ac off
```

You can turn the battery status to the options unknown, charging, discharging, not-charging, or full as follows:

```
power status full
```

You can turn the battery present state to true (or false) as follows:

```
power present true
```

You can turn the battery health state to the options unknown, good, overheat, dead, overvoltage, or failure as follows:

```
power health good
```

You can show the current power settings by issuing the following command:

```
power display
```

Typical results from this request look something like this:

```
power display
AC: offline
status: Full
health: Good
present: true
capacity: 99
OK
```

Using Other Console Commands

There are also commands for simulating hardware events, port redirection, and checking, starting, and stopping the virtual machine. For example, quality assurance personnel will want to check out the event subcommands, which can be used to simulate key events for automation purposes. It's likely this is the same interface used by the ADB Exerciser Monkey, which presses random keys and tries to crash your application.

Enjoying the Emulator

Here are a few more tips for using the emulator, just for fun:

- On the Home screen, press and hold the screen to change the wallpaper.
- If you press and hold an icon (usually an application icon) from within the All Apps launcher, you can place a shortcut to it on your Home screen for easy access. Newer platform versions also enable other options, such as uninstalling the application or getting more information, which is very handy.
- If you press and hold an icon on your Home screen, you can move it around or dump it into the trash to get it off the screen.
- Press and fling the device's Home screen to the left and right for more space. Depending on which version of Android you're running, you find a number of other pages, with App Widgets such as Google Search and lots of empty space where you can place other Home screen items.
- A way to add widgets to your Home screen is to launch the All Apps screen, then navigate to Widgets. There are many different widgets available, and selecting one is how you can add those widgets to your Home screen, as shown in Figure B.12.

Figure B.12   Customizing the emulator `Home` screen
with a `Power Control` App Widget.

In other words, the emulator can be personalized in many of the same ways as a regular device. Making these sorts of changes can be useful for comprehensive application testing.

Understanding Emulator Limitations

The emulator is powerful, but it has several important limitations:

- It is not a device, so it does not reflect actual behavior, only simulated behavior. Simulated behavior is generally more consistent (less random) than what users experience in real life on real devices.

- It simulates phone calls and messaging, but you cannot place or receive true calls or SMS messages. There is no support for MMS.

- It has a limited ability to determine device state (network state, battery charge).

- It has a limited ability to simulate peripherals (headphones, sensor data).

- There is limited API support (for example, no SIP or third-party hardware API support). When developing certain categories of applications, such as augmented reality applications, 3D games, and applications that rely upon sensor data, you're better off using the real hardware.

- Performance is limited (modern devices often perform much better than the emulator at many tasks, such as video and animation).
- There is limited support for manufacturer- or operator-specific device characteristics, themes, or user experiences. Some manufacturers, however, such as Motorola, have provided emulator add-ons to more closely mimic the behavior of specific devices.
- On Android 4.0 and later, the emulator can use attached Web cameras to emulate device hardware cameras. On previous versions of the tools, the camera would respond but took fake pictures.
- There is no USB, Bluetooth, or NFC support.

Summary

In this appendix, you learned about one of the most useful tools incorporated with the Android SDK, the Android emulator. The Android emulator is available as part of the Android IDE and is also available from the command line. The emulator is an effective development tool for simulating real devices. When your application requires testing on many different device configurations, rather than purchasing every device you would like to support, the Android Virtual Device Manager allows for varying emulator configurations, making testing cost-effective. Even though the emulator has limitations and is not meant to be a replacement for testing on real hardware, you have learned much of what the emulator has to offer and have discovered firsthand just how close to reality the emulator performs.

Quiz Questions

1. What is the keyboard shortcut to toggle networking of an emulator?
2. What is the keyboard shortcut for toggling between portrait and landscape modes?
3. What is the keyboard shortcut for emulating a trackball with your mouse?
4. Which `Activity` lifecycle events does pressing the `Home` key invoke?
5. What is the hardware configuration property for supporting GPU emulation within your AVD configurations?
6. What is the command for connecting to an emulator from the console?
7. What is the command for a simple GPS fix?

Exercises

1. Using the Android documentation, devise a list of the Android emulator category command-line parameters.

2. Using the Android documentation, name the command-line option for enabling GPU emulation.

3. Using the Android documentation, design a command for creating an AVD from the command line.

References and More Information

Android Tools: "Managing Virtual Devices":
  http://d.android.com/tools/devices/index.html
Android Tools: "Managing AVDs with AVD Manager":
  http://d.android.com/tools/devices/managing-avds.html
Android Tools: "Managing AVDs from the Command Line":
  http://d.android.com/tools/devices/managing-avds-cmdline.html
Android Tools: "Android Emulator":
  http://d.android.com/tools/help/emulator.html
Android Tools: "Using the Android Emulator":
  http://d.android.com/tools/devices/emulator.html
Android Tools: "android":
  http://d.android.com/tools/help/android.html

C

Quick-Start Guide: Android DDMS

The Dalvik Debug Monitor Server (DDMS) is a debugging tool provided with the Android SDK. Developers use DDMS to provide a window into the emulator or the actual device for debugging purposes as well as file and process management. It's a blend of several tools: a task manager, a profiler, a file explorer, an emulator console, and a logging console. This Quick-Start Guide is not complete documentation of the DDMS functionality. Instead, it is designed to get you up and running with common tasks. See the DDMS documentation provided with the Android SDK for a complete list of features.

When this appendix discusses an IDE, the focus is on the Android IDE. Whenever we refer to the Android IDE, the same instructions apply to Eclipse with the ADT plugin. Because the Android IDE and Eclipse with the ADT plugin are equivalent, from here on we will mention only the Android IDE.

Using DDMS with the Android IDE and as a Standalone Application

If you use the Android IDE, the DDMS tool is tightly integrated with your development environment as a perspective. By using the DDMS perspective (shown in Figure C.1, using the File Explorer to browse files on the emulator instance), you can explore any emulator instances running on the development machine and any Android devices connected via USB.

If you're not using the Android IDE, the DDMS tool is also available within the /tools directory of the Android SDK, and you can launch it as a separate application, in which case it runs in its own process.

Tip

There should be only one instance of the DDMS tool running at a given time. This includes the Android IDE perspective. Other DDMS launches are ignored; if you have the Android IDE running and try to launch DDMS from the command line, you might see question marks instead of process names, and you will see debug output stating that the instance of DDMS is being ignored.

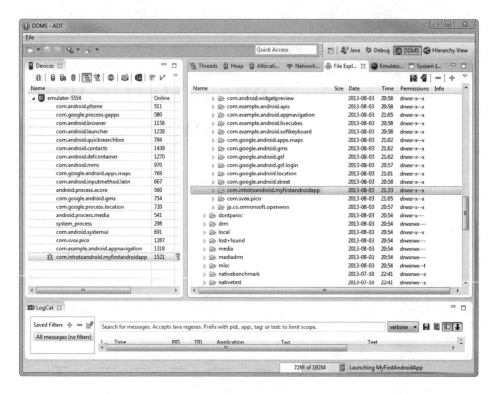

Figure C.1   The Android IDE DDMS perspective with one emulator and one
Android device connected in the Devices pane.

Warning

Not all DDMS features are available for both emulators and devices. Certain features, such
as the Emulator Control features, are available only for emulators. Most devices are
more secure than the emulator. Thus, the File Explorer may be limited to just public
areas of the device, unlike on the emulator.

Getting Up to Speed Using Key Features of DDMS

Whether you use DDMS from the Android IDE or as a standalone tool, be aware of a few
key features:

- The Devices pane displays running emulators and connected devices in the top-left
corner.
- The set of Threads, Heap, Allocation Tracker, Network Statistics, File
Explorer, and System Information tabs on the right side are populated with data
when a specific process on an emulator or device is highlighted in the Devices pane.

- The `Emulator Control` pane provides features such as the ability to send GPS information and to simulate incoming calls and SMS messages to emulators.
- The `LogCat` window enables you to monitor the output of the Android logging console for a given device or emulator. This is where calls to `Log.i()`, `Log.e()`, and other log messages display.

Now let's look at how to use each of these DDMS features in more detail.

Tip

Another Android IDE perspective provides direct access to the Hierarchy Viewer tool, which can be used for debugging and performance-tuning your application user interface. See Appendix A, "Mastering the Android Development Tools," for more details about this tool.

Working with Processes, Threads, and the Heap

One of the most useful features of DDMS is the ability to interact with processes. Each Android application runs in its own VM with its own user ID on the operating system. Using the `Devices` pane of DDMS, you can browse all instances of the VM running on a device, each identified by its package name. For example, you can perform the following tasks:

- Attach and debug applications in the Android IDE
- Monitor threads
- Monitor the heap
- Stop processes
- Force garbage collection (GC)

Attaching a Debugger to an Android Application

Although you'll use the Android IDE debug configurations to launch and debug your applications most of the time, you can also use DDMS to choose which application to debug and attach directly. To attach a debugger to a process, you need to have the package source code open in your Android IDE workspace. Now perform the following steps to debug:

1. On the emulator or device, verify that the application you want to debug is running.
2. In DDMS, find that application's package name in the `Devices` pane and highlight it.
3. Click the little green bug button () to debug that application.
4. Switch to the `Debug` perspective of the Android IDE as necessary; debug as you would normally.

Stopping a Process

You can use DDMS to kill an Android application by following these steps:

1. On the emulator or device, verify that the application you want to stop is running.
2. In DDMS, find that application's package name in the Devices pane and highlight it.
3. Click the red stop sign button (📵) to stop that process.

Monitoring Thread Activity of an Android Application

You can use DDMS to monitor thread activity of an individual Android application by following these steps:

1. On the emulator or device, verify that the application you want to monitor is running.
2. In DDMS, find that application's package name in the Devices pane and highlight it.
3. Click the button with three black arrows (📑) to display the threads of that application. They appear in the right portion of the Threads pane.
4. On the Threads pane, you can choose a specific thread and click the Refresh button to drill down within that thread. The resulting classes in use display below.

Note

You can also start thread profiling using the button with three black arrows and a red dot (📑).

For example, in Figure C.2, we see the Threads pane contents for the package named com.introtoandroid.myfirstandroidapp running on the emulator.

Monitoring Heap Activity

You can use DDMS to monitor the heap statistics of an individual Android application. The heap statistics are updated after every garbage collection (GC) via these steps:

1. On the emulator or device, verify that the application you want to monitor is running.
2. In DDMS, find that application's package name in the Devices pane and highlight it.
3. Click the green cylinder button (🗄) to display the heap information for that application. The statistics appear in the Heap pane. This data updates after every GC. You can also cause GC operations from the Heap pane using the button Cause GC.
4. On the Heap pane, you can choose a specific type of object. The resulting graph in use displays at the bottom of the Heap pane, as shown in Figure C.3.

Tip

When using the Allocation Tracker and Heap monitor, keep in mind that not all memory your app uses will be accounted for in this view. This tool shows the allocations within the Dalvik VM. Some calls allocate memory on the native heap. For example, many image manipulation calls in the SDK will result in memory allocated natively and not show up in this view.

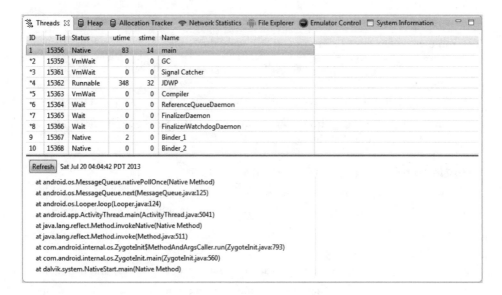

Figure C.2   Using the DDMS Threads pane.

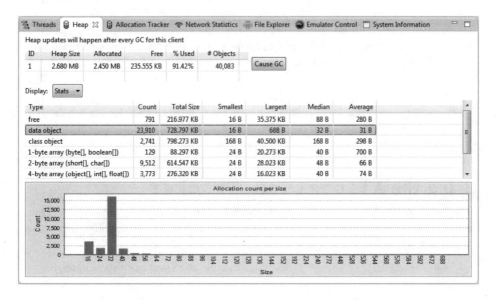

Figure C.3   Using the DDMS Heap pane.

Prompting Garbage Collection

You can use DDMS to force GC to run by following these steps:

1. On the emulator or device, verify that the application you want to run GC for is running.
2. In DDMS, find that application's package name in the Devices pane and highlight it.
3. Click the garbage can button (![icon]) to cause GC to run for the application. The results can be viewed in the Heap pane.

Creating and Using an HPROF File

HPROF files can be used to inspect the heap and for profiling and performance purposes. You can use DDMS to create an HPROF file for your application by following these steps:

1. On the emulator or device, verify that the application you want the HPROF data for is running.
2. In DDMS, find that application's package name in the Devices pane and highlight it.
3. Click the HPROF button (![icon]) to create an HPROF dump to be generated for the application. The files will be generated in the /data/misc/ directory.

For example, in Figure C.4, you can see the HPROF dump response in the Android IDE. You are switched to the Debug perspective, and a graphical trace is displayed.

Once you have Android-generated HPROF data, you can convert it to a standard HPROF file format using the Android SDK tool called hprof-conv. You can use whichever profiling tool you prefer to examine the information.

Note

You can generate HPROF files in Android using several other methods. For example, you can do it programmatically using the Debug class. The monkey tool also has options for generating HPROF files as it runs.

Using the Allocation Tracker

You can use DDMS to monitor memory allocated by a specific Android application. The memory allocation statistics are updated on demand by the developer. Follow these steps to track memory allocations:

1. On the emulator or device, verify that the application you want to monitor is running.
2. In DDMS, find that application's package name in the Devices pane and highlight it.
3. Switch to the Allocation Tracker pane on the right pane.

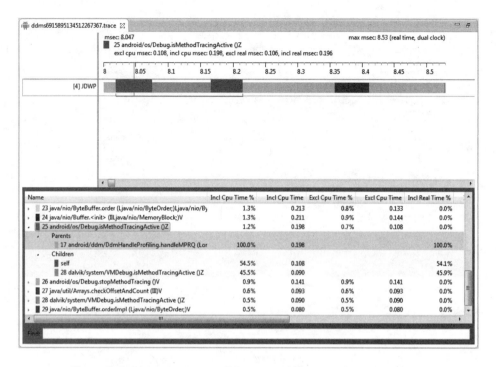

Figure C.4   Using the Android IDE to inspect HPROF profiling information.

4. Click the Start Tracking button to start tracking memory allocations and the Get Allocations button to get the allocations at a given time.

5. To stop tracking allocations, click the Stop Tracking button.

For example, in Figure C.5, we see the Allocation Tracker pane contents for an application running on the emulator.

The Android developer website has a write-up on memory analysis at *http://android-developers.blogspot.com/2011/03/memory-analysis-for-android.html*.

Viewing Network Statistics

You can use DDMS to analyze the network usage of your applications. This tool is useful for providing information about when your application performs network data transfers. The Android class TrafficStats is used to add network statistics analysis code to your application. To distinguish among different types of data transfers in your application, you simply apply a TrafficStats tag in your code before executing the transfer. Knowing

Figure C.5   Using the DDMS Allocation Tracker pane.

network statistics should help you make better decisions about how to optimize your network data transfer code. In Figure C.6, we see the Network Statistics pane contents for a Nexus 4 device.

Working with the File Explorer

You can use DDMS to browse and interact with the Android file system on an emulator or device (although it's somewhat limited on devices without root access). You can access application files, directories, and databases, as well as pull and push files to the Android system, provided you have the appropriate permissions.

For example, in Figure C.7, we see the File Explorer pane contents for the emulator.

Browsing the File System of an Emulator or Device

To browse the Android file system, follow these steps:

1. In DDMS, choose the emulator or device you want to browse in the Devices pane.

2. Switch to the File Explorer pane. You see a directory hierarchy.

3. Browse to a directory or file location.

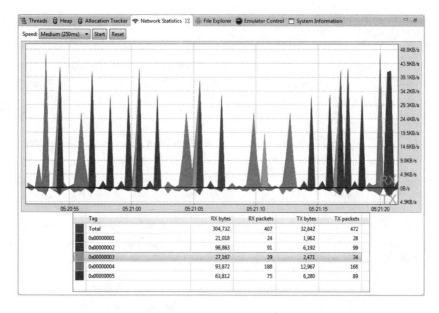

Figure C.6   Using the DDMS Network Statistics pane.

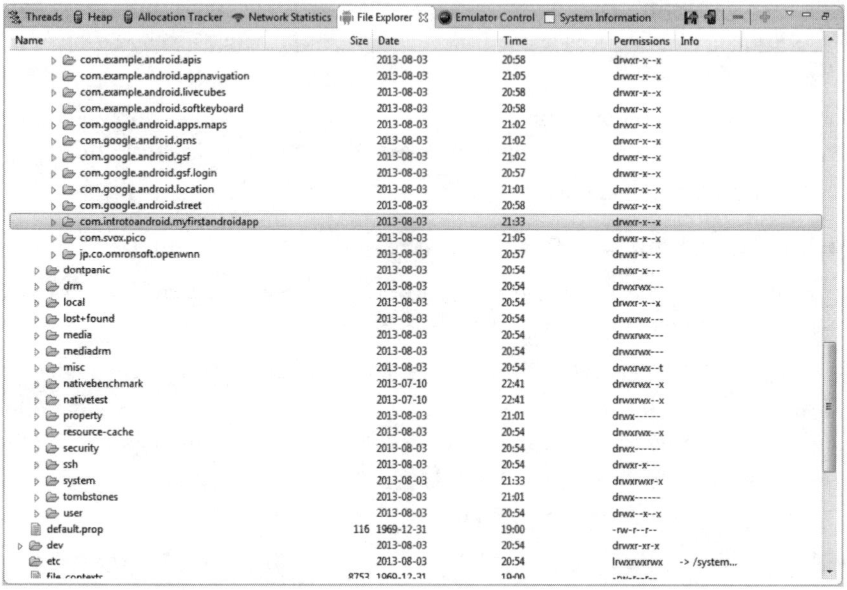

Figure C.7   Using the DDMS File Explorer pane.

Table C.1 **Important Directories in the Android File System**

Directory	Purpose
`/data/app/`	Where Android APK files are stored.
`/data/data/<package name>/`	Application top-level directory; for example: `/data/data/com.introtoandroid.myfirstandroidapp/`.
`/data/data/<package name>/shared_prefs/`	Application shared preferences directory. Named preferences are stored as XML files.
`/data/data/<package name>/files/`	Application file directory.
`/data/data/<package name>/cache/`	Application cache directory.
`/data/data/<package name>/databases/`	Application database directory; for example: `/data/data/com.introtoandroid.pettracker/databases/test.db`.
`/mnt/sdcard/`	External storage (SD card).
`/mnt/sdcard/download/`	Where browser images are saved.

Keep in mind that directory listings in the `File Explorer` might take a moment to update when contents change.

Note

Some device directories, such as the `/data` directory, might not be accessible from the DDMS `File Explorer`.

Table C.1 shows some important areas of the Android file system. Although the exact directories may vary from device to device, the directories listed are the most common.

Copying Files from the Emulator or Device

You can use the `File Explorer` to copy files or directories from an emulator or a device file system to your computer by following these steps:

1. Using the `File Explorer`, browse to the file or directory to copy and highlight it.

2. From the top-right corner of the `File Explorer`, click the disk button with the arrow () to pull the file from the device. Alternatively, you can pull down the drop-down menu next to the buttons and choose `Pull File`.

3. Type in the path where you want to save the file or directory on your computer and click `Save`.

Copying Files to the Emulator or Device

You can use the `File Explorer` to copy files to an emulator or a device file system from your computer by following these steps:

1. Using the `File Explorer`, browse to the file or directory to copy and highlight it.

2. From the top-right corner of the `File Explorer`, click the phone button with the arrow () to push a file to the device. Alternatively, you can pull down the drop-down menu next to the buttons and choose `Push File`.

3. Select the file or directory on your computer and click `Open`.

Tip

The `File Explorer` also supports some drag-and-drop operations. This is the only way to push directories to the Android file system; however, copying directories to the Android file system is not recommended because there's no delete option for them. You need to delete directories programmatically if you have the permissions to do so. Alternatively, the `adb` shell can be used with `rmdir`, but you still need permissions to do so. That said, you can drag a file or directory from your computer to the `File Explorer` and drop it in the location you want.

Deleting Files on the Emulator or Device

You can use the `File Explorer` to delete files (one at a time, and not directories) on the emulator or device file system. Follow these steps:

1. Using the `File Explorer`, browse to the file you want to delete and highlight it.

2. In the top-right corner of the `File Explorer`, click the red minus button () to delete the file.

Warning

Be careful. There is no confirmation. The file is deleted immediately and is not recoverable.

Working with the `Emulator Control`

You can use DDMS to interact with instances of the emulator using the `Emulator Control` pane. You must select the emulator you want to interact with for the `Emulator Control` pane to work. You can use the `Emulator Control` pane to do the following:

- Change telephony status
- Simulate incoming voice calls
- Simulate incoming SMS messages
- Send a location fix (GPS coordinates)

Change Telephony Status

To simulate changing the telephony status using the `Emulator Control` pane (shown in Figure C.8), use the following steps:

1. In DDMS, choose the emulator whose telephony status you want to change.
2. Switch to the `Emulator Control` pane. You work with the `Telephony Status`.
3. Select the desired options from `Voice`, `Speed`, `Data`, and `Latency`.
4. For example, when changing the `Data` option from `Home` to `Roaming`, you should see a notification in the `status bar` that the device is now in roaming mode.

Simulating Incoming Voice Calls

To simulate an incoming voice call using the `Emulator Control` pane (shown in Figure C.8), use the following steps:

1. In DDMS, choose the emulator you want to call in the `Devices` pane.
2. Switch to the `Emulator Control` pane. You work with the `Telephony Actions`.
3. Input the incoming phone number. This can include only numbers, +, and #.
4. Select the `Voice` radio button.
5. Click the `Send` button.
6. In the emulator, your phone is ringing. Answer the call.
7. The emulator can end the call as normal, or you can end the call in DDMS using the `Hang Up` button.

Simulating Incoming SMS Messages

DDMS provides the most stable method for sending incoming SMS messages to the emulator. You send an SMS much as you initiated the voice call. To simulate an incoming SMS message using the `Emulator Control` pane (shown in Figure C.8, top), use the following steps:

1. In DDMS, choose the emulator you want to send a message to in the `Devices` pane.
2. Switch to the `Emulator Control` pane. You work with the `Telephony Actions`.
3. Input the incoming phone number. This may include only numbers, +, and #.
4. Select the `SMS` radio button.
5. Type in your SMS message.
6. Click the `Send` button.
7. Over in the emulator, you receive an SMS notification.

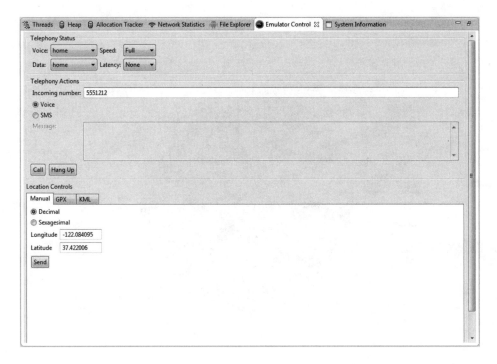

Figure C.8   Using the `DDMS Emulator Control` pane.

Sending a Location Fix

The steps for sending GPS coordinates to the emulator are covered in Appendix B, "Quick-Start Guide: The Android Emulator." Simply input the GPS information into the `Emulator Control` pane (shown in Figure C.8, bottom), click `Send`, and use the Maps application on the emulator to get the current position.

Working with the `System Information` Pane

You can use `DDMS` to analyze the system information of instances of the emulator using the `System Information` pane. You must select the emulator you want to analyze for the `System Information` pane to work. You can use the `System Information` pane like so:

1. In `DDMS`, choose the emulator or device you want to analyze.
2. Switch to the `System Information` pane.
3. Select from the drop-down the type of `System Information` you are interested in analyzing.

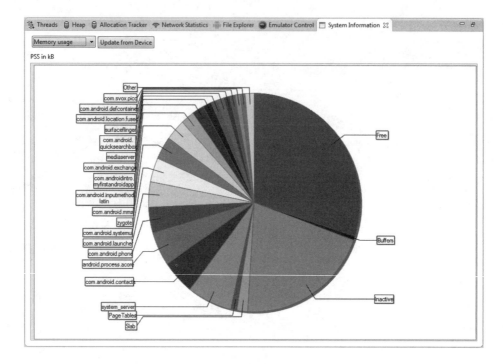

Figure C.9   Using the DDMS System Information pane.

4. If the screen is blank, you may need to press the Update from Device button.

5. You should now see a chart displaying the System Information, as shown in Figure C.9.

Taking Screen Captures of the Emulator and Device Screens

You can take screen captures of the emulator and the device from DDMS. The device captures are most useful for debugging, and this makes the DDMS tool appropriate for quality assurance personnel and developers. To capture a screenshot, take the following steps:

1. In DDMS, choose the emulator or device you want to capture in the Devices pane.

2. On the device or emulator, make sure you have the screen you want to capture.

3. Click the multicolored square picture button (📷) to take a screen capture. A capture window launches, as shown in Figure C.10.

4. Within the capture window, click the Save button to save the screen capture. Similarly, the Copy button stores the screenshot in your clipboard, the Refresh button

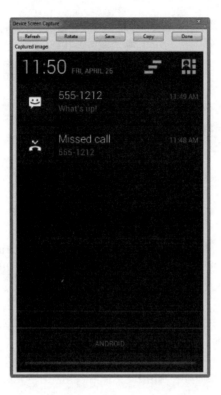

Figure C.10   Using DDMS to take a screenshot.

updates the screenshot if the underlying device or emulator screen has changed since you launched the capture window, and the Rotate button rotates the screenshot 90 degrees.

Working with Application Logging

The LogCat tool is integrated into DDMS. It is provided as a pane along the bottom of the DDMS user interface. You can control how much information displays by choosing an option from the log type filter drop-down. The default option is verbose (show everything). The other options correspond to debug, info, warn, error, and assert. When selected, only log entries for that level of severity and worse will display. You can filter the LogCat results to show just search results by using the search entry field, which fully supports regular expressions. Search terms can be limited in scope with prefixes, such as text:, to limit the following term to just the log message text.

You can also create saved filters to display only the LogCat information associated with particular attributes. You can use the plus (+) button to add a saved filter and show only

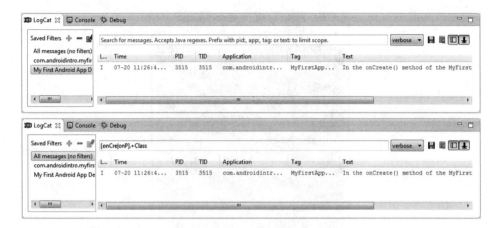

Figure C.11   Using the DDMS LogCat logging pane with a custom filter
(top) and a regular expression search (bottom).

log entries matching a tag, message, process ID, name, or log level. The strings for each
attribute filter can also be Java-style regular expressions.

For example, suppose your application does this:

```
public static final String DEBUG_TAG = "MyFirstAppLogging";

Log.i(DEBUG_TAG,

    "In the onCreate() method of the MyFirstAndroidAppActivity Class.");
```

You can create a LogCat filter using the plus button (⊞). Name the filter and set the
log tag to the string matching your debug tag:

```
MyFirstAppLogging
```

The LogCat pane with the resulting filter is shown in Figure C.11.

To search for the message if you don't need to create a full tab, you could type in
"MyFirst" and get all the results with tags and text fields containing this string.

Summary

In this appendix, you have learned many valuable features that DDMS provides. Many of
the DDMS tools are available from within the Android IDE or as standalone applications.
You learned that DDMS provides tools for monitoring your application's performance
while running on an emulator or a device. You also learned that DDMS allows you to interact directly with the file system of an emulator or a device. You should also feel comfortable interacting with an emulator or device, performing actions such as phone calls,
SMS, taking screenshots, or even logging application data.

Quiz Questions

1. What is the name of the Android SDK directory where the command-line DDMS application resides?

2. True or false: The DDMS tab for sending GPS coordinates to a device or emulator is called the Emulator Control tab.

3. Name some of the tasks that you can perform with the Threads and Heap tabs.

4. What is the name of the class used for adding network statistics analysis code to your application?

5. True or false: The LogCat tool is not part of DDMS.

Exercises

1. Launch a sample application, on either an emulator or a device, using a Debug configuration, and practice analyzing the application using the various DDMS tabs.

2. Practice interacting with an emulator or device by sending calls, SMS messages, and GPS coordinates, and then take screen captures of each interaction using DDMS.

3. Practice adding log statements to a sample application, and then use LogCat to view the logging information.

References and More Information

Android Tools: "Using DDMS":
   http://d.android.com/tools/debugging/ddms.html
Android Reference: "TrafficStats":
   http://d.android.com/reference/android/net/TrafficStats.html
Android Tools: "Reading and Writing Logs":
   http://d.android.com/tools/debugging/debugging-log.html
Android Reference: "Log":
   http://d.android.com/reference/android/util/Log.html

Android IDE and Eclipse Tips and Tricks

The Android IDE (a special version of the Eclipse IDE with the ADT plugin prein-stalled) is included as part of the Android ADT Bundle. The Android IDE (Eclipse) is one of the most popular development environments for Android developers. In this appendix, we provide a number of helpful tips and tricks for using the Android IDE to develop An-droid applications quickly and effectively. Even though you may choose to use your own copy of Eclipse and manually install the ADT plugin yourself, the instructions provided within this appendix apply to using either the Android IDE or Eclipse with ADT. Since the Android IDE and Eclipse with the ADT plugin are equivalent, from here on, we will refer only to the Android IDE.

Organizing Your Android IDE Workspace

In this section, we provide a number of tips and tricks to help you organize your Android IDE workspace for optimum Android development.

Integrating with Source Control Services

The Android IDE has the ability to integrate with many source control packages using add-ons or plugins. This allows the Android IDE to manage checking out a file (making it writable) when you start to edit it, checking a file in, updating a file, showing a file's status, and a number of other tasks, depending on the support of the add-on.

Tip

Common source control add-ons are available for CVS, Subversion, Perforce, Git, Mercurial, and many other packages.

Generally speaking, not all files are suitable for source control. For Android projects, any file within the /bin and /gen directories shouldn't be in source control. To exclude these generically within the Android IDE, go to Window, Preferences, Team, Ignored Resources. You can add file suffixes such as *.apk, *.ap_, and *.dex by clicking the Add Pattern... button and adding one at a time. Conveniently, this applies to all inte-grated source control systems.

Repositioning Tabs within Perspectives

The Android IDE provides some pretty decent layouts with the default perspectives. However, not everyone works the same way. We feel that some of the perspectives have poor default layouts for Android development and could use some improvement.

Tip

Experiment to find a tab layout that works well for you. Each perspective has its own layout, too, and the perspectives can be task oriented.

For instance, the `Properties` tab is usually found on the bottom of a perspective. For code, this works fine because this tab is only a few lines high. But for resource editing in Android, it doesn't work so well. Luckily, in the Android IDE this is easy to fix: simply drag the tab by left-clicking and holding on the tab (the title) itself and dragging it to a new location, such as the vertical section on the right side of the Android IDE window. This provides the much-needed vertical space to see the dozens of properties often found here.

Tip

If you mess up a perspective or just want to start fresh, you can reset it by choosing `Window`, `Reset Perspective`.

Maximizing Windows

Sometimes you might find that the editor window is just too small, especially with all the extra little metadata windows and tabs surrounding it. Try this: double-click the tab of the source file that you want to edit. Boom! It's now nearly the full Android IDE window size! Double-click to return the window to normal. (`Ctrl+M` works on Windows, `Command+M` on the Mac.)

Minimizing Windows

You can minimize entire sections, too. For instance, if you don't need the section at the bottom that usually has the console or the one to the left that usually has the `Package Explorer` view, you can use the minimize button in each section's upper-right corner. Use the button that looks like two little windows to restore it.

Viewing Windows Side by Side

Ever wish you could see two source files at once? Well, you can! Simply grab the tab for a source file and drag it either to the edge of the editor area or to the bottom. You will then see a dark outline (shown in Figure D.1) showing where the file will be docked—either side by side with another file or above or below another file. This creates a parallel editor area (shown in Figure D.2) where you can drag other file tabs as well. You can repeat this multiple times to show three, four, or more files at once.

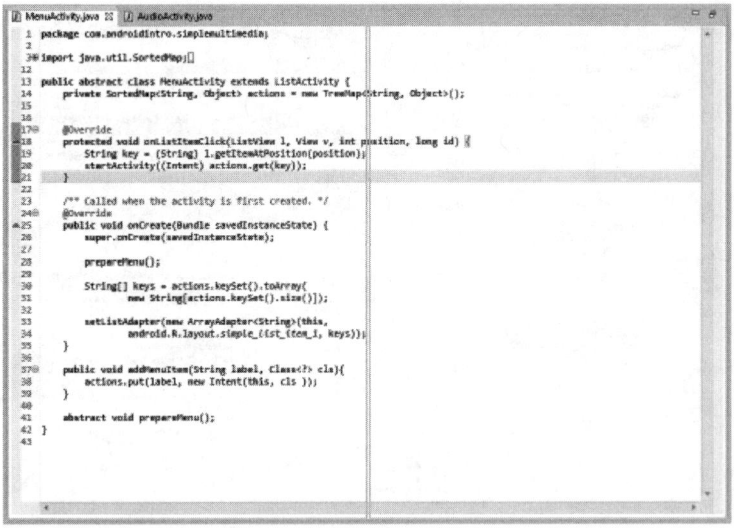

Figure D.1   A dark outline indicating how the windows
will appear when docked side by side.

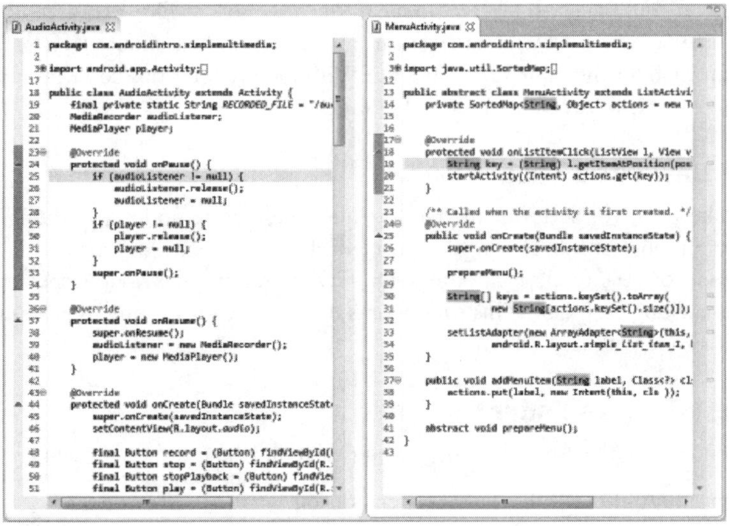

Figure D.2   Two windows docked side by side.

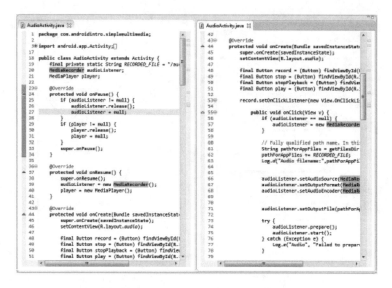

Figure D.3   Viewing different sections of the same file
in two different windows side by side.

Viewing Two Sections of the Same File

Ever wish you could see two places at once in the same source file? You can! Make sure the file is open and focused, select Window from the menu, then choose New Editor. A second editor tab for the same file comes up. With the previous tip, you can now have two different views of the same file (see Figure D.3).

Closing Unwanted Tabs

Ever feel like you have far too many tabs open for files you're no longer editing? We do! There are a number of solutions to this problem. First, you can right-click a file tab and choose Close Others to close all other open files. You can quickly close specific tabs by middle-clicking each tab. (This even works on a Mac with a mouse that can middle-click, such as one with a scroll wheel.)

Keeping Windows under Control

Finally, you can use the Android IDE setting that limits the number of open file editors:

1. Open the Android IDE's Preferences dialog.

2. Expand General, choose Editors, and check Close editors automatically.

3. Edit the value in Number of opened editors before closing.

This will cause old editor windows to be closed when new ones are opened. Eight seems to be a good number to use for the `Number of opened editors before closing` option to keep the clutter down but to have enough editors open to still get work done and have reference code open. Note also that if you select `Open new editor` under `When all editors are dirty or pinned`, more files will be open if you're actively editing more than the number chosen. Thus, this setting doesn't affect productivity when you're editing a large number of files all at once but can keep things clean during most normal tasks.

Creating Custom Log Filters

Every Android log statement includes a tag. You can use these tags with filters defined in `LogCat`. To add a new filter, click the green plus sign button in the `LogCat` pane. Name the filter—perhaps using the tag name—and fill in the tag you want to use. Now there is another tab in `LogCat` that shows messages that contain this tag. In addition, you can create filters that display items by severity level.

Android convention has largely settled on creating tags based on the name of the class. You see this frequently in the code provided with this book. Note that we create a constant in each class with the same variable name to simplify each logging call. Here's an example:

```
public static final String DEBUG_TAG = "MyClassName";
```

This convention isn't a requirement, though. You could organize tags around specific tasks that span many activities, or you could use any other logical organization that works for your needs. Another simpler way to do this is as follows:

```
private final String DEBUG_TAG = getClass().getSimpleName();
```

Although not as efficient at runtime, this code can help you avoid copy-and-paste errors. If you've ever been looking over a log file and had a misnamed debug tag string mislead you, this trick may be useful to you.

Searching Your Project

You have several ways to easily search your project files from within the Android IDE. The search options are found under the `Search` menu of the Android IDE toolbar. Most frequently, we use the `File` search option, which allows you to search for text within the files found in the workspace, as well as for files by name. The `Java` search option can also help you find Java-specific elements of your project such as methods and fields.

Organizing Android IDE Tasks

By default, any comment that starts with `// TODO` will show up on the `Tasks` tab in the `Java` perspective. This can be helpful for tagging code areas that require further implementation. You can click a specific task and it will take you straight to the comment in the file so you can implement the item at a later time.

You can also create custom comment tags above and beyond to-do items. We often leave comments with people's initials to make it easy for them to find specific functional areas of the application to code review. Here's an example:

```
// LED: Does this look right to you?
// CDC: Related to Bug 1234. Can you fix this?
// SAC: This will have to be incremented for the next build
```

You might also use a special comment such as //HACK when you have to implement something that is less than ideal, to flag that code as subject to further review. To add custom tags to your Task list, edit your Android IDE preferences (available at Window, Preferences) and navigate to Java, Compiler, Task Tags. Add any tags you want to flag. The tags can be flagged for a certain priority level. So, for instance, something with your initials might be a high priority to look at right away, but a HACK flag may be a low priority because, presumably, it works but maybe not in the best way possible.

Writing Code in Java

In this section, we provide a number of tips and tricks to help you implement the code for your Android applications.

Using Autocomplete

Autocomplete is a great feature that speeds up code entry. If this feature hasn't appeared for you yet or has gone away, you can bring it up by pressing Ctrl+spacebar. Autocomplete not only saves time in typing but also can be used to jog your memory about methods— or to help you find a new method. You can scroll through all the methods of a class and even see the Javadocs associated with them. You can easily find static methods by using the class name or the instance variable name. You follow the class or variable name with a dot (and maybe Ctrl+spacebar) and then scroll through all the names. Then you can start typing the first part of a name to filter the results.

Creating New Classes and Methods

You can quickly create a new class and corresponding source file by right-clicking the package to create it and then choosing New, Class. Next, you enter the class Name, pick a Superclass and Interfaces, and choose whether to create default comments and method stubs for the superclass for constructors or abstract methods.

Along the same lines as creating new classes, you can quickly create method stubs by right-clicking a class or within a class in the editor and choosing Source, Override/ Implement Methods. Then you choose the methods for which you're creating stubs, where to create the stubs, and whether to generate default comment blocks.

Organizing Imports

When referencing a class in your code for the first time, you can hover over the newly used class name and choose `Import "Classname" (package name)` to have the Android IDE quickly add the proper import statement.

In addition, the Organize Imports command (`Ctrl+Shift+O` in Windows and `Command+Shift+O` on a Mac) causes the Android IDE to automatically organize your imports. The Android IDE removes unused imports and adds new ones for packages used but not already imported.

If there is any ambiguity in the name of a class during automatic import, such as with the Android `Log` class, the Android IDE prompts you for the package to import. Finally, you can configure the Android IDE to automatically organize the imports each time you save a file. This can be set for the entire workspace or for an individual project.

Configuring this for an individual project gives you more flexibility when you're working on multiple projects and don't want to make changes to some code, even if the changes are an improvement. To configure this, perform the following steps:

1. Right-click the project and choose `Properties`.

2. Expand `Java Editor` and choose `Save Actions`.

3. Check `Enable project specific settings`, check `Perform the selected actions on save`, and check `Organize imports`.

Formatting Code

The Android IDE has a built-in mechanism for formatting Java code. Formatting code with a tool is useful for keeping the style consistent, applying a new style to old code, or matching styles with a different client or target (such as a book or an article).

To quickly format a small block of code, select the code and press `Ctrl+Shift+F` in Windows (or `Command+Shift+F` on a Mac). The code is formatted to the current settings. If no code is selected, the entire file is formatted. Occasionally, you need to select more code—such as an entire method—to get the indentation levels and brace matching correct.

The Android IDE formatting settings are found in the `Properties` pane under `Java Code Style`, `Formatter`. You can configure these settings on a per-project or workspace-wide basis. You can apply and modify dozens of rules to suit your own style.

Renaming Almost Anything

The Android IDE's `Rename` tool is quite powerful. You can use it to rename variables, methods, class names, and more. Most often, you can simply right-click the item you want to rename and then choose `Refactor`, `Rename`. Alternatively, after selecting the item, you can press `F2` in Windows (or `Command+Alt+R` on a Mac) to begin the renaming process. If you are renaming a top-level class in a file, the filename has to be changed as well. The Android IDE usually handles the source control changes required to do this, if the file is being tracked by source control. If the Android IDE can determine that the item is in reference to the identically named item being renamed, all instances of the name are renamed as well. Occasionally, this even means comments are updated with the new name. Quite handy!

Refactoring Code

Do you find yourself writing a whole bunch of repeating sections of code that look, for instance, like the following?

```
TextView nameCol = new TextView(this);

namecol.setTextColor(getResources().getColor(R.color.title_color));

nameCol.setTextSize(getResources().

getDimension(R.dimen.help_text_size));

nameCol.setText(scoreUserName);

table.addView(nameCol);
```

This code sets text color, text size, and text. If you've written two or more blocks that look like this, your code could benefit from refactoring. The Android IDE provides two useful tools—`Extract Local Variable` and `Extract Method`—to speed this task and make it almost trivial.

Using the `Extract Local Variable` Tool

Follow these steps to use the `Extract Local Variable` tool:

1. Select the expression `getResources().getColor(R.color.title_color)`.
2. Right-click and choose `Refactor, Extract Local Variable` (or press `Alt+Shift+L`).
3. In the dialog that appears, enter the `Name` for the variable and leave the `Replace all occurrences` check box selected. Then click `OK` and watch the magic happen.
4. Repeat Steps 1–3 for the text size.

The result should now look like this:

```
int textColor = getResources().getColor(R.color.title_color);

float textSize = getResources().getDimension(R.dimen.help_text_size);

TextView nameCol = new TextView(this);

nameCol.setTextColor(textColor);

nameCol.setTextSize(textSize);

nameCol.setText(scoreUserName);

table.addView(nameCol);
```

All repeated sections of the last five lines also have this change made. How convenient is that?

Using the `Extract Method` Tool

Now you're ready for the second tool. Follow these steps to use the `Extract Method` tool:

1. Select all five lines of the first block of code.
2. Right-click and choose `Refactor, Extract Method` (or choose `Alt+Shift+M`).
3. Name the method and then click `OK` and watch the magic happen.

By default, the new method is below your current one. If the other blocks of code are actually identical (meaning the statements of the other blocks are in the exact same order), the types are all the same, and so on, they will also be replaced with calls to this new method. You can see this in the count of additional occurrences shown in the dialog for the `Extract Method` tool. If that count doesn't match what you expect, check that the code follows exactly the same pattern. Now you have code that looks like the following:

```
addTextToRowWithValues(newRow, scoreUserName, textColor, textSize);
```

It is easier to work with this code than with the original code, and it was created with almost no typing! If you had ten instances before refactoring, you've saved a lot of time by using a useful Android IDE feature.

Reorganizing Code

Sometimes, formatting code isn't enough to make it clean and readable. Over the course of developing a complex `Activity`, you might end up with a number of embedded classes and methods strewn about the file. A quick Android IDE trick comes to the rescue. With the file in question open, make sure the outline view is also visible.

Simply click and drag methods and classes around in the outline view to place them in a suitable logical order. Do you have a method that is called only from a certain class but is available to all? Just drag it into that class. This works with almost anything listed in the outline, including classes, methods, and variables.

Using `QuickFix`

The `QuickFix` feature, accessible under `Edit, Quick Fix` (or `Ctrl+1` in Windows and `Command+1` on a Mac), isn't just for fixing possible issues. It brings up a menu of various tasks that can be performed on the highlighted code, and it shows what the change will look like. One useful `QuickFix` now available is the Android `Extract String` command. Use `QuickFix` on a string literal and quickly move it into an Android string resource file, and the code is automatically updated to use the string resource. Consider how `QuickFix` `Extract String` would work on the following two lines:

```
Log.v(DEBUG_TAG, "Something happened");

String otherString = "This is a string literal.";
```

The updated Java code is shown here:

```
Log.v(DEBUG_TAG, getString(R.string.something_happened));

String otherString = getString(R.string.string_literal);
```

And these entries have been added to the string resource file:

```
<string name="something_happened">Something happened</string>

<string name="string_literal">This is a string literal.</string>
```

The process also brings up a dialog for customizing the string name and which alternative resource file it should appear in, if any.

The QuickFix feature can be used in layout files with many Android-specific options for performing tasks such as extracting styles, extracting pieces to an include file, wrapping pieces in a new container, and even changing the widget type.

Providing Javadoc-Style Documentation

Regular code comments are useful (when done right). Comments in Javadoc style appear in code completion dialogs and other places, thus making them even more useful. To quickly add a Javadoc comment to a method or class, simply press Alt+Shift+J in Windows (also Alt+Shift+J on a Mac). Alternatively, you can choose Source, Generate Element Comment to prefill certain fields in the Javadoc, such as parameter names and author, thus speeding the creation of this style of comment. Finally, if you simply start the comment block with /** and press Enter, the appropriate code block will be generated and prefilled as before.

Resolving Mysterious Build Errors

Occasionally, you might find that the Android IDE finds build errors where there were none just moments before. In such a situation, you can try a couple of quick Android IDE tricks.

First, try refreshing the project. Simply right-click the project and choose Refresh or press F5. If this doesn't work, try deleting the R.java file, which you can find under the /gen directory under the name of the particular package being compiled. (Don't worry; this file is created during every compile.) If the Compile Automatically option is enabled, the file is re-created. Otherwise, you need to compile the project again.

A second method for resolving certain build errors involves source control. If the project is managed by the Android IDE via the Team, Share Project menu selection, the Android IDE can manage files that are to be read-only or automatically generated. Alternatively, if you can't or don't want to use source control, make sure all of the files in the project are writable (that is, not read-only).

Finally, you can try cleaning the project. To do this, choose Project, Clean and choose the project(s) you want to clean. The Android IDE removes all temporary files and then rebuilds the project(s). If the project was an NDK project, don't forget to recompile the native code.

Summary

In this appendix, you have learned useful tips and techniques for leveraging many powerful features provided with the Android IDE. You have learned quite a few tips for organizing your Android IDE workspace. You have also learned useful tricks for writing code for your applications in Java. The many features of the Android IDE (Eclipse) make this the best choice of IDE for developing Android applications.

Quiz Questions

1. True or false: It is possible to use source control from within the Android IDE.
2. What is the keyboard shortcut for maximizing windows within the Android IDE?
3. Describe how to view two source file windows at once.
4. True or false: It is not possible to view two different sections of the same file in two different windows within the Android IDE.
5. What is the keyboard shortcut for formatting Java code?
6. What is the keyboard shortcut for using the `Extract Local Variable` tool?
7. What is the keyboard shortcut for using `QuickFix`?

Exercises

1. Practice using the various keyboard shortcuts mentioned throughout this appendix.
2. Use the Eclipse documentation or the Internet to discover at least one other useful keyboard shortcut for Java development not mentioned in this appendix.
3. Practice rearranging the various UI elements within the Android IDE until you are comfortable with your arrangement.

References and More Information

Eclipse Resources: "Eclipse Resources":
   http://www.eclipse.org/resources/
Eclipse Resources: "Eclipse Documentation":
   http://www.eclipse.org/documentation/
Eclipse Resources: "Getting Started":
   http://www.eclipse.org/resources/?category=Getting%20Started
Eclipse Wiki: "Main Page":
   http://wiki.eclipse.org/Main_Page
Oracle Java SE Documentation: "How to Write Doc Comments for the Javadoc Tool":
   http://www.oracle.com/technetwork/java/javase/documentation/index-137868.html

E

Answers to Quiz Questions

Chapter 1: Introducing Android

1. The Brick
2. Snake
3. Android, Inc.
4. G1 was the name. HTC was the manufacturer. T-Mobile was the carrier.

Chapter 2: Setting Up Your Android Development Environment

1. Version 6
2. Unknown sources
3. USB debugging
4. android.jar
5. junit.*
6. Google AdMob Ads SDK

Chapter 3: Writing Your First Android Application

1. Snapshot greatly improves emulator startup performance.
2. The e means ERROR, w means WARN, i means INFO, v means VERBOSE, and d means DEBUG.
3. Step Into is F5. Step Over is F6. Step Return is F7. Resume is F8.
4. Ctrl+Shift+O on Windows and Command+Shift+O on Mac
5. Double-clicking on the far-left column of the intended line of code
6. Alt+Shift+S

Chapter 4: Android Application Basics

1. `Context`
2. `getApplicationContext()`
3. `getResources()`
4. `getSharedPreferences()`
5. `getAssets()`
6. The "back stack"
7. `onSaveInstanceState()`
8. `sendBroadcast()`

Chapter 5: Defining Your Application Using the Android Manifest File

1. `Manifest, Application, Permissions, Instrumentation, AndroidManifest.xml`
2. `android:versionName, android:versionCode`
3. `<uses-sdk>`
4. `<uses-configuration>`
5. `<uses-feature>`
6. `<supports-screens>`
7. `<uses-library>`
8. `<permission>`

Chapter 6: Managing Application Resources

1. False
2. Property animations, tweened animations, color state lists, drawables, layouts, menus, arbitrary raw files, simple values, arbitrary XML
3. `getString()`
4. `getStringArray()`
5. PNG, Nine-Patch Stretchable Images, JPEG, GIF, WEBP
6. `@resource_type/variable_name`

Chapter 7: Exploring User Interface Building Blocks

1. `findViewById()`
2. `getText()`
3. `EditText`
4. `AutoCompleteTextView, MultiAutoCompleteTextView`
5. False
6. False

Chapter 8: Designing with Layouts

1. False
2. True
3. `setContentView()`
4. False
5. `android:layout_attribute_name="value"`
6. False
7. False
8. `ScrollView`

Chapter 9: Partitioning the User Interface with Fragments

1. `FragmentManager`
2. `getFragmentManager()`
3. The fully qualified `Fragment` class name
4. False
5. `DialogFragment, ListFragment, PreferenceFragment, WebViewFragment`
6. `ListView`
7. With the Android Support Package

Chapter 10: Displaying Dialogs

1. `Dialog, AlertDialog, CharacterPickerDialog, DatePickerDialog, ProgressDialog, TimePickerDialog, Presentation`
2. False
3. `dismiss()`
4. `AlertDialog`
5. True
6. `getSupportFragmentManager()`

Chapter 11: Using Android Preferences

1. `Boolean, Float, Integer, Long, String, String Set`
2. True
3. `/data/data/<package name>/shared_prefs/<preferences filename>.xml`
4. `android:key, android:title, android:summary, android:defaultValue`
5. `addPreferencesFromResource()`

Chapter 12: Working with Files and Directories

1. `0, 32768`
2. False
3. `/data/data/<package name>/`
4. `openFileOutput()`
5. `getExternalCacheDir()`
6. False

Chapter 13: Leveraging Content Providers

1. `MediaStore`
2. True
3. `READ_CONTACTS`
4. False
5. `addWord()`
6. False

Chapter 14: Designing Compatible Applications

1. True

2. 99%

3. `<supports-screens>`

4. False

5. `ldltr, ldrtl`

6. False

7. `onConfigurationChanged()`

Chapter 15: Learning the Android Software Development Process

1. False

2. The lowest common denominator method and the customization method

3. Early, when project requirements are just determined and target devices are determined

4. False

5. Write and compile the code, run the application in the software emulator, test and debug the application in the software emulator or test device, package and deploy the application to the target devices, test and debug the application on the target devices, and incorporate changes from the team and repeat until the application is complete.

Chapter 16: Designing and Developing Bulletproof Android Applications

1. How many users install the application, how many users launch the application for the first time, how many users regularly use the application, what the most popular usage patterns and trends are, what the least popular usage patterns and features are, what devices are the most popular

2. Updating means modifying the Android manifest version information and redeploying the updated application on users' devices. Upgrading means creating an entirely new application package with new features and deploying it as a separate application that the user needs to choose to install and that does not replace the old application.

3. The Android emulator using different AVDs, DDMS, Hierarchy Viewer in Pixel Perfect View, `layoutopt`, Draw Nine-Patch tool, real devices, technical specifications for specific devices

4. False

5. The Android IDE, Eclipse with the ADT plugin, Android Studio, the Android emulator, physical devices, DDMS, `adb`, `sqlite3`, the Hierarchy Viewer

6. False

Chapter 17: Planning the Android Application Experience

1. The activities must reside on the same hierarchy level within the application, and a simple call to `startActivity()` is all that is required.

2. Define the `parentActivityName` and use the correct `Activity`.

3. `onBackPressed()`

4. `setDisplayHomeAsUpEnabled(true);`

5. `android:uiOptions="splitActionBarWhenNarrow"`

6. `getActionBar().hide();`

Chapter 18: Testing Android Applications

1. True

2. Test application integration points, test application upgrades, test device upgrades, test product internationalization, test for conformance, installation testing, backup testing, performance testing, test in-app billing, test for the unexpected, and test to increase your chances of being a "killer app"

3. JUnit

4. `.test`

5. `test`

6. False

7. `TouchUtils`

Chapter 19: Publishing Your Android Application

1. `ProGuard`

2. False

3. Google Analytics App Tracking SDK

4. `versionName` is used to display application version information to users, and `versionCode` is an integer that Google Play uses internally to handle application upgrades.

5. True

6. False

7. A Google Wallet Merchant account

Appendix A: Mastering the Android Development Tools

1. True

2. `/platform-tools`

3. False

4. Graphical Layout mode, XML editing mode

5. Hierarchy Viewer

Appendix B: Quick-Start Guide: The Android Emulator

1. F8

2. `Ctrl+F11/Ctrl+F12`

3. F6

4. `onPause()` and `onStop()`

5. `hw.gpu.enabled`

6. `telnet localhost <port>`

7. `geo fix <longitude> <latitude> [<altitude>]`

Appendix C: Quick-Start Guide: Android DDMS

1. `/tools`

2. True

3. Attach and debug applications in the Android IDE, monitor threads, monitor the heap, stop processes, force garbage collection

4. `TrafficStats`

5. False

Appendix D: Android IDE and Eclipse Tips and Tricks

1. True

2. Ctrl+M on Windows, Command+M on Mac

3. With two source file windows open, grab the tab for a source file and drag it either to the edge of the editor area or to the bottom.

4. False

5. Ctrl+Shift+F on Windows, Command+Shift+F on Mac

6. Alt+Shift+L

7. Ctrl+1 on Windows, Command+1 on Mac

Index

U